BURIED SECRETS

BURIED SECRETS

Truth and Human Rights in Guatemala

VICTORIA SANFORD

First published 2003 by
PALGRAVE MACMILLAN™
175 Fifth Avenue, New York, N.Y. 10010 and
Houndmills, Basingstoke, Hampshire, England RG21 6XS.
Companies and representatives throughout the world.

PALGRAVE MACMILLAN is the global academic imprint of the Palgrave Macmillan
division of St. Martin's Press, LLC and of Palgrave Macmillan Ltd. Macmillan® is a
registered trademark in the United States, United Kingdom and other countries. Palgrave
is a registered trademark in the European Union and other countries.

ISBN 1-4039-6023-2 hardback

Library of Congress Cataloging-in-Publication Data
Sanford, Victoria
   Buried secrets : truth and human rights in Guatemala / by Victoria Sanford.
     p.   cm.
   Includes bibliographical references and index.
   ISBN 1-4039-6023-2
   1. Mayas—Crimes against—Guatemala.   2. Human rights—Guatemala.
3. Mayas—Guatemala—Government relations.   4. Political violence—Guatemala.
5. Genocide—Guatemala.   I. Title: Truth and human rights in Guatemala.   II. Title.

F1435.3.C75S35   2003
972.8105'3—dc21

2002044984

Transferred to Digital Printing 2005

A catalogue record for this book is available from the British Library.

Design by Letra Libre, Inc.

First edition: May 2003
10 9 8 7 6 5 4 3 2 1

For the survivors and their children

CONTENTS

LIST OF ABBREVIATIONS

ACNUR—Alto Comisionado de las Naciones Unidas para los Refugiados (United Nations High Commissioner for Refugees)

AI—Amnesty International

AID—U.S. Agency for International Development

CALDH—Centro de Acción Legal de Derechos Humanos (Legal Action Center for Human Rights)

CEH—Comisión para el Esclarecimiento Histórico (Commission for Historical Clarification)

CERJ—Consejo de Comunidades Etnias Runujel Junam (Council of Ethnic Communities—"We are all Equal")

CIA—U.S. Central Intelligence Agency

CONAVIGUA—Coordinadora Nacional de las Viudas de Guatemala (National Coordinator of Guatemalan Widows)

CPR—Comunidades de Poblaciones en Resistencia (Communities of Populations in Resistance)

CUC—Comité de Unidad Campesina (Campesino Unity Committee)

EAFG—Equipo de Antropología Forense de Guatemala (Guatemalan Forensic Anthropology Team)

ECAP—Equipo Comunitaria de Ayuda Psico-Social (Psycho-Social Community Assistance Team)

EGP—Ejército Guerrillero de los Pobres (Guerrilla Army of the Poor)

FAFG—Fundación de Antropología Forense de Guatemala (Guatemalan Forensic Anthropology Foundation)

FAMDEGUA—Asociación de Familiares de los Detenidos-Desaparecidos de Guatemala (Association of the Families of the Detained and Disappeared of Guatemala)

FAR—Fuerzas Armadas Rebeldes (Rebel Armed Forces)

FRG—Frente Republicano Guatemalteco (Guatemala Republican Front)

GAM—Grupo de Apoyo Mutúo (Mutual Support Group)

HRW—Human Rights Watch

IGE—Iglesia Guatemalteca Exiliada (Guatemalan Church in Exile)

MINUGUA—Misión Naciones Unidas en Guatemala (United Nations Mission in Guatemala)

OAS—Organization of American States

ODHA—Oficina del Arzobispado de Derechos Humanos (Archbishop's Office on Human Rights)

ONU—Organización de Naciones Unidas (United Nations Organization)

PAC—Patrullas de Autodefensa Civil (Civil Defense Patrols, Civil Patrols)

PDH—Procuraduría de Derechos Humanos (Human Rights Ombudsman)

REHMI—Proyecto Interdiocesano de Recuperación Histórico (Interdiocesene Project for the Recuperation of Historical Memory)

URNG—Unión Revolucionaria Nacional Guatemalteca (Guatemalan National Revolutionary Union)

LIST OF PHOTOS

Photo 1. Site of clandestine cemetery under excavation in Acul graveyard in December 1997

Photo 2. Widows, orphans, and other relatives of victims of 1978 army massacre gathered at clandestine cemetery in Panzós 1997

Photo 3. Exhumation of clandestine cemetery in Panzós in September 1997

Photo 4. Antemortem interview with widow of massacre

Photo 5. Forensic anthropologist examines skeletal remains being exhumed in Acul

Photo 6. Widows of victims of La Violencia in San Andrés Sajcábaja help sift dirt from graves and sort through artifacts

Photo 7. A man places candles next to the remains of his brother

Photo 8. As remains are uncovered and identified in Acul, widows cover them with their shawls and offer candles, flowers, and prayers to the deceased

Photo 9. K'iche' priestesses perform a religious ceremony for the deceased in the plaza of San Andrés Sajcábaja while we carry out the exhumation inside the church

Photo 10. Reburial procession in Panzós in May 1998 on the twentieth anniversary of the massacre

Photo 11. Q'eqchi' *Reina Indígena* (indigenous beauty queen) participating in the reburial procession

Photo 12. The national Maya widows organization gathers in Nebaj on the day of the guerrilla reinsertion, March 1997

Photo 13. Achi in Plan de Sánchez prepare sacred maize for the feast to be held the following day commemorating the victims of the Plan de Sánchez massacre

Photo 14. Local Achi gather in the Plan de Sánchez chapel built at the site of the massacre, where the remains of victims were reburied following the exhumation

ACKNOWLEDGEMENTS

This book would not have been possible without the generosity, trust, and friendship of massacre survivors in the municipalities and villages of Chimaltenango, Cubulco, Nebaj, Panzós, Rabinal, San Martín Jilotepeque, and San Andrés Sajcábaja who shared their homes, their lives, and their personal and community histories. The commitment to justice and truth exemplified by these individuals in their daily work for peace, often at great personal risk, provided tremendous inspiration to me, especially on those days when the realities of the truths confronted overwhelmed me. Whatever insights this book may offer to understanding *La Violencia* in Guatemala are the result of the generosity and trust of survivors. Any errors are, of course, mine alone. While I would like to thank these friends by name, with few exceptions, I am unable to do so because daily life in Guatemala remains precarious for many—especially Maya human rights activists living in rural communities. This book is written for them.

The widows and mothers of the Grupo de Apoyo Mutúo (GAM), Coordinadora Nacional de las Viudas de Guatemala (CONAVIGUA), and the Familiares de los Desaparecidos de Guatemala (FAMDEGUA), as well as the rural members of Consejo de Etnias Runujel Junam (CERJ), Centro de Acción Legal de los Derechos Humanos (CALDH), Defensoria Maya, the Coordinadora de Viudas y Huerfanos de Rabinal, and many local committees taught me about personal courage and the power of truth by example. Again, I am unable to acknowledge most of them by name due to fear of retribution. Thus, I thank those who are publicly known rural human rights leaders and activists: Juan Manuel Gerónimo, María Maquín, Carlos Chen, Pedrina Chen, and Jesus Tec.

The Guatemalan Forensic Anthropology Foundation (Fundación de Antropologia Forense de Guatemala—FAFG), CERJ, the Equipo Comunitaria de Estudios y Ayuda Psicosocial (ECAP), and the Museo para la Paz have been a constant source of support, guidance and friendship throughout the research and writing of this book. Additionally, many

Guatemalans in the capital went to great efforts to share whatever experiences, documents, and/or contacts they had to support this project. For their support and courageous work on behalf of human rights, I gratefully acknowledge Felipe Sartí, Olga Alicia Paz, Rolando Alecio, Amilcar and Miriam Mendez and their family, Aura Elena Farfán, Miguel Angel Albizures, and Frank La Rue. I am indebted to Dr. Alain Breton and Luis and Anaite Galeotti for the personal and professional support they provided to me when I was affiliated with the French research institute CEMCA (Centro de Estudios Mexicanos y Centroamericanos) during my fieldwork. I also thank Carmen de la Rosa, Karen Fischer, Jorge Mario Garcia La Guardia, and Julio Arango Escobar for their generosity.

Working with the FAFG for nearly a decade has been an honor. I am especially appreciative of the support of Roberto Lemus, a Guatemalan judge who was forced into exile after pursuing the first exhumations in Guatemala. It was through the work Roberto did while in exile in California that I began my project with the FAFG. My deepest appreciation and respect goes to all the members (former and present) of the forensic team, especially to former president Fernando Moscoso Moller and current president Fredy Pecerrelli for always opening their offices to me and welcoming my participation at exhumation sites and also to Chemelo Suasnavar, Claudia Rivera, Leonel Pais, Renaldo Acevedo, Fernando Flores, and Marlon Garcia for making me feel like part of the team. Dr. Clyde Snow, who organized the international support and lent his forensic expertise to create the FAFG, continues to inspire us all with his work for human rights all over the world.

Other colleagues and friends have been generous with their time, friendship, and experience, especially Alberto Fuentes, Chico Mendez, Oilio Mendez and his extended family, Greg Grandin, Ramiro Avila Santamaria, Arienne de Bremont, Roberto Rodriguez, Leila Lima, Alan Meltzer, Graham Russell, Victoria and Camilla. Special thanks to Pablo, Juanita, Ana, Lucas, Jacinto, Dominga, Luisa, Angela, and other research assistants who helped tremendously in the gathering of archival data and transcribing of testimonies. Robert Leventhal and Elisa Irwin made their home seem like my home when I was in the capital on holidays and Sunday evenings. I will always appreciate Daniel Rothenberg's generosity of spirit and unflagging support each time I reached the capital exhausted, ill, and/or with a carload of friends from villages who needed medical attention, legal assistance, or simply wanted to visit the city for the first time. I also thank Puri and Guillermo for their hospitality and for teaching me how to make Spanish tortilla.

Friends and colleagues in Mexico have continued to support me over the years, especially Licha Walker, Louisa Greathouse, Teresa Siera, and Francois Lartigue. The spirit, friendship, joy of life, and commitment to justice of Oscar Walker, Cesar Pellegrini, Severo Martínez Paláez, and Lorena Otero continue to move me even after their passing. The Mothers of the Disappeared in El Salvador, the faculty of the Universidad de Centroamericana, Mario Pozas, Father Bernie, and Maria Teresa Tula helped me understand Guatemala in a regional context. A fellowship from the Inter-American Institute for Human Rights in the summer of 1994 provided me the opportunity to study human rights law in Costa Rica with Latin American human rights leaders and activists.

Over the course of this project, I have met many new friends and colleagues who have sharpened my scholarship and inspired me with their shared commitment to justice. They include Marvyn Perez, Serena Cosgrove, Neil Harvey, George Lovell, Lucia Ann McSpadden, John Mowitt, Arif Dirlik, Helena Pohlandt-McCormick, Michael McCormick, my compadres Ada Gonzalez and John Peterson, Gilberto Arriaza, Naomi Roht-Arriaza, Noelle Thomas, Karen Musalo, Richard Boswell, Holly Hololsberg, John Collins, Louis Bickford, Harold Trinkunas, Gastón Gordillo, Noel Corea, Valerie Zamberletti, Betsy Konefal, and Marcos and Jacinto Yoc and their family. I thank Michael Ondaatje for his friendship, understanding, and *Anil's Ghost*. I also thank Philippe Bourgois and Arturo Arias for encouraging me to pursue this project and providing continued support at critical moments over the years. In San Francisco, the Comité Maya Ku Same Junam, Guatemala Unity Committee, and the Guatemala News and Information Bureau have always been generous with their time and open to sharing whatever information they had available.

The research and writing of this book would not have been possible without the support of the Inter-American Foundation (IAF), Fulbright-Hays, MacArthur Consortium at Stanford University's Center for International Security and Cooperation (CISAC), Bunting Peace Fellowship at the Radcliffe Center for Advanced Study at Harvard University, a Rockefeller fellowship at the Virginia Foundation for the Humanities and Public Policy (VFH), and the University of Notre Dame. The Shaler Adams Foundation provided me with the opportunity to research and write about nongovernmental organizations in Guatemala as well as numerous opportunities to meet with women's human rights activists from around the world. The Peace and Life Institute supported research on women and violence in Guatemala. At the University of Notre Dame, the Department of Anthropology, the Kellogg Institute for International Studies, the Kroc Institute for International Peace Studies, and the Institute for Scholarship in the Liberal Arts have provided me with the time and resources to complete this book.

Beyond the financial support, these fellowships were supervised by wonderful people who marked my research with their insight, experience, and creativity. IAF academic advisors Mitch Seligson, Billie Jean Isbell, and Beatriz Manz provided support and encouragement throughout my research. Michael Orlansky made the Fulbright-Hays a great experience with his limitless enthusiasm, and Carmen Foncea introduced me to Guatemalan women writers and her own beautiful poetry. At CISAC, Lynn Eden and Pam Ballinger challenged me to think about anthropology and my work through interdisciplinary lenses. I thank Lucia Ann McSpadden, formerly of the Peace and Life Institute, for excellent feedback on my research in Guatemala and for continuing to include my work in human rights forums. The Bunting Fellowship Program provided a tremendously supportive environment for writing. It also afforded the opportunity to learn from brilliant women doing interesting projects in a wide range of fields. For this I thank Rita Brock Nakashima, Renny Harrigan, Julie Burba, Lyn Oconor, and all the Bunting fellows—especially Patricia Mcanany, Rosemary Taylor, Suzy Becker, Margaret Lee, and Francesca Polletta. Bunting Peace Fellows, former and present, have been among my best teachers and friends as I have written. Thanks to: Sam Barnes, for your boundless generosity and friendship and for sharing your vast knowledge on demilitarization following armed internal conflicts; Pumla Godobo-Mazikewela, for your good spirit and sharing your own personal and political experiences on the Truth and Reconciliation Commission in South Africa; Anita Mesiah, for your humanity and example working for peace in Sri Lanka; and, Marguerite Feitlowitz and your generous heart, for writing one of the best books I have ever read about terror and providing me with emotional and intellectual support at the most difficult moments in my project. Cheryl Laguardia at Harvard Library gave tremendous bibliographic assistance and Janice Randall of the Radcliffe Institute provided venues for the presentation of my work. Anna Haughton and Newton made Cambridge a fun place to live and write.

The tranquility and hospitality of the Institute on Survival and Violence at the VFH offered the perfect environment to complete the writing of this book. Institute director Roberta Culbertson embodies empathy and commitment to truth and healing in both actions and words. Anne White Spencer and Judy Moody attended to any and all administrative needs with grace and good humor. Susan Pennybacker, Delora Wojchewska, Len Smith, and Claudia Fermin became a second family. At Notre Dame, Father Patrick Gaffney and Father Bob Pelton have provided enthusiastic support and thoughtful reflection on my work. Kroc director Scott Appleby, my faculty mentor Ivan Jaksic, and *Notre Dame Magazine* editor John Monczunski each generously provided comments on the entire first draft of this manuscript. Ken Garcia and George Lopez always made time to listen when I needed a sympathetic ear. Notre Dame gave me a reduced teaching load, financial support, and leave, creating a model for the type of institutional support all universities should provide to junior faculty. The cheerful and highly organized presence of my research assistants Catherine Oakar and Kristin Kajdzik made the final stages of formatting a pleasure rather than a source of anxiety. I am also indebted to Faith Martin and Anne Gurucharri for their research assistance, and thanks to Claire McAuliffe for creating the maps.

Stanford University provided consistent support through graduate studies and beyond. Beyond the financial support of fellowships from the anthropology department, the Center for Latin American Studies, and the Office of the Dean, which allowed me to begin my research during my first year of graduate school, I have been personally enriched by and my book has greatly benefited from a very dedicated committee of advisers. Bill Durham helped me to integrate material realities of rural life with testimonies; Purnima Mankekar introduced me to feminist anthropology and inspired me to explore my own personal experiences in fieldwork; and Akhil Gupta encouraged me to explore subaltern studies and seek balance between theory and narrative by insisting on the inclusion and analysis of life histories. I also thank Sylvia Yanagisako, Arthur Wolfe, Hil Gates, John Rick, Benjamin Paul, Renato Rosaldo, Ellen Christiansen, Beth Bashore, Shelly Slingsby, and Nanaz Rohni. Anthropology graduate students created an intellectually challenging and mutually supportive environment, especially Liliana Suarez, Bill Maurer, Genevieve Bell, Diane Nelson, Ramon Gonzalez Ponciano, Constanza Ocampo, Aida Hernandez, John Davis, Don Moore, Lok Siu, Shari Seider, and Robin Baliger, among others. Other anthropologists have kindly supported my research and encouraged me by their example, including: Carol Smith, Carolyn Nordstrom, Kay Warren, Linda Green, Victor Montejo, Joanne Rappaport, Stefano Varece, Charlie Hale, and Terrence Turner. Veena Das, Debbie Poole, Tlal Asad, Pradeep Jeganathan, Marianne Fermé, Laurence Cohen, and Janet Roiteman provided (perhaps unknowingly) invaluable feedback for the conceptualization of this book at a School of American Research seminar. From her extensive writing on social suffering and violence to public presentations and casual conversation, along with the humility with which she shares her brilliance and insights as well as the ease with which she supports junior colleagues, Veena Das exemplifies the very best of public anthropology and deep commitment to teaching and knowledge.

The Center for Latin American Studies at Stanford (CLAS) was my second home during graduate school. Terry Karl made CLAS an intellectually stimulating and mutually supportive place to be. As my professor, adviser, mentor, colleague, and friend, she provided me with the gifts of her insight, creativity, and experience; guidance and feedback on this project since its inception; and personal and institutional support for academic panels and symposia on human rights. I thank her for the model of commitment, integrity, scholarship, and teaching she has given me. Kathleen Morrison, Beth Frankland, Alicia Heramschuck, Jutta Mohr, Iñigo Bryce, Joshua Paulson, Joan Kruckewitt, Evelyn Casteñeda, and Ricardo Huerta provided feedback at critical moments in my project. My students Jesse Aaron, Antonia Welsh, Jenny Terry, Stephanie Weisner, Jocelyn Weiner, Tseday Aleghan, and Rebecca Crocker reaffirmed that teaching is always a great opportunity for learning. At CLAS, I also had the tremendous opportunity to work with Eduardo Galeano, whom I thank for his support of my research and especially for his feedback on testimonies of Maya youth. Eduardo is an inspiration as a writer and a teacher.

Stanford law professor Sophie Pirie has made a tremendous contribution to the analytical and literary growth of this project. I thank her for believing that an anthropologist could have something meaningful to say about human rights law and for being an excellent teacher and mentor. I also thank the Stanford Native American Graduate Students Organization, especially Victoria Bomberry and Renya and Gil Ramirez, and the Guatemala Scholars Network, especially Marilyn Moors.

I am especially grateful to Kristi Long at Palgrave Macmillan for supporting this project from its early stages and providing consistently excellent feedback about all aspects of the writing and production process. Roee Raz, Jen Simington, and Donna Cherry generously provided the support to get through final revisions and make production run smoothly and swiftly. I also thank Barbara Rothenberg for kindly sharing her lovely artwork for the cover of this book.

I thank Stephen Dunstan for giving me the rapture of writing in solitude without the isolation of seclusion. I sat at my desk on the upstairs porch of his home overlooking the rolling farmland of Central Virginia, where he gave me a place to write, read, and reflect. His unconditional support, generosity, and good humor keep me sane.

In the end, this book became part of the lives of close friends and family who have supported and inspired me in more ways than they know over the years. Phyllis Beech, goddess of editing, has read and edited innumerable drafts of this book (though of course, errors and/or typos are mine); she also became a lawyer and represents refugees, asylum-seekers and other immigrants. Michael Bosia has graced my life with charm, wit, wisdom, and fierce loyalty since we first became political activists, when we were little more than kids. Carol Wolchok has tirelessly struggled for the rights of political asylum seekers and refugees for more than twenty years. Erika Bliss, who is truly blissful, is an inspiration as a doctor, a colleague, a friend, and a sister. Lotti Silber and Shannon Speed motivate us all with their ability to keep their commitments to social justice and reach wide audiences with their work while becoming mothers. Julia Leiblich elegantly writes about pain, loss, and faith as she moves through this world with a generous heart, an open mind and a deep empathy for human suffering. Kathleen Dill, who is herself writing about Guatemala today, has given me boundless patience, love, friendship, and trust. Asale Angel-Ajani has inspired me with her unwavering commitment to social justice and scholarship as well as her talent for revealing the literary beauty located in the tension between truth and testimony. I also thank Carlos Hernan, Steven Obranovich, Nils Frenzen, Dan Kesselbrenner, Noelle Thomas, Abdiel Oñate, Noel Correa, Victoria Sekula and Jolie Martin. Each of these friends sets an example about the difference one person can make in pursuit of a more just world.

Lastly, I thank my family: Elka, John, Sarrina, and Blake Suer; Jayme, John, Dominic, Alyssa, and Grant Daley; Rick Ludlow; Diana and Michael McCormick; Jean Highfield; and, my late grandmother Lucy de Belle, whose legacy was love. My greatest debt is to my mother, Hilda Mary Sanford (1915–2001), who taught me her love of travel, literature, truth, and justice. In 1937, she traveled across France with several friends hoping to join the Republican cause against fascism in Spain. A survivor of the London Blitz, she was an outspoken advocate of peace. Her wisdom, courage, and integrity marked all who knew her. She was a citizen of the world who cared deeply about the rights of all human beings. It is in her memory that I dedicate this book to the survivors of La Violencia and their children.

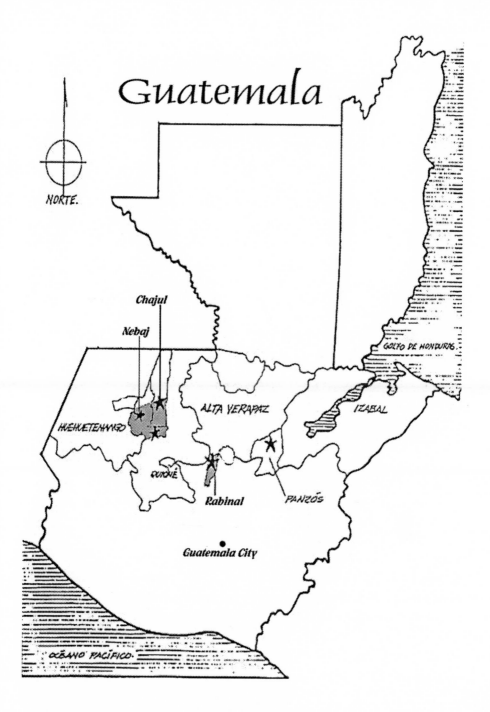

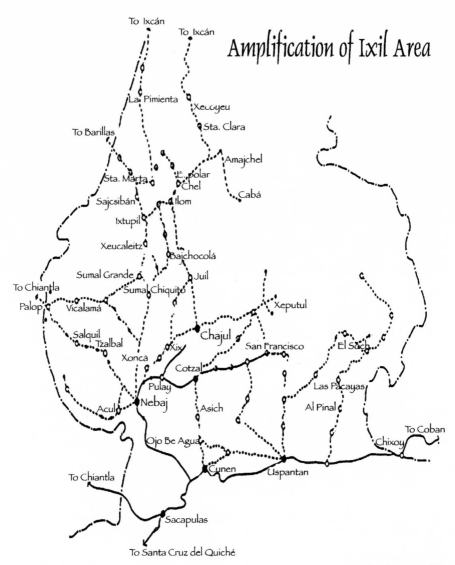

Amplification of Ixil Area

Created by Claire McAuliffe

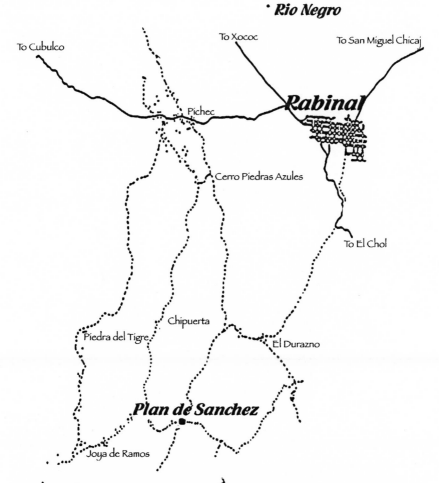

Amplification of Plan de Sanchez & Rio Negro in Rabinal

Created by Claire McAuliffe

PROLOGUE

If they ask you my name, tell them you don't know. Tell them you can't remember.

—Julia

Julia, my translator, arranged for many clandestine meetings in outlying villages. One of the first such meetings was in Tzalbal, which lies about an hour outside Nebaj by vehicle. I had never been there before and had not asked specifically that she set up these, or any other, meetings. In March 1997, several days before we went to Tzalbal, the first *guerrilla* combatants had come down the mountain to a United Nations reinsertion camp that had been built near Tzalbal in late 1996 as a part of the Peace Accords.[1] In Nebaj, the reinsertion camp became a topic of discussion—mostly still in whispers. I had heard some Nebajeños say, "Those from Tzalbal were always *guerrilleros*." I had heard others reply, "No more than anywhere else. But it will be hard for them to prove they are not guerrillero now." Others asked, "Who decides where these camps go? Why do they have to be near here?" Nearly everyone asked, "Is the army going to be angry with us because it is here?" Many hoped that if the army became "angry," it would limit its anger to Tzalbal.

I mentioned the reinsertion camp and the gossip to Julia as we drove up and down the dirt road winding through the mountains. It was early morning and we drank warm coffee from the thermos with *pan dulce* (sweet bread) sent by Julia's mother. "The people are not guerrilleros in Tzalbal," asserted Julia. "But it is the people from Salquil who are spreading this rumor. They have always had envy of the people in Tzalbal. But what will happen in Tzalbal when the guerrilla arrive? In Salquil, they say the army will be angry and punish Tzalbal, again."

No one seemed to know exactly how the reinsertion process was going to work. "What happened to the guerrilla from Salquil?" asked Julia. "They had guerrilla, too." Nebajeños seemed to think that everyone at the Tzalbal camp was from Tzalbal and would "reinsert" there because it was their home. The United Nations had done little to clarify any misinformation or disinformation. Perhaps because Salquil is the nearest village to Tzalbal, those living in Salquil may simply have wanted to distance themselves as much as possible from Tzalbal in the event that the army became "angry."

To my surprise and delight, the reinsertion camp was right there on the side of the road as we rounded a bend coming down the hill into the valley. (In Nebaj, I had been told it would be dangerous to travel, to Tzalbal in general and to the reinsertion camp in particular, and that it was very far away, unreachable by vehicle.) Surrounded by a cyclone fence topped with razor wire, the United Nations flag flying high, the UN camp was covered with white mushroom-like tents stamped ONU (Organización Naciones Unidas—United Nations Organization) popping out of the rich, red earth. The white tents, like the white four-wheel drive vehicles, all bore "ONU" on the sides and on top—even a helicopter would know it was a UN camp. Everything looked new and therefore very out of place. Even the red earth was brushed clean. The large black letters "ONU" marked the entire area as not Guatemalan. The fog still hovered low, clinging to the ground and floating between the tents. The barren white tents popped out of the ground, seeming like an apparition from the past or an omen for the future. I asked Julia if she felt comfortable stopping at the camp. I told her I would like to take some photographs. She told me that she did not think they would allow it but that she was interested. "If they let you in, can I go with you?" she asked. "It scares me a little bit, but I am very curious."

I took some photographs from the side of the hill because I did not believe I would be allowed to take any when I asked. It seemed better to take some before asking. As Julia and I approached the gate with my dog, we saw no one. When I called out *"Buenos días"* in a normal tone of voice and received no response, Julia recommended I shout, then giggled nervously as I followed her recommendation. After what seemed a very long time, a UN military officer came to the gate. "Dogs are not allowed in the area and you cannot park there," he said. "I am sorry, it is a UN rule in all the camps." In my mind, his comment did not bode well for my desire to enter the camp. He had not even said "good morning." Having spent some twelve months between 1994 and 1997 in different Maya communities, I had adopted some of the Maya understandings of human interaction without realizing it. *"Ni nos saludaron"* (They didn't even greet us) was often the beginning of a story of a negative encounter with authority, sometimes culminating in insult, often times ending with physical injury or worse. So when the UN officer failed to greet us, I understood his omission as a public display of power that would most likely lead to a negative encounter—in this situation, a refusal to allow me to take photographs.

I moved my car and left my dog inside with the windows opened about three inches. She is very smart and very protective, but not aggressive and not obedient. She opened a back window and jumped out. This happened several times. Though the camp was outside Tzalbal, it was right on the road, and because it was early morning, men were walking to their fields. It was not long before a laughing crowd watched me put my dog in the car, only to have her open the window and escape over and over again. Indeed, my dog Asha always drew a crowd. Forensic team members called her my "secret weapon" because rural Maya peasants were fascinated by her size and apparent docility. Massacre survivors reluctant to recount their experiences to outsiders would approach me to talk about Asha, and these conversations quickly led to testimonies of survival. Outside the camp, I paid a young man to watch my dog. I left her reluctantly, because I am always afraid that someone will steal my dog—even in Cambridge. Julia assured me that everything would be fine because she knew the young man's uncle. As time went on, it seemed that Julia, if not actually related to just about everyone we met in the Ixil area, at least knew one of their relatives.

Finally, we returned to the gate. This time the officer greeted us. We exchanged "*Buenos días,*" and I introduced Julia and myself and asked about taking photographs on the compound. He replied that he would have to ask his commander about the photographs, so we stood outside the gate for another ten minutes. Finally, another UN officer, younger than the first, approached and opened the gate. I explained that we were waiting for the commander because I wanted to take photos and needed the commander's permission. He invited us inside the dining tent for coffee and served us. The first officer we'd met smiled at us as he entered the tent. He introduced the second, younger officer as his commander. Julia could not contain her giggles because a military officer, a commander, was serving us coffee, putting sugar in our cups and stirring them. She leaned toward me and whispered, "They are not from my country. They are foreigners."

In the damp cold, we were grateful for the coffee. The commander left us with the officer who had met us at the gate, a Venezuelan colonel, who invited a U.S. officer, a Mormon captain from Utah, to join us. So, for about forty minutes, Julia and I had coffee with these two officers. During our conversation, I explained that I was a doctoral student in anthropology conducting research on the peace process—that was the easiest truth to explain. I saw the Mormon from Utah as a potential problem in my quest to gain permission to take photos. I considered telling him that the U.S. embassy was very supportive of Fulbright scholars but feared alienating the Venezuelan in the process of winning over the Mormon. My fear was that the Venezuelan colonel might dislike U.S. foreign policy and the U.S. captain most likely supported it—my reservations were based on experiences at the U.S. embassy, where many political and military staff still divided the geography of Guatemala into zones of either "subversive" or army control. Still, I felt I somehow needed to win them both to my side in order to take the photographs. I opted to tell the U.S. captain that I had a Fulbright-Hays doctoral research fellowship. He was duly impressed and told the Venezuelan colonel, "She has to be really smart to have a Fulbright." I felt like I had just been given the U.S. military stamp of approval—it was a disquieting sensation. The U.S. captain was in charge of food for both the UN compound and the URNG (Unión Revolucionaria Nacional Guatemalteca—Guatemalan National Revolutionary Union) reinsertion camp and talked about the logistics of ordering food and getting it prepared in Tzalbal. I shifted the conversation somewhat when I asked the Venezuelan about the role of the UN and its peacekeeping forces in the peace process. I found him extremely well-informed about the peace process and about Guatemala in general.

The U.S officer did not have the same kind of knowledge about Guatemala, stating "It is hard to find books about Guatemala in Utah." However, to participate in the conversation, he began to talk about the URNG combatants who were then in the reinsertion camp (which was separate from the UN compound). "The *comandante* is not Guatemalan," he declared. "He is Salvadoran. Boy, does he have stories. You know, he was trained in Cuba." The U.S. captain was proud that he knew this about the URNG commander and seemed especially content to be sharing it with a compatriot. I was somewhat horrified that the first URNG commander to demobilize troops to the Tzalbal reinsertion camp was a Cuban-trained Salvadoran—a cartoon-like, right-wing stereotype of who leads revolution in Central America. Yet, the man was Salvadoran, and the U.S. captain seemed mostly fascinated with the comandante's persona.

Then he added, "The war is over, we all just sit around and share war stories at night. The comandante is not breaching anything by telling me about his training." I appreciated that he added this comment to protect the guerrilla commander. After another moment of thought, he added,

"Here in the camp, we have soldiers from all over the world and the URNG combatants. In the end, we are all just soldiers." Perhaps he intended this commentary to protect himself from being labeled as a guerrilla sympathizer, and with each of these comments from the U.S. captain, the Venezuelan colonel seemed to smile a little more. "It is really interesting," concluded the captain. "You should get the comandante to tell you some stories." With what seemed to me to be self-satisfaction, the Venezuelan said, "That is a great idea." And I thought to myself, "I really doubt that the comandante is going to tell me that he is not Guatemalan, that he is Salvadoran, and that he was trained in Cuba." (And I was mostly correct.)

The Venezuelan colonel told the U.S. captain that he would take Julia and me on a tour of the UN camp, then on down to the URNG reinsertion camp. After inviting the captain to rejoin us at the URNG camp, he then excused us and took us on a brief tour. "I know a lot about Guatemala because we always had to study about it in the military academy," he explained. "I am just glad that I am part of the peace process, instead of something else." As we walked through the camp, we both made polite and sincere remarks about how "*amable*" (nice) the U.S. captain was. It seemed our way of acknowledging that the colonel and I shared a different understanding of the things the U.S. captain had said. Though he never said so, I also had the impression that the Venezuelan had known all along that the U.S. captain would tell me about the URNG comandante and had introduced us for that purpose. As we walked, I took photos of the UN camp.

We walked outside the cyclone fencing up to the top of a hill so that I could get a good shot of the entire UN camp, as well as some shots of the reinsertion camp. Then he explained that the UN could not give permission for me to go to the URNG camp but that he could introduce me to the comandante. "You will have to make your case for yourself," he said. Having never imagined that I would actually be able to go down into the reinsertion camp, I asked Julia if she wanted to accompany me or wait in the UN camp. "I am a little scared, but mostly I am curious," she said for the second time that day. I asked the Venezuelan if he thought I would be given permission to take photos. "I don't know, but you can't know if you don't ask," he responded with a smile.

The fog was beginning to lift by the time we made our way behind the UN camp, and the U.S. captain rejoined us on the trail. As the fog turned to mist, I could see beyond the path into the small valley that contained twenty-eight wood plank barracks built to hold some 350 combatants. The UN camp was there to protect the URNG combatants and to receive their weapons. The weapons would be turned in when all the combatants were in the camp. When we arrived, there were only thirty-five combatants in the camp—the first to come down from the mountains. Another 300 would be coming down later that week in a large convoy accompanied by United Nations military officers.[2] So when I entered the camp with the UN military officers and Julia, there were several dozen URNG combatants milling around the entrance of the communal dining barrack. Julia seemed startled, and I noticed each combatant wore his machine gun as someone nervous about being late might wear a watch—remembering its presence and experiencing its precision with a touch and a glance. The U.S. captain asked one of the combatants to call the comandante.

While the U.S. captain seemed to really like Comandante Zacarias, the Venezuelan colonel had a greater affinity with him. As I was introduced, the comandante looked at the Venezuelan, who said, "She has already interviewed us and taken photographs in our camp. We explained the rules to her, that it is your camp and your decision. So we will leave you to talk to her and let her explain what she wants." Looking at me, he shook my hand and said, "We will wait for you in our camp. Good luck," and they left.

With the arrival of the comandante (who also carried a machine gun) and the departure of the UN officers, Julia had shrunk back so far that she was at the end of the building, leaning against a wall. She had made herself almost invisible, a well-developed skill. She was within earshot and she listened to my conversation with the comandante. I do not know if the comandante was unaware of her or simply indifferent to the presence of a small Ixil woman in *corte* and *huipil*.[3] I explained my research and I told him about the exhumations and my interviews with massacre survivors.

The comandante was taller than I, probably about five feet, nine inches, yet I doubt he weighed more than 120 pounds. In fact, beyond the machine guns, the most striking attribute of almost all the combatants was their bony, angular faces. They looked like they had been in the mountains surviving on weeds for years. They looked hungry. The comandante's face was weathered, with deep creases and skin nearly blackened by the sun and years of exposure to the elements. He smiled as he listened to me. He told me he had joined the EGP (Ejército Guerrillero Popular—Popular Guerrilla Army) sixteen years earlier and he had been living in the Ixil mountains for those sixteen years—nearly half his life. I asked him where he was from. He looked at me and said, "Didn't they tell you I am from El Salvador?" I replied that they had, but I wanted to know what part. He smiled skeptically, "Or you wanted to see if I would tell you." I nodded my head and said, "That could be. One never knows because it could be that one of the officers made a mistake. Someone also said you were trained in Cuba."

"It is true," he said with a wide smile. "People say a lot of things and one can never know." He never did clarify if "it is true" that he was trained in Cuba or that people say a lot of things. That particular truth was not the issue. It was simply part of the dance of calculation, a political subtext. He asked me where I lived, how long I had been working in Guatemala, which parts of the country I knew. I told him some stories of the communities where I had worked. I also told him I had interviewed army officials who in 1994 had mostly denied army responsibility for massacres, and who, by 1996, attempted to explain them away by saying that both the army and the guerrilla had made mistakes. I explained the thesis of David Stoll's book that the Ixiles were caught between two armies and that the guerrilla had provoked the army massacres.[4] I told him that I wanted to have the guerrilla combatant's perspective. Operating under the assumption that I would not be given access for interviews, I asked for interviews *and* photos, hoping I would at least be given permission to take photographs. The comandante, much to my surprise, said, "The camp is open. We want people to come talk to us and meet with us. The war is over. You can interview anyone you want." Registering my amazement and further testing his response, I asked, "With my tape recorder?" He nodded in agreement. He asked me to write my name and address in a primary school spiral notebook that was to be the visitor's log. I was the first name in the book. I also gave him my business card with my U.S. and Guatemala addresses and phone numbers.

He gathered the thirty-four other combatants then in the camp and announced that I would be taking photographs of the barracks and of the combatants, as well as interviewing them. He ordered them to answer my questions and allow me to tape record. "She has my permission. She can walk freely wherever she wants and have private conversations with whomever she chooses," he said. I told the comandante that I would like to speak with the Ixil combatant who had been in the guerrilla the longest. Like the comandante, Compañero[5] Benjamín was the same age as I. As I began to talk to Benjamín, the comandante disappeared and Julia returned to my side. She said in Ixil, "I am her translator." We walked into the dining barrack. As we walked through, I saw several men I recognized from Nebaj who acted as if they had been caught doing something wrong and almost pretended not to recognize me. One of them, Rosalio, looked at the ground instead of at me. I had the feeling they were involved in some kind of clandestine meeting and did not want to be seen in the reinsertion camp. Benjamín said, "*Compañera* Victoria is going to interview me. I will be back when we are done." The men relaxed, nodded in my direction, and went back to whatever they were doing.

From the picnic-like dining tables and benches, I could see two women combatants cooking in the kitchen, their machine guns leaning against the wall. They served us large plastic cups full of a hot, sweetened corn drink that I wanted to hold because my fingers were numb and stiff with cold. Benjamín and Julia conversed in Ixil as my near-numb fingers fumbled with my tape recorder, tapes, and batteries.

Like many young Maya males, Benjamín's rite of passage to adulthood occurred at sixteen when he joined the guerrilla. At that time, I too was sixteen, but my rite of passage was taking the examination for my driver's license. Benjamín rested his machine gun on the table but continued to fondle it throughout the interview. He was a short, stocky man with very thick, large glasses covering nearly half his face. He looked at me intensely as he spoke, frequently glancing at Julia for approval or agreement. I wanted him to talk about why he joined the guerrilla as a youth, while he wanted to talk about the politico-military strategy of the URNG.

When I concluded the interview with Benjamín, Julia suggested we go on to Tzalbal because it was late. More than three hours had passed since we first entered the UN compound, and there were people waiting to give testimony in Tzalbal. If we failed to arrive, they probably would not all gather again. I also noticed that Julia had become increasingly nervous as I interviewed Benjamín. As we bid goodbye to the combatants in the camp, several called out for me to take another photo because they had not been in the first photos. In the thirty seconds it took me to pull out my camera, Julia had once again disappeared to the end of the wall—this time to avoid having her face recorded in the photo.

When we reached the car, there were several youngsters hanging about and looking at my dog in the car. I let her out and Julia suggested we walk her. We walked en masse and told the boys and girls about Asha. Julia proudly put her on the leash (which she neither likes nor needs). "She is not a coyote," Julia explained to the kids. "She is a German Shepherd." She seemed happy to be walking Asha, but I could tell that she was agitated. I felt very guilty about the entire camp experience because it had simply grown beyond anything I had anticipated. Had I known that I would be going in to the URNG camp, I would never have suggested that Julia accompany me because of the potential repercussions of her being seen entering the camp. We returned to the car, paid the young man who had watched the dog, and gave treats to everyone else.

Once we were alone, I apologized to Julia. I asked her if she was scared when she saw the guns. "Of course," she said, "but, Victoria, forgive me, forgive me a lot because I lied and forgive me even more because I ask you to lie to support my lie." She was even more agitated now. Registering my confusion about her "lie," she looked straight into my eyes and held my arm as she said, "And Victoria, be very careful because the comandante had a notebook that was like the notebook the *responsable*[6] used to have when he came through our village. He would write down names and then those people would disappear. Who knows what happened to them." Her grip on my arm tightened, and she said, "Do not tell them where you live. And forgive me because I lied."

As my fingers had fumbled with my tape recorder, Benjamín had asked Julia her name. "María," she had responded. She had lied about where she was from, where she lived, and where she worked. "Please," she implored, "if they ask you my name, tell them you don't know. Tell them you cannot remember." She gave a nervous laugh and added, "Tell them you work with lots of Ixil women and we all look alike because we wear the same clothes. Forgive me that I ask you to lie for me. And please be very careful. I do not want anything to happen to you. He had that notebook. That is what concerns me."

It was the first time I had ever seen Julia afraid. I reminded Julia that I never repeated the names of people we interviewed or ever told anyone her name or the nature of our relationship. I also reaffirmed that I would use "Julia," the pseudonym she had chosen, rather than her real name in anything I might write.[7] Still, I asked her if she wanted to return to Nebaj, offering to cancel the meeting in Tzalbal. I told her there was nothing so valuable that it was worth her being frightened. "No," she said. "Let's go to Tzalbal. They will be waiting and they want to tell their stories. They have no one to talk to. They will be disappointed if we don't arrive. But don't tell them we went to the camp." I asked her what would happen if the young man who knew her uncle or one of the other men said she had been in the camp. She laughed, "I told them I was trying to get a job cooking for the ONU and you were trying to help me."

IN TZALBAL

The layout of Tzalbal suggested the same temporal quality that both the UN and URNG camps possessed. It seemed as though the area had been randomly cleared of trees to create space for makeshift housing construction.

The houses were close together but bushes, small trees, *palos*[8] and barbed wire formed a tapestry that created the illusion of distance between the houses. Although the paths for the most part followed a grid pattern, they were so narrow that I had to leave my Trooper several blocks away from our destination. A flurry of activity and children dashing in and out of the house greeted our arrival. The wood plank house had a hard beaten dirt floor, a main room measuring about three meters by five meters, and a kitchen measuring approximately three meters by one meter. The main room had three windows and a door, while the kitchen had no windows and one door. Someone closed both doors and all the wooden window shutters as soon as we walked in. Two empty chairs were on either side of a small wood table in the middle of the main room. One was an adult's chair, the seat taller than the tabletop, which did not quite reach my knees. The other was a child's chair, the seat maybe six inches from the floor. I was invited to sit at the table. Not wanting to tower over the people I would be meeting, I chose to sit in the child's chair. Everyone laughed at my large body folded onto this tiny chair. They invited me to take the larger chair because "it is better." In the Maya villages where I work, few of the men and almost none of the women reach above my shoulders in height. Committed to not towering over the people any more than I already do, I declined, saying, "No, no, thank you. I am very comfortable here."

Julia instructed me to get out my tape recorder because people would be arriving. Two women scurried about in the kitchen—one adding wood to the stove and the other making tortillas. I laid my tools on the table: tape recorder, cassettes, batteries, notebook, pen, and camera. Julia was talking with the women in the kitchen. I wanted to join them but decided to wait for Julia to invite me. Julia introduced me to Patricia, saying "This is her house. She has invited people we trust to come over to talk to you." Patricia gave me a cup of coffee. Still chilled to the bone, I quickly drank the warm mixture of coffee, sugar, and grain (equal thirds). Having had numerous cups of coffee all morning, I was thinking that I would have to use the latrine, there being no private bush, since the houses were so closely packed together. There was so much activity that I never had a chance to get up. The children continued to run in and out of the house as more people arrived. Soon there were thirteen people sitting on a bed that was pushed against the wall. It was the only other piece of furniture in the house. We chatted about Asha. I explained that she is a German Shepherd, not a coyote, and that there are breeds of dogs, just as there are breeds of chickens. As usual, they collectively agreed in Ixil that she is a coyote and that I don't know it because I am a *gringa*.[9]

I was quite taken with this group of people, who all took time out of their work day to meet with me. There was an older man who looked to be about sixty-five. There were several men and women between the ages of thirty and fifty. There was a very young man who looked to be no more than eighteen and a girl who was probably about sixteen. I thought about my full bladder as we all received more coffee. Soon everyone was talking about Asha and petting her. I was wondering what I was going to do with thirteen people and asked Julia for her thoughts. I forgot about my bladder. She explained that the person talking would sit with me at the table and the others would wait quietly on the bed. The thirteen people stopped talking. I caught a short wave of conversation in Ixil in which each person expressed his or her desire to speak. They thought I was saying that thirteen was too many people, meaning that everyone would not be heard. I told the group in Spanish, and Julia translated to Ixil, that I would speak with each and every person but thought it was better to do so in private. Soon, half the people were in the kitchen and the other half went home to await their turn. I assumed they were not coming back. I asked what had happened to the children and was told they were "*cuidando*" (taking care of/watching out for). They had been placed on the four corners of the house and would whistle if anyone walked by. Everyone was concerned that other people in Tzalbal might find out that they were talking and what they were talking about.

Before we began the interview, Julia cautioned, almost scolded, each individual not to tell anyone else in the village what we were doing. "If they ask what the gringa is doing here," she said, "tell them she is a student and she is doing an investigation on development. Tell them you hope it brings help, but probably not because she is only a student. Say you think she might buy some weavings. Do not tell anyone what we are really talking about." And so began my new identity in Nebaj. "Patricia is a afraid that some people in Tzalbal will be angry with her if they know she is talking about this," Julia explained to me. "So we only invited people we trust and we have to remind them not to tell." Curious about the composition of the group, I asked Julia what brought these particular people together to talk to me. "We used to be neighbors before," she said. "This man was my father's best friend. I know he won't tell anyone he came here and he knows a lot. The only person who might know more is my father, but he died."

Julia and I explained to Don Marcos that I wanted to know about *La Violencia* in Tzalbal. How was life before? How did the violence arrive? What happened? We explained that I would not use his real name.

He interrupted Julia's translation and said in Spanish, "Use my name. I have nothing left to lose. I am going to tell the truth and I am not ashamed." Julia and I thanked him but suggested he still might want to use a pseudonym and that he should think about it. Don Marcos spoke Spanish quite well but said he preferred to tell his story in Ixil because it was easier for him. I explained that I wanted him to tell me his story and that I would not interrupt him. I would write down my questions and wait until the end to ask new questions or clarify points he made.

As the day wore on and each person came to the table, Julia began to explain our procedure without waiting for me to say it in Spanish. My first thought was to stop her and ask her to wait to translate, but I realized her explanation was important for several reasons. First, it gave her a central role in the interview process and made her more than a translator. Second, she had well-developed relationships with these individuals and they trusted her. Third, when she explained the process straight out, they were more likely to ask her questions, and the people were more comfortable asking those questions without my participation. A critical question people always asked Julia in Ixil was: "Do I tell her everything?" Julia always answered, "Yes, everything. She is trustworthy." As I attempt to synthesize the stories and experiences, both mine and theirs, I now do so out of commitment to honor the enormous trust and faith Julia and the dozens of men and women we interviewed together placed in me. For it is somewhere in this willingness to trust that hope is expressed, and the right to justice is asserted in the sharing of painful fragmented memory. In a world where the emotional pain and its very causes are either denied or blamed on the victims themselves, the mere sharing of pain through memory is a proclamation of identity, a shedding of misplaced culpability. The transformation of a private memory creates a public space, however small, where survivors learn to speak; it breaks down externally imposed understandings and chips away at the power structures imposed through silent negotiation of life-shattering events. This book is my humble attempt to share what I have learned and what I have not, what I understand and what I do not. Borrowing words from Ariel Dorfman, "Let me tell you something. Even if I had been there I could not have told their story."[10]

INTRODUCTION

We want peace. We want people to know what happened here so that it does not happen here again, or in some other village in Guatemala, or in some other department, or in some other country.

—*Juan Manuel Gerónimo*

INDELIBLE MEMORIES

A cool blue river cutting through green pastures loses its colors. The crispness of water rushing over white rocks is silenced. The fresh scent of damp earth is soured. The river is a weapon. A handmaiden to pain. It quenches no thirst. It denies air. Instead of green and blue, the mind's eye sees the struggle to breathe. The effort to lift a broken limb. The water hits the rocks like elbows, ankles, and knees. A face is lost as it grates across a boulder. A boulder smooth and slick only to the hand that slides over it, grasping. Nails ripping. Teeth breaking. The water cold, almost frozen. Moving. Rocks bloodied. Everything hurts. The body is thrown to shore. Crumpled. Empty.

The river carries away the evidence. Washes the pain off the rocks. Carries it down through the valley, where women collect drinking water and children bathe. A child finds a tooth and tosses it to shore, where it turns into sand. The tooth is lost, forgotten. A missing part of the landscape of the scarred face. Its absence, like the empty army camp, a reminder of terror.

Terror is a place that occupies memory long after the base has closed. It is a filter that becomes the lens through which we understand the past and interpret the present, and upon which we base our hopes for the future. To find a path to understanding Guatemala's current transition from authoritarian rule and efforts to construct a democratic society based on rule of law, we must first seek an understanding of how the majority rural Maya experienced state and insurgent structures of terror and how they internalized these structures of terror as part of their individual and collective identities.[1] As Mahmood Mamdani suggests in his work on genocide in Rwanda, " . . . atrocity cannot be its own explanation. Violence cannot be allowed to speak for itself, for violence is not its own meaning. To be made thinkable, it needs to be *historicized*."[2] I suggest that those best able to historicize violence are those who have survived it.

LA VIOLENCIA

In any book or article about Guatemala, one is bound to come upon statistical data about *La Violencia:* 440 massacres in villages burned off the map by the Guatemalan army, one and a half million people were displaced, 150,000 fled into refuge, and 100,000–150,000 were dead or disappeared.[3] The 1999 release of the Report of the Commission for Historical Clarification provided evidence of massacres in 626 villages and raised the number of documented dead or disappeared to more than 200,000. It further identified 83 percent of the victims as Maya and attributed blame to the Guatemalan army for 93 percent of the human rights violations, violations that were so severe and systematically enacted against whole Maya communities that the CEH (Comisión para el Esclarecimiento Histórico—Commission for Historical Clarification) determined that the army had committed acts of genocide against the Maya.[4] The numbers are staggering for any country and especially for a country of only nine million citizens. But often times, when people become numbers, their stories can be lost.

In the rural communities of the departments of Chimaltenango, Baja Verapaz, Alta Verapaz, Huehuetenango, and El Quiché, where I have worked, rural Maya emphasize the form and content, as well as the magnitude of the violence. They use "La Violencia" to name the time in the life of their communities when they suffered extreme violence at the hands of the state, and sometimes at the hands of the guerrilla. But what does the term "La Violencia" really mean? What does it reveal, what does it mask? And to whom does it give voice? In urban Guatemala, "La Violencia" generally refers to the years 1978 to 1982. This is a periodization of the violence perpetrated under the regimes of General Lucas García (1978–82) and General Ríos Montt (March 1982–August 1983). This usage of the term implies a time-bounded definition of La Violencia, relegating the Guatemalan experience of selective state terror in rural and urban Guatemala and its transition to mass terror culminating in the genocide of the "scorched earth" campaign to the status of an event within a linear chronology. While rural invocations of La Violencia might include the time period between 1978 and 1982, they are just as likely to include 1978–85 (from the terror of the military regimes to the 1985 elections), 1978–90 (from selective violence to the last bombings in the Ixil mountains in 1990), or even 1978–96 (from selective violence through to the disarming of the last civil patrols with the signing of the 1996 peace accords).

For rural Maya survivors, both victims and victimizers, La Violencia represents more than an event or a historical marker of a discrete period of extreme state violence. It represents the continuum of lived experience. It represents not only the actual violent events (indeed most Maya begin their testimony of La Violencia with the first act of violence in their community, an act that typically foretold a wave of extreme and widespread violence) but also the experience of that violence and its effects. These effects included silencing the Maya through the near total closing of opportunities for social and political participation, which in turn further curtailed whatever freedom of speech they may have had. Thus, the impossibility of contesting terror was one of the effects of La Violencia, and this powerlessness is implicit in La Violencia in both its definition and usage. In this way, the term "La Violencia" is also used as a demarcation between the violence of the past and a contemporary, ongoing contestation of that violence.

When I first visited Guatemala in 1990,[5] I was struck by the use of the term "La Situación," which is how people named the violence when they were living it. "La Situación," or the use of this term, is a by-product of the terror and reflects the internalization of both previous and ongoing violence by the government.[6] By 1994, the change in vocabulary from "La Situación" to "La Violencia" reflected as much a change in state terror as it did a change in the experiential space of social and political participation. To say "La Violencia" was to assert an opening for freedom to speak. The term was perhaps limited in its ambiguity but was nonetheless active in its denouncement of the past—La Violencia could only be publicly named as "La Violencia" when it became the past. In other words, the ability of victims and survivors to say "La Violencia" instead of "La Situación" represents a shift in power for the individual and community—they have the power to name the lived experience and to do so with a far more explicit name than "La Situación."

Though one might argue that "La Violencia" is a somewhat neutral term in that it lacks explicit reference to repression, terror, and state responsibility for genocide, I would argue that its meaning has shifted as Guatemalan society has begun to come to terms with its violent past through various forms of truth telling. Moreover, the term "La Violencia" embodies the relationship of the military state with its citizenry, and the shift from naming this relationship "La Situación" to naming it "La Violencia" marks a shift in the balance of power defining the relationship between the state and its citizens.

All told, La Violencia is a sociopolitical phenomena both veiled and revealed in its history and naming. Like the terror of its past, its memory is a contested terrain upon which the shifting tensions and allegiances of all sectors of Guatemalan society create, adapt, and lose control in their conflicting struggles for domination, liberation, and peace. In this way, while the phenomenon of La Violencia must be understood as a result of terror (and ultimately genocide) designed and carried out by the Guatemalan state against its citizens, resistance to terror, both insurgent and democratic, as well as the role of elite economic sectors and international interests, must also be contemplated. By maintaining the tension between the engagement of structure and agency, this framework not only recognizes the significant roles of Generals Lucas García and Ríos Montt in the design and execution of state terror but also provides the opportunity to behold the myriad political spaces created by sectors of civil society under the most repressive of conditions.

FORENSIC ANTHROPOLOGY AND THE STUDY OF VIOLENCE

Most research on violence focuses on individual, community, or national interpretations of social, cultural, and political phenomena.[7] These patterns of analysis reflect conceptual research approaches that are based on very specific case studies or global analyses. My research is different in that I use a heterodoxy of methods, including quantitative and qualitative, to move from the micro to the macro by documenting popular mobilization of indigenous communities around issues of past violence and its relationship to ongoing efforts to institutionalize democratic practices in Guatemala.

To carry out this research, I selected communities where massacres had occurred during La Violencia. I began my preliminary fieldwork in 1994, working with the Guatemalan Forensic Anthropology Foundation (Fundación de Antropología Forense de Guatemala—FAFG)[8] on an exhumation in Plan de Sánchez, an isolated village in the mountains of Rabinal, Baja Verapaz. As I moved forward in my research design, I chose a multisite approach that included Ixil, K'iche', Kaqchikel, Q'eqchi', and Achi[9] villages from the northwest highlands to the central lowlands to the eastern mountains. This multisite approach allows for an analysis of violence that is specific to historical contexts of different communities while at the same time offers opportunities for generalized conclusions about the similarities, contradictions, and complexities of the lived experiences of violence for the majority rural Maya throughout Guatemala. During my research, it has been, and remains, my intention to use the strengths of anthropological ethnographic research to engage debates not only in my own discipline but also in history, political science, and critical legal studies, as well as public policy debates.

The process of the exhumations also begs the question "how silent are silences?"[10] Mass graves of massacre victims are referred to as clandestine cemeteries. Yet a cemetery is generally understood to mean a sacred place where the rites of burial and mourning are publicly observed and the remains of the deceased are entombed. These clandestine cemeteries were hidden in that they were silenced, but survivors, witnesses, and most community members know the locations of these graves. Thus, they are truly clandestine only in the official negation of their existence and the silence imposed on communities. They are cemeteries, albeit illegal cemeteries of mass graves, in that despite the imposed silence and fear, community members clandestinely left flowers at the grave sites to acknowledge their relationship with the deceased.

As an exhumation begins, the site of a mass grave containing the remains of massacre victims (often the actual site of the massacre, as well) becomes a community space for local healing and a site for the reconstruction of larger social relations. A space for the physical exhumation of bones and artifacts, as well as the excavation of individual and collective memory. In this book, I look at the exhumations not only as the evidence gathered by forensic archeologists and forensic anthropologists but also as the process of the excavation of memory and retaking of public space. The survivor testimonies I have gathered provide the context of the physical evidence, and the collection of these stories is integral to the forensic investigation. The theoretical relationship between the physical evidence and the stories echoes the methodology of anthropology as a discipline.[11] The exhumation demands a coming to terms with space: physical space for the excavation, public space for memory, political space created by the exhumation, and the individual and collective giving of testimonies, each of which creates new space. Moreover, beyond the forensic value of the testimonies, I suggest that the language used in the testimonies is itself evidence of the genocide. The language used in testimonies is not just a collection of words randomly strung together, nor is it simply a story of the genocide. The language itself is a part of the genocide.[12] The legacy of trauma is embedded in the language, just as it is embedded in other structures of the culture. The language is one of extremity, of surviving a violence so extreme that it falls into the category of what many have called "limit events."[13]

In my fieldwork, I collected more than 400 lengthy testimonies from massacre survivors, former soldiers, civil patrollers, and insurgent combatants in rural areas. I also conducted interviews with rural and urban leaders of human rights organizations, high-ranking military officers, and government officials. My approach allows me to analyze how violence is remembered and experienced before and after a public space for memory of violence is established, while measuring shifts in political space created by the exhumation of clandestine cemeteries and the excavation of collective local memory.[14] Significantly, I was able to interview these leaders several times between 1994 and 1998 and meet with many again in 2002. This has allowed me to describe shifts in their perceptions of La Violencia over time. Interviews with military and guerrilla leaders have provided unexpected insight.

Initially, the army denied having committed massacres and the guerrilla denied having committed any atrocities. By 1997, five years of exhumations of clandestine cemeteries of army massacre victims had firmly placed army responsibility for the slaughter of civilians in the public consciousness. This has forced some military officials to recognize the army role in massacres—albeit with many reservations and justifications. Following the 1999 release of the final report of CEH,[15] which found the guerrilla had committed three percent of the human rights violations, guerrilla leaders were forced to publicly come to terms with violence committed against civilian populations. Though just as apt to use the same types of reservations and justifications as the army, though through a different ideological lens, the URNG (Unión Revolucionaria Nacional

Guatemalteca—Guatemalan National Revolutionary Union) publicly apologized to the Guatemalan people. The army, whom the CEH found responsible for 93 percent of human rights violations, remained silent despite CEH urging that both armed parties had a moral obligation to make an apology for their atrocities.[16] Guatemalan President Alvaro Arzú fell in line with the army denying "that there was a genocide during the armed conflict, disagreeing for the first time with the Historical Clarification Commission."[17] At the same time, President Bill Clinton affirmed the CEH's findings with his unequivocal condemnation of past U.S. intervention and support for four decades of Guatemalan state terror: "For the United States, it is important that I state clearly that support for military forces and intelligence units which engaged in violence and widespread repression was wrong, and the United States must not repeat that mistake. We must, and we will, instead, continue to support the peace and reconciliation process in Guatemala."[18]

Clinton

Despite the recalcitrance of the Guatemalan army and president, these reluctant and limited acknowledgments of responsibility represent the intersection, or perhaps clash, of political space with new public space for memory. Interviews (even with military officials) become a space where something happens between political and public space. Army officials on the one hand speak in a collective official voice, yet on the other also convey something of their own individual experience. One high-ranking official told me that when he thought of human rights workers, prior to meetings with me and with a South American human rights activist, he had envisioned someone "wearing a Ché Guevara beret with a star and carrying a machine gun."[19] Shifts in their perceptions represent changes in official and individual understandings, as well as the coming to terms, both institutionally and individually, with new political space created by physical and discursive evidence gathered in exhumations.

Archival research in municipal offices, particularly reviews of death registers from 1978 to 1990, provided critical data documenting waves of violence at the local level. Working with an archival research team from the FAFG, we were able to amass and analyze a tremendous amount of data from municipal archives. A comparison of this type of data from five different communities across the country illustrated national shifts in violence. The most surprising aspect of this research for me was the great detail with which assassinations and massacres were documented in death registers that frequently named the responsible institution. This was surprising given the amount of fear, secrecy, and shame surrounding massacres and extrajudicial killings. With the help of research assistants in Guatemala, I was able to carry out an extensive archival review of Guatemalan newspapers and their coverage of La Violencia between 1978 and 1984.[20] Significantly, I had the privilege to work closely with several CEH investigators in the field and also serve as a research consultant to the FAFG for their report to the CEH.

As is often the case in fieldwork, upon my return to the United States, I found that my research had both affirmed and changed my approach. A central theme of this book is that redress for past human rights violations is a critical component to transitions from military regimes.[21] My research reaffirms and provides evidence to support this theory. At the same time, my research also demonstrates that truth, memory, community healing, and justice are integral to a successful transition from an authoritarian regime and that there can be no rule of law or democracy without attending to issues of truth and memory.[22] Redress for past human rights violations is the cornerstone to rule of law and, importantly, this redress transcends narrow legal definitions because it can take many forms. For example, exhumations, collective remembering, public acknowledgment, burial, and public mourning are all forms of redress. And like the trials of perpetrators that victims seek, none of these forms of redress offers a singular, comprehensive resolution. While my research challenges simplistic conceptualizations of reconciliation often proffered by international agencies, it also suggests that peaceful community reconstruction is possible after genocide.

ON TRANSLATION AND VOICE

I worked with Spanish-speaking Maya and monolingual speakers of Achi, K'iche', Kaqchiquel, Q'eqchi', and Ixil. I chose my translators from among the Spanish speakers I most trusted and believed would not translate through the ideological lens of the army or guerrilla. Choosing my translators from among those Spanish speakers I had already interviewed gave me insight into their understanding of La Violencia and their own interest in understanding it better. I most often chose women translators because I found that Maya men and women trust women more than men because men can too easily be identified as "guerrilla" or "army," and most Maya men were in the army, civil patrols, and/or guerrilla during La Violencia. Thus, men are always viewed with suspicion.

Additionally, women survivors are more willing to discuss war crimes against women with other women survivors. Quite simply, to both rural Maya men and women, Maya women translators can ask questions that men cannot.

After establishing strong ties with these translators, I often conducted interviews in Maya languages even with bilingual Maya because the victims and survivors were more comfortable recounting their lived experiences of violence in their Maya language. They experience their lives and culture in their language—Spanish being an "outside" language. Working with trusted Maya women from the community in Maya languages, I gained more of an "inside" position. From my translators, I learned a great deal about communication in the villages. In addition to learning some of the language, in each community I learned much about local culture and custom. In a sense, my translators translated me, not just my words, so that I was understandable to the community.

Ultimately, these translators opened up their lives and their communities to me. They were the ones who translated systems of thought and approach. They made arrangements for me to conduct clandestine interviews in villages where people were still too frightened to be seen in public speaking with an outsider. We went to army bases and guerrilla reinsertion camps. I lived these experiences not only as a researcher but also as shared experiences with my translators. These women were not just translators; they became my most trusted friends. My research became part of their experience with La Violencia. We compared their experiences as survivors to those of others we interviewed. We sought understanding together. We shared insight and pain on those days that overwhelmed. "Aren't you overwhelmed?" I asked Julia after the fourteenth testimony on a particularly cold, damp day as I looked out at the line of survivors still waiting to give testimony. "Of course, Victoria," she responded. "But they want to talk and who else will listen?"

We guided one another through the process. All the translators were tireless. They were peasant women accustomed to rising at four in the morning and working until after dark by the light of a fire. They worked me from five or six in the morning until nine or ten at night. They laughed when I would tell them I was exhausted. There was always one more interview, one more testimony, or one more house to visit. They made me tireless, too. I learned things about La Violencia in rural Maya villages that I have never seen in any literature on Guatemala nor heard discussed on any academic or policy panel.

Most importantly, what I learned about La Violencia was taught to me by survivors. They taught me of their human agency. They shared with me what was most significant, what most marked their public and private lives. In this process of sharing, they too marked my life. My research and subsequent writings are now a part of their experience with La Violencia and their memories of La Violencia are a part of my life. Dominick LaCapra has called this "a kind of virtual experience" whereby the secondary witness who takes or listens to testimonies of survival experiences transference. This "[o]pens oneself to empathetic unsettlement," which he considers to be "a desirable affective dimension of inquiry which complements and supplements empirical research and analysis."[23] So now, as I contemplate theoretical issues involving redress for past human rights violations in transitions from military regimes, I do it through the multiple lenses of survivors of La Violencia.

The collection of testimonies has forced me to challenge every aspect of my research from the complex and contradictory perspective of survivors. I feel a great responsibility to the communities in which I worked.[24] I also believe that I must honor the words shared with me, lived experiences of violence as understood by survivors. The taking of testimony, the interview, provided a space for survivors (1) to tell of their experiences, (2) to teach a larger community of their history (and of this they were always conscious), (3) to create an open space and be accompanied as they came to terms with what had happened to them as individuals and communities, (4) to provide context to the physical exhumation, and (5) to be heard and have their words valued rather than negated. The very process of taking testimonies reveals a new kind of agency, one that historicizes and attempts to make sense and provide context for both the speaker and the listener.[25] This parallels the physical process of digging up bones and artifacts and conducting scientific analysis of forensic evidence to reconstruct the crime scene (the massacre), the returning of the remains to the community, proper religious burials, community and national recognition of massacres, and the building of memorials for the historical memory of future generations.

TRUTH, MEMORY, AND HUMAN RIGHTS

This book is about La Violencia in Guatemala from the perspective of rural Maya survivors. Yet it is not frozen in their histories of the past.

Rather, it is a chronicle of the present in which memories of La Violencia are embedded in contemporary discourse and practice. Though the research presented here focuses on Guatemala, the theoretical and practical political issues it raises resonate with current internal turmoil in Colombia, East Timor, the former Yugoslavia, South Africa, Rwanda, Burma, Sri Lanka, and other countries in which unsettled histories of past repression continue to form much of the terrain for contemporary power struggles. Moreover, observations and analyses about La Violencia offer new ways of understanding the necessary components for national reconstruction and peacebuilding in Guatemala and beyond. Among these components are truth, memory, history, terror, and genocide.

Before I could begin to explore the current transition from authoritarian rule, efforts for national reconstruction, and establishment of rule of law in Guatemala, I found that I had to first problematize the slippery concepts of terror and genocide. In the process, I discovered that truth and memory are as integral to analyses of terror and genocide as the latter are to transition from authoritarian rule and societal reconstruction. These considerations raised more questions than they answered. How do we think about human agency? What is the relationship among culture, politics, language, race, ethnicity, class, and gender? What is truth? How is it historically constructed? How is history created, written, challenged, and rewritten? How do we understand terror? What is the interaction between memory and history? How do we understand human rights after genocide?

To explore the discourse and practice of human rights, it is necessary to enter the structures, their effects, and how they are experienced to understand the types of possibilities presented by the different ways one might approach research on the topic.[26] Human rights implies a series of domains: human beings and the meaning of being human and the relationship between the state and "bare life," and the variety of local, national, international, and nongovernmental institutions that define, create, and enact human rights discourse and practice.[27] Given the multiple locations in which the qualities and rights pertaining to the condition of being human are constituted and formalized as human rights, there is no reason to assume that there must be a single epistemological space in which to explore human rights as an object of anthropological inquiry. The anthropological method provides an opportunity for critical exploration of the theory and practice of human rights in its multiple locations and contexts.

Anthropologists are concerned with boundaries and their different configurations. Anthropology can make connections among the local, national, and international expressions of human rights practices as well as local appropriations of global rights discourses.[28] Because anthropologists can have close relationships with those who are the victims of human rights violations and those who organize their communities for recognition of their rights, anthropologists can greatly enhance legally bound understandings of human rights.[29] Indeed, "owing to our knowledge and experience, our theoretical and practical research skills, we are in a unique position to further the causes of human rights and justice."[30]

In the case of Guatemala, while David Stoll creates a binary between the army and guerrilla in which the Maya were caught "between two armies," Linda Green identifies fear in Guatemala as a chronic condition embedded in social memory.[31] In her analysis of La Violencia, Judith Zur asserts that this "memory is not only a personal, subjective experience but also a social phenomenon."[32] On the role of the anthropologist studying terror, Kay Warren observes that "while there are horrors I know but cannot recount," it is still possible for anthropologists to "work to understand the violence of memories only partially revealed and partially revealable."[33] Are narratives of terror evidence of the process "whereby a culture of terror was created and sustained," as Michael Taussig suggests?[34] Does survival of terror signify "a new understanding of meaning and action," as Carolyn Nordstrom asserts?[35]

What of E. Valentine Daniel's claim, in his work on Sri Lanka, that if one looks for the causes of violence and possible solutions "they may well rest in forgetting the causes and remembering the carnage in 'paradise'?"[36] Describing his survival in Auschwitz, Primo Levi wrote, "History had stopped."[37] If history can be stopped, how can it be started again? Can remembering the atrocities without benefit of the context of history explain anything beyond the acts of violence themselves? Is it even possible to remember the violence without remembering the history? Is the giving of testimony a means through which survivors can face their "past and at the same time interface with the present," as Yazir Henry writes of his own survival under apartheid and his testimony before the Truth and Reconciliation Commission?[38]

The burgeoning literature on terror suggests agreement on the value of work aimed at understanding extreme violence and/or its aftermath. Though the approaches may differ, most of the literature also suggests a desire to confront and seek understanding of the causes of violence.

Yet the observations, analyses, and interpretations are as striking at the nexus of their contradictions as they are in their points of agreement. Michael Taussig, Nancy Scheper-Hughes, and Kay Warren, among others, argue that anthropologists have an ethical and moral obligation to write against terror.[39] Nordstrom, Green, and Zur have attempted to do this in their anthropological work, in which one finds active engagement with and a conscious struggle to enact this obligation. It is not only anthropologists who consider this moral responsibility. Through his life's work on the Holocaust, Primo Levi insisted that "it is everyone's obligation to reflect on what happened."[40] In her work on Argentina's Dirty War, Marguerite Feitlowitz made clear that "testimony fulfills the sacred obligation to bear witness, and however discomfiting it may be for us, our pain, though great, is minor compared with that of the victims."[41] Elaine Scarry asserts that "acts that restore the voice become not only a denunciation of the pain but almost a diminution of the pain, a partial reversal of the process of torture itself."[42] Is there meaning to be found beyond the researcher's obligation and the survivor's need for healing?

If we preface our analysis of terror with an exploration of agency, how might that shift analyses? Recent scholarship in subaltern studies[43] and Latin American *testimonio*[44] offer a different theoretical vantage point from which to problematize truth, memory, and terror. Subaltern studies bring the issue of agency to the forefront, and testimonio presents lived experience from the perspective of the Latin American subaltern. What new ways might we find to theorize agency and memory if we bring the subaltern and testimonio literatures into dialogue with cultures of violence and structures of history? How might this in turn impact how we theorize terror? How might terror problematized through agency and memory shift the grounding from which we observe and analyze transitions from authoritarian regimes and measure the construction of rule of law? Finally, what types of redress and reconstruction might be revealed by this new subaltern view?

This book offers new ways of addressing these largely philosophical, yet inherently practical, political questions in Guatemala and beyond. Further, my research makes clear that the subaltern view opens new paths to understanding the synergetic structural relationships among terror, memory, and history. The exploration of truth and human rights in these various domains has allowed for the development of three ethnographic themes throughout the book.

The forensic investigation that outlines the scientific process of the exhumation of clandestine cemeteries and the integral role of testimony to the excavation process is the first theme. This ethnography, which unfolds throughout the book, becomes a framework for understanding local attempts to make meaning of the experience of survival, community interaction with the exhumation and forensic team, as well as my own experience as an ethically engaged witness and participant-observer. It is the totality of the exhumations (excavations, testimonies, archival research, and laboratory analysis) that reveals the perpetration of genocide against the Maya and its intellectual and material authors, as well as contemporary local efforts to rebuild Maya communities.

The second theme is an ethnography of massacres and genocide based on participation in the exhumation of clandestine cemeteries in six different communities and field research on massacres in seven other communities. Just as the forensic investigation becomes a framework for revealing evidence of the massacres and genocide, this ethnography, based on testimonies of survivors, interviews with perpetrators, and archival research, provides an opportunity to understand the structure and context of La Violencia from the lived experience of survivors. This perspective is critical for understanding the contemporary transitional justice in which survivors live and seek to rebuild their lives and communities.

Local community mobilizations for truth, justice, and healing are the third theme. This ethnography follows communities from the first exhumations in the early 1990s to their current and ongoing efforts for justice. How did communities move from requesting proper burials to demanding public recognition of truth? How did survivors add justice and prosecution of perpetrators to their demands? What is the relationship between justice and healing in the Maya communities? Is reconciliation related to truth? To justice?

Chapter one begins with my own account of participating in the Guatemalan Forensic Anthropology Foundation's exhumation of a clandestine cemetery in Plan de Sánchez in 1994. I discuss the four phases of the FAFG's forensic anthropology investigation and interface it with massacre survivors' experiences and the Guatemalan court system. Through Plan de Sánchez massacre survivor testimonies, I also begin the history of exhumations in Guatemala.

In "The Silencing of Maya Women," chapter two, I explore the political consciousness, self-representation, and action of Maya women on the one hand and their continued exclusion from "official" local and national politics on the other. The intersections of truth, memory, and history; representations of "political" Maya women; and the discursive violence to which they have been subjected, from the martyred Mamá Maquín to Nobel Laureate Rigoberta Menchú, are ethnographically critiqued. Specifically, this chapter analyzes and challenges revisionist representations made by David Stoll in his reconstruction and deconstruction of Guatemalan history through the life of Rigoberta Menchú.[45] Finally, this chapter points to the urgency to include the voices of survivors (and particularly women) in analyses of violence, not simply as descriptive contextualization but as lived experiences that provide interpretation and give meaning to the very structures of state violence.

Based on research in the municipal archives, witness interviews, and the 1997 archeological excavation of massacre victims in Acul, chapter three raises the question of how we think about human agency and how we decide what is "true." Truth and memory are explored, beginning in 1978 with community responses to increasing violence in the Ixil Area and continuing through to the report of the CEH. In addition to my narrative, the story of Acul is recreated through multiple voices of survivors with a particular focus on Don Sebástian, a principal (Maya religious leader), and Doña Elena, a young widow of the massacre.[46]

Chapter four follows the massacre survivors in flight from army attacks in the mountains. In the voices of survivors, it chronicles their travails during the two years they fled army attacks. With the same voices, it explores their return to Acul and the subsequent reconstruction of their community under army control. This chapter continues the story of Acul and builds on discussions of agency, truth, and memory in previous chapters.

In chapter five I introduce the schema of the phenomenology of terror that I have developed based on ethnographic research working with survivors of massacres in villages in the municipalities of Chimaltenango, San Martín Jilotepeque, San Andrés Sajcabajá, Santa Cruz del Quiché, Chichicastenango, Nebaj, Cotzal, Chajul, Ixcán, Panzós, El Estór, Rabinal, Cubulco, Salamá, Cobán, San Miguel Acatán, and San Miguel Chicaj. Through comparative presentation of ethnographic data from these different communities, the phenomenology of terror becomes a means of understanding and contesting the violence of the past and the fear that continues to thrive long after actual physical violence dissipates. This comparative analysis of my ethnographies in tandem with the findings of the Commission for Historical Clarification also provides sufficient evidence for the identification of Guatemalan state violations of specific

United Nations conventions and protocols as well as the American Convention on Human Rights.

In chapter six, I demonstrate how massacres as a strategy of state terror shifted systematically to a decade-long series of army genocide campaigns against the Maya. I provide evidence to prove that each of the three campaigns of genocide I have identified is a clear violation of the United Nations Genocide Convention and that each of these campaigns was designed and implemented by the Guatemalan army with the intention of genocide.

Ranajit Guha's "prose of counterinsurgency" and Michel Foucault's "Fearless Speech" serve as theoretical frameworks to contrast official and academic discourses on La Violencia to survivor testimonies in chapter seven.[47] By presenting abbreviated life histories of survivors in contrast to academic and other elite representations of La Violencia, this method of presentation allows us to consider the different conclusions that can be drawn about the causes of La Violencia, depending upon which voices are privileged, and shows how genocide can be shrouded by the unwitting adoption of official discourse.

In chapters eight, nine, and ten, I return to Plan de Sánchez and other villages in Rabinal, where I began my fieldwork in 1994, to explore the impact of exhumations and truth telling on local communities and contemporary understandings of La Violencia. In chapter eight, through the testimonies of Juan Manuel Gerónimo and Pablo, we learn about life after the massacres in Rabinal: the militarization of villages through army-controlled civil patrols, who benefited financially from the massacres, how survivors carefully mobilized to dismantle civil patrols in their communities, how they organized to collectively request exhumations, and the danger and death threats they experienced throughout the process. This chapter ethnographically explores how people understand and experience the state and create new local, national, and transnational organizations in the aftermath of extreme violence. Testimony and its relationship to community reconstruction are considered through community experiences and reflections on the exhumations and truth.

In chapter nine, I continue with the ethnography of Plan de Sánchez and explore the impact of the 1994 exhumation on the larger Rabinal community and shifting power in civil/military relations at the local level. I track the founding of a community healing project in Rabinal, the Archbishop's *Nunca Más* investigation, and the work of the Commission for Historical Clarification.[48] In this way, I examine not only the organization and impact of the CEH but also the genesis and organization of local community healing projects from the perspective of citizens in marginalized communities who have a very real stake in undoing the ambient violence that engulfs them. I look at the way local communities respond and recuperate by mobilizing local culture and material resources to create new public political space and new healing practices and sites for individuals and communities.

In chapter 10, "Genocide and the 'Grey Zone' of Justice," I focus on the 1999 trial and murder conviction of military commissioners for their participation in the massacre of Río Negro, the exhumation of clandestine cemeteries, and other current rural Maya human rights initiatives. This final chapter discusses contemporary debates about truth versus justice, international tribunals versus domestic prosecution, a nation's international legal obligations, and the interplay of these practices and discourses at the local level. I call attention to the myriad ways in which rural Maya have created and seized new political spaces in Guatemala's nascent democracy, thereby making Maya community human rights organizing a nexus of engagement between Maya citizens and the nation. This chapter points to the absolute necessity of Maya participation in constructing national and community political structures and practices in order for these projects to truly realize their creative intention of developing a new moral vision of equality and human rights in Guatemala.

One

"THE BONES DON'T LIE"

I raffled the truth to declare the truth. Before the exhumation, all the people hid everything inside.

—*Juan Manuel Gerónimo*

In June 1994 I began my fieldwork, which focused on the Guatemalan Forensic Anthropology Foundation (Fundación de Antropología Forense de Guatemala—FAFG) exhumation of a clandestine cemetery in Plan de Sánchez. After a six-hour bus ride, Kathleen Dill and I reached Rabinal— a small rural town of about 6,000 inhabitants with some 18,000 more living in surrounding villages.[1] It was in the late afternoon on a Thursday, and we noticed that all the doors and windows of all the houses were shut. We reached Rabinal just as the forensic team was departing for Guatemala City for the weekend to take care of some paperwork. We had missed the FAFG's first week of work at the site. They offered us a ride to the city in the back of the truck, but by then, it was nearly four o'clock and we had been in transit (on buses) since six in the morning. We decided to stay for the weekend. There was no public transportation to Plan de Sánchez and it wasn't safe for us to walk to the village alone, so we waited until Monday, when the FAFG returned in the early morning, to go up the mountain. Though just eight kilometers above Rabinal, it took some forty minutes for a four-wheel drive vehicle to climb the mountains to reach the small village. It lies so high in the mountains that we left the fog of the morning behind in the valley of Rabinal. We reached the clear morning sky at the top of the mountain, and looking down, we saw a blanket of clouds resting in the valley.

When we reached Plan de Sánchez and began to hike up the hill to the clandestine cemetery, my body was overcome with a cold sweat. My hands were alternately hot and cold, and sweating regardless. I felt light headed and my stomach started to cramp. I remembered having seen a video of the first FAFG exhumation in El Quiché. In the video, Dr. Clyde Snow[2] was holding what looked like a reddish brown walnut in his hand and saying, "This is a piece of brain matter." My feet felt heavy as I continued the short walk up the hill. I began to concentrate on not fainting. I felt like I was going to vomit. "Don't faint. Don't vomit. I won't faint. I won't vomit," I repeated to myself as the conversations around me seemed to drift far away. Then I began to panic. I thought, "I can't faint and I can't vomit. If I do, I will be humiliated in front of the survivors with whom I want to work and I will be incapable of carrying out my research. This is too important." Then, we were at the site.

Much to my relief, there were no visible skeletons because, as I later learned, the team never leaves any exposed. They always complete as much as they can before leaving and cover any incompletely excavated skeletons. Recovering from the negative rush of adrenaline, I still felt like I was outside my body. As I stood above a large open pit watching the archeologists uncover half-excavated skeletons, the lead archeologist, Fernando Moscoso, handed me a chopstick and a small paintbrush. He pointed to a section of the grave and said, "If you please, why don't you begin by cleaning out that area over there." I was lost somewhere in what Trinh Minh-ha calls "being in the in-between of all definitions of truth."[3] The "in-between" of I'm not vomiting, I haven't fainted, what a beautiful valley, everything is greener than green, those are real bones, my god 200 people were massacred here, their relatives are watching. Self-consciously, I felt as if all the people (and especially the peasants) were registering my discomfort until I realized that Fernando was talking to me. Without thinking, I obediently accepted the chopstick and brush. I climbed into the grave, slowly walked over to the section he had indicated, and gingerly began to clear away loose dirt. My training in anthropology prepared me to study sociocultural structures from the community to the nation state. I had no training in the archeological skills of site excavation or any osteological knowledge, which was necessary to analyze skeletal remains. As I reluctantly began to brush away the earth, I didn't even notice that my friend Kathleen had been sent to work with another archeologist. Unlike me, Kathleen was well prepared for this type of work because, due to time spent as an x-ray and surgical imaging technician, she had extensive knowledge of the human skeleton and skeletal trauma. She also had some training in archeology. Kathleen was an immediate asset to the team.

As for me, I imagine that as he watched my tentative and clumsy movements, Fernando realized I had no idea what I was doing. He came over and showed me how to break the dirt and brush more systematically. Soon, I was caught in the intricacies of the excavation and its many puzzles. When I discovered a bone, I had to think about which bone it was, which meant I also had to learn the human skeleton. I had to think about how the skeleton was positioned and how best to uncover it. I had to learn the intricacies of an incredibly tedious process. Fernando supervised my work. He had a lot more confidence in my abilities than I did. When I completed the process of brushing the earth away from a skeleton, Fernando would join me. He would lift and examine each bone. He would show me whatever signs of trauma or damage he found. I would inventory the bones, record any observations of trauma, mark the bags in which the bones were to be stored, and pack them away. As the day ended, I was relieved that I had not had to sit and watch all day. I found patience doing the digging and it was a patience I knew would have eluded me had my role been restricted to that of observer.

The exhumation of a clandestine cemetery is much more than the archeological excavation of the graves. Each exhumation has four phases. This methodology of the forensic anthropology investigation has been developed by the FAFG through its experience working in Maya communities, often under difficult circumstances, including geographic inaccessibility of isolated communities and lack of adequate facilities in which to carry out the work.[4]

The methodology of the forensic anthropology investigation has four phases. The first phase includes antemortem interviews, collection of survivor testimony, and archival research. The antemortem interview is conducted with surviving relatives about the height, weight, and physical health history of the victims; this includes any particular life events, such as broken bones, dental work, or abnormalities. This basic information is used to reconstruct the osteological biography of each of the victims, with the goal of using this information in the identification process.[5] Later each bone will be compared to each section of the antemortem interview both manually and through the antemortem interview database program.

These interviews are conducted by FAFG forensic anthropologists and expert consultants, generally with a translator, since the majority of survivors are monolingual speakers of one of the twenty-one Maya languages.

Survivor and witness testimony is collected with the objective of locating the mass graves as well as reconstructing the events leading up to the massacre, the massacre itself, and its aftermath. Archival research consisting of review and analysis of all available official, academic, and media documents pertaining to the massacre assists in both forensic research and historical reconstruction.

This first phase is conducted simultaneously with phase two, which is the actual archaeological excavation, because many survivors and witnesses come forth for the first time when the ground is broken to begin the excavation and others continue to come forward throughout the excavation. Thus, antemortem interviews and the collection of testimony usually continue throughout most of the exhumation.

The archaeological excavation begins with the identification, mapping, and excavation of the massacre site, which is, in forensic terms, the crime scene. It is concluded with the exhumation of the remains and recuperation of all associated artifacts including personal belongings, clothing, bullet and grenade fragments, etc. This phase utilizes archeological techniques and each step is documented with technical drawings, photographs, and video because the archaeological context of the clandestine cemetery is completely destroyed by the end of the exhumation. These drawings, photographs, and video are vital to documenting the crime scene—for example, they provide documentary scientific evidence of the massacre and its specifics, including cause of death, whether victims' hands and/or feet had been bound together, and whether victims were killed before or after being placed in the grave.[6]

In the months that I worked with the FAFG in Plan de Sánchez, I assisted in the excavation of more than two dozen skeletons. I learned osteology and forensic archeology while excavating clandestine graves. And I felt very fortunate because as Dr. Snow told me when he came to visit the site, "You couldn't have a better teacher. Fernando [Moscoso] is one of the best forensic anthropologists in the world." Dr. Snow added, "The thing that most people don't understand is that these guys are the real experts. We may have more advanced technology in our labs in the United States, but these guys have more experience with the bones than anyone else. Look at all the graves here. The bones don't lie and these guys know what they say. They are the real professionals of forensic anthropology."

Indeed, in 1994, FAFG lab analysis was much more laborious than it is today. The first limitation was the small size of the lab and the need to share equipment, which limited the number of skeletons that could be examined at any one time. The second limitation was that the location for storage and lab analysis was determined by the whim of the judge issuing the court order to investigate. In the Plan de Sánchez exhumation, the judge had ordered that we conduct lab analysis within the borders of the department of Baja Verapaz. Thus, we temporarily used the lab equipment and morgue of the hospital in Salamá, the departmental capital, to conduct lab analysis.

The laboratory analysis is the third phase of the exhumation. It consists of scientific examination of each of the bones (206 in total) of each skeleton after it is washed, marked, and reconstructed in the lab. This examination determines the cause of death, which refers to the trauma that killed the person (firearm injury, machete or knife wound, strike with blunt instrument, etc.); the manner of death (violent or natural); and the identification of the skeleton (through antemortem interview data, dental records, associated artifacts, and DNA). When it is determined that victims died from firearm projectiles or grenade fragments, lab analysis includes x-rays of affected remains to document fragments still present in bones. Thus, just like a murder investigation in the United States, the contextual, artifactual, and ballistic documentation is included in the osteological breakdown that forms a part of the forensic record.[7]

The most reliable scientific method for the identification of remains is mitochondrial DNA analysis, especially in the Guatemalan cases, in which the majority of indigenous victims lack medical registers and dental records. Mitochondrial DNA analysis compares the root of a hair or a blood sample of a maternal relative to a DNA bone sample taken from the remains of victims. Unfortunately, there is no mitochondrial DNA laboratory in Guatemala, making it necessary to consult with specialized labs in other countries.[8]

While I was waiting in the hospital corridor for the x-ray technician to complete his x-rays, I was surprised when one of the doctors approached me. He asked me if I was working on the exhumation. I responded affirmatively and explained my research project. He took me to the surgery section of the hospital. He told me that he had lived in Salamá throughout La Violencia. He shook his head and placed his gaze in a far away place. It was a gaze I came to understand as a signal that the grounding of time and space was shifting, a sign that I was no longer involved in a simple conversation, but rather a witness to memory.

"I was in this room," he said. "I was doing a surgery. My patient was a young man, maybe he wasn't yet 20. He had bullet wounds and knife wounds. The places that weren't bleeding were bruised from being beaten. I was young. I didn't have a lot of experience. I was just trying to stop the bleeding so I could determine what to do next." He broke his gaze and looked at me. "It was terrible and it wasn't the only time."

I said it must have been very difficult to be a young doctor trying to heal people in a time when so many were being deliberately harmed. He nodded in agreement, "Yes, Victoria, that is your name, right?" I nodded as he continued, "Yes, it was extremely difficult, but that isn't the story. The story is about impunity." He drifted back into the gaze. As he stared far off into the distance, he said,

What happened was that I heard loud shouts in male voices and I heard screaming. It seems like it was all in the same moment. I heard the shouts, the scream, I stopped what I was doing, I thought the scream came from a nurse, I lifted my head, and the door to surgery burst open—all at the same time. Then they came in. There were three of them. They had machine guns. One of them shoved me away from my patient with his machine gun as he said, "With your permission, doctor." He pushed me against the wall. I didn't give them my permission. Then, the three of them lined up in front of me laughing as they opened fire on my patient. I can't even describe what it was to watch them kill my patient in my surgery room right in front of me as I was trying to save his life. I remember how it felt to have my entire body against that wall. They were still laughing as they left. The same man said to me, "It looks like there's nothing you can do here. This time he's really dead. Go home to your family, relax. It's late."

What I want to tell you, Victoria, is that it is the impunity of the act. Those men didn't even wear masks to cover their faces. They are from here. One of them lives on the same street as I do. I tell you, each time I see him on my street, each time he greets me, I relive those moments. Those men should not be allowed to walk freely through the streets with no shame. I don't know why I told you this story. I never talk about it. I have never even told my family because they would just worry. But can you imagine? I see this man most every day and the impunity is so great, he doesn't even hang his head."

He hadn't spoken with anyone else on the forensic team about these experiences. Though, as team members admitted, they didn't tend to ask questions for fear of having trouble within the hospital. In 1994, there were very few out-of-towners in Rabinal and Salamá. Perhaps the doctor told me because I was a gringa who worked in the exhumations. As time went on, it seemed that everywhere I went, someone had a story to tell. In fact, one day in Rabinal as Kathleen and I were walking down the street, we heard footsteps running toward us. We turned around and saw a few Achi women walking. Then we heard the running steps again. We turned around, again we saw no one running. Then, the steps were right behind us. We turned around startled and expecting to see someone with some kind of weapon. We found a young Achi woman looking up at us with a huge smile and sweating because she had been running. "Are you the *forenses?* The forensic anthropologists?" she asked in a voice just above a whisper. "We work with the forenses," we responded. "We need an exhumation like the one in Plan de Sánchez," she declared.

The fourth and final phase of the exhumation is the processing of the data, interpretation of the evidence, and production of the final forensic report. After completing phases one to three, it is possible to determine the consistencies and contradictions between the written documents, interviews, testimonies, and material evidence from the excavation. The final interpretation is based on the analysis of all facts collected in all phases of the investigation. The information gathered in each phase of the investigation is recorded and processed in database programs. The most effective way to identify victims is to use a database to compare the information collected in antemortem interviews with laboratory analysis of remains. Such a process greatly reduces the possibility of error and increases the speed of identification.

The final report is prepared as forensic evidence for presentation in court. Survivors in the community also receive copies of the report. In Rabinal, the forensic team produced a book and a low-literacy monograph about the Rabinal massacres.[9] The monograph, *Nada Podrá contra la vida,* circulated in Maya communities throughout the country and became a teaching tool to prepare communities about what to expect in the exhumation process. Later when I was working in Nebaj, I mentioned to a few close Ixil friends that I had worked in some exhumations. For the rest of the day, that was all they wanted to talk about. They asked me for more information. The next time I was in Guatemala City, I picked up some copies of the low-literacy monograph. My friends then organized several private meetings in groups of three to four local Ixil leaders. Each time, the monograph was read aloud and the reading was peppered with comments that "the same thing happened here" and questions about how to organize and request an exhumation. Inevitably, the reading of the monograph was followed by a group discussion about La Violencia in different communities and other people who might want exhumations.

THE EXHUMATIONS OF RABINAL

Two years before Kathleen and I joined the team in Rabinal, the forensic anthropologists had just completed their second exhumation in the country, in the department of El Quiché in 1992. It was at this time that the FAFG first visited Rabinal at the request of the departmental human rights ombudsman of Salamá (Procurador de Derechos Humanos—PDH).[10] Survivors of massacres in the villages of Chichupac (January 1982), Río Negro (March 1982) and Plan de Sánchez (July 1982) had filed complaints with the PDH seeking exhumations and reburials. A single widow initiated the complaint for Chichupac. Jesús Tec, who was orphaned by the Río Negro massacre, organized several other Río Negro survivors to join in filing a complaint for his community. Plan de Sánchez widowers and orphans, including Juan Manuel Gerónimo, Pablo, and José, jointly filed a complaint.

"We organized a meeting with the priests of the Verapaces to explain the work of the FAFG," explained Fernando Moscoso, founding member and former president of the FAFG. "Our presentation caused great anxiety amongst the priests. After a very short discussion, they concluded that it would not be possible to carry out the exhumations in Baja Verapaz for at least two years—which was the amount of time they said they would need to 'prepare the communities' for the exhumations."

Despite the reluctance of the priests, the FAFG began the first exhumation in Chichupac just a few months later. This exhumation was the third in the nation. Like all exhumations, that of Chichupac was a legal process ordered by the court at the request of survivors. The FAFG had met with the priests to request their collaboration, not their permission.

In 1994, two years before the 1996 reform of the judicial system, exhumations were initiated by the PDH where requests for the investigation of human rights violations could be filed by individuals, organizations, and/or communities; these requests could also be filed anonymously. For an exhumation to proceed, a complaint had to be filed at the Superior Court. If approved by the Superior Court, it then had to be approved by the Appeals Court, which would then pass it on to the

Court of the *Primer Instancía,* the departmental administrative court, which would then issue an order to the local justice of the peace. It was then the task of the justice of the peace to solicit forensic experts to carry out the exhumation. Rabinal's justice of the peace sought out the FAFG because the forensic doctor in Rabinal worked only four hours a day and had no formal training in forensics. The FAFG was appointed as the court's expert and began its first exhumation in Rabinal (in the village of Chichupac) a few months after their meeting with the priests.[11]

The church was absent from the exhumation in Chichupac until months later, when the remains were returned for the burial, which was well attended by villagers from throughout Rabinal. The next exhumation was in Río Negro. The priest from Rabinal was frequently present during the exhumation and held mass at the site. Priests and religious workers from Cobán also provided support and visited the site throughout the exhumation. The PDH, the local justice of the peace, and representatives from human rights groups regularly visited both sites to accompany and support the survivors and the work of the FAFG. CONAVIGUA (Coordinadora Nacional de Las Viudas de Guatemala— National Coordinator of Guatemalan Widows) and GAM (Grupo de Apoyo Mutúo—Mutual Support Group) provided food for the forensic team as they worked and also provided the resources for the reburial of remains when they were returned to the communities.[12] Whereas previous exhumations had been initiated by these human rights groups by providing legal support and filing complaints at the request of survivors, the Rabinal exhumations were unique in that they were initiated by local residents with no apparent organizational support.

DECLARING THE TRUTH

Juan Manuel Gerónimo's Testimony

I raffled the truth to declare the truth. Before the exhumation, all the people hid everything inside. They concealed their feelings. No one would even talk about what had happened, much less make a public declaration. It just didn't seem possible that a person had the power to declare these types of things at the national level or international level. We decided that we were going to declare the truth of what happened. We were going to do it legally. We decided that we were going to do it together, all the families united. I encouraged everyone to participate. I told them, "Look, please, if they call us, we will all go together. We will all go together and we will go without this fear. I am not afraid. If you support me, you will give me more strength to do this." So, when the Ministerio Público (Public Ministry—Prosecutor) called us, we all went together. When the court called us, we all went together. We said, "We want a Christian burial for our families because they aren't dogs, and we don't want them piled up in those graves like dogs." That's how we did it.

So, we moved forward together. I said, "We won't be afraid. We will do this together. Because if we say that one person is in charge of this work, then we are just giving them a new martyr. But if we are all together, we can do this work. What we are doing is legal and the law isn't going to put all of us in jail." These were the ideas we had and this is how we worked together.

One day, the military commissioners from Chipuerta came here.[13] They had been sent by the chief in Rabinal. They wanted a report. They said, "Who is leading the exhumation here? Who is in charge?" But we just said, "We are all doing this together. We want a proper burial." After they left, we discussed this. Once again, we all agreed that no one would blame anyone else and that no one would say there was a leader. The next thing that happened is that I received a note from the chief of all the PACs in Rabinal. The note said that I was to go to Rabinal to meet with him because he wanted to talk to me. I didn't go.

Several days later, he found me walking down the street in Rabinal. He asked me, "Look, what's going on with this business up there?" I said, "What business?" Then he said, "Look, you, what's going on with this business up there? What's going on with this exhumation?" I said, "Do you mean how will it be done? First, we are going to exhume the remains and then we are going to rebury them. But I don't know when." Then he said, "Who has told you this? Who is behind this?" "No one," I said, "we are doing it by ourselves." "But you are working with an organization, aren't you?" he said. And I said, "No. The only institution is our own strength and commitment. So, if you would like to support us somehow with some money that would be helpful." He didn't know how to respond. He said, "How's that?" And I said, "Well, it would be like an institution helping us. We want to do the exhumation." He just accepted that and walked away confused because I hadn't told him anything.

CONAVIGUA was really helping us. The truth is they explained to us how we could make our declarations, how to complete the forms, and where to take them. We are very poor. We don't have any money for taking buses. So, whenever we had to go to the Ministerio Público or the court, they would reimburse our transportation costs. Thanks to God, they helped us a lot. I hope God repays them for their good deeds. They really struggled to help us. But we did our part. We did all the work ourselves. We made all the trips to file the paperwork. That is why it was important for all of us to go together to do these filings. The widows from CONAVIGUA were in agreement that no one should go alone. They said, "Believe us, if only one person goes by himself, somewhere along the road, in one of those holes, you're going to find him buried." This made a lot of the people scared, but we stuck together. I was never afraid. I don't know why, I just never was.

THE EXHUMATION IN PLAN DE SÁNCHEZ

There was always a lot of activity at the excavation site. Because exhumations are carried out as an investigatory procedure of the court, municipal police maintain a twenty-four hour presence to guard the site, observe the excavation, and conserve legal custody of all evidence exhumed. In 1994, Rabinal had only one police officer, so the court requested assignment of several customs police because neither the FAFG nor the community wanted soldiers or paramilitary police at the exhumation site. Four customs police were stationed for three weeks at a time in Plan de Sánchez. They set up a large tent at the base of the hill where they camped—supposedly providing twenty-four hour security to the area. Each day after the remains were catalogued and boxed by both the forensic team and the police, the boxes were transported to Rabinal, where they were stored in the modest office of the justice of the peace.

In tandem with the archaeological procedures, Maya rituals marked different moments of the excavation. Before the ground was broken, the Maya priest (*sacerdote* Maya) conducted a religious ceremony. Maya priests are the keepers of Maya religious tradition (*costumbre*) which the Maya have maintained and reinvented since the arrival of the Spaniards in the sixteenth century. While many have viewed Maya costumbre as a syncretic blending of Maya belief systems with Catholicism, the cult of Catholic saints is also a blending of Catholicism with Maya religion. Each religion reminds us that belief systems are never static but always changing. For the Achí, as for other Maya, it is sacrilegious to disturb the remains of the dead, because wherever the blood of the dead has spilled in burial, the spirits of the dead hover above.[14] To disturb the bones is to disturb the spirits. However, because it was the desire of the community that the truth of these clandestine graves be known, that their loved ones have proper religious burials, and that there be justice, the Maya priest performed a special ceremony before each grave was opened. While every culture places significance on its particular burial practices, Maya ritual practices at the graves of ancestors implicate not only the passing of the ancestor but also the identity, rights, and responsibilities of the living. Archeologist Patricia Macanany dates these practices back to before the Conquest and notes that "very few royal tombs were sealed and never revisited; most were periodically reopened for an elaborate ceremony of burning incense. It almost seems as though it was vitally important to maintain open pathways of communication with the ancestors." These rituals at burial sites implicate the enactment of deeply held beliefs about individual and community identity and reckoning in the past as well as the present.[15]

After lighting candles, burning copal incense, and adorning the area with red gladiolas and pine needles, the Maya priest would speak with God to explain why the exhumation should take place and ask permission from God to disturb the bones. Then the priest would call upon the spirits to explain to them that God had given permission for the exhumation to take place. He would plead with the spirits to heed God's call. Instead of using their powers against those who disturb the bones, the priest asked the spirits to use their powers to bless and protect the forensic team and all who worked at the exhumation.

Everyone in Plan de Sánchez worked to support the exhumation. The men organized a schedule so that everyone helped with the manual labor but also had time to tend their fields. I was struck by the volunteers who came from other areas representing popular human rights organizations. These peasant men and women were giving up their time working for their own livelihood to support an exhumation that wasn't even in their own communities. They said they came because they wanted to learn more about the exhumations and because they hoped people would come when they had their exhumations in their own communities. "If we are together, we have greater strength and less fear," explained a massacre survivor from a faraway Chichicastenango village in El Quiché. These volunteers came for ten days at a time. Within the village, each man gave several days a week of his time. All helped to do the heavy digging that was necessary before the delicate brushing work of the excavation could begin. They also carried all the dirt out of the graves to sift it. (This sifting is necessary for finding bullet and grenade fragments.) It was the rainy season, so shelters had to be built over the work sites and gullies had to be dug around the perimeter to prevent the water from flooding the open graves. The work was further complicated by the steep grade of the mountainside, where many of the graves were located. In all, there were eighteen graves, so there was a lot of digging, sifting, and building.

When I first arrived to the site, one of my fears was that I would be overcome by the smell of death. That first day, working in the graves that had been opened and exposed for several days prior, there was no smell, or if there was, I didn't notice it. The flesh had decomposed, and the remains were bones still dressed in the clothes that had not yet decomposed. Rather than the trepidation I had expected to feel about just being near the bones, I felt great tenderness because they seemed fragile, vulnerable, and somehow almost noble. These were the final traces that confirmed that a human being, this human being, had existed. Sometimes when we opened a new grave or if it was a damp day, a slight smell of life lingered. It wasn't a putrid smell; the earth had long since absorbed the rot of death. The scent that lingered was the light murky smell of birth or a stillborn puppy or that of wine fermenting in oak barrels—not a noxious aroma, but one of movement or transformation in rhythm with the mountains and its pine trees, flowers, rich earth, and luscious green grass.

The scent of burning *leña*[16] and the resin used to start cooking fires wafted over the site, blending with all the other smells. As their husbands worked on the exhumation of their first families, the current wives of these men (most themselves previously widowed by massacres) prepared food for the forensic team and anyone else who helped with the work. This meant grinding corn, patting out tortillas, and preparing a large cauldron of beans or soup for what usually amounted to some thirty-five additional mouths to feed each day. They also prepared *atol* (hot corn drinks) for us twice during the day.

As the forensic team and community members worked on the exhumation, *campesinos* from nearby villages walked as many as six hours to reach the site to observe the exhumation. These individuals, like the villagers of Plan de Sánchez, were expressing their support of the exhumation by their mere presence. They were seizing the political space opened by the exhumation and further extending it. Each day, dozens of people came. Not only was no one in Plan de Sánchez singled out, but the presence of villagers from other communities demonstrated that the people of Plan de Sánchez were not alone. It was a profound expression of what

Michel Foucault called "the power effects of truth," an idea that I will explore throughout this book.[17]

During the exhumation, local campesinos were always waiting and watching. While the excavation of massacre victims may seem like a gruesome endeavor, it is the presence of these local Maya peasants that enables the forensic team members to do their work. It is not simply the collaboration of local labor that helps. It is also the great respect for the dead and the living, and the spiritual and emotional strength that community members bring to the site, that encourages everyone involved to continue their work each day.

The police were always watching from a distance. They often stood behind a tree and would peek out to watch us. They weren't scared of us or the graves, they were scared of the photographers. A photographer demonstrated to me that all he had to do was take out his camera and the police would scatter, running behind trees. When I asked them why they hid, one of the police said, "If my picture is taken here, people might think I support it, that I am taking a side. I could lose my job." At the time, I just thought he meant that military institutions, including the customs police, were against the exhumations.

A few days later, I was excavating a skeleton. It was the skeleton of a woman who was face-down in the grave. She had a shawl wrapped around her upper body. As I opened her shawl, the skeleton of an infant was revealed. The same customs officer came out from behind his tree. He walked right up to the edge of the grave. As he leaned into the grave, he called the other three officers. He said, "Look. Look at this. It is a woman with a baby on her back. They told us these were pure guerrillas. These aren't guerrillas. That's a mother and a baby. That's a crime." As the other police came closer to watch, the villagers joined them. One of the police said, "A woman and her baby. Poor woman. Poor baby. I sure would like to machine gun whoever did that." And all the villagers quietly backed away to the other side of the grave. Still, after witnessing the excavation of this woman with a baby on her back, the officers stopped hiding behind trees and voluntarily began to help with the manual labor in the exhumation.[18]

"LEAVE THE DEAD IN PEACE"

Each Thursday afternoon we would return to Guatemala City to do paperwork, visit with friends and family, and rest. Before dawn on Monday, we would be on the road returning to Rabinal. When we reached Plan de Sánchez on the morning of July 25, there were only a few villagers from Plan de Sánchez waiting for us at the grave site and there were no villagers from outside—usually there were several dozen. The mood was somber and everyone was very quiet. The widowers of Plan de Sánchez met with us to explain what had happened.

The day before, on Sunday, the subcommander of the army base in Rabinal had ordered all men from the villages to attend a meeting at the army base. The order was received in the morning. By noon, there were several thousand men waiting in the sun at the base. At two in the afternoon, the subcommander greeted the crowd and began a lecture. He told the peasants not to pursue the exhumations. "The anthropologists, internationals and journalists are all guerrilla," he explained. "You know what happens when you help the guerrilla. Collaborating with the guerrilla will bring back the violence of 1982," he warned. "Now, I am going to give you an order," he said, "Leave the dead in peace."[19]

While the men attending the meeting at the base were too frightened to contradict anything the subcommander said, they were not dissuaded from continuing to work on the exhumation. They had increased local security by coordinating trips to their fields and to Rabinal to ensure that no one ever traveled alone and also to make sure that there were always some men in the village. They recommended to us that we not walk around alone in Rabinal during the daytime and that at night, we not walk around outside at all.

When we suggested that a delegation could go to the capital to denounce the army's threats, the villagers informed us that they had pooled their resources on Sunday afternoon to pay bus fare for several men to go to the capital to do just that. Thus, the army's threats were denounced to the human rights ombudsman, the court, and the national press. At the end of the week, the army made a public statement in which they claimed that the subcommander was not expressing army policy and that he had been transferred to another base. Word of this statement traveled quickly through Rabinal. By the following week, we were back to several dozen local visitors each day at the site.

Later, Juan Manuel admitted to me that the villagers had held a meeting to discuss what we (the forensic team) should be told about the assembly at the army base. Several people were worried that we might not complete the exhumation if we knew about the army's death threat. Though we never mentioned it to the villagers, we were concerned that they might pull out of the exhumation due to the threats. The consensus of this political chess game, however, of both the forensic team and the villagers, was that if the exhumation was not completed, then the army would have more power than it did before the exhumation began. This consensus revealed a highly nuanced understanding of the politics of power relations and also the palpable sensation that on any given day the balance of power could weigh in on the side of the army or civil society.

This was neither the first, nor the last, threat directed at the team or its work. As I write this in March 2002, eleven current and former FAFG forensic anthropologists are under twenty-four hour protection due to death threats. On February 21, 2002, they received individually type-written letters: "We will finish you off . . . you aren't the ones to judge us. If the exhumations don't stop, your families will be burying your bones and those of your children."[20] After more than 190 exhumations, these current threats are intended to intimidate these eleven anthropologists who will be called as forensic expert witnesses in forthcoming court cases against current and former high-ranking army officials.

In terms of the team's response to the 1994 death threat, some members of the forensic team recognized it as a death threat, while others categorized it merely as part of the army's campaign to discredit human rights work. Plan de Sánchez survivors, however, viewed the subcommander's statements not only as a death threat but also as an order for the civil patrollers to attack us—hence their recommendations about our safety in Rabinal. Though it heightened our consciousness of individual and group security practices, we continued our work routine as always—traveling en masse, never walking alone, never leaving the vehicle unattended, and never arriving or departing at exactly the same time (which was, more often than not, a result of lack of planning rather than the reverse).

Less than two weeks after the army's disclaimer, on August 10, the departmental human rights ombudsman in Salamá and the national PDH received identical death threats: "*deija* [sic] *en pas* [sic] *a los muertos Hijo de puta*,"—"leave the dead in peace son of a whore." At the same time, while in Guatemala City conducting interviews with government officials, a high-ranking member of the Guatemalan government's Peace Commission (then representing the government and army in peace negotiations) told me that "no member of the forensic team should believe themselves to be immune to violent reprisals." He also emphasized that a U.S. passport should not be assumed to provide protection from such reprisals. When I asked him if this was a threat from the army, he said,

"It doesn't matter where I heard this or who told me. And it isn't a threat, it is a warning."

When I later met with the national human rights ombudsman, Jorgé Mario García La Guardía, and asked him about the death threats the PDH had received, he shrugged his shoulders and showed me a stack of threats he had received. "This is the reality of our work," he said. "If I stopped to contemplate the implications of each of these threats, I would be immobilized." This reminded me of Fernando Moscoso, who once explained how he continued working even when he was tired, "When I am excavating, I am conscious that in a year, or two, or three, the skeleton in the ground might be mine."

By the end of my interview with García La Guardia, it was early evening. He offered me a ride to my next destination because I had mentioned to him that a man had attempted to mug me in Guatemala City several days earlier. When I told the friends I was meeting that the ombudsman had given me a ride and that his security was impressive (the driver and two guards each with automatic weapons), they retorted that I would have been safer walking. "No one rides with the PDH. Those guards and guns are worth nothing if someone drives by and opens machine gun fire."

"YOU ARE SEEING THE TRUTH"

After all the Plan de Sánchez graves had been exhumed, there were eighteen large holes in the earth. The sizes of the graves ranged from eight by ten feet to fifteen by twenty feet. Each was about four to five feet deep. Because it was the rainy season, the holes quickly filled with water. As I looked at the gaping holes in the earth, they seemed to be many things. They looked like miniature versions of the wounds left in the earth by nickel mines or gravel pits. They looked like muddy ponds. The area, which had always been filled with people, was deserted, and the holes heightened the empty feeling of absence. My thoughts were broken by the laughter of children who trailed Juan Manuel, Erazmo, Pablo, and José. We sat on a grassy knoll and looked at the empty spaces, the valley below and the mountain range beyond it.

"It looks sad here," said Don Erazmo. "But when we have a proper burial, everyone will live with tranquillity." He said this with the knowledge that it was unlikely he would receive the remains of his family members because it appeared that they had been among those who were burned beyond recognition. As he spoke, the children played with each other and climbed on their fathers, seeking embraces.

By the end of the exhumation, I had interviewed all massacre survivors still living in Plan de Sánchez. I asked them why they wanted the exhumation. In addition to not wanting their relatives buried "como perros"—like dogs, each person gave me several reasons beyond the proper burial.

The first and most stark reason is the concrete, the real, the hard evidence. You can touch it. It is the bones of the victims we pulled out of the earth. And, as Dr. Clyde Snow always says, "The bones don't lie." The army claimed there had been a battle with the guerrilla in Plan de Sánchez. The exhumation clearly showed that the vast majority of victims were women, children, and the elderly. Moreover, the forensic evidence unquestionably demonstrated that the skeletons in the grave were victims of a massacre, not an armed confrontation with guerrillas and not civilians caught in crossfire, as the army had asserted about mass graves throughout the country.[21]

Don Pablo asked me, "How could they say these were guerrilleros? How can an infant of six months or a child of five, six, or seven years be a guerrillero? How can a pregnant woman carrying her basket to market be a guerrillero?"[22] About the exhumation, Don Erazmo told me, "*Allí, no hay mentira. Allí, están veyendo la verdad*" (There, there is no lie. There, you are seeing the truth).

In 1994 I asked them why an already vulnerable community would put itself at greater risk by supporting and actively collaborating with the exhumation. Don Juan Manuel told me that the community supported the exhumation because they wanted "the truth to come out that the victims were natives of the area. Our children who knew nothing, who owed debts to no one. They killed women and elderly who did not even understand what they were accused of by the army. Campesinos, poor people. People who work the fields for the corn we eat."

The community wanted the truth to be known. Don Erazmo said, "We have worked in the exhumation. We have worked for truth." I asked what importance truth could have twelve years after the massacre. This is what I was told:

"We want peace. We want people to know what happened here so that it does not happen here again, or in some other village in Guatemala, or in some other department, or in some other country."

"We strongly support this exhumation and that everything is completely investigated because we do not want this to happen again."

"We do this for our children and our children's children."

"We want no more massacres of the Maya."

"We want justice. We want justice because if there is no justice, the massacres will never end. God willing, we will have peace."

Some said they wanted revenge. All said they wanted justice. There was great hope that someone involved in the massacre would be tried in court and prosecuted.[23] Just as army threats had sent tremors of fear through Plan de Sánchez, and indeed throughout Rabinal, the process of the exhumation restored community beliefs in the right to truth and justice. Rural Maya have a strong community tradition of publicly speaking their objections and seeking redress within the local hierarchy. Moreover, in rural Maya culture, the ancestors help the living move into the future. They continue to play a role in the life of the community. They play an important role in defining place and the significance of place as social space, as living space.[24] In this sense, the exhumations resuscitated local Maya cultural practices and created new space for the practice of citizenship.

It was the combination of the forensic evidence of the exhumations with the visible resuscitation of community beliefs in the right to truth and justice that threatened those implicated in the massacres. Denial that those killed had been unarmed civilians remained plausible only as long as the mass graves were untouched. Exhumations provided not only an accretion of truth within the public space of the community but also an accretion of forensic evidence for court cases and the beginning of a new national and international understanding of La Violencia. As exhumations have proceeded throughout the country, the collective evidence has pointed not only to army massacres of unarmed Maya but to a carefully planned and strategically enacted genocide.

THE SILENCING OF MAYA WOMEN

We speak from the heart.

—*María Maquín*

INTRODUCTION

The chronicle of Plan de Sánchez massacre survivors organizing for an exhumation in chapter one provides a powerful example of local Maya community mobilizations for truth and justice. In response to these types of initiatives, the Guatemalan army, elite interests, and some academics have attempted to represent Maya political activism as a manipulation of the Maya by the guerrillas and/or popular organizations and religious groups. These representations of the Maya tend to conflate or draw little to no distinction among these sectors, thus reinforcing the official conflation of ethnicity with political affiliation. I suggest that the perception of the "manipulated" Maya is a recovery and transformation of the official story intended to erase both community and individual memory and agency. Like the official story upon which it is based, this perception shares the same racist ideational foundation that denies political consciousness and free will to the Maya; to explain away Maya political action as a manipulation is to negate the memory and agency of Maya communities, families, and individuals. In this chapter,[1] I explore testimony, official discourse, and truth in popular memory in relationship to the still-contested reconstruction of Guatemalan history. The recovery and transformation of official discourse negates the agency of the Maya in general, and especially monolingual Maya women. And agency is one of the central themes of testimony. Understanding the political ideologies and mobilizations of these organizations through Maya experience (and especially Maya women's experience), instead of official state discourse, offers a more nuanced analysis of Maya political activism as experienced by the majority rural Maya, remembered within their world cosmology, and expressed in their political memory and agency as conscious subjects.

As philosopher Paul Ricoeur wisely noted, "To project our past, our future, our human milieu around ourselves is precisely to situate ourselves."[2] It is through awareness of the contemporary situated subjectivity of the majority rural Maya that we can seek broader understanding of the experience of surviving a seemingly endless chain of violent events; it is within this experience that we encounter the nuanced complexity and meaning of terror.

Moreover, lucid analysis and contestation can be found in the words of survivors. Marguerite Feitlowitz suggests that terror presents a cascade of "unthinkable options" in a world where torture and death are "castigations for thought," so people try "to stop thinking." In her research on torture in Argentina, she found that "language itself became a prison."[3] The narratives of survivor testimony presented throughout this book reaffirm the external and internal prisons in which massacre survivors have lived. For survivors giving testimony, the very act of verbalizing the experience and meaning of survival is a contestation and reshaping of the world. While it is painful to recount their experiences, it is also a cathartic relief because the pain is always with them. It is with them in their silence as much as it is with them as they give testimony. Theorist Elaine Scarry has written that "acts that restore the voice become not only a denunciation of the pain but almost a diminution of the pain, a partial reversal of the process of torture itself."[4] Moreover, this recounting of experience is particularly significant for rural Maya (and especially for Maya women) who are seldom, if ever, asked to reconstruct national history because they are seen as apart from history, not representative agents of it.[5]

In "The Small Voice of History," historian Ranajit Guha asks, "But suppose there were a historiography that regarded 'what women were saying' as integral to its project, what kind of history would it write?" Guha offers that a rewriting attentive to women's voices will (1) "challenge the univocity of state discourse" and (2) "put the question of agency and instrumentality back in the narrative."[6]

This is exactly what happened with the 1983 publication of Rigoberta Menchú's autobiography *Me llamó Rigoberta Menchú y así me nació la conciencia* (published in English as *I, Rigoberta Menchú—An Indian Woman in Guatemala* in 1984).[7] By asserting the political consciousness, self-expression, and political action of Maya women, Menchú challenged official histories of Guatemala and romantic representations of Maya women, which, each in distinct ways, negated the dynamic and varied political responses of Maya women to Guatemalan state violence. Recorded and written in Paris by anthropologist Elizabeth Burgos Debray, *I, Rigoberta* chronicles the life of Rigoberta's family, which becomes the vehicle for the outsider (both non-Maya Guatemalans and the international community) to understand the struggle of the Maya in Guatemala to defend their lands, communities, and culture in the face of ever-increasing state violence. Rigoberta's standing in the world community as Maya, female, and *campesina*[8] was transformed by her book and multiple speaking engagements in Europe and the United States. Thus, Rigoberta came to represent the antithesis of stereotypes of Maya women as silent, traditional, static, without politics, and without agency. Indeed, in *I, Rigoberta* and in her life, Rigoberta demanded recognition of Maya women as more than pawns of political processes designed and led by others. Rigoberta obliged the world to recognize Maya women as agents of their own history whose participation in political movements shaped those very movements regardless of their initial catalyst. Tenacity, commitment, and determination brought Rigoberta recognition as an international advocate for the rights of the Maya—culminating with the Nobel Peace Prize.

Published at the height of state terror in 1983 as the Guatemalan army continued its "scorched earth" campaign begun against the Maya in 1981, her book described the destruction of Maya villages and brutal killings of the Maya, including members of her own family. Sixteen years after the publication of her book, the Commission for Historical Clarification defined the "scorched earth" campaign as genocidal acts committed against the Maya.[9] But sixteen years earlier, Rigoberta's book, more than any other publication, drew international attention to the plight of the Maya. In the midst of genocide in her country, she offered an alternative vision to the official version of a "war on communism" and, in so doing, firmly placed herself as an active subject directly challenging state violence. Through her self-expression in her autobiography and her political action as a tireless speaker around the world, she put the Maya in general, and Maya women in particular, back into the historical narrative of Guatemala—and firmly placed Maya women in that narrative as conscious subjects, not malleable, manipulated instruments.

While Rigoberta's book and advocacy brought celebrity to her person and her cause, her efforts were not the first such attempts by Maya women to exercise political agency. Indeed, testimonies of Maya women, as well as archival and forensic research, again and again reveal Maya women as "agents rather than instruments" of political mobilization and contestation, which was "itself constituted by their participation."[10] As I have written elsewhere, Maya women did not have a homogenized response to state violence.[11] Some protested peacefully, some organized or participated in popular organizations, some joined the guerrillas, some fled into refuge in the mountains, Mexico, or the United States, and some suffered in isolated silence.

Moreover, avenues of protest and resistance were varied and often expressed in seemingly unusual places. For example, on June 15, 1978, two weeks after the Panzós massacre and five years before the publication of *I, Rigoberta,* Amalía Eróndina Coy Pop publicly asserted her political consciousness, self-expression, and agency when she was crowned Indigenous Queen of San Cristóbal, Alta Verapaz.[12] Speaking to the crowd of mostly Q'eqchi' and Poqonchi' onlookers in Poqonchi', she made reference to the Panzós massacre, which had occurred just two weeks earlier. Her statements were not without impact or retribution. A group of local *ladinos* (non-Maya), angered that she did not give her speech in Spanish and furious that she had spoken about the Panzós massacre, pressured the mayor of San Cristobal and the fair's beauty pageant committee to remove her title and crown.

On June 21, 1978, one week after her speech, a new pageant was held and the committee chose a new indigenous queen—who gave her thanks in Spanish and did not mention the army massacre in Panzós. The Guatemala City newspaper *El Gráfico* reported that the military base in Cobán had dispatched army personnel to San Cristóbal to investigate "the content and meaning" of Coy Pop's speech about Panzós. On June 26, 1978, less than one month after the Panzós massacre, Coy Pop traveled to Guatemala City to ask *El Gráfico* to "make public her energetic protest against the attitude of the group of ladinos[13] who stripped her of her crown and to also to publicly declare that no problems exist in her tranquil community."[14]

Amalía Eróndina Coy Pop is not alone—not as a woman, a Maya, or a beauty queen. Women of all backgrounds have long been active in

Guatemala's struggle for justice, and many of them have been brutally murdered.[15] Rogelio Cruz, a former Miss Guatemala, was a member of the Rebel Armed Forces (Fuerzas Armadas Rebeldes—FAR) in the 1960s. An architecture student from a middle-class family, she ran a clandestine hospital for the guerrillas in Guatemala City. She was kidnapped by paramilitary forces. Several days later, the former Miss Guatemala's lifeless, mutilated body was found at the side of a main road in Guatemala City.[16] Indeed, the Guatemalan state, like other military states, had a very gendered response to the political actions of women. Psychologist Nancy Caro Hollander has noted that during the military regimes of Chile, Argentina, and Uruguay, officers, soldiers, and paramilitary forces had free rein to express the "fundamentally misogynist attitudes of the military."[17] She explained: "Female political activists, who represented the antithesis of bourgeois femininity, became a special target of the terrorist state. They embodied not only a revolutionary challenge to existing class relations but an assertion of self that challenged male hegemony in the psychological as well as political domain."[18]

The point of introducing the actions of Amalia Erondina Coy Pop and Rogelio Cruz along with Rigoberta Menchú's is to underscore that while Rigoberta's life is widely known, neither her experience nor political action are unique. In this sense, *I, Rigoberta* rightly embodies the essence of testimonio, which is a "narration of urgency," "a powerful textual affirmation of the speaking subject itself," and a narration that "always signifies the need for a general social change in which the stability of the reader's world must be brought into question."[19]

THE PANZÓS PROTEST

Panzós is an isolated community in the lowlands of Guatemala. The journey to Panzós from Guatemala City requires, first, a five-hour drive to Cobán, Alta Verapaz. From Cobán, the traveler begins the descent from the cool mountains into the oppressive heat and humidity of the valley below, crossing twenty-six wood bridges, ninety-three small creeks or drainage tubes, three small rivers with no bridges, and two large rivers straddled by very old bridges (one of which is an iron bridge built at the request of large coffee growers in 1883 by the Passaic Rolling Mill Company of New Jersey).[20] This leg of the trip is relatively easy as long as none of the bridges are out. On my first trip to Panzós, one of the small wooden bridges had collapsed under the weight of a large commercial truck loaded with bags of cement. Our alternate route took us four-wheel driving around the nearby saturated fields, mostly cleared of trees and dotted with Brahmin cattle. We crossed through several creeks, to a point where the river was passable without benefit of a bridge.

The Polochic River and its dozens of tributaries dominate the landscape. The water is clear blue as it passes through the lush pastures, occasionally washing over a boulder. The climate is so humid and the red earth so rich and moist that all the embankments are thick with vibrant green foliage, which falls upon the water passing below. It seems that everywhere one gazes there is the green grass of pastures squared off by barbed wire fences that keep the cattle of the absentee landowners from drifting away. The cattle graze freely, and every now and again, the small thatched hut of a caretaker is seen in the middle of the pasture, or off to the side, but always next to a lone tree. The dirt road from Cobán to El Estór cuts through this scene. Though mostly out of sight, Lake Izabal parallels the road on the southern side of the pastures and fields. Above- and below-ground waterways so saturate the earth that visible steam rises from the ground throughout most of the day. Towering in the distance beyond the lake, the dry brown Sierra Las Minas mountains stand in contrast to the fast blue water of creeks, streams, and rivers cutting through the humid lowlands with no regard for fence posts, roads, or bridges.

An engineer who worked on development projects in the Panzós region between 1978 and 1981 also remembers the rivers and their wet, grassy banks. But in his mind's eye, they are littered with human corpses. He recalls that sometimes there were so many cadavers that they would choke the river like a logjam. The flow of water would create a funnel that would reproduce itself as a whirlpool of bodies carried downriver by the current, still spinning as it flowed out of sight. "Each day when I went to work I imagined they were the same bodies passing by, though I knew that could not have been possible. It is just that to realize each of these whirlpools had newly dead men and women each day was too much."[21]

On May 29, 1978, the Guatemalan army opened fire on several hundred Q'eqchi' campesinos who had gathered in front of the municipal offices of Panzós to protest for the return of their communal lands that had been illegally seized by local *finca* (plantation) owners. A few days prior to the massacre, these local plantation owners, the mayor, chief of police, and other municipal functionaries held a meeting in the town offices, where it was decided that they would request support from the military to defend their ill-gotten gains.

One of the former functionaries recalls, "It was a very friendly meeting. We had lunch. We were even celebrating a birthday. Then, after lunch, we had the real talk—that we were going to call in the army." During this discussion, the group sang a birthday song and shared a cake to celebrate the birthday of one of the functionaries.

AN OFFICIAL STORY: EL CANCHÉ ASIG

During an interview with police chief El Canché Asig, a former mayor, and several other former municipal functionaries (some of whom requested anonymity), Asig told me that about 800 *"indios"* (a derogatory term for Maya) came to the plaza angry and waving machetes in the air. Women had balls of something in their hands, which they raised in fists. He said there was blood along the edge of the machetes because the "indios" had practiced witchcraft before marching into the town plaza. Soldiers were stationed on top of the buildings around the plaza. A few were on the ground. Asig believes it was a platoon of sixty soldiers. He says he hid because he was afraid of the "indios" and their witchcraft because "they cast spells on people and bad things happen to them." He said the soldiers began to fire because someone took a machine gun away from a soldier and after getting control of it, did not know how to fire it. A few soldiers opened fire in self-defense, he said. Asig explained that only a few soldiers could possibly have fired because he remembers a short eruption of gunfire followed by screaming and running. He estimated that about thirty people died. He told me that one truck took cadavers up to the cemetery in two trips.

When I asked if the guerrilla had organized in Panzós, Asig said that it was more organized in the 1960s. To support his testimony, he called in the current mayor with the snap of his fingers and then sent him as messenger to request the presence of a retired mayor who immediately came to the municipal office and told me his story of the guerrilla taking Panzós on October 16, 1963. Indeed, the Panzós military base (which no longer exists) was established in the 1960s to combat the guerrilla, who at that time were based in the nearby Sierra Las Minas mountains. Archival records and newspaper accounts from October 1963 verify the guerrilla occupation of Panzós and the deaths of three soldiers during combat with the guerrilla.[22] By 1978, the army base still remained staffed, and the soldiers had expanded their living quarters to include the local community hall adjacent to the plaza. In our interview, Asig and the former mayor insisted Panzós had seen no guerrilla activity since 1963.

Four to five days before the 1978 massacre, a platoon of soldiers arrived in Panzós and installed themselves in the Municipal Salon. Asked about their arrival, one former functionary said: "Some soldiers arrived to Barrio Maw and they raped various women a few days before the massacre. Before the massacre, there was also a meeting of military officials at the school in Xaliha. In the municipality, there was also a meeting between municipal functionaries and the finqueros before the massacre. This was a very friendly meeting. There was a lunch. After this, the conversation about calling in the army arose."[23]

This friendly meeting ended with a birthday celebration and the agreement that soldiers would stay in the municipal salon facing the plaza in front of the municipal building. Thus, when protesters reached the town plaza, it was surrounded by a platoon of at least sixty soldiers. At the head of the protest was a sixty-year-old grandmother, Adelina Caal Maquín, affectionately known throughout the community as Mamá Maquín.

MAMÁ MAQUÍN AND THE PANZÓS MASSACRE

Though there are conflicting versions of exactly how the massacre began, it is certain that Mamá Maquín was at the front of the demonstration. Her granddaughter María, who was then twelve, remembers her grandmother telling the soldiers to put their guns down and allow her to speak with the mayor. María also remembers the sudden and loud crack of machine gun fire that separated Mamá Maquín's skull from her head. Mamá Maquín fell dead in the plaza along with thirty-four other Q'eqchi' men, women, and children.[24] Mamá Maquín spoke Spanish and had long been organizing her community in their ongoing struggle for land rights throughout the fertile Polochic Valley where Panzós is located. A 1981 guerrilla solidarity publication mentions Mamá Maquín as a "patriot" murdered by the military dictatorship.[25] By 1983, the same publication includes her in another article about Guatemalan women martyrs and also claims she "had joined the guerrillas in the 1960s."[26] Of the more than 200 survivors and widows interviewed for the Guatemalan Forensic Anthropology Foundation's (Fundación de Antropología Forense de

Guatemala—FAFG) report on the Panzós massacre for the CEH (Comisión para el Esclarecimiento Histórico—Commission for Historical Clarification), everyone remembered Mamá Maquín as a community leader and land rights advocate.

Whether Mamá Maquín had indeed joined the guerrilla in the 1960s is less the issue here than her tenacity in seizing whatever political spaces might be available for asserting land rights, whether in the 1960s or 1970s. Amongst elder leaders in Q'eqchi', Achi, Ixil, Kanjobal, K'iche', and Q'aqchiquel communities, it was common for them to begin the history of their communities within their lived experience of land struggles and confrontations with the state dating back to the near fourteen-year dictatorship of General Jorgé Ubico that ended in 1944.[27] The Democratic Spring (1944–1954) that followed the Ubico regime was an attempt at a capitalist revolution designed to break the feudal relations which defined the agro-export economy. Both nationalist and democratic, the government sought to integrate all Guatemalans, including the Maya, into a new, modern capitalist economy.

In 1952, when democratically elected President Jacobo Arbenz implemented his land reform program under Decree 900, the Q'eqchi' and Poqonchi' of Panzós participated in local government decision making for the first time. Local agrarian committees were formed and included local indigenous peasants in decision-making positions. These peasants, like other Maya peasants throughout the country, experienced a significant and memorable shift in public space and political action. The redistribution of lands to Q'eqchi' communities and the end to forced labor was remembered by community elders and passed on through the community's tradition of oral history. In 1996, a Panzós elder recalled, "During the time of Arbenz, they gave us land with coffee. The municipal authorities advised us on how to form our communities and we elected our own leaders."[28] Land reform did not survive the 1954 United States–backed overthrow of President Arbenz.[29] Still, the political space created by ten years of Democratic Spring, and the indigenous participation in its political processes, is remembered as much as its subsequent elimination. "When Jacobo [Arbenz] died," the Panzós elder recalls, "the mayor called us to a meeting. He said we were not going to work together like we had been [during the Arbenz land reform]. That is where our work in committees ended and our work on *haciendas* began again."[30] It is worth noting that for this elder, the overthrow of Arbenz is remembered as his death.[31]

The connection between these stories of living Maya elders and Mamá Maquín is that her political consciousness, self-expression, and action are representative of lived Maya experiences beyond her individual story. The leadership role she held in her community was based on Mamá Maquín's political experience and reputation within her community as someone who, in the words of a Panzós widow, "always struggled for our rights to land."

Though Mamá Maquín's voice was silenced by the massacre, her struggle and legacy as a leader have been memorialized by Guatemalan refugee women in Mexico who founded a refugee women's rights organization and named it "Mamá Maquín." Echoing *I, Rigoberta,* a foundational document of Mamá Maquín states, "Our history as refugee women is none other than the history of our country: a history of war, poverty, misery, pain and human rights violations."[32]

U.S. AMBASSADOR THOMAS STROOCK AND SISTER DIANNA ORTIZ

In 1987, Sister Dianna Ortiz, a U.S. nun, began working as a teacher in San Miguel Acatán, a small K'anjobal community high in the Cuchumatán mountains of Huehuetenango. Like other religious workers, she sought to minister those most affected by the poverty and loss of La Violencia. In the eyes of the powerful, her commitment to the poor was an act of subversion. In September 1988, a local bishop warned Sister Dianna that he had received an anonymous letter accusing her and the other sisters in San Miguel of working with the guerrilla. Later, Sister Dianna received two death threats. "Eliminate Dianna, assassinate, decapitate, rape," announced the first written threat. "The army knows who you are. Leave the country," warned the second one.[33]

On November 2, 1989, Sister Dianna was kidnapped from within the enclosed garden of a religious center. During her detention, she was burned with cigarettes, raped, and placed in a pit of rats and decomposing bodies with other still-breathing torture victims. At one point, a small machete or knife was placed in Sister Dianna's hands and her assailant, "placing his hands on hers, forced her to thrust it into the other woman's chest." Next, "a tall, fair-skinned man, whom she had heard them [her assailants] refer to as Alejandro, or 'the boss,' arrived. He ordered them to stop, saying that she was a North American nun and her disappearance had become public. He told her in unaccented English that the abduction had been a mistake and they had confused her with guerrilla leader Veronica Ortiz Hernández. And he said he would take her to a friend at the nearby American embassy, who would help her leave the country. When his jeep stopped in traffic, however, she opened the door and fled."[34]

After her escape, rather than investigate the brutal attack on a U.S. citizen, U.S. Ambassador Thomas Stroock questioned "the motives and timing behind [her] story" and wrote to then Secretary of State James Baker that Sister Dianna's kidnapping and torture could be "a hoax" to push for an end to U.S. aid to Guatemala. Guatemalan Defense Minister Hector Gramajo offered that rather than a victim of abduction and torture, the nun had invented the story to cover up a sadomasochistic "lesbian tryst." ABC News traced the lesbian rumor from General Gramajo back to Lewis Amselem, the U.S. Embassy Human Rights Officer at the time.[35] In 1994, a Guatemalan army officer smirked and told me that the easiest way for the Guatemalan army to defend itself against charges of torturing a woman was to "spread rumors that she is a lesbian and likes it rough."[36] When I didn't laugh at his joke, he asked me not to use his name in anything I might be writing.

When Stroock reviewed the State Department's 1990 Human Rights Report on Guatemala, he wanted to delete a section referring to the 111 burns on Sister Dianna's back that stated: "And a physician confirmed she had been burned." Stroock claimed the embassy did not know if it was true: "Her lawyers say it is, but we have no independent confirmation." However, in a 1992 cable, Stroock said that embassy officials believed the physician "who examined and treated her back wounds on the night of her release" and found his medical report credible. Yet when journalist Julia Lieblich interviewed Stroock in 1997, Stroock defended his previous position calling for the deletion of the reference to Sister Dianna's burns and their confirmation. Stroock claimed the physician had said "the lesions on her back *may* [have been] caused by burns." Stroock made no mention of the 1996 Inter-American Commission's Annual Human Rights Report, which quoted the same physician as concluding that Sister Dianna's "injuries were first or second degree burns." Lieblich also asked Stroock about another medical report completed by a New Mexico doctor that affirmed "one-hundred-eleven second-degree circular burns approximately one cm. across" on Sister Dianna's back. Stroock discounted this report and cast doubt on its validity, saying the doctor had "examined her after several months." Lieblich notes that in fact the medical report (to which the U.S. embassy had access) was written on November 8, 1989—less than one week after Sister Dianna escaped her captors.[37]

Finally, despite two 1989 independent physician reports about wounds inflicted on Sister Dianna, notwithstanding the 1996 findings of the Inter-American Commission that validated Sister Dianna's testimony of abduction and torture, and in direct contradiction to a 1990 letter to Ortiz's lawyer in which Stroock wrote, "No one in this Mission has any reason to disbelieve [her] sworn affidavit," Stroock warned Lieblich, "If you write a story that says it happened, you're liable to be in big trouble. There's not one shred of evidence to prove that it happened."[38] Thus, Stroock continues to cast doubt on Sister Dianna Ortiz and when confronted with corroborating evidence by a critical investigative journalist, his response is to admonish her that she will "be in big trouble" if she writes her story, implying that the doubt cast on Sister Dianna's credibility would by extension be cast upon Lieblich.

DAVID STOLL'S STORY OF RIGOBERTA MENCHÚ

In *Rigoberta Menchú and the Story of All Poor Guatemalans,* David Stoll discounts lived experiences of La Violencia in general, and Menchú's experiences in particular, by presenting conjecture and hearsay as fact in order to attack details of Menchú's testimony. While obliquely acknowledging army violence against Maya civilians in the final chapters of his book, Stoll uses La Violencia as a springboard to blame the guerrilla for army atrocities. Though somewhat buried in the work, he explains his motivations for scrutinizing Nobel laureate Rigoberta Menchú through his interpretation of *I, Rigoberta Menchú* based on (1) his concern that if Rigoberta Menchú's representation of La Violencia is accurate, then Stoll's previous work "was wrong about Ixil country" and (2) his "hope" that his work will "help the Latin American left and its foreign supporters escape from the captivity of Guevarismo."[39]

Stoll conflates solidarity activists with anti-intervention activists, with human rights workers, and with academics carrying out research.[40] Within this political schema, anyone who disagrees with Stoll is homogenized into someone who supported or supports the guerrilla. This is not unlike a recently released 1982 internal U.S. State Department document that concluded that Amnesty International and the Washington Office on the Americas had "successfully carried out a campaign of Communist-backed disinformation."[41]

Interestingly, although Stoll both constructs and deconstructs Rigoberta Menchú, his own book about Rigoberta cannot withstand the type of scrutiny to which he subjected her book. And, significantly, the places where this Stanford-trained anthropologist's research falls apart are exactly where concrete primary documents are available.

For example, Stoll provides a review of recent Guatemalan history in which he claims there was a lack of relationship between the United States government and the Guatemalan military regime in the 1960s.[42] This is a curious summary of an era that included an expanded continuation of counterinsurgency and intelligence training for Guatemalan military officers at the U.S. Army School of the Americas. In fact, documents of the School of the Americas date this training relationship with Guatemala back to 1947! Additionally, in the 1960s, meetings of Central American ministers of the interior (who have jurisdiction over police and internal intelligence) were organized and led by the U.S. State Department with assistance from the CIA, AID (U.S. Agency for International Development), the customs bureau, the immigration service, and the justice department. These meetings were "designed to develop ways of dealing with subversion," according to William Bowdler, who represented the State Department at the gatherings.[43] These meetings led to the development of paramilitary organizations throughout Central America, including the death squads known as the Mano Blanco (White Hand) in El Salvador, and the Mano (Hand) in Guatemala. The extreme terror waged against civil society in Guatemala in the 1960s resulted in the deaths of thousands of peasants and distinguished Guatemala as the first country where "disappeared" came to be used to describe the political condition of being kidnapped by government death squads, tortured to death, and buried in a clandestine grave.

Another egregious assertion in Stoll's rewriting of history is his representation that a massacre at the Spanish embassy in Guatemala in 1980 was actually a self-immolation coordinated by indigenous protesters.[44] Spanish military investigators in their 1981 report on the massacre and the 1999 report of the Commission for Historical Clarification concluded that the army carried out a premeditated firebombing of the embassy.[45] Indeed, all accounts of this massacre, except for the Guatemalan army's and David Stoll's, charge that the Guatemalan army committed the massacre (where Rigoberta Menchú's father, Vicente Menchú, was killed). In addition to blaming the victims of the massacre for their own deaths, in different points in his narrative, Stoll labels deceased Vicente Menchú as "a thief," "an illegitimate child," "not supplicatory," "bitter," and a "myth."[46] Stoll's narrative strategy, not unlike Stroock's, seems to be one that distracts from the culpability of the army for its atrocities, which claimed the lives of more than 200,000 Guatemalans, and, at the same time, makes suspect any sympathy one might feel for the victims and survivors of what the CEH qualified in legal terms as "genocidal acts committed against the Maya."[47]

All told, Stroock, Gramajo, and Stoll seek to promote an official contemporary history of Guatemala that is void of facts, lacks critical analysis, and has no room for the testimonies of survivors. In this official history and its regurgitation, survivors like Dianna Ortiz and Rigoberta Menchú are suspect. Victims like Vicente Menchú and others who perished in the Spanish embassy massacre are responsible for their own deaths. As the cases of the Panzós massacre, Sister Dianna Ortiz, and Rigoberta Menchú indicate, silencing victims and survivors by attacking their credibility is a practice that is enacted at local, national, and international levels. In other words, the attempts made by local officials in Panzós to attack the credibility of victims, survivors, and widows were not unique. Rather, they were in keeping with the politics of La Violencia in Guatemala.

THE PANZÓS MASSACRE AND THE COMMISSION FOR HISTORICAL CLARIFICATION

When the CEH decided that it wanted to carry out its own investigation of a massacre, including a forensic exhumation of the massacre victims, the Panzós massacre was always foremost in the discussions among the CEH and the human rights groups with which it consulted.[48] Among the hundreds of clandestine cemeteries of massacre victims, why did Panzós so easily bring consensus? Panzós was a large massacre. CEH and human rights leaders estimated the number of victims to be at least 200. Panzós was historically important because it was the first massacre in what came to be widely known as La Violencia. For many human rights leaders, Panzós was also the appropriate place to do an exhumation with the presence of the CEH and the UN Mission in Guatemala (Misión Naciones Unidas en Guatemala—MINUGUA) because by the late 1990s, the Polochic Valley was better known for drug trafficking than other exports, and UN presence would provide increased security for all involved in the exhumation. Additionally, Panzós had been the first such massacre and had resonated with urban dissatisfaction with the military. Because of this, it had galvanized significant urban attention, and, therefore, in contrast to other massacres, Panzós was remembered as a historical marker in the chronology of La Violencia. Through the CEH's investigation, Panzós would remain a historical marker, but with transformed meaning. The story of Panzós and its impact on the community would be a marker not only in the history of La Violencia but of historical clarification and truth—the very essence of the CEH's mission in uncovering the events and meaning of La Violencia.

TIME AND THE QUANTIFICATION OF GENOCIDE

The 1997 exhumation of the clandestine cemetery of 1978 plaza massacre victims recovered the remains of thirty-five people. This number was significantly lower than had been expected by the FAFG and the CEH. Indeed, as we began the exhumation, popular knowledge of the Panzós massacre placed the death toll between 100 and 200 victims.[49] When dealing with an event such as a massacre, how do you define "victim"? While this might seem intuitively obvious, in fact there are a number of distinct ways of defining and counting victims, and the Panzós massacre offers an instructive example of how this process works.

In our forensic investigation, the collection of survivor testimonies revealed numerous deaths and disappearances following the actual massacre. These provided a lens to community understanding of the massacre as a part of a continuum of violence, rather than as a discrete incident. Moreover, research in the Panzós municipal archives corroborated survivor and widow testimonies of deaths preceding and following the massacre. Oral historian Alessandro Portelli's "grammar of time" sheds light on the survivors' understanding of their lived experience of violence. Portelli writes, "Time is a continuum; placing an event in time requires that the continuum be broken down and made discrete."[50] No doubt, choices made in the breaking down of moments on the continuum into discrete events reflect cultural cosmologies. Still, one wonders about the source and propagation of the widely held belief of popular organizations, academics, and others that more than one hundred people were killed in the Panzós massacre.

In my review of fifty-five paid advertisements placed in the Guatemalan newspaper *El Gráfico* in 1978 by various popular organizations, I found a June 18 full-page ad that provided a list of sixty-eight named victims of the Panzós massacre. I have cross-checked the names in this ad with the names of victims listed in reports prepared by the FAFG, which named the thirty-five skeletons exhumed; the Archbishop's Human Rights Office *Nunca Más* report, which named eight of the massacre victims, and the CEH's *Memory of Silence* report, which named fifty-three victims.[51] Portelli's "grammar of time" is also important to consider in reviewing these varying numbers because he draws attention to the often overlooked variable of the timing of the researcher: the moment in the life of the subject's history in which the researcher makes his or her entrance. This issue of timing can also be extended from the life cycles of individuals to the life cycles of communities.

First, there were thirty-five skeletons in the mass grave of victims—no more, no less. Of the thirty-five skeletons, the FAFG named twenty-five victims based on forensic identification, including probable identification of twenty-three based on antemortem interviews and two positive identifications based on antemortem interviews in tandem with laboratory testing of skeletal remains. The possibility of DNA testing was eliminated because all the skeletons displayed an advanced stage of decomposition due to the high acidity level of the soil. Insufficient scientific data prohibited the positive identification of the remaining ten skeletons as well as the scientific confirmation of the additional ten names I collected through testimonies.

The Archbishop's *Nunca Más* report, also known as the REHMI (Proyecto Interdiocesano de Recuperación Histórico—Interdiocesene Project for the Recuperation of Historical Memory) report, most clearly raises the variable of timing in research, as well as access to survivors and witnesses. When the REHMI project began its far-reaching investigation utilizing the infrastructure of the Catholic Church in municipalities throughout the country, many survivors and witnesses still feared coming forward and many local REHMI investigators had to be extremely cautious about their own security as well as that of their witnesses. Unlike our forensic investigation of Panzós, REHMI investigators were not able to hold large public gatherings on a daily basis for three months while conducting their research. Nor did they have the benefit of the frequent visits by the prosecutor, MINUGUA and CEH representatives, the human rights ombudsman, national and international press, and human rights observers. No doubt, the forensic team's access to survivors and witnesses was greatly increased by the presence and support of all these individuals and organizations. Indeed, their presence, and our access to local survivors and witnesses, was largely the result of previous investigative work conducted in the area and support given to community members by REHMI and also by MINUGUA. The willingness of witnesses and survivors to come forward was also increased by the signing of the peace accords, the demobilization of civil patrols, and the reinsertion of the guerrillas into civil society—each of which took place prior to our arrival in Panzós. Whereas we were able to collect 200 testimonies in our forensic investigation, the REHMI report, which named eight victims, was based on four testimonies.[52]

Because the CEH report was written after the commission received our forensic report on the exhumation, the CEH list of fifty-three named victims is extremely interesting. In its final report, the CEH noted that the forensic report revealed thirty-five skeletons in the mass grave. The CEH investigation, however, in addition to the thirty-five victims in the grave, included those who were injured in the plaza and died after fleeing the army massacre, those who drowned in the river fleeing, and those who were executed by security forces shortly thereafter. Thus, the CEH concluded that "the Guatemalan army arbitrarily executed fifty-three people and attempted to kill another forty-seven who were injured in the plaza massacre" resulting in "a grave violation of the right to life."[53] The CEH's methodology, which was legally based in international human rights law and the collection of legal evidence of human rights violations, encompassed violations occurring in the actual massacre as well as those occurring shortly thereafter that could be tied to the violence meted out by the army in the plaza and in the days immediately following.

While the REHMI report was affected by timing and access to witnesses and survivors, the forensic report was limited by the parameters of forensic science that define what is and what is not considered to be positive scientific evidence. The CEH's timing and legal methodology allowed for a more comprehensive analysis of the violence experienced in the Panzós massacre than the forensic or REHMI reports. The 1978 popular organization's ad naming sixty-eight victims was based on whatever information was provided by the witnesses and survivors to whom they had access in the nineteen days following the massacre.[54]

A commonality in the production of knowledge created by each of these organizations' methodologies in compiling a list of victims was the grounding of each project, in varying degrees, in the collection of survivor testimony. And testimonies, as theorist John Beverly has noted, are the narrated memories of real people "who continue living and acting in a real social history that also continues.[55] Both the testimony of the witness as well as the involvement of whoever listens to the testimony and produces it in written form are also part of that real and continuing social history in the making. In this sense, the lists of names can be understood as more than a naming of victims of the massacre. They can also be understood as "the real and significant historical fact" beyond the names underscored by the testimonies of survivors, which is "memory itself,"[56] and this memory is one of genocide. The only certainty one can have in the study of genocide is that for all we can learn and document from investigating these types of atrocities, regardless of our methodologies, the very destructive force that is the essence of genocide impedes our ability to ever fully document, know, or understand the totality of the devastation.

TRUTH, REBURIAL, AND THE RESHAPING OF HISTORY

On May 28, 1998, twenty years after the Panzós massacre, I had the privilege of accompanying the FAFG to return the boxed skeletal remains of the victims to their wives, mothers, fathers, daughters, sons, and grandchildren. This concluded the investigation we began in July of 1997 for the CEH to document the Guatemalan army massacre of Q'eqchi Maya peasants in the plaza of Panzós.

It was a long, hot ride to Panzós because the rains were unusually late, thus making the roads extremely dusty. The sky was hazy from the floating ash of a recent volcanic eruption as well as from the expansive fires raging out of control in the nearby Peten. Add to this the seasonal slash-and-burn farming technique still favored by most farmers of maize and you get visibility of less than one hundred meters due to the density of smoke. The mountains of Cobán and the hills of the lowlands were hidden behind a thick haze. Chunks of ash lightly gliding through the air left marks of soot in the hands that grabbed them. Months without rain had transformed the road to Panzós into a path of white powder. Peasants walking along the road scurried out of the path of oncoming vehicles, which left a cloud of white dust, leaving everyone and everything looking as if they had been dipped in flour.

The late afternoon heat was intense and extremely humid. Lacking air-conditioning, we had all our windows open. By the time we reached Panzós at six in the afternoon, the sun was still burning through the smoke-filled sky and we each looked as if we had been rolled in white talc. Everything seemed to be impregnated with the dust that whitened our hair, covered all our belongings, and formed dark shadows and lines across our faces damp with sweat.

As we wound around the bend that passes the cemetery, there was yelling, applause, and the honking of a handheld horn. We were stopped in the middle of the road, surrounded by a cheering crowd. More than 400 people were waiting by the cemetery near the entrance to Panzós. We forgot we were hot. We forgot we were dirty, tired, and hungry. As we got out of the truck, widows I had interviewed nine months earlier laughed and shouted. They greeted and embraced each of us. Many smiled as tears ran down their faces.

The widows had arrived at seven that morning and had stayed all day for fear of missing us. We had been in the prosecutor's office in Cobán until nearly three in the afternoon. It was only due to the dedication and persistence of the prosecutor and the forensic team that we were able to reach Panzós that day with the remains. Despite having earlier agreed to release the skeletons to the survivors for burial on the twentieth anniversary of the massacre, the presiding judge had that morning unexpectedly decided that if the skeletons were returned to the community then the survivors would abdicate their right to a criminal trial—which, along with proper religious burials of massacre victims, is a central goal of legal and forensic investigations into massacres. After writing, signing, and sealing many legal documents throughout the day, the prosecutor was finally able to convince the judge to allow us to take the remains to Panzós for burial on the anniversary of the massacre without survivors losing their right to pursue legal remedies in the criminal court proceedings.

When we reached Panzós, before we could take the bones to the municipal center to place them in coffins, the community wanted us to unload the cardboard boxes at the cemetery. Everyone wanted to help unload the trucks. Each woman wanted to carry a box. The elder women performed a Maya *costumbre* until the sky opened in a heavy downpour. We all ran the half mile down the road to the church, the women running with the boxes on their heads.

When we reached the church, the women had placed the thirty-five boxes at the altar. It did not seem to matter that the speakers were almost completely blocked out of sight by the boxes. Everyone was wringing the rain out of their skirts and shirts. Most everyone was smiling—even those with tears running down their faces. There was a collective sense of victory. These monolingual Q'eqchi' women had successfully stood up to those who threatened them, to those who killed their husbands, sons, fathers, and brothers. Several different Q'eqchi' men stood at the podium speaking in Q'eqchi'. The widows continued to talk among themselves in an oddly festive atmosphere. Smiling as they dried their faces, they seemed almost oblivious to the men speaking to them from the podium on the altar of the church.

Just as I was wondering if any of the widows would have an opportunity to speak, María, Mamá Maquín's granddaughter, approached the podium. María nervously looked down at the podium. Lifting her head, looking out across the crowd filling the church, she said, "I am not afraid. I am not ashamed. I am not embarrassed." All the widows stopped talking and focused their attention on her. All the scattered conversations in the church stopped. And the church fell silent except for her words and the slapping of water upon the roof and ground outside. A bilingual health worker approached me, "This is important," she said, and she began to translate María's words from Q'eqchi' to Spanish.

"I cannot tell lies because I saw what happened and so did a lot of other people. That is why there are so many widows and orphans here," she affirmed in a quiet voice. The widows in the pews looked at one another, nodding in agreement. "Twenty years ago, they did many things to us. Bad things. The blood of our mothers and fathers flowed in these streets. They tried to kill me, too."

The widows began to rock their whole bodies in agreement with María's words; her cadence became rhythmic, near hypnotic. "I thank god for giving me life. Our mothers and fathers did everything possible to try to make a better life for us. The blood that ran in the streets ran for God, too. Because we are all from the same blood and same body. The same God."

For a moment, she paused to gather her thoughts, to gain her composure. In this moment, everyone in the church looked toward the altar, waiting in a hush for her to continue. "We are very poor," she said. "Because of our ignorance, they took advantage of us. They did not think we have the same god. They paid no attention to the harm they caused us as they stole our lands. To them, we were nothing more than animals. That day in the plaza, I realized this. They chased after me, they tried to kill me."

When she says, "They tried to kill me," she begins to shake. She begins to cry. As she wipes the tears from her cheeks with her bare hands again and again, she continues to speak. I glance at the widows, who continue to rock. Many of them now crying, reaching out to one another. María speaks louder and with greater force. She is still crying, but no longer shaking. She says, "I had to throw myself in the river. I lost my shoes. The current carried me down. I hit myself on rocks. When I finally got out of the river, I was covered in mud and full of thorns." María shakes her head at the implausibility of the truth and says, "But this happened to everyone. The army and the *finqueros* did this. But we are still alive."[57] The widows look at one another, nodding in agreement and repeating her words, "We are still alive."

Through irregular breaths of sorrow, she says, "They thought that they would always be able to treat us like animals, that we would never know how to defend ourselves. But, we also have rights. We have rights from the same laws that they have rights. We have the same rights."

"I decided to speak tonight because I was in the plaza the day of the massacre. Today I am giving my testimony in public. We have to tell everything that happened to us in the past so that we won't have fear in the future." All the widows are attentively listening. They continue to nod in agreement to the rhythm of her words.

María is no longer crying. She stands before her community at the altar of the church. She takes a deep breath and declares in a loud voice that fills the church, "I am still in pain. I have such sorrow. I lost my mother, my father, my grandmother, and I was only twelve. The people who did this to us, they live here with their families in tranquility. That is why I say tonight," and then she states firmly and loudly, "I AM NOT AFRAID."

Tranquility seems to replace the pained look on her face. She almost smiles and says calmly, "Before, there was fear. But not now. That is why I speak clearly of the pain I have suffered." Her words pass over the crowd as a wave of satisfaction, almost a happiness.

"We are here to receive the remains of our loved ones and I thank the forenses," she says and all the widows make eye contact with each of us and smile. "We are in total agreement that the truth be known. We don't want to suffer like in the past. We don't want problems. If we can talk about the past and all the bad things that happened, then we can say 'never again.'" The entire crowd seems to vibrate in agreement. Everyone is looking at one another and nodding in agreement.

María is filled with the energy the crowd has returned to her. She asserts herself with great authority: "Even those people who did these terrible things, they can't do them again. They can't do it again because there are people who help us and we are no longer afraid. We will move forward and never ever repeat the past. They said that we were worthless. We are humble people and they humiliated us. We must leave our fear behind. We must leave our shame behind. We all share the same soul. We all want to live in peace."

In this moment, she has the entire crowd mesmerized and waiting for her words. She concludes, "I love God, life, and law. A man has no right to break the law of God. Man is not God. Only God can take life. We speak because we are not afraid. We speak from the heart."

In *The Book of the Embraces,* Eduardo Galeano notes that the root of *recordar,* to remember, is from the Latin *re-cordis,* which means "to pass back through the heart."[58] The public remembering of María Maquín, this passing back through the heart before her community, is the very essence of the discourse and practice of human agency, of political consciousness, self-representation, and action. Her story is not the story of dead people, though the dead are present. These stories from Panzós, like other testimonies in this book, are stories of the living—those who survived and have much to share when given the opportunity to speak. Human agency is silenced through death, but it is also silenced in other subtle and not so subtle ways. Army massacres driving people into the mountains, the scorching of abandoned villages, and the bombing of mountains where survivors fled for their lives silenced human agency but did not eliminate it. Forced participation in army-controlled civil patrols and community life regimented by an occupying army also silenced, but could not do away with, human agency. Mamá Maquín was silenced in the Panzós massacre, but her memory grew far beyond the confines of Panzós. María Maquín broke the silencing of the Panzós survivors with her public testimony in 1998, as Rigoberta Menchú broke the silencing of the Maya with her testimony.

Through a translator, Feliciana, a monolingual Ixil speaker, once said to me, "I don't know if my words have value, but I want to tell you my story." I believe the words of María, Feliciana, and other survivors have great value for survivors and researchers alike. I am not alone in this belief. In his work on history, memory, and the Holocaust, philosopher Dominick LaCapra affirms that "Testimony is a crucial source for history" and that it is "more than a source" because it "poses special challenges . . . for it raises the issue of the way in which the historian . . .

becomes a secondary witness . . . and must work out an acceptable subject position to the witness and his or her testimony."[59]

When anthropologists, sociologists, and historians fail to consider the Maya as actors in their own history, they commit a discursive silencing of human agency. They compound the terror of La Violencia by not taking into account the voices of the survivors—in effect, they silence them. Thus, however unwittingly, they compound the political, social, cultural, physical, and material violence with discursive violence.

Twenty years after the Panzós massacre, I sat with María as the massacre victims were buried and remembered in a Maya religious ceremony. We shared a bag of water in the heat. Her eight-year-old son picked up a pamphlet about the Panzós massacre. She smiled proudly, almost mischievously, and nodded at him with approval. Just as she was her grandmother's faith in a better future, her son is hers. Easily and quickly, he read the words of Mario Benedetti: *"Cantamos porque los sobrevivientes y nuestros muertos quieren que cantemos."*[60]

APPROPRIATION, AGENCY, AND THE ACCRETION OF TRUTH

While "official" histories may be used to justify and maintain military regimes or the authoritarian tendencies of civilian governments, history can also become a tool for the empowerment of the hitherto powerless.[61] Much has been written in testimonial, subaltern, and anthropological literature about the dynamics of representation and appropriation in the relationship between those who give testimony and those who write it. Literary theorist John Beverly suggests that while we should be watchful of "the idea of literary transculturation of the colonial and postcolonial subaltern from above," we must also consider and "admit to the possibility of transculturation from below."[62] In the case of *I, Rigoberta,* he suggests we should "worry less about how we appropriate Menchú" and rather seek to "understand and appreciate how she appropriates us for her purposes."[63] Building on Beverly's suggestions regarding literary transculturation, I suggest we consider Maya appropriation and enactment of external political discourse and action to understand contemporary Maya political activism. At the Panzós church, the night before the reburial of the exhumed remains, María Maquín said, "If we can talk about the past and all the bad things that happened, then we can say, '*Nunca más.*'" Was María using her own words, was it the discourse of outsiders or human rights discourse, or was someone else talking through her, as several anthropologists have suggested to me? Or was her discourse and her political action of speaking publicly an instance of Beverly's "transculturation from below" and an appropriation of global discourse for local purposes? Was María, as Beverly suggested of Rigoberta Menchú, "appropriat[ing] us for her purposes"?

Unless we go beyond the "safe, exclusive" theorizing and "condemnation of certain *representations* of violence," literary theorist Rosemary Jane Jolly argues that "we cannot identify how our present vocabulary contributes to a violent reality."[64] One way to heed her concern is to seek an understanding of the content and meaning of the violence experienced by subalterns from their perspective. In my fieldwork, I have found that each testimony creates political space for another survivor to come forward to give her own testimony. Moreover, this giving of individual testimony represents an expansion of both potential and real individual agency that, in the collectivity of testimonies, creates new political space for local community action. Michel Foucault argued that repression, in fact, "works through language and that the struggle to overturn repression includes speaking out against it. . . . Speaking out, not theorizing, constitutes a counterdiscourse, and it is produced by those involved 'radically' and 'physically' with existence."[65] Moreover, the very organization of speech and silences expressed in speaking "reveal[s] the speakers' relationships to their history."[66] Indeed, Maya political activism resonates with sociologist Francesca Polletta's research on the U.S. civil rights movement, which indicates that "the experience of 'standing up' [speaking], of demonstrating collective determination and resistance in the face of repression, may in fact be an instrumental benefit, a measure of movement success" and, furthermore, "the chance to 'stand up' against repression may be enough of a political opportunity to motivate collective action."[67]

In their testimonies, both public and private, Rigoberta Menchú, María Maquín, and other massacre survivors shared "not just what people did, but what they thought they wanted to do, what they believed they were doing, and what they now think."[68] Dominick LaCapra has observed that "for memory to be effective at a collective level, it must reach larger numbers of people. Hence, the acts or works that convey it must be accessible."[69] Further, he identifies the witnessing of the giving of testimony as a "necessary condition of agency."[70] He explains:

> It is altogether crucial as a way in which an intimidated or otherwise withdrawn victim of trauma may overcome being overwhelmed by

numbness and passivity, reengage in social practice, and acquire a voice that may in certain conditions have practical effects (for example, in a court of law). But just as history should not be conflated with testimony, so agency should not simply be conflated with or limited to, witnessing. In order to change a state of affairs in a desirable manner, effective agency may have to go beyond witnessing to take up more comprehensive modes of political and social practice.[71]

In Panzós, these modes began with the community organizing and "standing up" to request an exhumation and ultimately succeeding not only in the exhumation but also in the retaking of public spaces—the municipal plaza, the church, and the cemetery. As a community, survivors challenged these public spaces as mere reminders of Q'eqchi' loss and remade them into sites of popular memory contesting official stories. Further, these same survivors and widows seized the space they had created not only to publicly adjudicate collective memory but also to move forward with legal proceedings against the intellectual and material authors of the massacre and to seek resolution of the very land claims that had driven the Q'eqchi' to the plaza on May 29, 1978. Thus, in Panzós as elsewhere in Guatemala, "emancipation would be a process rather than an end and women its agency rather than its beneficiaries."[72]

ON DISTORTION AND CREDIBILITY

I do not know whether Asig or the other functionaries, both current and former, knew that FAFG members Leanor, Miguel, María, and I had collected dozens of testimonies about Asig's involvement in disappearances and threats. I do know, however, that it was very much in his interest to share his experience of the Panzós massacre. He told me that he felt the story of the Panzós massacre was "an unjust stain on the integrity of Panzós because 200 people were not killed." Certainly, Asig knew that in the end the FAFG would find the number of people buried by digging up the skeletons in the grave. If he could prove that the massacre was a lie, then he could cast doubt on other testimonies and perhaps exonerate himself, as well as other local thugs, from involvement in and responsibility for the disappearances and deaths that preceded and followed the massacre. The formula is not uncommon: to believe that those who are not guilty of one crime are therefore innocent of another and that those who tell one story with incorrect facts can be assumed to be lying when telling another story. Thus, Asig and the others implicated in the disappearances of local Q'eqchi' were counting on sharing what they knew about the Panzós massacre in a way that would cast doubt on the credibility of massacre survivors and relatives of the disappeared. In so doing, at least proportionally, they might increase their own credibility by lessening the credibility of survivors and victims.

Indeed, the cases of Sister Dianna Ortiz and Nobel laureate Rigoberta Menchú are two examples of distortion being used to chip away at the credibility of victims and survivors of La Violencia and indicate how widespread this strategy has been at all levels of Guatemalan society—from officials in isolated municipalities to U.S. academics and journalists writing about La Violencia, to the U.S. ambassador to Guatemala.

In its final report, the CEH concluded that the Panzós massacre was an illustrative case of "the undue influence exercised over the state apparatus by the agricultural sector to beneficially resolve land conflicts in their favor by involving the army in agricultural conflicts using violence against poor peasants." Further, the local landowners "not only requested the presence of the army, but also favored the creation of a hostile environment against the peasant population."[73] Thus, more than twenty years after the massacre, the nationally and internationally supported CEH affirmed the 1978 claims of the Panzós survivors and popular organizations, stating that the massacre was indeed the result of army intervention on behalf of local landowners. While the Panzós survivors lived in near total silence during the twenty years between the massacre and the investigation, the Panzós massacre as a metaphor for land rights and army repression was sustained in the popular imaginary. The investigations of the ODHA (Oficina del Arzobispado de Derechos Humanos—Archbishop's Office of Human Rights), the FAFG, and the CEH helped break the silence of Panzós, and the survivors seized the opportunity to define and seek local justice by appropriating the discourse of the peace process, which included human rights discourse. In so doing, Guha's "small voice of history" got a hearing in the survivors' account of the massacre by "interrupting the telling in the dominant version, breaking up its storyline and making a mess of its plot."[74]

CONCLUSION

In my quest to document massacres, colleagues in other disciplines (most notably in political science) have suggested on the one hand that I categorize the "worst" massacres and develop data sets, and on the other that narratives based on survivors testimonies are too "anecdotal" or that descriptions should be more "conceptual." When we first began to take survivor testimonies in Panzós, after three days and dozens of testimonies, we had only three testimonies from survivors of the plaza massacre. The rest of the testimonies came from widows, mothers, and daughters of the disappeared and assassinated. When we asked if those who came to give testimony could organize themselves, prioritizing plaza massacre survivors, one of the widows responded, "I am a widow. My husband died in the plaza but it isn't right to not listen to all the widows. We all suffered equally." If I were to construct a framework driven by categories of massacres and academic concepts rather than survivor testimonies, the voices of Maya women would be largely lost and we would learn little of the nuanced experiences of survival. This brings us back to the question of what constitutes "fact" or "knowledge" and how we count victims. While for well-meaning outsiders, massacres may represent little more than something to be counted to prove a violation of international law, for survivors, the living memory of La Violencia is integral to the local production of knowledge and the purpose of that knowledge in the production of new regimes of meaning. Within these new regimes, Maya women's voices challenge not only the Guatemalan army and government but also human rights workers and academics seeking to understand La Violencia.

Three

"IT FILLS MY HEART WITH SADNESS"

Ethnography of Genocide Part I

We were forced to do it. We are full of fear. We are trembling while we are there.

—*Don Sebastián*

In December 1997, I assisted the FAFG in its forensic investigation of the April 1981 army massacre of civilians in Acul and its subsequent report to the Commission for Historical Clarification. To reach Acul from Guatemala City, you leave the noise and grit of the city by taking a scenic and winding four-hour drive through the green grass and red earth of the lowland mountains of Chichicastenango and Santa Cruz del Quiché. You leave Santa Cruz on a dirt road. You drive for another hour or so, passing small communities of subsistence corn farming on a dirt road that covers everything with dust in the dry season. The looming purple and blue mountains in the distance suddenly appear closer as you reach the seemingly fertile oasis of Sacapulas and the river you must cross. If you are lucky, the bridge is not "out of order." If you cannot use the bridge, then you look for the place where the river is widest and, if you are like me, you hold your breath when the water rushes over the top of your engine hood as you drive across the river.

By the time you four-wheel drive through the sandy dirt road up to the top of the mountain to cross the crest that leads to the Ixil valley, you have risen to nearly 3,000 meters above sea level. Looking down on the Sacapulas side of the mountain, everything is dry and dusty except for the oasis bordering the river. From a distance, the valley below begins to look like green, brown, yellow, orange, and blue chalk. A clear day reveals an immense white, gray, brown, and blue valley with two volcanoes peaking out from behind the cloud-shrouded mountain range on the southwestern horizon. Then, just as suddenly as the mountains were upon you, you cross the crest of the mountain from the dry valley over to the moist, green land of the Ixiles. The air is crisp and cool, offering the fragrances of pine trees and wildflowers instead of dust. The clean air and vibrant greens, purples, and reds make you forget the fatigue from the long drive. As you drive down the mountain road, you see the Catholic church of Nebaj—a white spot amongst the red tile roofs in the distance. In 1981, the population of the Ixil Area was estimated at 80,000, with over 90 percent of the residents identified in a national census as Ixil.[1]

After the six-to-seven hour drive to Nebaj, you can reach Acul by driving northwest for about forty minutes. When you turn off the main road to go south for about ten minutes, to your right you will see a rushing river cutting through lush green grass. This river accompanies you until you reach the town square of Acul, which is marked by a small, whitewashed Catholic church facing a simple building that houses the local government. Nearly midway between the buildings is a tremendously large tree trunk, painted white and topped by bright green branches that together form a perfectly round treetop. It is only when you look down the road to the east between the church and government building that you realize Acul is in the valley directly to the west of Nebaj, with a mountain standing between the village and the municipality.

In Acul, in addition to participating in the FAFG (Fundación de Antropología Forense de Guatemala—Guatemalan Forensic Anthropology Foundation) archeological excavation of the clandestine cemetery containing the remains of the victims who were buried en masse, I worked with the FAFG to develop a methodology for the historical reconstruction of the massacre for their report to the CEH (Comisión para el Esclarecimiento Histórico—Commission for Historical Clarification). This investigation included an extensive review of municipal archival documents and the collection of lengthy testimonies from both survivors and witnesses.[2] As has been my experience in other research locations, as well as that of the FAFG in numerous investigations throughout Guatemala, this research reaffirmed that to understand the massacre and its impact on Acul residents, we had to also learn how Acul residents experienced life both before and after the massacre. The truth of the Acul massacre is not simply the recounting of the violent event but also the increasing militarization of village life leading up to the massacre and the lived experiences of survival in the midst of terror and the ongoing decimation of community life and structures.

In this chapter and chapter four, I offer an ethnography of Ixil Maya life and community structure before, during, and after the 1981 Guatemalan army massacre of Acul. Though each massacre I have investigated has its own particularities, there is more than sufficient consistency in army violence (before, during, and after massacres) to identify systematic army strategies, intent, and enactment of genocide in Maya communities throughout the country. In these two chapters, I also introduce the three campaigns of genocide that I have identified in my research on army violence and that I further explore in chapter six: (1) the massacre; (2) the sustained hunt for survivors in flight; and, (3) the systematic militarization and deliberate infliction of harm on survivors forcibly relocated into army-controlled camps that were called "model villages" in the army's "Poles of Development Plan."[3] Thus, this ethnography of the exhumation in Acul is also an ethnography of genocide.

ANTES . . . (BEFORE)

Most Acul residents remember first hearing of army and guerrilla violence in the Ixil Area between 1976 and 1977, when they witnessed the initial expansion of army troops and increasingly frequent military maneuvers throughout the Nebaj area. In the late 1970s, most had also heard of the guerrilla, though many had never actually seen guerrilla combatants. Some knew the guerrilla as the EGP or Ejército Guerrillero de los Pobres (Guerrilla Army of the Poor). Others referred to them as the *guerrilleros.* Many simply called them *los subversivos,* parroting army propaganda about "subversives" from cartoon pamphlets that depicted guerrilla combatants with Cuban revolutionary icon Ché Guevara's face and signature beret on a sinewy animal-like body with devil's tails and horns.

Still, the violence of the guerrilla and army seemed far removed from the daily life of Acul Ixiles. Their peasant community was relatively prosperous. Most families had sufficient land to grow enough *milpa* (maize) for subsistence farming. The land was productive, and each year usually brought two harvests of maize. People worked hard and usually had money for such luxury items as soap and oil. If crops failed or if a family wanted to purchase furniture, more land, or save money for a religious celebration, the men, and sometimes the entire family, went to the coast to work in seasonal coffee harvests.

Doña Elena[4]

Doña Elena is a widow of La Violencia. She is thirty-five years old and has one son, born after the murder of her husband. She is calm and carries herself with great dignity. She wears the red Ixil corte[5] with many bold and bright vertical gold lines—the quantity, depth of color, and width of these gold lines are the measure of the corte's quality. Her hair is braided and perfectly bound with a bright red, green, and white woven cloth. Her intricately embroidered huipil[6] is of top quality work and representative of the most prized clothing Ixil women can possess. Quality huipiles like Doña Elena's take an average of three months to weave and embroider. Today, few Ixil women have huipiles of this high quality because few have the level of skill to produce so perfect a weave and even fewer have the 1,000 *quetzales*[7] needed to buy such a huipil. While once a mandatory component of the Ixil bride's wedding trousseau, today most Ixil women wearing this type of huipil are the few who have bought it for themselves after completing their teaching studies and taking their first jobs. In rural communities, only expert weavers who can make their own still possess and wear such lovely huipiles, and most who make them sell them out of need.

Doña Elena is thin but appears healthy. Unlike the majority of Acul residents, she does not appear to have a respiratory or eye infection. Though weathered beyond her years, she retains a youthful glow in her skin and eyes. Her hands are those of a weaver and a woman who has daily worked the earth, hand milled corn, made thousands of tortillas, and washed her clothing in the cold waters of the river. Though we are seated on a grassy knoll far away from anyone who might hear, she speaks very softly, just above a whisper. Still, her words are firm as she gazes into the distance, occasionally glancing past the translator to look in my eyes when she is making a point, perhaps to be sure I am really listening, perhaps to measure trust or gauge understanding through my expressions. Having worked through translators in five different Maya languages, I have learned that body language often communicates as much as the spoken word, if not always in explanation, at least in intention. Having asked Doña Elena about her life before the violence, she begins firmly and proudly: "My husband worked hard. He grew our food in Acul and worked on the coast. That's why he always bought my clothes. I had five cortes and five huipiles. He bought me my food, my dishes, and a cabinet to keep my belongings. We had a table and chairs. A radio. I had a place to put away my things, not like today with everything in cardboard boxes. We always had a lot because my husband worked very hard."[8]

*   *   *

In Acul, as in other villages prior to the massacres, houses were much larger than today, averaging fifty square meters with walls of wood planks and solid foundations of rock and cement. The majority of houses were constructed with hand-planed walls of cypress boards and roofs of sun-baked clay tiles. Most families had a principal home of residence as well as another home under construction—either for an elder son's wedding present or as an inheritance to be left for grandchildren. Many families also had a smaller house for short-term housing in far away fields. Prior to the massacre, every household had livestock and domestic animals, furniture, several changes of clothing for each family member, pots, pans, dishes, and farm tools. Most had transistor radios and batteries to keep them running. Some even had musical instruments, including guitars and marimbas. Community life and the passage of time were marked by the celebrations of Maya costumbre and the rituals of the Catholic Church, as well as ceremonies commemorating the advent of marriage, birth, and death.

Throughout my fieldwork in Guatemala, whenever I have asked massacre survivors about their losses and their needs, I have found that *vivienda* (housing) is always one of the main worries. While to many outsiders peasant lifestyles may appear to be uniformly poor, for peasants, the size of a house and the materials of its construction have great implications for the comfort and health of a family. In addition to general comfort and space to move around, a larger space decreases the spread of illness, and increased doors and windows improve ventilation and air circulation, which is also critical for good health—especially when wood-burning stoves are used for cooking.

DON SEBASTIÁN'S HOUSES

Don Sebastián is seventy years old. He is a principal of the community.[9] His thinning white hair is short and unevenly cropped. For several hours as others gave their testimonies, he has waited patiently for his story to be heard. When it is his turn, he hurries to seat himself, takes off his hat, and puts it under the chair. In stark contrast to his white hair, his skin is darkly bronzed from decades of working the fields below the sun. Don Sebastián is so thin, his knees, elbows, and collarbone poke out of his pants and shirt—each of which have been constructed by sewing together worn-out remnants of several other pieces of clothing. I offer him a juice and some cookies. He tentatively accepts them, then devours them. It is one in the afternoon. He hasn't eaten since five this morning, when he had six tortillas before going to work in the fields for several hours, prior to getting in line to share his story. I give him more cookies and juice.

He begins by asking me the identity of all the other people who have been asking for information because he is unfamiliar with them and with their organizations. "Are they *forenses*?[10] A man with glasses wrote down my *cédula* number.[11] I am scared because I don't know why he did it or who he is. I am still scared." We tell him we will find out who took the information and let him know as soon as we do.[12]

Despite his fear, Don Sebastián wants to share his experience and denounce the murderer of his only child, his son. As he struggles to speak, his face fills with pain:

> My house before was built of pure wood. It had 2,300 tiles. Before, there used to be very good wood. Cypress. We would walk up into the mountains to bring it down. We thought about the future, but we did not know what was about to happen to us. I worked for the future. Cypress is hard wood to work with because you have to go far up in the mountain and then bring it down. But it is good wood. It will last for more than one hundred years. I thought it would be an inheritance for my children. I built my house for the future. If I had known what was going to happen to us, I would not have worked so hard. We did not know that the army was going to come to Acul and burn all of our houses. It brought me great pain to see the foundation of the house I built. [13]

The day before our interview, we had gone with Don Sebastián to the site of his home before the massacre. With agility and speed, Don Sebastián chopped back the vegetation to reveal the rock and cement foundation. As we measured and examined the foundation, Don Sebastián called our attention to the burned remains of wood beams that had once supported his home. Just as Bertolt Brecht once wrote, "I'm like the man who took the brick to show how beautiful his house used once to be,"[14] Don Sebastian said, "My whole house looked just like this. Pure carbon. This is proof that what I say is true. The base of this beam in the foundation is burned because they burned down my whole house. The army burned it down."

Don Sebastián explained the other losses that the loss of his house represented:

> It fills my heart with sadness how much it cost me to build this house. I cannot reconstruct this house. I cannot reconstruct my family. What you have come to see is what existed before. You are now witnesses to what happened before. You have seen the bones of our children massacred by the army and the foundations of our burned houses. Before, I used to think that here I would live my future with my children and my grandchildren. But they killed my son and burned my houses. I am old and alone. My grandchildren would be with me, but I don't have them because the army killed my son. So his wife had to find another man because I had nothing to give them. I have nothing.[15]

*   *   *

Despite the relative prosperity of Acul peasants prior to La Violencia, life was not easy. It was the difficult and arduous life of subsistence milpa farmers dependent on good weather and pest-free crops for an abundant annual harvest. *Curanderos* (healers), *juezeros* (bone setters), and *parteras* (midwives) provided most medical care because clinic-based medical care was expensive and far away, both culturally and geographically. There was no electricity. There was no potable water. For Acul residents, the only means to reach Nebaj, located on the other side of the mountain, was a three-and-one-half hour walk up the mountain from Acul and down the other side to Nebaj. The same walk awaited outsiders seeking to reach Acul, unless they had a helicopter.

In the late 1970s, Acul residents began to take advantage of the skills-building training and resources made available to rural communities through Catholic Action and peasant organizations. These programs were especially attractive to young men who, having completed between one and four years of primary school, tended to be semiliterate and functionally bilingual Ixil/Spanish speakers. In Acul, these semiliterate Spanish-speaking young men were attracted to agricultural training programs to improve and diversify crop production for market, as well as to popular literacy, health, and catechist projects.[16] These young men became the cultural brokers for their community and, because of their greater understanding of the Spanish-speaking world outside Acul, they also became advocates for anyone wronged by an outside individual or institution.

WHEN THE ARMY AND GUERRILLA ARRIVED

Don Paulino and Doña Luisa

Acul residents say that in 1980 on the road from nearby Chemala to Nebaj, the guerrilla killed approximately twenty-eight soldiers when they ambushed two army trucks carrying soldiers and *leña* (firewood) to Nebaj. According to the Nebaj Death Register, some fifteen soldiers were killed on April 2, 1980, in Chemala.[17] Following the guerrilla ambush, army soldiers began to arrive in Acul and other neighboring *aldeas* (villages) to question everyone about the guerrilla. Soldiers went house to house and aldea to aldea searching for weapons and questioning men, women, and children. Don Paulino, whose son was killed in the Acul massacre, remembers army soldiers arriving en masse in Acul: "They climbed up on top of our roofs and from there they would give their speeches."[18]

It was at about this same time that guerrilla representatives also began to arrive in Acul. They met first with one family in one house, then with the next family in another house in small private meetings. Doña Luisa recalls that the first guerrilleros to arrive in Acul were unarmed. "The EGP [Guerrilla Army of the Poor] came to give speeches and to organize us, nothing more," she explains. "They asked for nothing." Later, the guerrilla would call community-wide meetings explaining their armed struggle and revolutionary program for the future. This pattern of moving from initial individual contact to wide-scale community meetings and the building of clandestine organization was repeated throughout the Ixil Area, as well as in other departments in Guatemala.

Doña María

As the exhumation in Acul proceeded, men and women traveled long distances by foot to reach Acul. They came because they had heard we were listening to their stories. I first noticed Doña María as a new face approaching the Acul women with whom I had been working. They pointed in my direction, nodding to her and to me. She came straight over to me, crossed her arms decisively, shyly looked down at her feet, abruptly raised her head, looked me straight in the eye, and said, "I walked here to give my testimony of La Violencia. I am not from Acul. I do not have a relative in the grave, but what happened here happened in my village, too. It happened everywhere."

I asked her why she came to Acul when many people were still afraid to speak. She told me that she had heard that there was a gringa listening to women. "I was a girl when it happened, but I am a woman now. I want to tell my story. Will you listen?" She told me her village had been burned by the army the same day as the massacre in Acul. Doña María wanted to talk about the army and the guerrilla. She remembered the first time she saw the guerrilla, "They told us, 'We are the army of the poor.'"[19]

Don Martín and Doña Angela

Like many of the men giving testimony about the destruction of Acul, Don Martín's son was killed in the army massacre. When he begins to speak of the arrival of the guerrilla, he explains that even though Acules are poorer today than they were before La Violencia, "We have always been poor."[20] It was this poverty that the guerrillas recognized and addressed in their speeches. The absence of electricity, only footpaths for transportation, the lack of educational opportunities, and the exploitative working conditions for seasonal laborers on the southern coast were among the issues initially raised in the battle cry of the EGP to galvanize popular support from Ixil villages. Don Martín recalls, "They told us, 'The president is receiving aid and none of it is reaching us. That is why we will struggle together.'"

Throughout her testimony, Doña Angela's large, almond-shaped eyes are brimming with tears. Each time I think they will spill down her face, she takes a deep breath, swallows, looks off into the distance and continues, her voice just above a whisper. Her arms are folded across her chest. Her hands never move from tightly holding her forearms. She is tapping her foot throughout our meeting. Her tapping accelerates each time she speaks of the army and guerrilla. "The Responsable counseled us. He told us we had to hold meetings," she says. "They told us there were people in the mountains who needed food. They said, 'So, you are going to do the favor of making food for the people with guns in the mountains.'"[21]

Don Manuel, Doña Josefina, and Doña Rosario

The majority of Acul residents followed guerrilla instructions and dug *buzones*[22] for storing food and clothing. Don Manuel echoes numerous survivors when he states, "They explained how to build a buzón. How to conserve and conceal the food and clothes we would need in special holes we dug in the earth. Almost everyone had food and clothing stored away."[23] While interviews with survivors support Don Manuel's assertion that nearly everyone had a buzón, there existed dissension about these constructions not only within the community but also within families. Doña Josefina, widowed by the massacre, agreed that nearly every household in Acul had a buzón of food and clothing, but she did not agree with their construction, nor with community support (whether voluntary or coerced) for the guerrilla. Her husband participated in the guerrilla-mandated activities, but she chose not to. "I did not participate because I did not know its implications or purpose," she explains. While Doña Josefina is aware that her husband's participation and societally imposed gender division of decision-making responsibilities allowed her the luxury of choosing not to participate, this did not stop her from disagreeing with her husband and her neighbors. "We have robbed nothing. Why do we have to hide our belongings?" She asks me the same question she asked her husband. She pauses and looks at me, as if awaiting an explanation.[24]

Whether acquiescing to guerrilla pressure to support insurrectionary actions or out of ideological affinity to a cause that promised liberation, Acules agree that the guerrilla began to prepare them, both materially and psychologically, for flight from the village and war. Another massacre widow, Doña Rosario, sums up myriad reasons for community participation in guerrilla preparations. She repeats an EGP warning shared with the community, an explanation of why Acules built buzones regardless of their level of support for, frustration with, or fear of the EGP. Buzones should (and ultimately would) be built and stocked because: "Maybe the army will come and kill all of you. You have to be prepared."[25] Some Acul residents organized meetings and activities for the EGP. The majority participated because it seemed "like a good idea" and because Acul residents had experienced the injustices outlined by the EGP and had reason to believe EGP warnings of future army attacks.

* * *

For Acul Ixiles, like most Maya, "If there are enough tortillas for four people, there are enough for five." Though the reproduction of Maya peasant culture is dependent on individual agricultural production, it is also equally dependent on community collaboration in difficult times.

Acul Ixiles gave food to both army soldiers and guerrilla combatants. Most gave tortillas, beans, and shelter to EGP combatants passing through because it is a common practice to give food and lodging to travelers. Both the army and the guerrilla banked on this customary reciprocity and hospitality—indeed, this is one of the very bases of guerrilla organizing strategy. Still, there is an unquantified, yet shared, rule in every culture that recognizes what is appropriate behavior for both the giver and the receiver. When and how did it come to pass that the Ixiles came to feel drained and, later, used and/or abused by army and guerrilla demands for continued "hospitality?"

Don Miguel and Don José

As time wore on, both army and guerrilla discourses became more aggressive and accusatory. Acules grew tired of the near-continual presence of armed soldiers and combatants and its implication for the family food supply. Still, they continued to share their small stock of food because the EGP combatants and Guatemalan soldiers were armed. "We were frightened because it would be worse if we don't give them food because they can kill us," relates Don Miguel, "It is better that we just give them food."[26]

As support (whether enthusiastic or reluctant) for the guerrilla increased in Acul and other Ixil villages, guerrilla presence in and around Ixil villages also increased. It became increasingly common to run into EGP combatants on the footpaths outside Acul. Sometimes the combatants were known to local villagers, sometimes they were unfamiliar faces, sometimes they were neighbors. By this time, most households had guerrilla-mandated buzónes. Acules had seen small groups of armed and unarmed guerrillas in Acul and had given them food. Still, local villagers were startled to meet the armed combatants in the mountains—especially when they were strangers. "I went to work in the fields and I ran into two EGP. They grabbed me and asked me who I knew and where I was going," remembers Don José. "I was very afraid."[27]

THE ARMY ATTACKS CIVILIANS

Doña Jacinta, Doña Josefina, and Don Sebastián

This increasing guerrilla presence did not go unnoticed by the army. "The EGP came to organize the people," explains Doña Jacinta. "In the end, the army heard about it and within the year the army came to my house." Doña Jacinta was lying in bed with her newborn son when the army burst in.[28] The soldiers asked her, "What are you doing there?" Doña Jacinta pulled her son close to her breast and answered, "Me, nothing. My son was just born." Though the soldiers moved on to another house, their violent entry marked both the birth of her son and the beginning of a new era of violence in Acul.

As happened in other villages throughout Guatemala, the violence eventually began to directly affect Acul Ixiles. Very late on the night of October 12, 1980, the army carried out its first military operation against civilian Ixiles in Acul. In a predawn, house-to-house search, the army dragged nine young men out of their beds. Doña Josefina remembers, "It was before the massacre. We saw the army take them away because these men were our neighbors. Later my husband went with the other men to look for them. They found them and buried them."[29]

Don Sebastián was unaware of what had happened until dawn, when the families of the abducted began to cry out, "They've taken our sons! They've taken our husbands! We are so sad!" The men of Acul formed groups to search for the missing men. They looked all over the outskirts of Acul but did not venture far up the mountain paths for fear of running into the army platoon. The dead bodies of the nine men were left high above Acul on a mountain path halfway to Nebaj. "We found them about a week after. We brought them down and buried them," says Don Sebastián. "Some were strangled to death with a rope and others were killed by the force of a knife driven through them." He is silent for a moment. Then he looks straight at me and says, "The army did it."[30]

THE GUERRILLA ARMY OF THE POOR RETALIATES

Seven months after the army attack on Acul, the community suffered its second loss of life to La Violencia and its first at the hands of the EGP. In the afternoon of April 12, 1981, and on the same path where the nine victims of army terror had been found in October, the EGP was holding a meeting with community members from Acul and other nearby villages.

Doña Magdalena

Doña Magdalena is among the first group of widows who present themselves to give testimony about the Acul massacre. She is completely disheveled. Her general disorderliness makes her stand apart from the other women. Instead of the strictly symmetrical wrapping of the corte, with the huipil tucked underneath and neatly held together by a brightly woven *faja*,[31] her corte is crooked. It sticks up under the faja unevenly and her huipil appears to be on backwards and is not completely tucked in. While her clothes are old and worn, they are no worse than those of many other poor peasant women; they just lack the fastidious presentation to which I have become accustomed. Instead of having her hair neatly wrapped on top of her head or held in a ponytail with a barrette, it seems to be flying in all directions and looks as though she may have arranged it once several days earlier, but not since then. Her dark eyes dart in all directions. I can feel her fear. Her damage is visible in her carriage, her voice, and her body language.

On the morning of April 12, 1981, her husband and son left home early to begin the ascent of the mountain to Nebaj in the cool morning mist. As they reached the midpoint of the path before it descends down the mountain, they were stopped by EGP combatants. "The guerrilla came out on the path and asked, 'What are you doing here? Are you Orejas[32] for the army?'" Doña Magdalena says almost with disbelief. "Then, they grabbed my husband and son and took them away and killed them. The people who were at the meeting with the EGP told me what happened and they helped me find and bury them."[33]

Doña Magdalena explained that her husband and son were buried legally in the cemetery, but that she wanted to give her testimony. She had heard that we were listening to everyone who suffered, not just to the survivors of the massacre. She told me that after her husband and son were killed, "Something went wrong inside of me. I cannot explain what happened, but nothing mattered anymore. I didn't leave my house. I didn't eat. I didn't cook. I still had one child. I had a daughter. She was two. I lost her. I don't know what happened to her. I think she left and went looking for food. I never saw her again."

*   *   *

Between 1977 and 1980, residents of Nebaj and its surrounding communities suffered a twenty-fold increase in violent deaths. In 1977, there were five violent deaths recorded in the Nebaj Death Register. Thirteen deaths were recorded in 1978 and also in 1979. By 1980, the Death Register records one hundred people as victims of violent deaths caused by gunfire, strangulation, knife wounds, and internal hemorrhaging caused by trauma to the abdominal area and trauma to the cranium.

In 1981, one hundred new violent deaths were recorded in the first six months of the year. By the end of 1981, the toll of recorded violent deaths reached 172. Close to eighty percent of the victims were residents of outlying aldeas and caserios. Nebaj residents account for 13 percent of violent deaths. Seven percent of victims are recorded as nameless "XXX," with neither place of origin nor place of death noted.[34] This escalation of death did not go unnoticed by the Acules. "Each day, there were more dead, more disappeared and more tortured in the eighties," declares Doña Josefina.[35]

THE MASSACRE

On April 21, 1981, the Guatemalan army surrounded and occupied Acul.[36] At 6:00 in the morning, when the men got up to go work in their cornfields, they discovered their community surrounded by the Guatemalan army and the civil patrol from Nebaj. Men on their way to work were captured en route to their fields and taken to the Catholic church in Acul.

Don Salvador, Doña Juana, and Don Sebastián

Don Salvador was one of the young men taken to the Catholic church. He is now forty-nine years old. He seems nervous, more embarrassed than frightened. He looks at his feet as he expresses concern that he has no money to rebury his brother after the exhumation. "I offer my apologies for my question, but I am poor. I have no money. I hardly have any food. I want justice, but how will I pay to bury my brother?" he asks as he looks at me for the first time. After I explain that one of the human rights organizations will provide wood for caskets, as well as resources for the burial ceremony, he relaxes and begins his story, "There were two soldiers and one civilian. The civilian wore a mask. They caught us as we walked to our fields. They tied up my older and younger brothers. They tied me up, too. They began to interrogate us then and there." During this interrogation, another man from Acul walking with his young son came upon the scene. "The army told the little boy to cross the river to see if he had been given his guerrilla training. But the truth is that we are just simple peasants. The child had no idea how to do what the army told him to do. The river carried him away."[37]

While Don Salvador and his brothers were being interrogated on the banks of the river, the men of Acul were being taken to the church plaza.

Don Sebastián was among them, "We were perhaps 300 and they told us to crouch down on the ground, to put our heads down and not look at anything. If you look at anything, there were some soldiers who would break your head just for looking."

As those on paths leading to the fields were rounded up, the civil patrollers went house to house looking for both older and younger men. "The patrollers went house to house and they came in and took my son while the army waited outside," says Doña Juana. "They only picked up the men. Whoever they were, whoever they could find. They grabbed the youth, the elderly, all of them. The thing is, they just grab them and take them away."[38]

Doña Juana was in her home when the patrollers broke down the door, came in, and dragged away her son, "They did not say anything, not one word." For a moment, she falls silent. She is large for an Ixil woman. She is probably close to five feet, four inches and quite plump. Her massive gray hair is gracefully swept on top of her head and neatly wrapped in a woven cloth. She is sixty-five years old and should be enjoying her grandchildren. She holds her chin in her hand rocking back and forth as she remembers, "The thing is if we speak, they are going to kill us. That's why we just watched them take him away without saying anything."

In a house next to the school, the army placed all the elders of Acul. These elders are called *principales* because they hold the secrets of the past and carry on the Maya religious tradition of costumbre. The elders waited in fear, waited in silence.

One of the members of the civil patrol wore a mask. People later identified him as a seventeen-year-old youth from a neighboring village. While the elders were held in the house, the military walked the rest of the captured men by this young masked man who pointed at each individual and then pointed at either the school or the church. The men put in the church had their hands tied behind their backs. The men not sent to the church were placed in the school. Don Salvador was sent to the school. His brothers were not so lucky.

Inside the church, the soldiers ordered the men to lay face down on the floor. The soldiers walked around the church kicking and beating the men. Then, they covered the beaten men with a blanket of leaves and dirt. Meanwhile, the principales were taken by another group of soldiers to the cemetery and ordered to dig a grave. Don Sebastián recounts, "We were forced to do it. We are full of fear. We are trembling while we are there."[39]

While the elders were digging the grave, the young men detained in the school were taken to the church and ordered to run and jump on the piles of leaves and dirt. "With the dirt and leaves on top of them, it was as if there weren't any people underneath, " explains Don Salvador. "The soldiers ordered us to hop and jump and run inside. We had to do what they ordered because we were threatened with death and they were beating and torturing us."

As they hopped and ran and jumped in the church, the soldiers were beating them in the head and ribs with the butts of their machine guns. Several of the young men sustained broken ribs and fractured skulls. The beatings intensified as they tried to stop jumping because they felt human beings, their brothers, cousins, and neighbors, writhing with pain below their feet. Then, these young men were ordered to lay face down on top of the earth and leaves covering the other young men below. "Though I was face down, I could see a little," recalls Don Salvador. "A soldier slammed me in the head and ribs with his machine gun and asked, 'What are you looking at?' I fractured some ribs from these blows and kicks."[40] As they lay face down upon the men covered with earth and leaves on the floor of the church, the soldiers continued to beat them.

While all this was happening, the elders of the community were digging a grave. They had been ordered to dig a deep grave, deeper than their height. When they finished digging the grave, they were made to stand in it. The elderly men believed they were going to be killed. "The soldiers were laughing and aiming their weapons at us," says Don Sebastián. "I thought to myself, 'This is where I die!'"[41] Then, as suddenly as they had been ordered to dig and stand in the grave, the soldiers ordered the elders out of the grave and marched them back to the plaza in front of the church.

The young men who had been trampled on the church floor were brought out, their hands still tied behind their backs. The young men from the school were brought out as well. The soldiers now reorganized these three groups of men into two groups. The young men with their hands tied behind them who had been covered with leaves and dirt and tortured in the church were placed on the left and told they were "hell." The elders who dug the grave and the young men who had been forced to run and jump upon the bodies of their cousins and brothers were put into a group on the right and called "heaven."

Then, one man from "hell" was singled out. "He was a brother, what I mean to say is an evangelical. He was innocent," clarifies Don Salvador.

"The soldiers said, 'This is to make an example of you even though you read the Bible. This is the real commander of the guerrilla,' they said this to each side, to 'heaven' and to 'hell.' Then, they carried out the execution of the evangelical brother." After the soldiers tied Roberto, the evangelical brother, to the tree in the plaza in front of the church, they obligated each man to hit or kick him. When it was over, "The army said, 'Now he is dead. Now he is finished. Now it is your turn,'" remembers Don Salvador. Then the soldiers began to talk among themselves. The men could hear them saying, "These are the people to be killed. They need to be taken up to the cemetery. We'll kill the rest of them later."[42]

The young men in the group called "heaven" were sent back to the school. Some still had their hands tied behind their backs. The army separated the elders out of "heaven" and ordered them to go to "hell" and get their sons and nephews. The elders were ordered to take their sons and nephews to the grave in the cemetery. As Don Sebastián recounts the cruelty of taking his son to the grave, he begins to cry softly. He continues to speak, to tell the tale of terror as his quiet weeping swells to loud sobs. He rocks back and forth, running both hands all over his face, then drying them on his pants. Despite the laborious breathing that accompanies his tears, he only stops speaking long enough to take another deep breath to continue, "They told us, 'Now that you have finished the graves, each one of you must take a person. You must choose your sons and then you will be the ones to take them away. The men of heaven must take the men of hell to the cemetery.'"

As the elders took their sons and nephews up to the cemetery, the soldiers said, "This is what happens when you let your children help subversives. Now you will see what happens when you do not raise your children properly."[43] The soldiers put the young men in rows in front of the grave and they put the elders on the sides to watch. Then, the soldiers lined up and began to fire into the young men in the first row. They fired directly into their faces, their chests, and their stomachs. The first row of young men fell into the grave. Then, the soldiers pushed the remaining rows of men into the grave on top of those already shot. They then fired into the grave.

It is painful for Don Salvador to remember that while his brother was sent to "hell," he was sent to "heaven." "I felt his sorrow. The principales told me that the soldiers shot my brother three times, but even with three bullet wounds he didn't die. He tried to climb out of the hole of dead. He tried to crawl out of the hole." When the soldiers realized the young man was not dead they beat him in the head with their machine guns. "Directly they smashed his head, but he still wasn't completely dead. He was still breathing when they buried him," Don Salvador laments.[44]

The soldiers ordered the elders to bury the dead. The old men covered the dead and near-dead bodies of their sons and nephews with earth. When they had finished filling the grave with earth, the soldiers said, "Wait, you haven't finished yet. You still have more work to do. Now, we are going for a walk." Still sobbing, Don Sebastián recalls, "We thought, 'Now the soldiers are going to kill us. They have taken our children away. Certainly, they are not going to let us live. They are going to kill us now. We are going to join our children in heaven." He looks up at me, for a moment almost breathing regularly, and says in a firm voice, "Our children are not in hell."

But instead of killing them, the army sent the elders to pick up the bodies of the five men killed by soldiers early that morning as the men walked to work in the cornfields. The elders carried these bodies back to the grave site. Next to the grave of thirty sons and nephews, they dug a second grave and buried these five bodies. After they had buried the bodies, the soldiers said, "Why are you all so sad? You shouldn't be sad. It is not just here that there are problems. There are dead everywhere. There are dead in Cotzal and Chajul. So, you have to have a little, too. Why are you so sad? It has to be this way."[45]

Indeed, the Acul massacre was but one of seventy-nine massacres carried out in the department of El Quiché in 1981. These massacres and others like them were the Guatemalan army's first campaign of genocide against the Maya. These massacres followed a systematic genocidal pattern, which I discuss further in chapter six.

Don Sebastián remembers, "Then, they asked us, 'What have you observed here? What is it that you have seen?' We did not answer them because we knew that they had killed our sons. We just didn't respond." The soldiers did. They said, "You don't answer us because you don't take good care of your sons. These sons of yours are involved with the guerrilla. That's why you don't answer us. Now, you've seen the dead. You have to return to your homes. You must go tranquil. Go home and eat, relax, and sleep. Don't do anything. You have done good work here. Go home. Go home tranquil."

The sobbing swells again and Don Sebastián almost shouts, "But we are not tranquil. We are sad. We went home, but we didn't eat. We are crying. We are not content because we know what they have done. They killed our sons. I couldn't eat for more than a month." He doubles over, burying his face in his hands between his knees. Still rocking his body, his sobs dwindle to whimpers. I turn off my tape recorder. Without a word, Julia and I stand, then crouch, on either side of Don Sebastián. We half embrace him, half caress his back. I can feel each rib, each vertebrae. He is so thin. Powerlessly, I whisper, *"Lo siento."* (I am sorry.) Julia says, *"No es justo. Sufrimos mucho. Todos sufrimos."* (It is not just. We suffered a lot. We all suffered.) He lifts his head out of his hands. His hard, callused hands pat our arms. He gains composure as he comforts us. "I am still not finished," he says, almost in apology. "There is still more. I want to tell more."[46]

* * *

In the frenetic escalation of painful memories, there is always more. It seems each time, when I thought we had reached the final ebb, when I felt overwhelmed with their memories of terror, when there just could not possibly be more horror that a human being could suffer and endure, these new friends who accepted me as their confidante would say, "There is more." For the outsider seeking to understand La Violencia, the trick is to assume nothing. One must accept the survivor as the guide through the labyrinth of terror. Embrace the path of the memory and allow the survivor to carry it to its closure. Even if the path to closure is far beyond the untested limits of one's imagination.[47]

AFTER THE MASSACRE

Don Salvador
Before the dead were buried by the elders, the young men of "heaven" who had been forced to witness the brutal murder of their brothers, cousins, friends, and neighbors, were marched back to the school. The soldiers began to interrogate them collectively, "What are you thinking now? Are you going to take us to the buzones? Is that where you have the weapons? The claymores? The mines that you use on the roads?" The men responded, "How can we answer your questions when we don't even know what you are talking about?"

One by one, the soldiers grabbed the men and threw them on the floor. Repeating their questions to each survivor, they formed a human pyramid, soldiers flattening the man at the bottom. The weight of the soldiers pushed the air out of the men's bodies and prevented them from breathing. "I almost died," says Don Salvador as he takes a deep breath, remembering the torture in both mind and body. "I almost died, but I survived."

None of the men answered the questions. After each had been tortured, they were taken outside the school and forced to eat their lunches. Below the soldiers' gaze, they ate the tortillas, eggs, beans, and honey they had been carrying with them as they walked to the fields to work in the morning. Then, once again, they were returned to the school. The soldiers began to beat them in the head and stomach with the butts of their machine guns. "Blood began to run out of our noses, our mouths, our ears and other parts of our bodies," says Don Salvador. "We were still breathing, but not normal breathing, because we were close to death. The soldiers recognized this and asked us, 'Are you thirsty?' They gave us water to drink, but it is not water. It was the urine of a soldier." These men were held and tortured in the school until seven in the evening.

When they were finally released, despite their extreme physical and emotional pain, they began to look for their tools. The tools they would have been carrying home from the fields had the army not swept down upon Acul that morning. "I had been carrying my machete and hoe to work, and my radio. There was a man in the patrol who I knew. So, I called him by name and said, 'Vicente, where is my satchel, hoe, machete, and radio?' He responded, 'How can you think about your things and not your life? Aren't you grateful to be alive? Look, there is going to be a meeting of all the communities in Nebaj on Thursday. You have to go.' I thought to myself, they are going to kill me. So, that Thursday, after the massacre, I did not go to the meeting."

As the men slowly made their way back to their houses after their release, they saw no one. The paths were vacant and the houses were empty. Almost everyone had fled. Don Salvador was too weak from torture to go anywhere beyond his house. Five days after the massacre, with much trepidation, his father and a friend returned to Acul searching for Salvador. "They had to carry me. It took two months for me to recover," Don Salvador explains. "I could not eat anything for more than twenty days, not even a bite of tortilla.[48] I lived on water and *aguardiente* (grain alcohol). Only with this could I escape the pain. In time, I began to feel better. After some twenty days, I ate a tortilla. But we were still fleeing the army in the mountains. I fell in a river and the river carried me away. I survived, but it gave me another illness."

When Don Salvador once again began to eat and his physical injuries began to heal, he felt stronger. "More or less, I felt normal," he recalls. "But then, I remembered my brother. How can I tell you what happened? It filled me with such profound sadness that I stopped eating. I didn't eat anything for another two months for the sadness of thinking about what had happened and how we are living. This is what I thought about the entire time in the mountains. I was always sad thinking about these sorrows."[49]

*   *   *

In the first few days following the massacre, most of the families of Acul fled into the mountains. Within two weeks, the village was empty, and the army burned every house and field of corn in Acul. The only building left standing was the Catholic church. Though not burned, it was not left untouched. The religious images of saints inside the church were stolen. Later, these images were found in the church in Nebaj, presumably taken there by Nebaj civil patrollers, but the silver crowns that had for years adorned the saints were never recovered.

Four

THE EXHUMATION AND THE ANTI-CHRIST

Ethnography of Genocide Part II

The pastors say you will sell the bones because you are the Anti-Christ.

—*Doña Fermina*

LIFE IN FLIGHT IN THE MOUNTAINS

The first few days following the massacre, the Ixiles of Acul slept in the mountains at night. In the day, the women returned to their houses to prepare food, and the men went to the fields to work. "But then, the army burned everything. So we stayed in the mountain," Doña Ana explains. "We did not have anywhere else to go."[1]

Doña Joséfina and Don Salvador

"The army obliged us to go into the mountains," says Doña Joséfina. "We suffered hunger, cold, and illness. We were like hostages. Those who fled the massacres were pursued and killed by the army. Those who fled the hunger of the mountains were also killed for being accomplices of the army."[2]

Despite life in flight, survivors attempted to grow milpa and whatever else they could in patches of land in the mountains. "But the army continued to pursue us and they found these places and cut down our milpa," laments Don Salvador. "They killed animals: cows, sheep, chicken, everything. Whatever they could grab, they killed."[3]

This destruction of crops and livestock was devastating for survivors. Doña Joséfina shakes her head, "There was nothing. There was no food. We ate the grasses, weeds, and roots we found in the mountain. Water with weeds, water with roots, that is all we ate." When the dry season came, the survivors had been driven so far up into the mountain that they were far from any river. Weak from months of hunger, they now had no water supply. "There was no food. There was no water," explains Doña Joséfina. "We looked for a root that has almost a teaspoon of water. If you couldn't find that root, then you died of thirst."[4]

*   *   *

Massacre survivors fled in groups as small as one to two families, others in groups of eleven to fifteen families. Many later joined larger, more or-ganized groups of 150 to 300 people. As each survivor recounted the search for the root with one teaspoon of water, I imagined these thou-sands of Ixiles clambering all over the mountain searching out the root, and the profound defeat of arriving to an area that should have had the roots of water, only to discover that another family or community had found them first.

THE DAILY SEARCH FOR FOOD AND WATER

Don José, Doña Angela, and Don Eulalio

They lived each day in search of food and water, and in fear of army ground attacks and aerial bombings, in fear of guerrilla justice, and with the constant gnaw of hunger and the preoccupation of a slow death from starvation or illness. "People were always dying," says Don José. "Every day or two, someone died from hunger."[5] Doña Angela's mother died of hunger in the mountain. "Many people died this way," she says, "there in the mountain, they are buried."[6] While some died from hunger, others died from the violence and retribution of war. "Many people died of hunger, but they also died from the gunfire of the army and, then, the guerrilla killed, too," says Doña Feliciana.[7]

Despite the hunger, thirst, violence, and extreme privations of sur-vival in the mountains, as relatives and friends died, the living sought to continue life by marking the passage of death through burial ceremonies. Don Eulalio was ten years old when he fled with his widowed mother to the mountain, "I am still so sad about what happened. There are more than fifty people I know buried in the mountain. The army would arrive and we would have to bury them quickly. It fills me with grief."[8]

Doña Petrona, Doña Magda, and Doña Martina

Children, especially babies and very young children, were extremely vulnerable to starvation. Babies died because their mothers' bodies would stop producing milk from malnourishment. In desperation, mothers would try to sustain their babies with water that they broke out of the roots they could find. "We were eighteen families fleeing together," says Doña Petrona. "Both my children died of hunger."[9] Death from hunger is painful, ugly, and slow. The body becomes debilitated. "My son became all puffy," says Doña Magda. "Many people became all puffy and swollen. Their feet and legs swell and swell until they can't walk. My son, I had to carry him. He died all swollen in the mountain. He was fourteen years old."[10]

Though babies, children, and the elderly may be at greatest risk of starvation, adult men and women did not escape hunger and its ravages. Doña Martina lowers her voice, her face flushes, "A man asked me for a tortilla. He said, 'I will trade you my millstone for one or two tortillas. I am hungry. I think I am dying. I can't get up. Please get me something to eat.'" But Doña Martina had nothing. She had not eaten any food for twenty days. There was no food. "But, I thought to myself, 'Tomorrow I will find him something, if only a root for the poor man.' It was already nighttime, so I told him, 'Just rest now and tomorrow I will find you something.'" The next morning, Doña Martina awoke with the rising sun. Next to her, the man was lying on the ground embracing his last possession in the world, his millstone. As she remembers the morning, her face flushes again, "He was dead. It's true, he was dying of hunger."[11]

THE STRUCTURE OF LIFE

Don Salvador

Most surviving residents of Acul lived in the mountains under guerrilla control and army attack for two years. When they first arrived in the mountains, their greatest fear was of the army who, after burning the villages and crops, continued to attack them. "First when we saw the EGP (Ejército Guerrillero de los Pobres—Guatemalan Army of the Poor) with their weapons, we had little fear because the EGP told us, 'It is not you that we are killing. We are killing the army. You don't need to be afraid of us. We are poor like you and we have no right to kill you,'" explains Don Salvador.

Three or four months after the massacre, the army began a major offensive against the civilian populations in flight in the mountains. While the army carried out ground and aerial attacks against the unarmed civilians, in the valleys below the civil patrollers searched out and destroyed newly planted crops, stole whatever livestock they found, and burned any stored food they unearthed from the buzones. Any remnants of previously inhabited villages that remained after the massacres and burning of homes were again attacked with fire until there was nothing left.

Fire was a tool of the army's offensive in the mountains, as well. Soldiers would encircle large areas of the mountain where they believed the civilians were hiding. They would set fire to the trees and grass, filling the air with smoke. People fleeing the fires often suffocated while hiding in holes in the earth or drowned trying to cross rivers to escape.[12] Others were simply shot. "The army had to encircle the population and scorch the earth because the only defense of the people is the mountain," explains Don Salvador. The army now sought to take the mountain away from the survivors because General Ríos Montt sought to destroy the fish (the guerrilla) by destroying the water (the Maya).[13] "Many people died in the mountain. Many died from this army offensive," says Don Salvador. Along with the fires and ground attacks, "They bombed the entire mountain. Many people died from these bombs. Many people died from hunger."[14]

*   *   *

Food was scarce for the guerrilla, as well. It seems certain that while the EGP had organized communities to store food and clothing, they had anticipated neither the level of army destruction nor the number of civilians who would be forced to flee to the mountains for survival. Indeed, a CIA document from February 1982 notes that there are "possibly thousands of refugees in the hills with no homes to return to. The EGP apparently cannot protect and feed such large numbers. . . ."[15] Certainly, the guerrilla did not anticipate years in the mountain without support from local communities, communities that were effectively erased from the map by the army's scorched earth campaign. As the war raged on, EGP recommendations to the civilian population became orders.

Don José, Doña Angela, and Doña Jacinta

In the midst of the army attacks, "The EGP arrived and asked us for food because they had nowhere to go for food. Even they didn't have food in the mountain," says Don José incredulously. "The work of the EGP is only to fight with the army, but they didn't have food. The populations had to collaborate and were giving them food, but we had to look for it because we didn't have any food either. Almost everyone gave them food because if we don't, they get angry with us. We are respecting them and giving them food. If we don't, suddenly, they might kill us. That is why we are respecting them."[16]

Many survivors of the mountain came very close to being killed by foot soldiers. Doña Angela remembers, "The army was very close to us, not more than two meters away. We were trembling with fear. They killed ten people. Women with children, and men. Later, a little girl who had escaped the soldiers found us. She had been raped. When she arrived, she said, 'My mother is dead. I am so sad and sore.' We left the dead where they had been killed because we had to flee."[17]

If there had ever been a logic to the daily balancing acts of survival between hunger, the army, and the guerrilla, this logic soon evaporated. "It felt like we were animals because of what the army was doing to us," says Doña Jacinta. "My husband and my brother died. The army killed my husband. The EGP came and grabbed my brother. They took him away. They are the same, the EGP and the army."[18]

Sometimes under guerrilla order, usually out of desperation to survive, the civilian populations begin to mimic guerrilla strategies of keeping watch for the arrival of the army. "In the end, we organized ourselves. Even I was organized," exclaims Don José. They placed lookouts at opposite points outside the community's hiding place. "When we heard the noise of the army, we used a signal to warn everyone so that there was enough time for the 300 people to move. I didn't have a weapon. Only the EGP has weapons. We didn't even have one gun."[19]

*   *   *

The army massacred unarmed Maya in their villages, then burned down every structure and destroyed all crops, leaving the survivors homeless and with no food source. The systematic implementation of massacres of

Maya in 626 villages throughout Guatemala was undoubtedly a campaign of genocide. But it was only the first; the second began with the sustained army hunt for survivors in flight.

THE ARRIVAL OF NEW LIFE

Doña Elena

Life in flight was particularly severe for pregnant women and widows with small children. Doña Elena was just over one month pregnant when her husband was killed in the Acul massacre. Her son was born in the mountain. "I had no food. I had nothing," she says. She spent eight months of her pregnancy hungry and in flight in the mountain. Often, she had to run in a different direction from the group because her pregnancy slowed her down. Later, she would look for the group. Each time the civilians fled, they found themselves farther away from the mountains they knew. "We had been running and running until we reached a very faraway mountain," says Doña Elena. "At eight that night, my son was born. At five in the morning, I had to get up and start running again because the army was upon us. I was bleeding a lot and very weak. I fell into a river with my newborn baby on my back. I thought I was going to die when we fell in the river because I had pain in my heart, pain in my head. I was so pale. I was bleeding so much. But, I didn't die. We were saved."

The river's current tossed Doña Elena, with her baby still on her back, to the shore. It was a cold and damp day. Her clothes were soaked with river water and stained with blood. She had no change of clothes, no food. She had given birth less than twelve hours earlier and she was hemorrhaging. "There was so much blood," she says, "I had to find another river to wash my corte. A woman helped me because I was so weak. My corte wasn't even dry. I had to put the same wet corte back on after it was washed. Only God is watching out for me. Almost nothing happened. My son lived, too. I don't understand it."

Giving birth in the mountain was only the beginning of the difficulties confronting women. The guerrillas told the women, "You have to cover the baby's mouth with a cloth." Many babies and younger children were killed this way. "They told me, 'You have to cover its mouth,'" says Doña Elena. "I responded, 'I would rather die with my son. I am not a dog. I am not going to throw my son down here. We are not dogs!'"

Initially, the guerrilla told the women to cover the mouths of the babies because they made too much noise, noise that could alert the army as to their whereabouts. Later, they told the women to toss their babies and leave them behind or to suffocate them by covering their mouths with a piece of cloth because of the noise and because few babies survived the hardships of life in the mountain. "Many children died in the mountain from having their mouths covered," says Doña Elena. "The guerrilla told us, 'Cover their mouths so they die because their crying is alerting the army.' I didn't do it. My son is alive because I didn't cover his mouth. How am I going to kill my son? He is my only keepsake of my deceased husband. Maybe twenty-five or thirty children died this way. If someone had a dog, they killed it as well."

When women like Doña Elena refused to kill their children, their refusal was a decision to brave life in the mountain alone with their child or children. When Doña Elena left her community, she said, "Maybe I will die. Maybe my son will die. But we will die together. The army killed my husband. I can't kill our son. If I do, I am no better than the army. We are not dogs."[20] When she left, she was still hemorrhaging. An older woman accompanied her to help. Together with her baby, they spent forty days hiding in a cave as she lay hemorrhaging. The older woman would spend the day searching for edible plants and roots, returning with whatever she found at the end of the day. As Doña Elena's health improved and the bleeding subsided, they continued to stay in the cave until the army, once again, forced them to flee.

THE BREAKDOWN AND RECONSTRUCTION OF FAMILY INSTITUTIONS

Doña Manuela, Doña Fermina, and Doña Esperanza

As the war raged on, EGP orders to kill babies were expanded to include young children, anyone who was unable to contribute to the survival of the community. Like Doña Elena, Doña Manuela also chose a life of flight alone in the mountains over killing her own children. At the time, she had four children. The eldest was six years old, the next was four, another was two, and the baby not quite a year. "They told me, 'you have to cover their mouths. They make too much noise and give nothing to the community.' So, I left. I said, 'If they die, they die with me struggling.'"

While carrying the baby on her back, the two year-old on her hip, and holding the hand of the four year-old, with the six year-old trailing behind, Doña Manuela walked out into the mountain alone. With her small children, she spent every day searching for edible plants, fleeing the army, and looking for a safe place to sleep. One day, instead of food, she found a little girl all alone in the mountain. "She was an orphan. She couldn't have been more than five," remembers Doña Manuela. "She had no one. I could not just leave her there all alone. If something were to happen to me, I hoped someone would take my children." At the risk of less food for her own hungry children, Doña Manuela added the girl to her entourage. "All of my children survived. So did she. I love Esperanza as my own daughter. Today, she is married," she muses with the satisfaction of a proud mother.[21]

Some communities in the mountains did not enforce guerrilla orders to kill children. Still, as survival became more tenuous, solidarity weakened. "I suffered by keeping them," recalls Doña Fermina. "I had one child on my back and one in each hand. Some people are kind and they would come by and help me move my children. But, there are other people who aren't kind and they don't help at all. I always moved little by little in the mountain, very slowly. I had to be sure I wasn't near anyone else because the army might hear my children."[22] Doña Fermina was less fortunate than Doña Manuela and Doña Elena. One child died of hunger in the mountain. The others became ill. One died shortly after leaving the mountain.

Though now twenty years old and married, Esperanza is not much larger than a girl of twelve. She begins by telling me that the army killed her father and that her mother died of hunger in the mountain. "I was five years old. There was no one to defend me," she explains. "Instead of killing me, they just left me alone there in the mountain. I wandered the mountain all by myself for about six months. I passed each day looking for roots to eat as I had with my mother before she died. Doña Manuela found me there. Her heart is very large. That is why I am alive today."[23] She smiles at me and nods in agreement with herself.

HUNGER'S VICTORY

While the initial military strategy of the army and guerrillas was one of territorial dominion, the massacres expanded the struggle for dominion to include control of the surviving populations. To keep civilians with them in the mountains, the EGP used methods ranging from deception to coercion. The EGP began to hold meetings with the communities in the mountains. They would tell the civilians, "It is better if you don't go to Nebaj because the army is waiting there to kill you. It is a trick. None of you should go to Nebaj." Soon, the guerrilla began to lie to the populations who had lived for nearly two years in isolation from the municipality, "Nebaj no longer exists. It is burned to the ground just like the villages. Everything is burned. There is nowhere to go. You have to stay here."[24]

Acul survivors had reason to believe the EGP because it seemed that everywhere they went in their daily search for food and water they came upon Ixiles from other aldeas who were fleeing army attacks and massacres. These Ixiles told stories mirroring the Acul experience: "The army came; they killed everyone they found; they killed and stole domestic animals; they burned down all the houses; they destroyed all the milpa." For the sick and starving survivors of massacres living under constant army bombardment in the Ixil mountains, it appeared that there was nowhere for them to go.

Doña Antonia, Doña Cristina, and Doña Elena

When hunger drove the civilians to attempt the descent to Nebaj despite the EGP warnings, they were accused of being army spies. "The EGP did not want us to go to Nebaj," explains Doña Antonia. "There were people who tried to go to Nebaj and the EGP hung them along the path to Nebaj."[25] Word of the warnings, dangers, threats, and deaths traveled quickly from community to community in the mountains. Families began to leave secretly at night. Doña Cristina fled the mountains as she had fled Acul, "We went to Nebaj without advising anyone because if we say we are going to Nebaj, they want to kill us because they don't want anyone to go to Nebaj."

Doña Elena decided to try to leave the mountain. The guerrillas had told her that if she went to Nebaj, the army would kill her. "But, I had no food and I was sick," she explains. "In the end, I decided to enter Nebaj without advising the guerrilla because if we tell them, then they kill us."[26]

Whether one decided to stay or leave, there was no safe haven. The only certainty was the knowledge that neither the guerrilla nor the army could be trusted. "Sometimes, there is just no difference between the two," explains Doña Cristina. "If we go over to one side, we are afraid, but we are afraid of the other side, too. The only difference is that the EGP doesn't rape women because it is prohibited."[27]

*   *   *

For both the army and the guerrilla, control of civilian populations living in flight in the mountains became the key to military victory. The army's new campaign was called *"Fusiles y Frijoles"* (rifles and beans) and offered "amnesty" to survivors in exchange for community acceptance of and participation in army-controlled civil patrols. This amnesty was offered in Ixil through loudspeakers from a helicopter crisscrossing the mountains where families had struggled to survive for two years.[28]

Doña Lucia

Still, despite their fear of EGP reprisal and doubts about the safety of surrendering to the army, civilians in the mountains were driven by hunger, disease, and desperation to seek survival in army-controlled Nebaj. In a world of life in flight with few choices, surrender to the army offered a new opportunity—especially for women struggling to keep their children alive. Doña Lucia recalls, "We were always thinking, thinking, 'where can we go?'"[29]

With the passage of time, there were also guerrilla combatants who tired of the mountains. "In the end, we decided to go to Nebaj," says Doña Lucia. "The URNG (Unión Revolucionario Nacional de Guatemala—Guatemalan Revolutionary National Union) said, 'It is better if you go to Nebaj and we are going to see what happens to you because we are tired. We don't have any food. We don't have anything to shoot or do anything.'" So Doña Lucia went to Nebaj. A few weeks later, the combatants who had advised her to leave the mountain arrived in Nebaj with their weapons. "There were about ten URNG who entered Nebaj. Nothing happened to them because they went directly to the army [base]. The army didn't kill those URNG," says Doña Lucia somewhat bemused. These seemingly confused descriptions of events can best be understood within the logic of the army's drive to gain control of the civilian populations and draw guerrilla combatants out of the mountains by offering amnesty. It also indicates the army's nuanced understanding of the identity of the combatants versus civilians. Doña Lucia's memory of the guerrilla saying they had nothing to shoot most likely reflects the breakdown of communication and supplies within the guerrilla. A former high-ranking EGP leader in the Ixil Area told me that by the beginning of 1982, orders originating from the guerrilla directorate were reaching combatants four months after they were issued and that these orders were often time-sensitive military maneuvers.[30] Additionally, just as the chain of communication between the comandantes and the combatants had been broken by the army destruction of the villages and constant flight of massacre survivors, so too had the passage of supplies.

* * *

A common theme in the testimonies about departure from the mountain and surrender to the army in Nebaj is that it was a surrender of choice and, for many, a surrender of hope: a choice made with few options, a personal decision. On the one hand, the very act of making a decision, however limited, is experienced as reinvoking some of the dignity and solidarity lost in massacres, in flight, and in the search for food. On the other, the surrender is experienced as relinquishing the hope that the army would lose the war. Again and again, hunger drove survivors out of the mountains. They went to Nebaj not because they were captured but because a certain death from hunger awaited them in the mountains.

Doña Juana, Don Salvador, Doña Martina, and Doña Cristina

Doña Juana entered Nebaj alone with her family. "I went to Nebaj because I was suffering from hunger in the mountains," she says. "I had nothing to eat. I had no clothes. I had nothing. So, I thought, 'Maybe it is better if the army kills me. I am going to Nebaj to see what will happen.' I went with my family. We were not captured by a patrol. We went to Nebaj of our own will."[31]

"I wanted to stay in the mountains and defend my family," says Don Salvador. "Look what the army did to us. I didn't want to surrender, but my family was starving. We didn't flee the guerrilla and we didn't surrender to the army. Hunger defeated us."[32]

Doña Martina was very ill when she decided to go to Nebaj. "I was sick. I was empty because it is not food that we are eating. There was nothing," she says. "I decided to go to Nebaj. The EGP said, 'Fine, if you want to go to Nebaj, then you will see if they kill you. I don't know.' But the problem is that we have no food. Even if we had had money, there was nothing to buy. I was in the mountains for two years."[33]

Doña Cristina says, "A plane flew over us and there was a person talking from the plane. He said, 'Please. You populations are going to go to Nebaj because now you are free. Now there is liberty. Now you can go to Nebaj.' In Ixil, they told us that now we are free. But, we weren't really free."[34]

SURRENDERING TO THE ARMY

Doña Luisa and Doña Catarina

By late 1983, the majority of surviving Acul residents had fled the starvation, guerrilla control, and the terror of constant army attacks and bombardments in the mountains in exchange for food under army control first in Nebaj, then later in Acul. Most Acul Ixiles spent several weeks or months in Nebaj after surrendering to the army. Both men and women were first taken to the Nebaj army base for interrogation. Most Acul women were interrogated briefly, then freed. Some women and most men were held at the base for several days to several months. During this time, they were tortured and interrogated. Several boys (age ten to twelve) were put in army uniforms, taken back into the mountains by the army, and forced, under torture and threat of death, to lead the army to civilian camps in the mountains.

After Doña Luisa made her way down through the mountains with close to one hundred civilians, arriving in Nebaj in the darkness of early morning, they turned themselves in to the army base. "It was a little bit calm," she says. "There was a little bit of freedom. We walked into Nebaj." Nonetheless, the one hundred massacre survivors who arrived weak and hungry were interrogated before receiving any assistance— assistance that had been promised from the amplified army helicopter voice to those below. "'Who brought you here?' the commander asked. 'We came of our own free will,'" we answered.

"We were hungry, thirsty, and weak," Doña Luisa explains. "Mostly, we were terrified. We didn't know what would happen next. If we would live or die. 'Who brought you here? Who brought you here?' They shouted at us over and over."[35]

Don Paulino was among the one hundred who had walked through the mountain all night to reach Nebaj. After being questioned, they were lined up with no explanation. "We were all sick, seriously ill. Everyone was swollen with sickness. We were all so weak, tired and hungry," he says, "we were frightened. Maybe they will kill us. We didn't know what would happen next. They gave us injections because we were sick, but we didn't know that was what they were going to do. That is why we were so scared. Then, they gave us some beans and tortillas. We could hardly eat because it had been so long since we had real food."[36]

Doña Catarina and her husband fled the mountain together. They arrived to the base alone. As they presented themselves at the gate, soldiers grabbed her husband and dragged him away. "I sat inside the base for two days," she remembers. "I knew my husband was in one of the buildings, but the soldiers became angry whenever I asked about him."

ARMY INTERROGATIONS

Doña Catarina and Doña Elena

For two days, Doña Catarina's husband, Juan, was beaten and interrogated by an army officer assisted by soldiers. In between beatings, he was placed alone in a small room. As the soldiers continued to beat him for nearly two days, Don Juan continued to refuse to answer their questions. He feared they would kill him after they had the information they needed. He also feared the guerrilla would kill him if they discovered he had talked.

Half way through the second day, a former guerrilla commander entered the small room. "He knew my husband because he was a commander and he knew my husband sometimes collaborated with the EGP," Doña Catarina explains. "This guerrilla commander helped my husband. He told him, 'You have to tell the truth because we know you are collaborating with the EGP.' In the end, he told the army everything because the guerrilla commander helped him. But when he was released, he was very badly beaten, bruised and bloody."[37]

Being female in no way guaranteed exclusion from brutality within the base. Before Doña Elena turned herself in to the army, as she came down the mountain, she had recovered a huipil and corte from a hidden buzón. Upon arrival to the base, the good condition of her clothing singled her out. "You are pure guerrilla wandering around in that new huipil. There is no doubt your husband is guerrilla and came to Nebaj to buy that for you," shouted the soldiers. "Tell me the truth or I will kill you."

"An officer put his gun right here on my neck," says Doña Elena, indicating the jugular vein just below her jaw. To the army who had killed her husband in the Acul massacre and pursued her throughout her pregnancy, Doña Elena responded, "My husband is already dead. If you do not believe me, then kill me." The officer withdrew the gun from her neck and motioned toward her brother with a nod. The soldiers dragged away her brother, kicking him behind the knee and slamming the butts of their machine guns in his back. "They beat him for three days." Doña Elena looks at the ground shaking her head, "they let him go, but he died from *susto*[38] and the blows of the soldiers."[39]

THE USE OF CHILDREN

Don Eulalio

Before the Acul massacre, Don Eulalio was a ten-year-old Ixil boy with a mother and father. Afterward, he fled Acul with his widowed mother. After two years of life in flight, his mother was very ill. At only twelve years of age, he decided to slip out of the mountain and down to the base to find out if freedom really existed and if the army would really help his mother. "When I arrived to the army base, they gave me food and clothing. An army uniform and boots," he recalls. After he had eaten and put on his new clothes, an officer told him that he had to lead a platoon of soldiers to his community in the mountains. "I didn't want to do it and they beat me. They beat me terribly," he says with a grimace. "There was blood pouring out of my nose and mouth. In the end, I agreed to take them. I was still bleeding when we left the base."

They climbed up through mountain paths for most of the day. When they finally reached one of the CPR (Comunidades de Poblaciones en Resistencia—Communities of Populations in Resistance) encampments, no one was there. Everyone had already fled to another site. "They beat me again. They called me a liar, a guerrilla," he recalls shaking his head in disbelief. "I was bleeding even more. I took them to another camp and no one was there either. So they beat me again, even harder and longer. This happened several more times: another camp, no one is there, they beat me. Harder and harder."

After several days of unsuccessfully searching for Eulalio's community's camp, the platoon returned to the army base, dragging Eulalio back with them. "They gave me no food and no water. They stripped me of my uniform. They took away my boots. They threw me naked outside the base. I begged them for the boots or a bit of clothing because I had nothing, nothing. They just kicked me again and again."[40]

CONFESSING TO THE ARMY

Doña Lucia

Despite their hunger, privation, and fear, many families chose to continue the struggle to survive in the mountains. Many stayed for the same reasons others gave themselves up. Still, not everyone arrived in Nebaj of their own free will. Lucia and her family were captured by soldiers in the mountain and taken to Nebaj by helicopter. "They beat and beat my husband," she remembers. Her husband was wearing a new hat and new boots. As they beat him with the butts of their machine guns, they shouted, "Where did you get these? You have to tell the truth!" When her husband did not respond to the interrogation, he was taken away from Lucia and the rest of the family. "They put him in a room within the army base and they wouldn't let me see him. They just kept beating him. I was so sad, so worried," says Doña Lucia.

They had been held in the base for nearly fifteen days when a cousin of Lucia's who was a civil patrol chief spoke with the army. Doña Lucia's husband had not responded to any of the army's questions because "the EGP had told us that we could not tell the army anything at all or they [the EGP] would kill us," explains Doña Lucia. "The truth is that my husband really did not know anything. He had none of the information the army wanted. He didn't even understand their questions because he doesn't speak Spanish."

After the appearance of the cousin advocating on their behalf, a former EGP commander then working with the army spoke to Doña Lucia's husband and later "helped my husband tell his story to the army," says Doña Lucia. "The army wanted information. They said, 'you have to show us the weapons. Where are they? Show us where they are stored!' But the truth is my husband did not know anything about this."[41]

THE SEARCH FOR A LOST HUSBAND

Doña Angela

During two years of life in flight, many families had become separated in their struggle to survive in the mountains. It was not unusual for people to leave the mountains to surrender to the army in their search for family members. Doña Angela went to Nebaj in search of her husband. "I went to the base three times asking for my husband," she explains. "The soldiers told me that the army does not capture people. They told me that I was an idiot to wander about asking for my husband."

The third time she went to the base, the soldiers said, "If you do not stop bothering us, we will kill you." Her experience with the army gave her every reason to believe their threats. "I was scared," she says wringing her hands, "and I did not know what to do." So, she went to the mayor and waited in the long line to speak with him, to ask for his help. "I asked him to speak with the army commander," she recalls. "I asked him to help me find my husband. The mayor told me, 'Even though we are mayors, they kill us, too. There are so many dead, not just in the aldeas, but also in Nebaj. I will tell you what to do. Take care of your children and do not go back to the base. There is nothing I can do.'" Doña Angela's eyes well with tears. She bows her head down as she explains, "So, I stopped going to the base and I never found my husband."[42]

Once the survivors were interrogated and released, they found themselves homeless in Nebaj. Some were sent to reeducation camps, some were sent to Las Violetas or other model villages under army control in Nebaj. Many survived exchanging work for meager food rations from the army and occasional shelter from friends, extended family, or strangers.

THE COLONEL ON THE HORSE

Don Sebastián

Beyond the disorientation and suffering of displacement, it was not unusual for massacre survivors to find their own belongings—things they had owned prior to the massacre—in the possession of army personnel. After all, when the soldiers and civil patrollers massacred villagers and burned down village hamlets, they also looted. Acul was no exception. Army soldiers and civil patrollers had both killed and stolen the livestock of massacre survivors. (Indeed, just as in San Andrés Sajcabajá and Rabinal, among the most successful market butchers in Nebaj today are those who stole village livestock while patrolling, massacring, and burning villages for the army.)

After a few days in Nebaj, Don Sebastián was walking the streets in search of work when he recognized the legs of his horse. He looked up to see Colonel Hilo perched upon his only surviving possession of the Acul massacre. Without thinking, Don Sebastián confronted the colonel, saying "That is my horse." The colonel looked down at him and said, "But, no. The horse is mine."

As the colonel began to ride away, again without thinking, Don Sebastián said, "I am not trying to steal the horse. The horse is simply mine. Please, give me back my horse." To this, the colonel stopped and turned around. With a smile, he looked down at Don Sebastián and said, "You lost this horse because your heart was with the guerrilla and that is why it is no longer your horse. Now, you will no longer think of the guerrilla. You will no longer think of the horse. Now you will think of nothing. Now, you have nothing." With that, the colonel rode away.

Recalling this incident, Don Sebastián again begins to cry. He says, "They never gave me my horse. Who knows where they sold it? It gave me great sorrow to watch the colonel ride away on my horse. He was a good horse. A beautiful horse. I loved that horse. I felt great sorrow because I lost him."[43]

THE CONSTRUCTION OF A MODEL VILLAGE

After passing through Nebaj for several weeks to several months, the Ixil men, women, and children who survived the Acul massacre and life in flight in the mountains now found themselves forced to build a road to Acul and to rebuild their village under army occupation. This forced labor was done under threat of army violence with frequent acts of physical abuse and punishment. Acul massacre survivors rebuilt their community in exchange for meager food rations from the army. They received no monetary remuneration. While this forced labor was compulsory, the army provided no tools to those charged with building a road and rebuilding a community. Survivors "rented" the necessary tools from other near-starving Nebaj Ixiles in exchange for part of their meager food rations. Many survivors continued to die from illnesses associated with malnutrition and starvation.

Doña Lucia

Doña Lucia's experience is representative of many. "We had to build a road. They gave us a little bit of corn and a small amount of beans," she says, raising her nearly closed hand to indicate a handful. "But, I did not have a machete or ax. My husband had to rent the tools, as well. I gave a little of my little bit of corn and a little of my little bit of beans to rent a machete and an ax so that I could do the work that the army ordered me to do so that the army would give me my little bit of corn and little bit of beans for doing the work."[44]

Men were organized into army-controlled civil patrols, and soldiers occupied their community for nearly two years. During this army occupation, all surviving widows of those killed in the 1981 massacre were repeatedly raped by soldiers, and at night soldiers would go to the houses of families with adolescent daughters and take the young girls back to the base. These girls were gang raped on the base and usually dumped off at the river the following morning. Many young men died from torture meted out to them by Acul civil patrollers under army order. Many young men were subjected to arbitrary punishment by army soldiers. Young men especially were repeatedly thrown into the river that passes through Acul or placed in pits of water for up to seventy-two hours. It was not uncommon for these young men to later die from pneumonia.

Doña Elena

"It wasn't long after we returned to Acul that the army began to harass us," recounts Doña Elena. The women of Acul were obligated to make tortillas and deliver them to the Acul army garrison each day before mealtime. Each woman in the village was given her "shift" for providing tortillas with no remuneration. "Each woman had her turn to give them tortillas," she explains. "It was nearly impossible to leave the tortillas there without a soldier grabbing you. They did this to the widows. They did this to all of us." She glances around the cemetery and exhumation site. With a sweeping gesture of her arm, she says, "All these mothers and widows waiting for the remains of their sons and husbands, the soldiers abused them. Everyone became pregnant. Half had children. The other half used a remedy."[45]

After recounting this violence meted out against the widows of Acul, Doña Elena returns to the story of her brother. Earlier, Doña Elena had given testimony about the army interrogating and threatening her at the Nebaj base. Following her interrogation, the army then interrogated and beat her brother for three days. Army persecution did not end with his release. Doña Elena remembers, "After the beatings on the base, the soldiers had to beat him again when we returned to Acul. They put him in a hole for twenty-four hours. They threw ten buckets of water on top of him in that hole. They mixed soap, oil, and salt and forced my brother to drink it. After that, he was vomiting and vomiting in that hole. They threw him in that hole twice. They threw him in the river twice. They made him drink that mixture of soap, oil, and salt two times."

Doña Elena, widowed by the massacre, pregnant in flight, alone with her baby in the mountains—a proud woman who told the colonel to kill her when he put his gun to her throat, crosses her arms, looks off into the distance, and rocks back and forth. She bites her lower lip. She turns to look me straight in the eyes. She says, "My brother was very sad after all these tortures. He was so sad, so very sad. He was thirty-three years old. He became ill from susto and the beatings. He died."

*   *   *

These lived experiences as recounted by Acul massacre survivors are corroborated by files in the Nebaj archives. Acts of violence against civilians in the municipality of Nebaj and its surrounding villages remained high despite the "amnesty." Between 1983 to 1986, for the town of Nebaj alone, the Death Registers record eighty-eight violent deaths. Though one might argue that this is a significant decrease from the 1978–81 yearly average of 156 violent deaths, at an average of twenty-nine deaths per year between 1983–86, it is still nearly six times as many as the five violent deaths for the entire municipality of Nebaj and all its surrounding villages recorded in 1977, before the wave of terror began.[46] Also, it is important to note that these eighty-eight violent deaths do not include the numerous "natural" deaths due to illnesses and other complications related to malnutrition and starvation. If any lesson can be learned from La Violencia, it is that a decrease in the number of human rights violations is not enough.

THE ARMY'S REDISTRIBUTION OF ACUL LANDS

When Acul massacre survivors returned to their village with the army, they found their entire community destroyed. There were no houses, no crops, no animals. The church on the plaza was the only building left standing. The church became the residence of the commander of the army garrison in Acul. As Acul Ixiles rebuilt their village under army occupation and order, their houses were not rebuilt where they had been before, nor were they the same size. Under army order, houses were built on a grid pattern using whatever and whoever's land stood in the path of the army's design. Few Acul residents got all their land back and many community divisions grew out of the army distribution of houses and land. In 1998, Acul residents described their land situation as *"revuelto"* (scrambled). The forced relocation into so-called "model villages," the dismantling of traditional Maya community structures through the total militarization of the community, the deliberate mental and physical harm systematically inflicted on Maya living under army control in villages, and the continued hunt for survivors in the mountains was the third campaign of genocide.

Doña Angela

"When I returned to Acul," explains Doña Angela, "there were people building on my land. What was I to do with these people? What could I do? They already had a house on my land. The land isn't theirs, the land is mine." Doña Angela asked them to pay her for the land. "They paid me forty quetzales for my sorrow. There are a lot of people who occupy land that isn't theirs. The army decided how, who, and where. We are all mixed up. There are K'iche's. There are Ixiles. But we all suffered the violence."[47] This mixing of Ixiles and K'iche's was a deliberate move by the army to further break community solidarity.

For Acul Ixiles, on average, the houses inhabited by Acul residents today are half the size of the houses in which they lived prior to the violence, and today's homes are built of inferior materials: cement blocks and *lamina*.[48] Before the violence, like Don Sebastián's home, Acul houses were built with cedar, and the roofs were covered with tiles.

CIVIL PATROLS AND THE REINFORCEMENT OF COMMUNITY MILITARIZATION

Even after the soldiers departed Acul in late 1984, the community remained highly militarized through the civil patrols, which continued to bear arms and do the bidding of the army until the signing of the Peace Accords in December of 1996—more than fifteen years after the massacre. Acul was the first model village built by the army and its civil patrol was among the last in Guatemala to be disarmed and disbanded. And, despite implementation of the army's model village as part of its Poles of Development Plan, Acul residents, like other massacre survivors throughout Guatemala, have yet to recuperate the economic losses caused by the Scorched Earth campaign.

These already desperate conditions awaiting those who returned to Acul were further compounded by the violence of the army-controlled civil patrol. Acul Ixil boys, men, and elderly (ages thirteen to seventy) found themselves placed at the front and back of army platoons patrolling through the mountains. Civil patrollers were poorly armed, and, in the instances where there was an armed encounter with insurgent forces, civil patrollers would be the first to die because they were essentially being used as human shields by the army to protect its soldiers from guerrilla fire. Additionally, while food and other provisions were brought in by helicopter for army soldiers, civil patrollers were given no rations.

The first few days of patrol, they would eat the tortillas they had brought with them. But not being able to carry more than a few days worth of tortillas, once again they found themselves foraging for roots in the mountains for up to three weeks at a time. The male population of Acul found itself spending at least half of its days, and sometimes more, patrolling for the army. In addition to the deprivation, torture, violence, and coercion of compulsory participation in the army-controlled civil patrols, the men of Acul paid a high price in the loss of time that would have been better spent tending crops to feed their families and rebuilding their homes. It also further exacerbated their already poor health.

For the majority of men who patrolled from 1983 to 1996, the compulsory patrols were "thirteen years of punishment."[49] Taking into account extended patrols of up to three weeks during 1983–85 and rotations of three to four twenty-four hour shifts per week, which later decreased to one twenty-four hour shift per week, on average, Acul civil patrollers gave 686 days of free labor to the army's civil patrols between 1983 and 1996. In addition to the physical and emotional trauma of patrolling, and the complete absence of any monetary remuneration for lost time, each patroller lost more than one year and ten months (and this is by calculating with twenty-four hours a day—eight hours a day would mean five and one-half lost years) of labor that could have been used in reconstructing the community rather than extending and reproducing a culture of terror and insecurity within the community.[50]

Was this civil patrol an autonomous community force, as claimed by David Stoll?[51] Did the Ixiles of Acul and elsewhere take the civil patrol (an army-imposed structure) and turn it into some kind of autonomous force that protected the community from both the army and the guerrilla, as Stoll claims?

PATROLLING IN ACUL

Don José, Don Pedro, and Don Erick

When I asked if Acul men continued to patrol because the civil patrols had eventually become autonomous, Don José looked at me incredulously. Then he responded, "We patrolled because we feared the army. The soldiers patrolled with us the first few years."[52]

"The civil patrol chiefs are in command," explains Don Pedro. "So, we are all very frightened of them and so is everyone else because if you don't do what they want, then they beat you or throw you in the hole."[53]

Beatings from army soldiers or civil patrol leaders were common, the severity of the beating seemingly determined more by its location than the actual "violation." Don Erick explains, "They beat people when we were in the mountains patrolling. But here in Acul, if a man was sick or couldn't patrol, they really beat him hard. The soldiers beat him, they threw him in the hole. Then, they tossed ten buckets of water on top of him. He had to stay there for at least a day and sometimes two or three. They thought nothing of throwing us in the river." Don Erick draws his thin jacket tighter over his chest. The day of our interview is cold, damp, and foggy. He pauses. We both look toward the river. He clears his throat. "Here in Acul," he says, "they punished people until the peace accords were signed."[54]

"It is not fair being forced to give away our days," declares Don José. "The soldiers receive a salary. We never received any salary. I hope that someone explains to the president that they never even paid us for our work. I hope someone explains to the president that we are owed something."

"Today, we have nothing," adds Don José. "We have no animals, no house. We have nothing like before. What happened here is that what we always have is fear.[55]

THE EXHUMATION AND THE ANTI-CHRIST

In December 1997, when the FAFG (Fundación de Antropología Forense de Guatemala—Guatemalan Forensic Anthropology Foundation) embarked on the exhumation of the clandestine cemetery containing remains of the 1981 massacre victims, only immediate relatives of the victims came to the first meetings. The mothers, fathers, widows, and children of the victims explained that the vice-mayor of the village and various evangelical pastors were advising the Acules to neither attend nor support the exhumation. Doña Angela agreed that there were more Acules who wanted to come to the exhumation but did not. "There are people who don't come," she said. "It is because others are telling them that after you leave, there will be more dead. The mayor of Acul has counseled our poor people not to come here."[56]

Doña Angela

The widows echoed Doña Angela's explanation, "The mayor of Acul is telling people not to come." When pressed for an explanation of why massacre survivors who wanted proper burials for their sons and husbands would accede to the village mayor's counsel, Doña Fermina looked away with embarrassment. "They say that you are all going to sell the bones and make yourselves rich," she said. "The pastors say you will sell the bones because you are the anti-Christ and they tell the people not to give their testimonies."[57]

The FAFG had the good fortune to receive support from the municipal mayor of Nebaj, a well-respected Ixil leader. He came to Acul to meet with the community and talk about the exhumation. He said, "There are people who say the forenses are the anti-Christ and they will enrich themselves selling our bones. If this was true, we Ixiles would all be rich because of all the skeletons throughout the Ixil Area." This commentary made people attending the meeting laugh in agreement with the mayor. He continued, "The Forenses work for the good of the people, they work for truth." After the Nebaj mayor's visit, many more Acules, as well as residents from other nearby aldeas, came to give their testimony of the violence and its aftermath, in which they continue to live.

Don Pedro

Even though Don Pedro had drawn a clear line between the violence that preceded the signing of the peace accords and the disbanding of the civil patrol, he insisted that local power structures continued to be shaped, both openly and covertly, by wartime power structures. I asked Don Pedro how the war had affected relationships within the community. "Those who were the civil patrol chiefs continue to order us around and are always on the side of the army," explained Don Pedro. "The URNG does that, too. When there is a responsable who has an official post, they think they are important. They both think they are big and important. They order us around, they reject and abuse us."

For Don Pedro, as for many Maya throughout Guatemala, understanding of the world continued to be divided between those who gave and those who followed orders. He said, "There are some people who don't obey the orders and they are mistreated for lacking respect." Still, Don Pedro was quick to point to ambient fear and violence that continues to inhibit community cohesion. "There are some men who are always angry. Others are stealing or fighting over women," he explained. "Even though these problems have always existed, the violence has made it worse. That is why so many people in Acul are angry or sad."[58]

Sadness certainly resonated throughout the community. When Acul survivors came to give their testimonies, they were unsure of the structure and purpose of our meetings. Though they had been told at community meetings that we would be meeting with them to get information about their dead and missing loved ones, most had little idea of how this would happen. They were drawn to these vague meetings because they wanted to talk about their loved ones and about their loss. While we sought certain types of antemorten information specific to the massacre and the physical appearance of those killed, the testimony was only very loosely directed. Each person defined the space in which they wished to speak. Word of this space traveled throughout Acul and to nearby communities. People began to line up with the express purpose of "declaring my sorrow." Several returned to speak more. As in Panzós, the exhumation opened a public space that expanded as those giving testimony gained individual and collective strength in the experience of giving testimony, reaffirming the importance and validity of their experiences. Women would bring other women by the hand and send their sons and brothers. These men, in turn, would send their friends and relatives. In methodological terms, the exhumation was the catalyst for a self-producing snowball sample.

The Acules shared their pain and entrusted me with their stories. In our conversations, we shared a common goal: to seek understanding of what had happened and how it had affected individuals, families, and communities. "I am always with sorrow, always with sadness," offered Don Sebastián in a quiet moment. "Since the problem with the violence, I am always sad just like the others. It is shameful what happened to us. That is why I am not well. I am always sick because I always remember my children and how they all died. I will never forget that. Never."[59]

In the midst of all this pain and suffering, mixed in with the emotional need to be heard and the stark physical needs presented by extreme poverty, there is anger and there is hope. One day during the exhumation as I sat with the widows, sharing their coffee by a fire just above the grave, Doña Elena waved her arm expansively across the grave. "I hope that you will show the government and that you will show the guerrilla commanders, show both of them, that they have to recognize the unjust judgment that was passed upon us," she said. "Why did they do all of this? I hope that you show them these bones. That you take them to the commanders of the army and the commanders of the guerrilla just to see how they will respond to this unjust judgment they passed upon us."[60]

Five

THE PHENOMENOLOGY OF TERROR

We are always afraid.

—*Don Sebastián*

INTRODUCTION

In 1978, the same year as the Panzós massacre, the Guatemalan army began a selective campaign of political disappearance and assassination in Guatemala City and other urban centers.[1] It also accelerated construction of military bases throughout rural Guatemala. Prior to 1979, the army had divided the country into nine military zones, each centered around a large army base. By 1982, the army had designated each of the twenty-two departments as a military zone, accompanied by multiple army bases in municipalities and army garrisons in villages throughout the country.[2] Forced recruitment into the Guatemalan army ensured the requisite number of troops for this extension of the military infrastructure.[3] Some of these large army bases, such as those in Rabinal and Nebaj, are structures that have endured to the date of this writing. Other more temporary locations, such as the churches in San Andrés Sajcabajá, Acul, Sacapulas, Joyabaj, Zacualpa, San Pedro Jocopilas, Nebaj, Chajul, Cotzal, Uspantán, Chiché, Canillá, and the Marist monastery of Chichicastenango, which were used by the army as jails, torture and interrogation centers, and clandestine cemeteries, no longer house the army.[4] The army grew to have a significant presence in the Ixil area with multiple bases in Nebaj, Chajul, and Cotzal. Soon the Ixil area became known by its army designation as the "Ixil Triangle"—referring to its three municipal centers, Nebaj, Chajul, and Cotzal, within a military schema composed of bases in each of the municipalities as well as many of the surrounding villages. This expanded army presence was accompanied by an acceleration of army violence, from selective assassinations to disappearances to multiple village massacres.[5]

A central thesis to this book is that the efficacy of peace processes and democratic transitions can best be understood from the ground up—that we can learn more from rural to urban analyses than we can from urban to rural when we seek to understand catastrophic levels of state terror in predominantly rural societies. That is to say, we can learn more from the situated subjectivity of rural Maya peasants than from the elites who claim to represent them. Guatemalan guerrilla organizations (like insurrectionary groups in much of the world) chose to focus their struggle in rural communities. These military strategies of rural to urban victory were usurped, effectively replicated, and more violently implemented by the Guatemalan army. Therefore, to understand state terror, we must endeavor to understand how militarization has been experienced by the majority rural Maya.

Here in chapter five, through a phenomenological presentation of the phases of terror I have identified in La Violencia and its aftermath, I explore the complex constitution and reconstitution of civil society and the lived experiences of massacre survivors as they negotiated and renegotiated individual and community practices and identities in their struggle to survive. The purpose of the phenomenology is to make the experience of surviving intelligible and increase the legibility of the state in order to document as clearly as possible the extent and complexity of the army's militarization of rural Maya life and the living memory of terror produced by this militarization.[6]

By making an in-depth study of the phases of the phenomenology of terror in El Quiché, we are offered an opportunity to understand the structure of genocide and terror from survivor experiences and memories of those experiences. The categories of the phenomenology put into words that which language often seems incapable of communicating about terror.[7] It also allows us to see quite clearly that when the Guatemalan army shifted its policy of repression from selective assassination to large-scale killings, it shifted to a prolonged series of genocidal campaigns against the Maya. These genocidal campaigns began with selective massacres in Maya villages all over the country and soon shifted to massacres of entire communities.

For massacre survivors fleeing in the mountains, surrendering to the army, and later rebuilding their villages and their lives under army control, surviving these phases of terror has meant living daily life in extremely militarized circumstances for up to fifteen years following a massacre. When the overt expressions of militarization are withdrawn, internalization of encounters with terror continues to shape and define individual relationships within families and communities, as well as community relationships with the nation-state. Survivor testimonies, viewed in the context of the discourse and practice of the various phases of state terror, help us to understand that while the torture victim's missing tooth may be interpreted as a sign of survival and the empty army base as a victory for peace, each also represents a living memory of terror that continues to shape and define daily life.

In this chapter, I provide an overview of the seven phases of violence I have identified in my research, which I refer to as the "phenomenology of terror."[8] These include: (1) premassacre community organizing and experiences with violence; (2) the massacre; (3) postmassacre life in flight in the mountains; (4) army captures and community surrenders; (5) model villages; (6) ongoing militarization of community life; and (7) living memory of terror. Within this phenomenology of terror, I identify violations of specific United Nations conventions and protocols as well as of the American Convention on Human Rights.

PREMASSACRE COMMUNITY ORGANIZING
AND EXPERIENCES WITH VIOLENCE

In 1979, arbitrary executions of local village leaders had become a systematic practice of the Guatemalan army. Among the victims were an evangelical pastor, a cathechist, and leaders and members of the Campesino Unity Committee (Comité de Unidad Campesina—CUC).[9] As early as 1980, civil patrollers and military commissioners participated in army-ordered kidnappings and arbitrary executions. These acts of state violence involving local community members were also directed at local village leaders. For example, in November 1980, PAC (Patrullas de Auto-Defensa Civil—Civil Patrol) members and army troops executed

Francisco Reynoso López, a member of the local cooperative of Macalajau in the municipality of Uspantán. Before leaving the area, they set fire to the victim's home.[10]

The army's selective execution of local leaders was not limited to civil society leaders but included elected members of local governments. One such example is when the army burned down the Nebaj village of Ixtupil in 1980. Felipe Raymundo, auxiliary mayor of Ixtupil, burned to death when the army torched the offices of the auxiliary mayor.[11] This type of public execution and arson became prevalent in 1980, setting the stage for the army's later Scorched Earth campaign (1981–1990).[12] Indeed, this acceleration and intensification of selective violence in 1980 was in fact accompanied by the initiation of the army's campaign of massacres, which became its first campaign of genocide.

The municipality of Chiché, El Quiché, is an illustrative case of the impact of the army's campaign of selective violence preceding massacres. In 1980, army repression first targeted the disappearance and assassination of catechists, teachers, local elected officials, members, and leaders of Catholic Action and CUC, as well as those of local village development/improvement committees. Military commissioners (civilians named as such by the army) and army informants provided lists of names of these local leaders to the army, who then accused the leaders of being guerrillas. The CEH (Comisión para el Esclarecimeinto Histórico—Commission for Historical Clarification) was able to document that following this selective violence, the army carried out thirteen massacres in the municipality of Chiché and its surrounding villages between 1981 and 1982.

In San Andrés Sajcabajá, local CUC members and leaders were taken from their homes to the "convent-base" the army had established in the colonial Catholic church in the municipal plaza in 1981. Many, like Pedro Pacheco Soc, Antonio Cipriano Chach, and Domingo Choc were never seen again. One local resident recalled, "We all knew that civilians who went in there never left, or if they did, they were dead."[13] Widows from the village of Piedras Negras were forced to wash laundry for the soldiers, prepare their food, clean their quarters, and gather wood for fires. Many of these widows were raped by soldiers.[14]

In April of 1997, the FAFG (Fundación de Antropología Forense de Guatemala—Guatemalan Forensic Anthropology Foundation) began an exhumation of the clandestine cemetery inside the church. Each day, dozens of local K'iche's traveled up to four hours to assist us in the labor of the excavation. Many hoped we would find the remains of a disappeared loved one. Dozens of men and women from the municipality came to give testimony of the selective violence and massacres they had survived. The testimonies I gathered in 1997 reaffirmed those I had previously gathered from a small group of Piedras Negras widows in San Andrés Sajcabajá in 1995.

The exhumation was particularly challenging and spoke to centuries of religious desecration and shifting religious practices. The first trench we opened in the center of the church floor revealed a post-Classical Maya floor from the Maya religious site upon which the Spaniards had built the colonial church.[15] The second trench in the front corner of the church floor revealed the colonial remains of dozens of infants who had been buried in the church because they had died before they had been baptized. In the third trench, we uncovered empty cans and plastic wrappers from army food rations. We decided to continue the excavation there because the hole was quite deep for burying garbage (which is usually incinerated), and a torture survivor of the convent-base had identified this particular spot as the site of a clandestine grave. As we continued digging, we came upon several picture cards of women in pornographic poses. Right below this, we found the first skeleton of one of the victims of the convent-base. In all, the FAFG exhumed the remains of twenty-six victims. We were unable to complete the exhumation because a new church building, with a cement foundation and floor, had been erected in the church garden, which contained several other graves. The CEH was able to identify seventy-two victims of arbitrary executions and disappearances.[16] This quantification of violence does not include the victims of massacres that followed the army's campaign of selective repression.

These premassacre community organizing and community experiences with La Violencia are extremely important because they (1) provide us with an entre to the escalation of violence from the perspective of those most affected by La Violencia; (2) reveal a military state that, even before the massacres, failed to make the distinction between dissent and subversion as the army selectively targeted and assassinated local leaders from church groups and peasant unions; and (3) demonstrate that local Maya identities were (and are) overlapping and that these identities are not singular or static, rather, they are located on a continuum of identity experiences, including: political, ethnic, religious, class, gender, and educational, among others.

For incidents of both community organizing and acts of violence against civilians, I have categorized commonplace occurrences into those that can be identified as those that *sometimes* happened prior to a massacre and those that *always* happened before the massacre. This is phase one of the phenomenology of terror.

In the dozens of massacres I have investigated,[17] there was *always* some kind of community organizing prior to the massacre. Activities usually began in both village communities and municipalities following the 1976 earthquake that devastated much of Guatemala and significant parts of the predominantly Maya Highlands. Thus, *always* present community projects were focused on one, or any combination, of the following: development, cooperatives, agricultural production, textiles, potable water, vaccination campaigns, primary education, literacy, and general health. Additionally, building on Vatican II Liberation Theology and its commitment to ministry to the poor, many of these predominantly Catholic communities had active catechists promoting community projects and organizing them through Catholic Action. These post-quake community organizing projects, which became models of local collective action to address community poverty were, to some degree, replicated throughout most of rural Guatemala—even in communities left unscathed by the earthquake.

Guerrilla organizing falls into the category of *sometime* present activities prior to the massacre. These guerrilla organizing activities include one or any combination of the following: guerrilla representatives clandestinely building on already existing community organization as a part of guerrilla strategy without organization member knowledge (i.e., participants were sometimes unaware that their local group was coordinated by the guerrilla), knowing community participation in clandestine meetings with

Phase One Premassacre Community Organizing and Experiences with Violence

Community Organizing	
Always Present	*Sometimes Present*
Church- and community-based organizing projects	Guerrilla organizing

Acts of Violence against Civilians	
Always Present	*Sometimes Present*
Guatemalan army operations	Forced recruitment of civil patrols
Participation of civil patrols in acts of violence in communities where civil patrols existed	Participation of civil patrols in acts of violence against community
Ambient fear	Guerrilla military operations

guerrillas, publicly called meetings with guerrillas in the central village plaza, recruiting guerrilla cell leaders and informants, heightened community participation in publicly known or clandestine guerrilla organizations, guerrilla preparation of unarmed civilian sympathizers, selective arming of community members designated as *responsables*[18] by the guerrilla, guerrilla military operations including threatening and disappearing community members identified as army informants, and discovery of the dead bodies of "accused" army informants in outlying areas of village.

At the same time, in each community that suffered a massacre, prior to the atrocity there were *always* Guatemalan army operations in the community that included: soldiers marching through the community and occupying it for several hours to several days, recruitment of army informers, soldiers going house to house looking for weapons and accusing community members of "subversive activities," direct and indirect death threats to community leaders, illegal arrest and disappearance of community leaders by government soldiers, soldiers threatening and beating civilian men, women, and children in public places, and discovery of dead, mutilated bodies of community leaders on village paths or in surrounding fields. In the category of *sometime* present army activities prior to a massacre, there is the recruitment and organization of army-controlled civil patrols (PACs) in municipalities and the *sometime* participation of these civil patrollers in army-ordered violence against civilians, including massacres.[19] This civil patrol participation in army operations appears to have taken place in every community where civil patrols were organized. Thus, civil patrol participation did not happen in every community prior to a massacre because every municipality did not yet have a civil patrol when massacres began, but it did *always* happen in every community where there was a civil patrol prior to the massacre.

Within the United Nations system, these army operations of disappearances, extrajudicial executions, torture, inhuman and degrading treatment and punishment, and arbitrary detention violated numerous articles of the Universal Declaration of Human Rights (UDHR), the International Covenant of Civil and Political Rights (ICPR), and the Convention Against Torture and Other Cruel, Inhuman or Degrading Treatment or Punishment.[20] Some articles of some conventions are derogable, meaning that a signatory (state party to the convention) can sign on to the convention, covenant of protocol, on the condition of not being held to the standard of particular articles which the state party identifies as derogations prior to signing. Articles 6 and 7 of the ICPR, which guarantee the right to life and freedom from torture respectively, are non-derogable. Articles 1 and 2 of the Convention Against Torture provide for no exceptions ever permitting torture: "No exceptional circumstances whatsoever, whether a state of war or a threat of war, internal political instability of any other public emergency, may be invoked as a justification for torture."[21] The Guatemalan army operations outlined in phase 1 also violated Articles 1, 3, 4, and 5 of the American Convention on Human Rights, to which Guatemala was one of the founding signatories in 1969. Articles 3, 4, and 5, which guarantee the right to juridical personality, right to life, and freedom from torture, respectively, are all non-derogable. Indeed, army operations in phases one to six of the phenomenology of terror violate these international human rights contracts, to which Guatemala is a signatory.[22]

Not surprisingly, in communities that experienced any level of guerrilla organizing, known and presumed army informants disappear or are found dead following selective campaigns of army terror against community leaders. These army campaigns of terror, again not surprisingly, led to increased participation of community members, who sought to defend themselves by joining guerrilla organizations. Over time, the pre-massacre violence of the army became increasingly systematic and was replicated in rural Maya communities throughout Guatemala. At the same time, while patterns of guerrilla violence can be identified, prior to the massacres such violence does not appear to have been systematic but rather was haphazard.

THE MODUS OPERANDI OF ARMY MASSACRES

The massacre is phase two in the phenomenology of terror. After investigating massacres in villages in twenty-one municipalities and reviewing FAFG, ODHA (Oficina del Arzobispado de Derechos Humanos—Archbishop's Office on Human Rights) and CEH reports on massacres, I find it virtually impossible to identify any single massacre as the biggest, the worst, or unique. Rather, each was representative of a wide-scale military strategy that did not distinguish between civilians and combatants,[23] a strategy that first used terror and psychological cruelty to force communities to accede to army control. Massacres should not be seen as discrete and one-time-only incidents of state violence but rather as integral strategic operations that in their sum form the army's first genocide campaign.

Nonetheless, each massacre is still significant in that it embodies the moment in which violence explodes into the lives of civilian villagers and forever changes the lives of citizens in Guatemalan society both locally and nationally. It is within the tension of this local and comparative national analysis of the massacres that we can best understand the meaning of the Guatemalan genocide.

The modus operandi of the massacres in the department of El Quiché fits the general blueprint for massacres carried out by the army throughout Guatemala.[24] The army was *always* inside and surrounding the village by dawn (i.e., villagers would awaken to find their community occupied and controlled by at least one platoon of soldiers). Villagers were violently awoken. All men in the community were *always* rounded up and always assembled in the village center or plaza. Women were *sometimes* instructed to stay in their homes and *sometimes* instructed to accompany the men to the assembly. Through 1981, for the most part, the army carried out selective massacres of men in Maya communities. These selective killings of men were usually, but *not* always, carried out with a hooded man, who often showed visible signs of torture, fingering the men who were to be killed—ostensibly indicating which men in the community were guerrillas or subversives. Those most likely to be targeted as guerrillas or subversives were catechists, literacy promoters, agricultural cooperative leaders and members, health promoters, or anyone else who stood up for the rights of his or her community. As one widow who lost her only son to La Violencia said, "After they killed my son, there was no one left to speak for us."

Civil patrollers and paramilitaries were *sometimes* with the soldiers. Whenever civil patrollers and/or paramilitaries were present, they *always*

Phase Two The Modus Operandi of Army Massacres

Always	*Sometimes*
Army surrounds village by dawn	Civil Patrollers are present
Villagers are violently awoken to community occupied by at least one army platoon	Paramilitaries are present
	Women are ordered to stay home
Civil patrollers and paramilitaries participate if they are present	Women are ordered to accompany men
	Women are raped
All men are rounded up and assembled in a central, public place	A hooded man, often showing visible signs of torture, identifies men to be killed by pointing at them as they file past him
Massacre is committed in public place	
Ambient fear	

participated in the army-ordered massacre. In the Ixil area, in the last six months of 1980, eighty-three Maya lost their lives in army massacres in five Ixil communities. By 1981, PACs (Patrullas de Autodefensa Civil— Civil Patrols) were systematically incorporated into the army's massacre campaign. Indeed, out of seventy-nine army massacres carried out by the army in El Quiché during 1981, local PACs participated in twelve (fifteen percent).[25] By 1982, the army had committed 131 massacres in El Quiché and local PACs participated in forty-one of these massacres— doubling PAC participation in army massacres to thirty-one percent.[26] No doubt, this increase in PAC execution of army strategy represents both the expansion of the army's Scorched Earth campaign as well as the growth of army-controlled civil patrols throughout the region.

In its comprehensive investigation, the Commission for Historical Clarification (CEH) found that 18 percent of human rights violations were committed by civil patrols. Further, it noted that 85 percent of those violations committed by patrollers were carried out under army order.[27] It is not insignificant that the CEH found that one out of every ten human rights violations was carried out by a military commissioner and that while these commissioners often led patrollers in acts of violence, eighty-seven percent of the violations committed by commissioners were in collusion with the army.[28]

Less than one month after the army organized all the men of San José and San Antonio Sinaché, Zacualpa, into a PAC, army-ordered PAC violence began within the community. On May 24, 1982, the army called all the 800 patrollers to gather in front of the church in San Antonio Sinaché. After chastising them for failing to turn in any guerrillas in the preceding weeks, the army lieutenant sent them on a fruitless march through the mountains searching for guerrillas. When they returned empty handed, the army and patrollers who had remained showed them the dead bodies of four PAC members and two local women. After ordering the patrollers to relinquish their *palos* (sticks) and machetes, the lieutenant accused Manuel Tol Canil, one of the local PAC chiefs of being a guerrilla. Two other patrollers protested that Canil was not a guerrilla and had committed no crime. The lieutenant then accused those two patrollers of also being guerrillas.[29]

The hands of the three men were bound behind their backs and they were tied to a tree in front of the church. The lieutenant ordered the patrollers to form a line in front of the tree. He picked up one of the machetes, gave it to the first man in line, and ordered him to "Kill them like this. If you don't kill him, then I will kill you." Taking turns, the men were ordered to not hit the men with lethal blows because their deaths should be slow to extend their suffering. When the first victim died after three machete blows, the lieutenant said, "That's too bad that he couldn't tolerate more, he died with only three blows of the machete."[30] After all three men had been killed, the patrollers were ordered to bury them. One patroller recalled returning home after the killings, "We came home cold, we were all frightened. The elders were crying as we walked down the path. The thing is that we were all crying."[31] Another former patroller explained the impact of this army-ordered violence in his community, "We began to drink more *guaro* [grain alcohol] to make our hearts more tranquil to try to pass through the pain these events brought to us."[32]

POST-MASSACRE LIFE IN FLIGHT

The story of the lived experience of massacre survivors would be incomplete without including the hardships and suffering of survival in the mountains. Much of civilian life in flight from the army in the mountains has been romanticized through stories of Communities of Populations in Resistance (Comunidades de Poblaciones en Resistencia—CPRs).[33] Daily life, however, was far removed from the propaganda stories of adults farming communally and children learning to read and write with carbon and wood. While life in villages had always been a life of want and lack of basic goods and services required to ensure human dignity, life in the mountains was even more precarious, the realities of staying alive day to day were so harsh as to deny both humanity and dignity to massacre survivors. Civilians in the mountains suffered extreme hardship with no shelter, no clothing, no medicines, and no stable food or water sources. People survived by eating roots and weeds. Families dedicated most of their time to the search for edible plants. Much anxiety was focused on thirst and the desperate search for and digging up of small roots that contained approximately one teaspoon of water per root . In the case of Acul, survivor testimony indicates that one-third of massacre survivors died in the mountains from hunger and diseases associated with exposure to the elements and starvation. Postmassacre life in flight in the mountains is phase three of the phenomenology of terror.

Army ground troops were *always* in pursuit of whole villages in flight. The soldiers would attempt to surround large sections of the mountain and move forward, shooting with the hope of driving the community into the gunfire of soldiers on one side or another.[34] These ground maneuvers were backed up with aerial bombings of the men, women, and children in flight in the mountains. At the same time, the army continued to burn abandoned villages and crops on a daily basis, thus destroying massacre survivors' access to food sources.

Also in the category of *always* is some degree of civilian population contact with guerrilla in the mountains. This contact took any one of various forms: communities armed by the guerrilla and living under guerrilla control; communities living within the sphere of guerrilla control, but unarmed with no means of self-defense against the army; communities living with guerrilla protection from the army; the guerrilla alerting the communities to army maneuvers in the area; the guerrilla warning communities of impending army attack; or sometimes no more than a one-time-only encounter with the guerrilla soon after flight from the village. While communities living under heightened guerrilla control are logically more commonly found in regions with higher incidence of guerrilla activity, these variations in civilian population contact with the guerrilla in the mountains existed in each of the communities in which I have conducted research.

While there was *always* some level of contact with the guerrilla, guerrilla actions are highly varied and fall into the *sometimes* category. These

Phase Three Postmassacre Life in Flight

Always	Sometimes
There is some degree of civilian contact with guerrilla	Guerrilla kill civilians
	Guerrilla provide communities with food
Army kills fleeing civilians	Guerrilla obligate communities to provide food
Army ground troops pursue and fire upon whole villages	
	Guerrilla arm men, women, and children
Army bombs men, women, and children	Guerrilla provide no weapons
Army burns abandoned villages	Guerrilla help starving civilians flee
Army burns all crops it encounters	Guerrilla use lies and coercion to obligate civilians to stay in mountains
Army steals and/or kills livestock	
Civilians die from war-related injuries	
Men, women, and children starve to death	
Men, women, and children die from illnesses associated with starvation and exposure to the elements	
Ambient fear	

sometime guerrilla actions in the CPRs ranged from providing food to communities to obligating community members to collectively farm and gather food for the guerrilla; from arming men, women, and children (including using girls as young as twelve and boys as young as nine as lookouts, and girls as young as thirteen and boys as young as twelve as combatants) to providing no weapons for community self-defense. Some guerrilla platoons assisted civilian villagers in their attempts to flee and find safe passage out of the mountains, other platoons used lies and armed coercion to obligate whole communities to stay in the mountains. In desperately coercive environments, guerrilla justice ranged from lying to communities, telling them that the army had burned municipalities as they had burned villages, to summary execution of entire families attempting to flee, to obligating mothers to suffocate their babies so the army would not hear them crying, to forcing abandonment of children up to age four in the mountains because such young children contributed nothing to community survival. In the collection of testimony of more than 400 survivors, I have documented more than sixty army massacres and have been able to document only two instances of guerrilla massacres, and each of these guerrilla massacres is already well-documented in existing literature.[35]

ARMY CAPTURES AND COMMUNITY SURRENDERS

By late 1983, the majority of massacre survivors had fled the starvation, guerrilla control, and the terror of constant army attacks and bombardments in the mountains in exchange for food under the army's *"Fusiles y Frijoles"* campaign (Rifles and Beans campaign, also referred to as Beans and Bullets campaign).[36] Whether those in flight surrendered or were captured by the army, they were first taken to the army base in the municipality. Among both the captured and those who surrendered, the return to the municipality was harrowing. Soldiers threatened, beat, tortured, and often killed or disappeared young men among those surrendering.

It is important to note here that significant numbers of massacre survivors in northern El Quiché (including, but not limited to, survivors from the Ixil area and Ixcán) continued to live in internal refuge in the CPRs into the 1990s. The CPRs continued the struggle to reconstruct self-sustaining communities, building makeshift shelters in scattered villages and attempting to plant and harvest milpa while in ongoing flight from army attacks.

One such CPR example is that of the Amajchel area. Between 1982 and 1983, soldiers from the army garrisons of La Perla, Juil, and Chajul, supported by soldiers from other Ixil army bases and garrisons, razed every village and all crops in the Amajchel area including Ilom, Sotzil, Jua, Chel, Visich, Viciquichum, Finca Estrella Polar, Caba, Amajchel, Finca Santa Clara, and Xeccoyeu.[37] Massacre survivors fled to the most northern parts of Amajchel. They were joined there by massacre survivors from other parts of the Ixil area. These internal refugees rebuilt the villages of Xecoyeu, Santa Clara, Amajchel, and Cabá. From 1983 to 1990, the army continued its military offensives against these communities of survivors, including attacks on fleeing civilians, aerial bombardments, the razing of the newly built villages, and the burning of maize crops. These army attacks would force the men, women, children, and elderly of the CPRs to retreat, once again, to the mountains without shelter, food, or other protections from the elements. Upon return to the charred remains of their makeshift village, they would find their crops destroyed, which meant another season of certain hunger and death, struggling to survive on weeds and roots. Though CPRs attempted to resettle high in the mountains, their life in flight from army attacks continued through the 1980s. In late 1984, many massacre survivors who had sought refuge in Mexico returned to Guatemala rather than be forcibly moved farther into the interior of Mexico to the states of Campeche and Quintana Roo. In September of 1990, the CPRs made public their existence and demanded national and international recognition as civilian populations.[38]

In the Ixil area, most survivors who came down from the mountains in the 1980s (whether through surrender or capture) spent several weeks or months in Nebaj. Men, women, and children were first taken to the Nebaj army base for interrogation. Most women were interrogated briefly, then freed. Some women and most men were held at the base for several days to several months. During this time, they were tortured and interrogated. In Eulalio's testimony, boys (aged ten to twelve) were put in army uniforms and taken back into the mountains by the army and forced, under torture and threat of death, to lead the army to civilian camps in the mountains.[39] Many adult men also suffered this same fate. As was Eulalio's experience, men and adolescent boys frequently left their families in the precarious "safety" of the mountains when they surrendered to the army. Lacking secure knowledge of fair treatment, they surrendered themselves alone with the hope that if the army did not kill them, they could later return to the mountains for their families and lead them to safety. Thus, the men sometimes returned willingly to the mountains hoping to find family members from whom they had been separated. These family rescues were carried out at great personal risk under army threats and with the knowledge that returning to the mountains, with or without soldiers, would mark these men as army collaborators in the eyes of the guerrilla.

Regardless of whether the family or community was captured by the army or surrendered to the army, these civilians were *always* subjected to the army's threats and acts of violence. Civilians were *always* taken to the army base or garrison where they were *always* threatened and interrogated. Once the interrogation ended, civilians were given small daily food rations that were *always* given only in exchange for work. Because the army provided no tools for their work projects, civilians had to use a portion of their daily food ration to rent the necessary tools to carry out army road building and construction projects.

Phase Four Army Captures and Community Surrenders

Always	*Sometimes*
Army carries out threats and violence against captured and surrendering civilians	Civilians are captured in the mountains
Army takes civilians to the army base	Civilians surrender
Army interrogates civilians	Civilians are detained
Army threatens civilians	Civilians are beaten and tortured
Civilians work for army in exchange for food	Women are raped on base by soldiers
Civilians build roads in exchange for food	Civilians are disappeared
Civilians rent tools, paying with food rations	Civilians are released
All men are organized in civil patrols	Civilians are taken back to mountains to show army CPR camps
Army orders civil patrollers to commit acts of violence against civilians	Civilians are taken to army re-education camps
Civil patrollers carry out acts of violence against civilians under army order	Guerrilla tries to stop civilians from surrendering
Civil patrollers are punished for any infraction, or perceived infraction, against army authority	Guerrilla assists civilians seeking to leave mountains
Civil patrollers accompany army into mountains	
Local army base commander is ultimate authority	
Ambient fear	

Among the returning communities, all men aged fifteen and older were *always* required to participate in army-organized and -controlled PACs. Army officials and army-appointed military commissioners *always* ordered civil patrollers to commit acts of violence against civilians in their own or neighboring communities. Under threat of certain torture and probable death, civil patrollers *always* carried out acts of violence against civilians under army order. Civil patrollers *always* patrolled nearby mountains with or without soldiers. Civil patrollers were *always* punished by army soldiers, military commissioners, and other patrollers for any infraction, or perceived infraction, of PAC or army authority—including not patrolling due to illness. The local army commander *always* had ultimate and total authority in all decisions affecting the community.

Sometimes the guerrilla used deception, coercion, or violence to dissuade families and communities from surrendering. *Sometimes* the guerrilla assisted families and communities in their efforts to seek safe passage from the mountains to the municipality. Among those who surrendered to or were captured by the army, civilians were *sometimes* detained for days, weeks, or months at the army base or garrison. They were *sometimes* beaten and tortured during their detention. Women were *sometimes* raped. Some of the detained civilians were never seen again after entering the base or garrison and, therefore, are now counted among the dead and disappeared. Civilians were *sometimes* released within the municipality and *sometimes* taken back to the mountains to serve as guides in the army's search to locate CPR camps and villages. *Sometimes* civilians were sent to army re-education camps in the area.

The re-education camp of Xemamatze, just outside Nebaj, was "a muddy place about the size of a football field within a horseshoe-shaped collection of dank, foul-smelling buildings with raw, sheetrock walls that accommodated about 600 people and a couple dozen heavily armed soldiers."[40] Re-education consisted of lessons in saluting the flag, singing the national anthem, and learning about the dangers of communism.[41]

The ideological content of the re-education camps was the army's attempt to impose a new ideological order on Maya who had been surviving collectively in the mountains. One re-education camp teacher described the work as follows:

At 5:00 A.M., everyone wakes up. From 5:30 to 6:00 A.M., we perform the flag ceremonies at the National Tent. From 6:00 to 6:15, we give a civics lecture. From 6:15 to 7:00, everyone eats breakfast. From 7:00 to

8:00, ideological lecture. After that, we give lectures on civil patrol techniques: if there is someone suspicious, how one denounces them; how to check people's documents; how to turn people in . . . all this is self defense for the civil patrols. . . . Afterwards we have health lectures; then a little snack. Then we give a lecture on how to prepare the food we distribute. An so on. We have ideological lectures about ten times a day. We emphasize and re-emphasize "Your nation is Guatemala. The flag is blue and white. The coat of arms is the quetzal bird. Our independence day is September 15, 1821. The national flower is the white orchid. The national anthem. . . ." We have to work them, to raise their consciousness. Our work is like erasing an old cassette tape and recording something new. We have to start with them like with little children. It could take months to get them ready to return to their homes. One, two, three, even six months.[42]

MODEL VILLAGES

Model villages were an integral part of the Army's Poles of Development campaign, which theoretically provided for rural development. In reality, the model villages, like the poles of development, were army-controlled resettlement work camps developed as a means of maintaining absolute control over Maya communities. The construction of the model villages was among the first "food for work" projects that returning massacre survivors were forced to build. Most of these villages were built upon the burned remains of villages razed by the army. Indeed, massacre survivors often returned to their villages of origin to rebuild under army order. Because the composition of villages was determined by the army, many villages were rebuilt with Maya from different villages as well as other ethnolinguistic communities. Thus, as previously noted, many Maya today describe their communities as "revuelto" (scrambled). In addition to the villages, survivors were also forced to build access roads for army vehicles.

Just as hunger had driven massacre survivors to surrender from the mountains, hunger also drove them to work for food. "No work projects, no food. A great way of doing things," said Sergeant Corsantes, one of the commanders at the Saraxoch model village.[43] Indeed, the 1980 Santa Fe Committee's "A New Inter-American Policy for the 80s," which served as a blueprint for the Reagan administration's Latin American policies, cynically stated "Food is a weapon in a world at war."[44] The Guatemalan army journal *Revista Militar* noted, "In twenty four hours, it is possible to assemble 3,000 or more voluntary workers to undertake construction of a road, a school, irrigation projects, a whole city. . . ."[45]

Within the model villages, residents were called to line up in formation and register in the morning, the afternoon, and the evening. Each day at midday, residents were also required to participate in antiguerrilla, pro-army

Phase Five Model Villages

Always	Sometimes
Civilians return to charred remains of village	There are PAC/army confrontations with
Houses have been burned	guerrilla
Crops have been destroyed	
Animals have been killed or stolen	
Civilians rebuild village under army control	
Army configures land for houses in grid pattern	
Army does not return land to original owners	
People live in barracks while building village	
Army commander distributes land and houses	
All men patrol	
Men who decline to patrol are tortured	
Some local men are publicly killed	
Men, women, and children work under army supervision	
PAC structures of command are organized by army	
Military commissioners are appointed by army	
Soldiers occupy village	
Adolescent girls and women are raped	
Army orders PAC to dig large pit for torture	
People cannot leave village without written army permission	
People spy on neighbors	
Local base commander is the ultimate authority	
Military commissioners displace traditional leaders	
PACs displace traditional community power structures	
Villages are contained in defined territory	
Military garrisons are among first forced construction projects	
Each model village has a heliport and airstrip	
Ambient fear	

confessional rituals in which several local men would recount how they had been betrayed by the guerrilla and helped by the army. Residents were not allowed to leave model villages without army permission.[46]

The construction of model villages was reminiscent of the strategic hamlets developed in Vietnam by the United States and the South Vietnamese army during the Vietnam War. Model villages included at least one, and often two, military detachments of 150 soldiers who were permanently housed in army garrisons built within the village. These garrisons were most often located close to the village entrance, allowing soldiers to monitor daily activities within the village. Model villages each had army/PAC patrol posts at the entrance and exit of the village. A soldier in the model village of Chisec explained, "We have a list of names. If their names appear on the list, we take them." Responding to a question about the fate of those taken away, the soldier said, "They die."[47] Thus, the grid-pattern construction plan of model village housing, its garrison layout, and land distribution were designed for army surveillance and control of the population, not for the functional development of productive agrarian communities, as the army claimed in "Poles of Development" propaganda. The model village plan destroyed the traditional village layout of scattered housing, a layout that allowed for cultivation of crops and care of livestock, replacing it with rows of tightly packed housing placed in a grid pattern, thus destroying agrarian production. The militarization of model villages is evident in the disappearance of army activities in the *sometimes* category and the consistent experience of army control through the systematic and organized use of terror outlined in the *always* category.

ONGOING MILITARIZATION OF COMMUNITY LIFE

One of the more obvious questions raised by the militarization of daily life in model villages under army control is whether the closing of army garrisons and the departure of military detachments allowed for more individual and community freedom. This would be true if PACs were voluntary, as the army claimed, and if PACs were able to become "autonomous" from the army, as David Stoll has claimed.[48] Yet it is not simply the army's presence that regulated daily life, it is the village infrastructure developed and implemented by the army—of which the PACs were an integral part—that regulated community life.

Following the departure of army detachments from model villages, the army continued to maintain tight surveillance and control of the community through the continuing structure of PACs, led by army-appointed military commissioners within the community. In 1992, Dr. Christian Tomuschat, United Nations expert on Guatemala who would later lead the CEH, concluded, "The civil patrols have become an institutionalized element of uncontrollable violence." He continued: "Contrary to what is indicated [by Guatemalan authorities], many inhabitants of the rural areas continue to be compelled to join the ranks of patrols. Anyone who refuses to join a patrol is accused of being a guerrilla or of collaborating with the guerrillas and is persecuted, threatened, ill treated or tortured, or even extrajudicially executed."[49]

For the majority of rural Maya, participation in the PACs was required for personal and familial security and performed under duress. Even a 1991 U.S. State Department memo noted that "Credible reports say that those who refuse to serve in the civil patrols have suffered serious abuse, including death."[50] Moreover, the PACs attacked nascent civil society organizations and especially human rights groups.

In many communities, the PACs in general and military commissioners in particular wielded the military authority vested in them for both army objectives and their own personal gain. Military commissioners used their power (to create lists of subversives for the army) to force neighbors to provide free labor and even forced neighbors to sign over land titles. Commissioners frequently raped local women and did so with impunity because of their power.[51] Even the departure of army detachments did not curtail the excessive surveillance and military control of villagers, who continued to be required to report to the PAC post before entering or leaving the village. They were required to provide information as to where they were going, with whom, and for how long. This information was noted and passed on to the army base.

Moreover, the army continued to arm the PACs. Army commanders met regularly with military commissioners to assess the community and review the PAC. In July 1992, one patroller explained: "We have patrol meetings every fifteen days with all the patrollers. The chiefs and military commissioners have meetings with the municipal chief of the patrols, Francisco Ixcoy, every eight days. They have to report about suspicious activities in the village so that Francisco can take that to his meetings with the army. They come back from the meetings with orders from the military to control nonpatrollers and members of human rights groups."[52]

Phase Six Ongoing Militarization of Community Life

Always	*Sometimes*
Army regularly visits	PAC/army has confrontations with guerrilla
Military commissioner and PACs must provide army with names of "subversives"	
Military commissioner and PACs must regulate entry to and exit from village	
PACs patrol village and surrounding mountains	
PACs denounce and torture other villagers under orders from military commissioner and army	
Villagers must have written permission to leave village	
All movement in and out of village is reported to army	
Amount of tortillas men are permitted to carry to work in field is limited to four	
Military commissioners abuse power	
Community divisions are exacerbated	
Local base commander is ultimate authority	
Military commissioners displace traditional leaders	
Public torture of "subversives" carried out by PACs under order of military commissioners	
PACs displace traditional community power structures	
Military commissioners report to army base commander	
PACs participate in public demonstrations under army order	
Ambient fear	

In 1992, the army continued to monitor villages and secure local participation in the PACs through intimidation. A patroller from a Quiché village recounted: "On May 2, 1992, the army arrived. . . . Some soldiers were dressed in civilian clothing and others were in green army uniforms. They called the civil patrollers together and said that all the men had to patrol, as, if they did not, then the violence would return as it was in 1978, '79, '80, '81, the periods of the most severe repression."[53]

Also, in 1992, PACs in El Quiché were used to organize a demonstration against the Quiché-based human rights group CERJ (Consejo de Comunidades Etnias Runujel Junam—Council of Ethnic Communities—"We are all Equal")[54]and to specifically condemn its founding leader, Amílcar Méndez. CERJ was founded to promote the human rights of the Maya and specifically challenged forced participation in the PACs. Méndez traveled from village to village collecting thumbprint signatures on petitions requesting the withdrawal of PACs from villages. He collected more than 13,000 signatures despite threats of violence against local CERJ members and Méndez himself. In response to the army order to protest CERJ, some 500 civil patrollers participated in the demonstration shouting slogans such as, "Amílcar Méndez and CERJ pretend to be leaders for human rights. Instead of applying the law, they kill humble peasants."[55] Amílcar Méndez and his family were repeatedly threatened and attacked by security forces. On May 10, 1992, a grenade was thrown at the Méndez family home in Santa Cruz del Quiché. In their efforts to silence Méndez, family members became the target of armed attacks, including the kidnapping and gang rape of a female relative and the kidnap-for-ransom of a nephew in 1997.[56] Anti-CERJ activities were not limited to army-ordered protests, nor was this violence directed only at Méndez. Between 1988 and 1992, twenty-five CERJ members were murdered, and CERJ recorded more than 400 acts of violence and intimidation against members, including: disappearances, kidnappings, threats, and torture.[57] In her comprehensive report on PACs for the Robert F. Kennedy Memorial Center for Human Rights, Alice Jay wrote, "civil patrollers routinely threaten, intimidate and harass CERJ members. Civil patrollers control the movements of CERJ members, accuse them of collaborating with the guerrillas, and threaten CERJ members with death."[58]

Thus, long after the soldiers left the army garrisons in villages, the military structure of the army continued to be reproduced by the PACs under army order. Like the model villages of phase five, the ongoing militarization of phase six reveals that army activities were absent from the category of *sometimes* because the militarization of communities by the army was systematically implemented and rigorously maintained by the army-controlled PACs throughout Maya communities.

LIVING MEMORY OF TERROR

Violence was not merely an effect of state terror; rather, it was one of myriad instruments used by the state to assert its domination. Violence against individuals and communities was selectively and massively enacted as an instrument of state terror throughout the country in the early 1980s. Despite an internationally brokered peace process, as we enter the second millennium, violence has yet to become an artifact of the past. Rather, for both victims and victimizers, the experience and survival of particular instrumentations of state violence fuse discrete experiences of physical and psychological violence, for both individuals and communities, within a continuum of survival. Over time, the making and remaking of this continuum of survival creates a living memory of terror wherein the memory of surviving a past physical or psychological act of violence is as real and current as today's experience with an act of violence, or its threat.

This living memory of terror can reinvoke the physical and psychological pain of past acts of violence in unexpected moments. A tree, for example, is not just a tree. A river, not just a river. At a given moment, a tree is a reminder of the baby whose head was smashed against a tree by a soldier. The tree, and the memory of the baby it invokes, in turn reinvoke a chain of memories of terror, including witnessing the murder of a husband or brother who was tied to another tree and beaten to death— perhaps on the same day or perhaps years later.[59] Unfortunately, these are not exceptional stories of the horrors of war. As evidenced by numerous testimonies, these were common occurrences in Maya villages throughout La Violencia and now form a part of both individual and collective memory, what I call "living memory" of terror. It is this living memory of terror, internalized in individual and community identities, that demarcates and defines contemporary life and culture for the majority rural Maya today.

Phase Seven Living Memory of Terror

Always	Sometimes
Former military commissioners attempt to maintain local power	Army sporadically occupies village
Community divisions impact community life	Former military commissioners continue to threaten village residents
Communities participate in civil society groups	
Villagers fear being "punished" for participation in civil society organizations	
Religious divisions and political divisions continue	
Ambient fear	

"We are always afraid" and "the fear never leaves" were among the most common statements survivors of La Violencia shared in testimonies. Though the *always* present ambient fear of survivors could be traced back to the army, recent threats and acts of violence *always* came from former military commissioners who sought to maintain their power (and that of the army by proxy) through ongoing intimidation. This resulted in the continuation of community divisions that had been exacerbated by all the phases of terror. Still, in every community, survivors *always* sought to organize civil society organizations to improve community life. Local projects sought to address immediate development needs such as potable water, literacy, health, agricultural and textile production, as well as justice issues such as land distribution, exhumations, human rights education, and community healing. Because of community divisions, any success in projects, even those as seemingly innocuous as potable water, were often met with *"envidia"* (envy) and accusations of *"interes"* (self-interest). Social justice organizing was *always* met with accusations of leaders being "subversive" or "guerrilla." These accusations heightened community fears of the army "punishing" them for these activities. Threats from military commissioners, sporadic army occupations of villages, and assemblies of civil patrollers at local army bases to denounce human rights activities reinforced the ambient fear of the living memory of terror. It is within this memory that courageous community leaders came forward in the 1990s to demand justice.

CONCLUSION

While focusing on the Maya experience in K'iche' and Ixil communities in El Quiché, the phenomenology of terror resonates with experiences of other Maya communities throughout Guatemala. In my fieldwork, I have found the presence of these phases in villages in the departments of Chimaltenango, El Quiché, Huehuetenango, Alta Verapaz, and Baja Verapaz. An in-depth review of the twelve-volume CEH report further confirms the presence of these phases in other Maya communities where massacres took place. I have chosen phases, rather than stages, as markers of identification because there is no evidence to suggest a functional evolution of terror through an experientially ordered passage of causally driven and independently reproducing stages. Still, while these phases are not causally related, the replication of massacres in Maya communities throughout Guatemala must be problematized and explained.

If there is no evidence to suggest a functional evolution of terror, why is each phase present, even if in varying degrees, in each massacre studied? The phases of terror I have identified and the consistent presence of these phases of state violence in villages throughout El Quiché, as well as other departments, represent widespread implementation of an army strategy in Maya communities—not phase one of terror leading to phase two, or phase two causing phase three. In her work in the Guatemalan army, Jennifer Schirmer has noted, "separation is purely rhetorical" and killings are not "accidental 'abuses' or 'excesses'; rather, they represent a scientifically precise, sustained orchestration of a systematic, intentional massive campaign of extermination."[60] And, as is argued throughout this book, the instrumentation of violence through massacres was a systematic and intentional genocide carried out by the Guatemalan army against the Maya.[61] These distinctions between stages and phases, and causal production versus strategic implementation, will become increasingly important to understanding the phenomenology of terror as we continue to witness La Violencia as experienced by survivors. Did the guerrilla provoke army massacres? Did army-imposed civil patrols become local autonomous institutions? These are not rhetorical questions. They are questions that matter greatly, and responses to these questions can have significant impact on the outcomes of peace efforts and democratization projects.[62]

Through schematic description of shifts in army counterinsurgency strategies and guerrilla responses, I have demonstrated that massacres represented a crescendo of violence that simultaneously destroyed villages and their community structures and increasingly polarized and isolated both the army and the guerrilla, thereby eliminating whatever consensual relationships they may once have had in Maya communities. Further, survivor testimonies throughout this book illustrate how this isolation and polarization of communities from both the army and guerrilla created community relations heavily, if not wholly, dependent upon and defined by armed coercion. I have focused on the Maya experience in the department of El Quiché to outline the consistencies, variations, complexities, and contradictions in lived experience of seven phases of terror identified during my research on massacres in Guatemala.[63] In communities such as Acul, Nebaj, which continued to be armed and highly militarized by the army until the signing of the Peace Accords in December of 1996, it is impossible to argue that such a community regimented by an army-controlled civil patrol could be anything other than dominated by the army.[64] Moreover, the phenomenology of terror, like testimonies from Acul, Panzós, and Plan de Sánchez massacre survivors, again reminds us that a massacre is not a discrete event—each massacre was part of a larger system of genocidal terror that is remembered as La Violencia. Taken as a whole, understanding the phases in the phenomenology of terror posits new ways of understanding the meaning of La Violencia within contemporary Maya political and social culture. Further, the narratives of lingering fear or living memory of terror indicate that La Violencia is as embedded in Guatemala's present as it is in its past. And, as Michael Taussig suggests, "the narratives are in themselves evidence of the process whereby a culture of terror was created and sustained."[65]

In this chapter, I have attempted to delineate a phenomenology of terror as a means to understanding and contesting the violence of the past and the fear, borne of this violence, that continues to thrive long after actual physical violence dissipates. To construct a democratic society with respect for human rights and dignity, structural terror must end. State infrastructures of institutions and laws that, in the past, employed violence as an instrument of imbuing society with terror must be dismantled and rebuilt upon a foundation of democratic values and practices, without violence as the primary recourse of the state. Yet, even these grand and significant gestures offer no guarantee to consolidate peace in fledgling democratic structures, because long after state structures of violence are dismantled, living memory of terror continues to exist and is reinvoked (with each new act of violence or its threat) in individual, community, and national consciousness. This living memory of terror thus forms a part of the psyche and identity of the individual, the community, and the nation, and greatly impacts individual and community capacities to embrace and reproduce the democratic values and practices necessary to consolidate democratic institutions and laws at the local and national levels.

Six

GUATEMALAN ARMY CAMPAIGNS OF GENOCIDE

> The army came with their guns. The people they found, they killed. The crops they came upon, they destroyed. Our clothes, our dishes, our tools, they broke them or stole them. And all our animals, our cows, goats, chickens and turkeys, they killed them too. They destroyed and ate everything on the path of their persecutions against the people.
>
> *—Alejandro, Ixil massacre survivor*

In this chapter, I demonstrate how massacres as a strategy of state terror systematically shifted to a tripartite, decade-long campaign of genocide against the Maya. It is when this shift happens that the Guatemalan army's human rights violations are no longer limited to the human rights instruments previously mentioned in chapter five.[1] It is here that the army moves to a new level of atrocity and violates the Convention on the Prevention and Punishment of the Crime of Genocide.[2] Critical to understanding why these massacres constitute the beginning of an intentional genocidal campaign is the fact that the army did not use massacres as a singular tactic, but rather combined massacres (its first campaign of genocide) with a "Scorched Earth" campaign; this included not only the complete destruction of villages and surrounding fields but also the relentless hunt for survivors, with army helicopters dropping bombs upon displaced civilians in the mountains and ground troops encircling and firing upon those fleeing aerial attacks (which comprise the second genocidal campaign). The third genocidal campaign is the simultaneous forced concentration of Maya survivors into army-controlled "re-education camps" and "model villages" and the continued hunt for massacre survivors who formed the Communities of Populations in Resistance (Comunidades de Poblaciones de Resistencia—CPRs) in their flight from terror. In this chapter, I provide evidence to prove that (1) each of the three campaigns of genocide I have identified is a clear violation of the UN Genocide Convention; (2) each of these campaigns was designed and implemented with the intention of genocide; and (3) the Guatemalan army genocide is not unique but rather fits a pattern of genocide wherein perpetrators use code words and expressions, such as "scorching communists," in order to detract from and neutralize their activities and "render them acceptable domestically and internationally."[3]

At the height of La Violencia, army justification of massacres in rural Maya communities rested upon its claims that the army was, in the words of former military dictator Efraín Ríos Montt, "scorching communists."[4] Moreover, the transnational nature of the Guatemalan army's campaign against the Maya was revealed in an October 5, 1981, Department of State memorandum classified as "secret." The memorandum acknowledged that then-dictator General Romeo Lucas García believed that "the policy of repression" was "working," and the state department official writing the memo described the "extermination of the guerrillas, their supporters and sympathizers" as the measure of a "successful" policy of repression.[5] The Guatemalan army used ground troops and aerial forces to saturate the mountain with firepower in its attempt to exterminate the unarmed Mayan men, women, children, and elderly who had fled the massacres and destruction in their communities.

In its final report, the CEH (Comisión para el Esclarecimiento Histórico—Commission for Historical Clarification) concluded that army massacres had destroyed 626 villages, that more than 200,000 people were killed or disappeared, that 1.5 million were displaced by the violence, and that more than 150,000 were driven to seek refuge in Mexico. Further, the commission found the state responsible for 93 percent of the acts of violence and the guerrillas for 3 percent. All told, 83 percent of the victims were Maya and 17 percent were ladino.[6]

DEFINING GENOCIDE

The Genocide Convention was adopted by the United Nations General Assembly on December 9, 1948. Rafael Lemkin, author of *Axis Rule in*

The Impact of *La Violencia*[7]

Known Impact of Violence Before Commission for Historical Clarification	Findings of CEH Final Report
440 villages massacred	626 villages massacred
1.5 million people displaced	1.5 million people displaced
150,000 people fled into external refuge	150,000 people fled to refuge in Mexico
100,000–150,000 dead or disappeared	More than 200,000 dead or disappeared

Who were the Victims of La Violencia?
The vast majority of the victims of acts of violence committed by the state were civilians.
83 percent of victims were Maya
17 percent of victims were ladino

Who Is Responsible for These Acts of Violence against Civilians?
93 percent of acts of violence committed by state
3 percent of acts of violence committed by guerrilla

Occupied Europe, drafted the convention, which was then debated and amended by the General Assembly. In the convention, "genocide means any of the following acts committed with intent to destroy, in whole or in part, a national, ethnical, racial, or religious group, as such

(a) Killing members of the group;
(b) Causing serious bodily or mental harm to members of the group;
(c) Deliberately inflicting on the group conditions of life calculated to bring about its physical destruction in whole or in part;
(d) Imposing measures intended to prevent births within the group;
(e) Forcibly transferring children of the group to another group."[8]

Moreover, Article 1 clearly states that "genocide, whether committed in time of peace or time of war, is a crime under international law which they [the signatories] undertake to prevent and punish."

Given that 87 percent of the victims of La Violencia were Maya, that all 626 massacred villages were Maya, and based on data presented in this and previous chapters, there is no doubt that the Guatemalan army violated the United Nations Convention on the Prevention and Punishment of Genocide. In this first campaign of massacres, the army unequivocally killed members of the group, caused serious bodily and mental harm, and deliberately inflicted conditions of life calculated to bring about the physical destruction of the Maya in whole or in part. Thus, at minimum, the Guatemalan army violated Articles 2(a), (b), and (c) of the Genocide Convention.

This alone, however, is not sufficient to prove genocide. Current legal debate about what constitutes genocide resides not just in determining the acts of genocide but also in proving that the acts were "committed with intent."[9] And, proving intent raises the question about what is acceptable as a standard of proof.

In its final report, the CEH (Comisión para el Esclarecimiento Histórico- Commission for Historical Clarification) concluded that the Guatemalan army had committed genocidal acts. However, in its discussion of genocide, the CEH wrote: "It is important to distinguish between a policy of genocide and acts of genocide. A policy of genocide exists when the goal of the actions is to exterminate a group in whole or in part. Acts of genocide exist when the goal is political, economic, military, or whatever other such type, and the method that is utilized to achieve the end goal is the extermination of a group in whole or in part."[10] Within the CEH interpretation, a policy of genocide has the end goal of genocide whereas acts of genocide are incidental to a plan that utilizes genocidal practices but has an end goal of something other than genocide. In this way, the CEH assumes that genocide was a means rather than an end. This then begs the question, how did the CEH come to this determination?

A CEH document used for internal discussion of genocide provides a lens to internal CEH debates on the topic. To the question, "Was there a genocide in Guatemala?" the document states: (1) at a national CEH forum to solicit recommendations from civil society, "only the indigenous communities requested that the CEH pronounce genocide"; (2) "not only the indigenous believe there was a genocide, but also some academics such as Falla, Churchill, and Sanford"; (3) others, including "[Hilde] Hey, the United Nations (UN) the Organization of American States (OAS) have proclaimed that "there were grave violations of human rights"; and, (4) the court cases within Guatemala "have been initiated [under the penal code] as common murder."[11] It is quite easy to understand these four points—none of which should be taken solely at face value. First, indigenous communities would request a pronouncement of genocide because they experienced it firsthand. Second, Ricardo Falla, Ward Churchill, and I have each spent extensive time in Maya communities, with displaced Maya, and with Maya refugees taking testimonies about La Violencia. In addition to this secondary witnessing, Falla lived with Maya in flight and documented the massacres of Ixcán.[12] Based on the evidence obtained through survivor testimonies, we each came to understand the systematic breadth of army violence for the genocide that it was. Third, Hilde Hey, the UN, and the OAS had made their determinations prior to the CEH investigations and without benefit of the immense data amassed by the CEH (indeed, their determinations were being discussed as the report was being internally debated and written). Fourth, massacre cases were initially filed with the Guatemalan courts as murder cases because those filing the cases felt they would be more likely to gain prosecution for murder because individual murder cases were not exempted from prosecution under the amnesties granted to perpetrators at the end of the military regime.

This same CEH document then explains that "in the epoch of greatest repression (scorched earth campaign) . . . it was believed that there was a relationship with the guerrilla (as a social base) and for this reason to be indigenous was to be stigmatized as a guerrilla or communist."[13] The next question raised is "Why did they kill the Maya?" The first response is that not everyone who died was Maya (13 percent were ladino). The second point is that "the Maya who died were not [killed] for their membership in an ethnic group, but for being considered "subversives."[14] It is this second point that is critical to understanding the CEH separation between a policy of genocide and acts of genocide— neither of which has anything to do with the technical aspects of the law of state responsibility.[15]

The memo then attempts to circumvent the exclusion of the category of political group[16] from the protected groups (national, racial, ethnic, or religious) of the Genocide Convention by arguing that the Guatemalan army sought to destroy a national group, "the Guatemalan citizens who had communist beliefs or who simply exercised their rights and demanded better living conditions, these were considered [by the army] to be 'subversive.' In this manner, they constitute a national group."[17] The document concludes that indeed there was a genocide of this national group.[18]

Based on the findings of the final report, it appears that after internal discussion, the CEH discarded the proposed national group thesis but accepted its underlying argument that the army's goal was to kill "subversives." Thus, within this faulty logic, genocide of the Maya was a means to an end (presumably the elimination of subversion). This CEH interpretation supports my earlier assertion that the Guatemalan army genocide fits a pattern of genocide wherein perpetrators (both individual and institutional) use code words and expressions to neutralize their activities.

In this case, rather than genocide, the CEH finds genocidal acts—a finding that is, though ambiguous, nonetheless significant. In addition to pointing out the specific and varied roles of the executive, judicial, and legislative branches of the Guatemalan government in violating the human rights of its citizens, the CEH attributed direct responsibility to the state and its agents for the construction of the counterinsurgency state and for the state's complete failure to comply with its obligation to investigate and prosecute human rights violations. At the public presentation of the CEH report in February 1998, CEH President Christian Tomuschat stated: "On the basis of having concluded that genocide was committed, the Commission also concludes that, without prejudice to the fact that the participants in the crime include both the material and intellectual authors of the acts of genocide committed in Guatemala, State responsibility also exists. This responsibility arises from the fact that the majority of these acts were the product of a policy pre-established by superior order and communicated to the principal actors."[19]

Moreover, we can deconstruct army claims of "scorching communists" and "killing subversives" as the goal of the genocide by analyzing the army's own words and interpretations of the massacres. Here I offer two declassified U.S. government documents that prove that the genocide was both a means and an end as well as under command responsibility of the hierarchy of the army.

First, a "secret" declassified CIA document from late February 1982, states that in mid-February 1982, the Guatemalan army reinforced its existing forces and launched a "sweep operation in the Ixil Triangle. The commanding officers of the units involved have been instructed to destroy all towns and villages which are cooperating with the Guerrilla Army of the Poor (EGP) and eliminate all sources of resistance."[20] Point one of the memo claims that civilians "who agree to collaborate with the army . . . will be well treated." Then, in point three of the memo the CIA acknowledges that "a large number of guerrillas and collaborators have been killed." Point three concludes with, "COMMENT: When an army patrol meets resistance and takes fire from a town or village it is assumed that the entire town is hostile and it is subsequently destroyed. . . . An empty village is assumed to have been supporting the EGP, and it is destroyed." Point four cynically concludes that the Army High Command is "highly pleased with the initial results of the sweep operation and believes it will be successful." The CIA then clarifies that "the army has yet to encounter any major guerrilla force in the area," and goes on to conclude that the army's "successes to date appear to be limited to the destruction of several 'EGP-controlled-towns' and the killing of Indian collaborators and sympathizers." Point four concludes with "COMMENT: The well documented belief by the army that the entire Ixil Indian population is pro-EGP has created a situation in which the army can be expected to give no quarter to combatants and non-combatants alike."[21] In the words of Jan Perlin, former legal counsel to the CEH, "The historic attribution of particular characteristics to the 'indigenous masses,' an integral part of the racist construct [of Guatemala], determined the choice of military tactics against geographically defined portions of this group when it was determined that 'they' constituted a threat."[22]

Second, as explained in the previously cited October 1981 declassified U.S. Department of State memorandum, General Lucas García believed that the "extermination" was the measure of the "success" of his "policy of repression."[23] Extermination was then not simply a means but a goal. Moreover, despite their convoluted language and censored presentation, these documents acknowledge Guatemalan army massacres of unarmed Maya and also concur with the Guatemalan army that all Ixiles are "pro-EGP." This concurrence between the CIA, State Department, and Guatemalan army represents the official conflation of ethnicity with political affiliation. Thus, the U.S. Embassy and its officers in Guatemala, the U.S. State Department, and the CIA justify Guatemalan army destruction of the social, political, and material culture of the Maya in general and the Ixiles in particular. Though this justification for genocide is based on the conflated idea that all Ixiles are pro-EGP, at no moment is ethnicity left out of the equation. Moreover, the 1982 CIA document makes clear that the Army High Command is not only informed about the massacres but that the "commanding officers of the units involved have been instructed to destroy all towns and villages. . . ." and that the Army High Command is "highly pleased with the initial results."[24]

Thus far, I have demonstrated (1) that army massacres of Maya communities violated Genocide Convention Articles 2(a), (b), and (c); (2) that though these massacres were directed at Maya communities in the name of "scorching communists," in fact, the Guatemalan army carried out its first genocidal campaign of massacres against the Maya because they were Maya; (3) further, that the army sought to cover this campaign against the Maya by conflating political affiliation with ethnic identity; (4) that because "extermination" of the Maya was, in the words of General Lucas García, a measure of the campaign's "success," the genocide was both a means and an end goal; and (5) based on declassified CIA and U.S. State Department documents, that the Army High Command ordered, was informed about, and "highly pleased with" army massacres in February 1982.

PROVING INTENT TO COMMIT GENOCIDE

This brings us back to the issues of intent and standard of proof, which are interrelated. First, intent is often confused with motive. In criminal law, intent means the deliberation behind the act regardless of the actual motive.[25] Intentionality defines intent.[26] Did the Guatemalan army intend to commit genocide against the Maya? Yes, because the army's commander in chief sought to exterminate the Maya with no distinction between civilians and combatants or between democratic opposition and armed insurrection.[27] Was the aim to destroy the Maya, as a group, in whole or in part? Yes, because (1) all Maya were at-risk of being "exterminated" by virtue of their indigenous identity; (2) massacres destroyed 626 Maya villages; and (3) all 626 villages were Maya.

By outlining the Guatemalan army's intent to commit genocide, I have also alluded to available evidence that leads us to the issue of standard of proof. Human rights law professor Dinah Shelton suggests that "*beyond a reasonable doubt* in common law court and *conviction in time* or its equivalent in a continental system" are internationally accepted standards of proof. Moreover, citing the Inter-American Court judgment in the Velasquez-Rodriguez case, she is "fully confident that proof can be inferred from a pattern or practice."[28]

Genocide scholar Ben Kiernan points out that "smoking gun" internal documentation is not necessary to prove intent—though the declassified U.S. government documents do provide this. Proof of intent can be inferred by "a proven pattern of actions, not just from a top-down written order."[29] "Serial killers who are convicted by showing patterns and inferred responsibility from circumstantial evidence"[30] provide one such example. Kiernan adds that "similar actions in a pattern across a territory can be proof of command intent."[31]

Declassified CIA and U.S. State Department documents provide evidence of intent to commit genocide. I would also like to suggest that intent is found in the very language of the generals in command during the "Scorched Earth campaign." While Lucas García spoke of "exterminating," General Efraín Ríos Montt spoke of "taking the water away from the fish" (quitar al agua del pes), the water being the Maya and the fish being the guerrilla. Even here, it is clear that the general made a distinction between the guerrilla (fish) and the Maya (water). If he truly meant to "scorch communists" and "eliminate subversion," the fish, rather than the water, would have been his military target. If he was unable to distinguish between the Maya and the guerrillas, the metaphor would have had no meaning. Ríos Montt, like Lucas García before him, wanted to eliminate the Maya. The massacres were a genocidal campaign, begun under Lucas García and continued under Ríos Montt, which intended to destroy the Maya because they were Maya. Seven months after Ríos Montt came to power, one Maya survivor said that after the massacres, "All that was left was silence."[32] Amnesty International issued a report condemning massacres of "Indian" peasants that resulted in more than 2,600 documented deaths, "many of them women and children," in the first six months of the Ríos Montt regime. Even with incomplete information, as early as 1982, it was clear to human rights observers that the Guatemalan "Indians" were the target of the army's campaign of terror.[33] Again, citing Perlin, "The truth of genocidal intent centers around the process of the construction of the 'other' as the enemy."[34]

At this point, I have demonstrated that the Guatemalan army committed genocide against the Maya with the intention to destroy the Maya in whole or in part and that genocide was both the means and the end, and furthermore, genocide was also the planned intent. Still, I want to offer further evidence of the army's strategic intent to commit genocide as well as some of the results of the genocidal campaign—both of which demonstrate that genocide was a consistent policy of the Guatemalan army through the dictatorships of Lucas García and Ríos Montt—each of whom had command responsibility.

The CEH found that the Maya had suffered 626 known army massacres. To date, the Guatemalan Forensic Anthropology Foundation (Fundación de Antropología Forense de Guatemala—FAFG) has carried out more than 190 exhumations. By combining the data collected on massacres by the FAFG and the CEH, we can further explore the intent and outcome of genocide.

GENOCIDE AS ARMY POLICY FROM LUCAS GARCÍA TO RÍOS MONTT

In general, the Guatemalan army has sought to elude responsibility for its genocidal campaign of massacres by claiming that massacres did not emanate from the army high command but rather from the actions of rogue field commanders. Former general Efraín Ríos Montt became president of Guatemala when he overthrew the dictatorship of Lucas García in March 1982. La Violencia was at its height during these two dictatorships. Still, Ríos Montt not only claims that he had nothing to do with the massacres but that his regime stopped the massacres begun by Lucas García.

Today, General Lucas García is withdrawn from the political scene due to Alzheimer's disease. Rios Montt, however, continues to play a powerful role in Guatemalan politics. His party, the FRG (Frente Republicano Guatemalteco—Guatemala Republican Front), holds a majority of seats in the Guatemalan Congress, over which Rios Montt himself presides as president of the Congress, and current President Alfonso Portillo came to office in an FRG landslide. When Rios Montt attempted to run for president in 1995, the Guatemalan Supreme Electoral Commission banned his candidacy (and his wife's) based on the Guatemalan constitution, which prohibits anyone who came to power through a military coup from running for president. The symbol of the FRG is a white hand on a blue background. When I asked Maya friends in El Quiché, Baja Verapaz, and Chimaltenango about the meaning of this symbol, I was always told, "It is the strong/tough hand" (la mano dura) and "the white hand" (la mano blanca). Both la mano dura and la mano blanca were names of death squads during La Violencia and death threats were often received with hand prints or drawings of hands.

Though current party politics are not my focus here, I do want to suggest that it is an ominous experience to be in a country of genocide survivors during an election with la mano dura plastered on every building, fence, and lamppost. Outsiders, both non-Maya Guatemalans and internationals, often ask why and how the FRG could win an election in communities of massacre survivors. Though a thorough explanation requires analysis of evangelical church affiliations with Ríos Montt as well as campaign practices,[35] I want to suggest that massacre survivors have little reason to believe that the power of Ríos Montt to exterminate their communities has diminished, given that he has an omnipresent political party with propaganda throughout Maya communities and that his party symbol is a signifier of terror.

In this section, through an analysis of the pattern of massacres in El Quiché during the last twelve months of Lucas García's regime (March 1981–82) and the first twelve months of Ríos Montt's reign (March

1982–83), I demonstrate that (1) massacres were *not* the result of rogue field commanders; (2) massacres were a systematic and strategic campaign of the army as an institution; and (3) Ríos Montt not only continued the campaign of massacres begun by Lucas García, but he actually further systematized the massacre campaign.

The Ixil and Ixcán areas are located in the northern part of El Quiché, with the Ixcán jungle north of the Ixil mountains. Between March 1981 and March 1983, the Guatemalan army carried out seventy-seven massacres in the Ixil/Ixcán region. There are 3,102 known victims of these massacres. If we locate the number of massacres and victims by date on the calendar of the regimes, Lucas García is responsible for forty-five massacres with 1,678 victims from March 1981 to March 1982, and Ríos Montt is responsible for thirty-two massacres with 1,424 victims from March 1982 to March 1983.[36]

If we focus only on comparing the number of massacres, we find a 15 percent drop in the number of massacres and 200 less massacre victims in the Ixil/Ixcán area during the first year of Ríos Montt. However, it would be misleading to simply conclude that the number of massacres and massacre victims decreased under Ríos Montt, because 1,424 Maya fell victim to thirty-two army massacres under his regime. Moreover, rather than a decrease in genocidal activities in the area, the number of victims per massacre actually increased under Ríos Montt from an average of thirty-seven victims to forty-five, or an 18 percent increase in number of victims per massacre. This increase indicates a more systematic genocidal policy that sought "efficiency" in killing ever-larger numbers of people in each massacre. Furthermore, if we limit the time of study to the last three months under Lucas García and the first three months under Ríos Montt, we find 775 Maya victims of twenty-four massacres under Lucas García and 1,057 victims of nineteen massacres under Ríos Montt. Though there is a 21 percent drop in the number of known massacres, there is a 72 percent increase in the average number of victims in each massacre under Ríos Montt. In the first three months of the Ríos Montt regime, the average number of victims per massacre increases from thirty-two to fifty-six. Further, the qualitative difference between an average of thirty-two and fifty-six victims is not village size, it is the systematic inclusion of women, children, and elderly in the slaughter. Whereas it is during the last six months of the Lucas García regime that the army began to include women, children, and the elderly as targets in some massacres, it is under Ríos Montt that their inclusion became a systematic practice.

If we broaden our analysis to the entire department of El Quiché, our conclusions about the strategies and patterns of massacres in the Ixil/Ixcán areas during the regimes of Lucas García and Ríos Montt are systematically reaffirmed.[37] From March 1981 to March 1982, 2,495 Maya were victims of ninety-seven army massacres in the department of El Quiché. Between March 1982 and March 1983, 3,180 Maya were victims of eighty-five massacres in El Quiché. Here again, while there is a 13 percent drop in the number of massacres under Ríos Montt, there is a 25 percent increase in the number of massacre victims during the first year of his regime. Again, under Ríos Montt, there is an increase in the efficiency of the massacres with 45 percent more victims per massacre, on average. And again, I want to emphasize that this 45 percent increase represents the systematic inclusion of women, children, and the elderly as massacre victims.

No doubt, the ever-increasing number of Maya massacre victims and the pattern from the Lucas García regime to the rule of Ríos Montt indicates an ongoing army strategy that was consistent in its target population (the Maya) and that became increasingly efficient. Moreover, this improved efficiency was no accident and certainly not the random and coincidental outcome of rogue commanders in the field. It was the field implementation of the Guatemalan army's "Plan de Campaña Victoria 82" (Victory Campaign Plan '82), which sought to "eliminate," "annihilate," and "exterminate" the "enemy."[38] A critical component to the campaign was the systematic organization of civil patrols that was begun, perhaps as a pilot campaign, under Lucas García but brought to fruition under Ríos Montt. Fully 64 percent of army massacres during the thirty-four year conflict occurred between June 1981 and December 1982.[39] According to a statistical analysis of the CEH findings, 14.5 percent of Ixil Maya were killed during La Violencia.[40]

INCLUSION OF PACS IN GUATEMALAN ARMY MASSACRES

Given that PACs were an integral component of the 1982 Plan Victoria, I want to again look at the massacres, this time analyzing the composition of the perpetrators. My questions here are: (1) Who carried out the massacres? (2) Does this reveal a pattern? (3) If there is a pattern, what are its implications?

In the department of El Quiché during the last year of the Lucas García regime, army platoons carried out ninety-seven massacres, but sixteen of these massacres were different from the rest because, for the first time, army platoons carried out massacres with local PAC participation under army command.[41] Under Lucas García, 19 percent of massacres were carried out by army platoons with PAC participation (under army command) and 81 percent of massacres were carried out by army platoons alone. Reviewing the number of victims of each massacre, one finds that 87 percent of the victims were killed in army platoon massacres and 13 percent of the victims were killed in joint army/PAC massacres.

Plan Victoria, developed under Ríos Montt, increased the centrality of the PACs to army strategy.[42] Thus, it should not be surprising that army massacres with PAC participation more than doubled to account for 41 percent of army massacres under Ríos Montt and that the number of victims of army/PAC massacres more than tripled to account for 47 percent of army massacre victims. This systematic pattern of incorporation of army-controlled civil patrols participating in army massacres at the same time that the army's official Plan Victoria campaign calls for increased organization of these PACs indicates "beyond a shadow of a doubt" that (1) massacres were carried out by army platoons and army platoons with PAC participation; (2) the pattern of army and army/PAC massacres from Lucas García to Ríos Montt indicates massacres as a result of widespread army strategy and command responsibility; (3) this pattern reveals a highly coordinated army campaign that increasingly and systematically included PACs in massacre operations under army command; (4) this pattern could only have existed as the result of a widespread army strategy with incorporation of PACs as a strategic component of the 1982 Plan Victoria; and (5) both Lucas García and Ríos Montt, as well as other army officials in the High Command, had command responsibility and were the intellectual authors of army and army/PAC massacres of the Maya during their military regimes. This sustained campaign of massacres was the army's first genocidal campaign against the Maya.

"HUNTER BATTALIONS"—THE GUATEMALAN ARMY'S SECOND CAMPAIGN OF GENOCIDE

As the Guatemalan army moved forward with Plan Victoria, committing massacres against the Maya in villages throughout the country, those who survived by fleeing into the mountains were pursued by the army.

Initially, massacre survivors fled to nearby villages in the mountains, seeking refuge from the army ground troops chasing them through the mountains as well as the machine gun strafing of army helicopters and the bombs being dropped from planes. These villages were soon attacked and destroyed by the army, which left only the mountain itself as refuge.

In July 1981, based on an interview with an unnamed U.S. intelligence operative who had worked in Brazil and Colombia, Everett G. Rafael reported in the *Wall Street Journal* that "the Carter Administration's policy of turning its back on a country that violates the human rights of its citizens during the fight against guerrillas 'is a coward's way out.'" Rafael also reported on the indoctrination of Salvadoran troops at a special training school. An unnamed Green Beret colonel explained the counterinsurgency techniques: "There aren't any such things as special forces camps or free-fire zones in irregular warfare. We are supposed to train the local forces to play guerrilla with hunter battalions that are moving all the time. . . . You make them realize their situation is hopeless and then you offer them amnesty."[43] These same techniques were taught to Guatemalan army officials and troops at the School of the Americas.[44]

Indeed, former soldiers involved in the pursuit of civilians in flight have referred to these operations as "hunting the deer" *(cazando el venado)*. The technique was to use multiple platoons to encircle a large area. These troops would be backed up by helicopter strafing and aerial bombardment. Soldiers would begin to fire into the forested areas of the mountains on all but one side of the circle, thereby forcing the civilians to flee in the direction that appeared to be safe for lack of gunfire. As civilians reached these areas, the soldiers would open fire directly onto the civilian populations. Testimonies from survivors of the Tzalbal massacres[45] are representative of testimonies I have taken in other parts of Quiché as well as Chimaltenango, Huehuetenango, Alta Verapaz, and Baja Verapaz.

Doña Eugenia fled the Tzalbal massacre with her baby on her back. She was one of thirty survivors fleeing from her village. She recalls:

> We were always asking each other, "'Where should we go? Where can we go? Is there a place we can go?" We were always looking for another place, a safe place. Many elderly died because we were climbing up and down steep mountains; the elderly cannot walk that much. They would stay behind resting. The army would find them and kill them. They killed lots of people: the elderly, children, babies, boys and girls, men

and women, our youth. There was a señora with us. She had one child, a boy. We were running from the army, she was carrying her son, she was holding him in her arms. A bullet hit her in the back, it came out through her stomach and went through her baby. She died there with her son in her arms. They died together.

When Doña Eugenia gave me this testimony, her sister Miriam was translating. We were at her mother's home and two other sisters were present. The family had been separated by the 1982 massacre of their village because they had fled in different directions. It was not until 1987 that they had all been reunited. Up until giving these testimonies, they had spoken very little about the massacre and even less about the specifics of surviving in the mountains. They had decided to stay together during the testimonies because they wanted to hear one another's stories of survival. Miriam had had the most contact with each of the sisters and her mother and had also initiated conversations with them about La Violencia. It was for this reason that her sisters were willing to speak to me with Miriam as their translator. As Doña Eugenia recounted the story of the señora dying together with her son in the mountains, her body began to shake. She clenched her jaw, stiffened her arms, and crossed them in front of her chest. She looked away from Miriam and stared out the window. She said,

> The same thing happened to me, except the difference is that I had my baby on my back. I felt the impact of the bullet, but I felt no pain. I touched my back and it was wet. When I looked at my hand, it was covered with blood. I kept waiting to collapse, but I didn't. I kept running, running from the soldiers shooting at us. It wasn't until hours later after we had hidden from the soldiers, I discovered my baby had taken that bullet. I am alive because my baby died on my back. I am always sad because of this. I am always remembering this sadness.

Between translating her sister's words, "I am always sad because of this" and "I am always remembering," Miriam adds her own words, "I knew the baby died in the mountains, but we didn't know how until today. That is why she is always so sad."

Doña Eugenia concludes her testimony: "What I am thinking is that it is not good what the army did because they were killing us. We are civilians,[46] we are not guerrilla—for example, my son who they killed. My son was not a guerrilla. We are nothing more than civilians and they killed us."[47]

While the army killed civilians in flight, they also forced these internal refugees to die from hunger. Empty villages were burned and their crops were destroyed by the army. Even those villagers who had dug buzones to hide and store corn and clothing had fared little better than those who had not. The buzones were most often found and destroyed by the army and/or civil patrols. Civilians in flight had little more than the clothes on their back, and whatever food they were able to carry lasted, at best, for only a few days. Civilians fled the army sometimes for days and sometimes for a week until they found a temporary safe haven where they would stay until the next army attack or until they drifted away in search of food and water. Wherever they landed, they were constantly pursued by hunger and thirst.

"We ate roots, we ate things we had never before eaten," explains Don Rafael. "We ate weeds and grass and animals. We tried everything—a little at first to see if it made us sick. If it didn't [make us sick], then we ate it. We even ate the bark off the trees. Hunger forced us to eat these things."[48] Writing of survival in Auschwitz, Primo Levi wrote: " . . . the physiological reserves of the organism were consumed in two or three months, and death by hunger, or by diseases induced by hunger, was the prisoner's normal destiny, avoidable only with additional food."[49] Indeed, in the hundreds of testimonies I have taken from massacre survivors, the power of the hunger, thirst, and illness of life in flight from army troops overwhelms even the event of the massacre because life in flight went on for years. During the years in flight an average of 30 percent of massacre survivors died from army attacks, hunger, and illnesses associated with hunger and exposure to the elements.[50] It was the desperation of hunger that drove massacre survivors to forage for edible roots, weeds, and bark in the mountains and also to search for any abandoned crops of milpa missed by the army's Scorched Earth campaign. Don Silverio recalls, "It had been more than eight days without food. We were far in the mountain, but we could see the milpa. The soldiers had left. There was a youth who was very brave, he said he was going to investigate and bring back maize for all of us. We heard the explosion. Poor youth. The army had mined the milpa. In other places where we found milpa, the soldiers had shit on our sacred milpa."[51]

"In the mountains, we were always living under the threat of the army, under the violence, all our sufferings. The people suffered greatly. There was so much hunger and rain. In these places there was so much mud and there we were sleeping in the mud—with no blankets, maybe under a piece of plastic, but when it rained everything got wet," explained Don Miguel.

Doña Claudia remembers the cold of the mountains, "I was always only wet, very wet. I slept in the same wet clothes without drying them. I slept in wet clothes in the rain. I was always crying in the mountains, crying for the massacre in my village, my house that had been burned, my animals that had been killed. We were all crying there in the mountain without food."[52]

For those who were children at the time of the massacres, the memories of life in flight are no less vivid and perhaps even more disturbing. "I remember the bombs dropping from the airplanes and helicopters full of soldiers firing machine guns and throwing grenades at us," recalls Ana. "Day after day they pursued us. We were cold and wet. Hiding in the rain, our clothes never dry. And we were hungry because they burned our milpa. I remember watching it burn. I remember the smell and the flames. My father died when the soldiers were shooting at us in the mountain. I was five years old." Ana is twenty when she gives her testimony. "I still have susto from running past all the dead in the mountains; the dogs and the hawks were eating them. I always have susto and I am always sad because I remember the milpa burning, I remember the hunger, the cold and the wet, and I always remember the dead and the pieces of the dead in the mountain, but I can't remember my father's face."[53]

Each survivor is more deeply marked, or more readily able, to talk about certain privations or sufferings in the mountains. Levi wrote that Auschwitz prisoners were scarcely able to "acquire an overall vision of their universe . . . [because] the prisoner felt overwhelmed by a massive edifice of violence and menace but could not form for himself a representation of it because his eyes were fixed to the ground by every single minute's needs."[54] For me, a professional anthropologist and witness to these testimonies of survival, it has taken nearly five years to be able to move beyond my own visceral memories of the testimonies and sufficiently assimilate the hundreds of stories in order to portray the overall experience of life in flight in the mountains without losing the voices of the survivors. And still, I know, although I give my best to this writing, I am incapable of conveying my own understanding of these deprivations and violence, much less the "real" experience of survivors. What does it mean to experience a hunger, thirst, wetness, or cold so profound and unrelenting that its memory causes one to shiver? Levi wrote, "our hunger is not the feeling of missing a meal . . . our way of being cold has need of a new word. We say 'hunger,' we say 'tiredness,' 'fear,' 'pain,' 'winter' and they are different things."[55] Still, Levi understood testimony to be "an act of war against fascism"[56]; it is in this spirit of opposition to evil that I plod forward as a witness to testimonies of survival, despite my own limitations.

"It was for the grief and torment that we were crying with hunger, with thirst. Pure thirst because there was no water. We would reach a place and there would be no water," explains Don Jacinto. "If there were rivers, there was no tranquility to carry the water. The sun would warm us, but when it was cloudy, we would tremble with cold. I would feel hunger for a while and then I wouldn't feel it because the sadness filled me. Worse still, in the morning, there would be more bombing and each day we would be fucked in another way yet again."[57]

"Thirst," wrote Levi, "does not give respite. Hunger exhausts, thirst enrages."[58] When not cold and wet from the constant rain of winter, massacre survivors in flight were hot and in search of water in the unrelenting heat of summer. Without water, there can be no life. What kind of life is there when water is so limited that one does not know from one day to the next if there will be water enough to drink? What does it mean to bring new life into the world in such dire conditions? Doña Juanita gave birth in the mountains when there was no water: "My son was born in the mountain. He was born without clothes. He was born without food. We didn't even have any water. When my son was born, I couldn't even change because I had no other clothes and I had to stay in my own filth because there was no water. We suffered greatly in the mountain."[59] Even when there was enough water for bathing, there was never any soap. In place of soap, people used ashes when they bathed.

In May 1982, the Campesino Unity Committeee (Comité de Unidad Campesina—CUC) issued a condemnation of army massacres, the slaughter of survivors in flight, and the forced concentration of Maya men into army-controlled civil patrols. CUC declared:

> Those of us who remain hidden in the mountains are suffering the worst hardship. We have no food and in some places we survive by eating roots and plants. The Army has depleted our corn reserves, which had to last us until the end of the year's crop. We are sharing the little that has not been burned, but there are too many mouths to be fed with such small quantities of food. We have no houses, we are suffering of hunger and cold weather, our children are dying of malnutrition and ill-

nesses. There are already many cases of chicken pox and influenza. With the beginning of the rainy season the situation is bound to deteriorate, especially for the children and elderly. We are afraid of widespread epidemics. All of this is caused by the Army's occupation of our towns and villages.

The CUC declaration calls for an end to U.S. military support of the "junta of generals and colonels" and asks the "people of the world" to "give their total support to our just struggle to end once and for all the repression, exploitation and discrimination that we are suffering. . . . STOP THE GENOCIDE."[60]

Less than two months later, the Reagan administration declared that Guatemala was "not a gross violator of human rights." In August 1982, the House Banking Subcommittee on International Development Institutions held a second hearing on human rights violations in Guatemala, and after survivor testimonies of violence, the subcommittee reaffirmed its objection to an $18 million International Development Bank (IDB) loan to Guatemala for telecommunications. Two months later, the Reagan Administration notified the House Banking Committee that it was changing its voting policy on Guatemala and would support nonbasic loans. Shortly thereafter, six IDB and World Bank loans (including the $18 million for telecommunications) were approved. In December 1982 the United Nations passed a resolution expressing grave concern about human rights violations in Guatemala. That same month, after meeting with General Efraín Ríos Montt, President Reagan declared that he was "inclined to believe" that the general "had been given a bum rap."[61] Within one month of this meeting and despite UN condemnation for human rights violations, The U.S. State Department approved more than $6 million in military assistance to Guatemala.[62]

Just as massacres were not the result of rogue army commanders, the hunt for Maya civilians in flight in the mountains as well as all the resulting death, privations, and sufferings were the systematic enactment of the Guatemalan army's second campaign of genocide against the Maya. The goal of this campaign, which was supported by the U.S. government, was to eliminate those Maya who survived the hundreds of army massacres. The army's third genocidal campaign was the forced concentration of Maya survivors in army-controlled work camps, which the army named "model villages," and the simultaneous and continuing hunt for civilians who organized themselves into CPRs. However, in order to understand the panorama of this third campaign, it is necessary to first briefly contextualize life in the municipalities, army captures of civilians, and civilian surrenders to the army as well as army re-education centers. Because I began this section with the Ixil village of Tzalbal, I will focus on the municipality of Nebaj.

LIFE IN NEBAJ DURING THE ARMY'S "SCORCHED EARTH" CAMPAIGN

As early as 1980, residents of Nebaj were required to identify themselves when entering, exiting, and even simply walking within Nebaj. Army soldiers and military police were everywhere. "'Who are you?' 'Where are you going?' 'What are you doing?' These were the questions they asked us each day," explains Don Leonel, a primary school teacher. "We saw this as an illness in our pueblo, the people were ill, the occupation was like an illness. I could no longer talk to my friends and we could not talk to our neighbors. There was nothing one could do other than to fall silent. We fell silent. The streets were silent with fear."

Army soldiers patrolled neighborhoods and went house to house investigating people, interrogating people about their activities, relatives, and neighbors. It became increasingly difficult for rural teachers to leave Nebaj to go to the villages in which they taught—partly because of army control at the entrances to Nebaj and throughout the town, but also because many villages no longer existed after army massacres.

In 1981 the army and military police gathered all the men in Nebaj in the central plaza. They were forced to line up to identify themselves and interrogated by the army. More than 300 of these men were pulled out of the group, tied up and forced to lay face down in the municipal salon as the soldiers called them in one by one for further interrogation, which took nearly four days. For three nights, these men lay on the floor, tied up, and without food or water. Don Leonel, recalls the fear and degradation, "Those poor men, urinating, dirtying themselves. One of the teachers gave himself up to the army, he began to accuse others to save his life. I was scared. I had been a catechist. He gave up other catechists. Somehow, I was able to walk away. Those other men were never seen again."

After the massive interrogation, there were daily disappearances as well as the discovery of mutilated bodies along the street each morning. "They were everywhere," says Don Leonel, "in the streets and hanging in the parks. The only thing that was certain was that each day there were more dead. There was tremendous confusion."

Also in 1981, as the army moved through outlying villages massacring residents, burning houses, and destroying crops, the teachers no longer left Nebaj. "All the teachers, we had to leave our villages, we had to concentrate here in Nebaj," recalls Don Leonel. "We couldn't leave. By this time, no one could leave without permission from the army. What is more, to go to Guatemala City, I had to have this permission that identified me as being with the army. If someone didn't have that permission and the bus got stopped, the army would take him off the bus and he would never be heard from again."

In 1982, the army organized the teachers into the first civil patrol. "They gave us rifles and grenades," explains Don Leonel. "They told us, 'We are going to combat the guerrilla.' We began to patrol that very night. There were four men who are my neighbors; they liked patrolling. They became the commanders. We had to respect their orders. The kidnappings began. I was only involved in four of these cases. I tried to stay at the tail end of the patrols. I didn't like what we were doing."

The teachers began to kidnap and kill under army order. Don Leonel becomes very agitated as he remembers his involvement. We are talking in the early evening in his one-room house. It is quite warm because he has closed the doors and windows. He becomes increasingly impatient with his children, who are laughing and playing just outside the door. He intermittently shushes them as he continues with his testimony. "We would arrive at midnight . . . to kill. Within two months, everyone in town was afraid of us," he recalls. "Even the children were afraid of us. They didn't know which days we would be teaching and when we did teach, they were careful never to talk about anyone. Soon, the army had every man in Nebaj patrolling. We stopped and searched everyone, children, women, whoever was out." Within months, the army had the Nebaj civil patrols participating in army operations in villages where the teachers had previously taught. "We knew the mountains, we knew all the paths. The army didn't care about us, they cared about what we knew," explains Don Leonel. "There must have been one thousand men. We went to Tzalbal. There was maize, flour, beans, tortillas, sugar, cortes, clothes, machines. It was somewhat strange. We went there to destroy everything. Some of the patrollers took these things. What wasn't taken, we destroyed. In a path of destruction, we went with the army from one village to the next. When we were alone [without the army], we didn't do anything because we felt badly, but when the army was there, we burned everything. We captured people and there was torture. This was how we had to be."[63]

ARMY CAPTURES AND CIVILIAN SURRENDERS

When the army helicopters flew over the massacre survivors in the mountains and announced that the army would give them "amnesty" if they surrendered, many gave themselves up to the army while others were captured. All of this happened while the army continued to pursue those who did not surrender and burned the fields of those who had resettled farther up in the mountains. Don Jacinto told me that the people were not caught between the army and guerrilla, "we were caught between the army and hunger." Indeed, Levi wrote, "In the space of a few weeks or months, the deprivations to which they were subjected [in Auschwitz] led them to a condition of pure survival, a daily struggle against hunger, cold, fatigue and blows in which the room for choices (especially moral choices) was reduced to zero."[64]

Doña Dominga's family decided to surrender, but in route to Nebaj, they were captured by the army. Eventually, a platoon of soldiers was moving some 500 refugees on foot. A few hours outside of Nebaj, the soldiers caught a Maya youth attempting to rig a Claymore mine along the path. In case there were other mines laid ahead, the soldiers ordered some of the civilians to walk in front of the group. Then, they tied up the Maya youth and dragged him along on the ground. As she gives her testimony, we watch her fourteen-year-old son carry cement blocks, two at a time on his back, from the center of the new Nebaj community of displaced people in which she lives to the site of her home under construction. Dominga remembers:

> They grabbed him and told him to show them where the other mines were. He said nothing. He was the only one they caught and they began to stab him. They stabbed him here in the arm and here in the head and here in the back. Wherever they wanted to, they stabbed him. I began to cry. I said, "Don't hurt him. If you want to kill him, then kill him, but not like this." They kept stabbing him over and over. Then, they nailed him to a piece of wood. They said, "Crucified! Look at this—he is shameless. It is people like him who have hurt all of you and your families." While they were doing this, they were giving us water and

bread and tortillas to eat. They said, "Perhaps you have been suffering because you haven't eaten." Then they shoved him and made him walk, bleeding and dragging the wood. It wasn't wood; it was like a small tree trunk. They would push him and poke him with their knives. I cried. I didn't want to see anyone like this. I cried for the man. "Why don't you untie him?" I was fifteen, I didn't understand. I cried, "What is it that you will do with me? Let him go. Maybe he did something bad. Maybe he didn't mean to do it." My father shouted at me to be quiet, "Callanse!" When we got to town, they crucified him again. They said, "He is the one who has done all this harm to you."

"It was not about the army or the URNG," explains Don Jacinto. "We didn't even talk about the guerrilla anymore. It was because of the food, the clothes; my wife had no clothes. We were hungry and in rags, then we caught malaria. I was half-captured and half-surrendered."[65] Don Jacinto spent several days in a small army encampment in Sancaba. While there, he was given sugar cane to eat. "That was all we had. We peeled sugar cane and ate it. Peeled it and ate," says Don Jacinto. "The soldiers said, 'Wait until you get to Xemamatze, there you will have food, clothes, a petate to sleep on. They will give you bread, rice, chicken. You will have everything because the government gives you what you need and the army gives you what you need.'"[66]

ARMY RE-EDUCATION CAMPS AND HUMANITARIAN AID

Whether captured by the army or surrendering, the starving massacre survivors, after months or years in flight from the army, were taken to a re-education camp. Most spent three months in Xemamatze, Las Violetas, or some other army-controlled location designated by the military. Just as many survivors in flight had reluctantly surrendered and accepted camp conditions in exchange for food, humanitarian aid organizations were also presented with a dilemma. On the one hand, there was no doubt that the Maya within these army camps were in desperate need of food, clothing, medical attention, and other such assistance; on the other, humanitarian aid to these camps inevitably supported this next phase of army destruction of the Maya and lent credibility to army claims of "development" when, in fact, the re-education camps, like the model villages to which they were a transition, had more in common with Nazi concentration camps (and the denial of their existence) than with late-twentieth-century

liberal development schemes for the poor.[67] Ideological, cultural, and political re-education was a cornerstone of the counterinsurgency campaign
that followed the campaings of army massacres and the hunt for survivors
in the mountains. Army re-education of Maya massacre survivors sought
"to turn Indian allegiances around on the most basic and traumatic truth
of all: that it was the army who massacred their families and destroyed
their villages in the first place. . . . [T]he army's entire strategy hinges on
its ability to deny or reverse the truth."[68]

   "Food for Work" was as integral to the army's transitional re-
education camps as it was to its model villages in its Poles of Development program. But, where did the Guatemalan army get support for its
"Food for Work" program? Though the U.S. Agency for International
Development (AID) claimed complete dissociation from the army's security operations (which were veiled in development language) in fact AID
provided several million dollars to the army's rural security. In 1986,
Sergeant Julio Corsantes, commander at the Saraxoch model village, said,
"Everything here came from AID: the new housing, the tin roofs . . .
down to the last nail." Corvantes continued, "No work projects, no food.
A great way to do things. Like it is written in the Bible, he who doesn't
work, doesn't eat. That's the philosophy of the World Food Program
(WFP)."[69] With or without UN approval, the UN WFP had relinquished
food distribution to the Guatemalan army and by the end of 1984, more
than 500,000 Maya massacre survivors were completing forced labor projects under army threat in exchange for WFP rations.[70]

   During the Guatemalan army's successive campaigns of genocide
against the Maya, international aid continued to flow into Guatemala.
Whether by design or through willful ignorance, U.S. AID, U.S. Food
for Peace, UN WFP, private voluntary organizations (now called
NGOs—nongovernmental organizations), and the countries of Israel and
Taiwan provided financial, technical, and material support to the
Guatemalan army. While new funds to Guatemala were blocked by the
Carter administration's human rights policy, previously authorized U.S.
monies continued to flow freely from the U.S. government to AID and
Food for Peace and then on to NGOs, who could provide humanitarian
assistance to only the locations and programs designated by the army-
controlled National Reconstruction Committee (CRN—Comité de Re-
construccion Nacional). Supplies for the Food for Work programs were
distributed by the World Food Program, Catholic Relief Services, and
CARE, among others. Indeed, Human Rights Watch concluded that in-

ternational food aid had become nothing more than "another instrument of army control."[71]

In 1982, a second wave of NGOs with fundamentalist and right-wing ideological practices burst onto the scene, openly supporting the army's "re-education" of the Maya. Ríos Montt was particularly attractive to the U.S. fundamentalist movement because he was evangelical and a member of Church of the Word (a branch of the very small California-based Gospel Outreach).[72] This fusion of evangelical fundamentalism with army authoritarianism led to a proliferation of Church of the Word and other evangelical churches throughout Guatemala. This, in turn, fueled the rapid development of Guatemala-based evangelical NGOs with ties to U.S. evangelical churches and the U.S. military. The Christian Broadcasting Network (CBN) and the Air Commandos (an organization of former and current members of U.S. Special Forces) raised monies for fundamentalist organizations in Guatemala that had continued to operate throughout the country with no incident even at the height of the violence because of their strong army ties. Guatemalan NGOs central to the army's counterinsurgency campaign include FUNDAPI (Foundation to Help the Indigenous People), the Carroll Behrhorst Foundation, and PAVVA (Program to Help the Residents of the Altiplano), among others.[73]

In Xemamatze, CEAR distributed food, clothing, and soap to the detainees, who were under constant army surveillance and compulsory participation in the daily two-hour re-education meetings. Despite the hardships within Xemamatze, Don Jacinto, like other detainees who had been captured by the army, worried that his wife and children were starving in the mountains. He went to the comandante and asked for permission to leave to go find his family to bring them back to Xemamatze. The comandante said, "Oh, you are sad without your wife. Go find one over there, we have so many widows here. Which one do you like? Do you want a younger one?" Don Jacinto told the comandate that he wanted his own wife and his daughters. To this the comandante responded, "Look, there are widows with two daughters, you can have them, take them." But Don Jacinto did not want a widow and he did not want the girls offered to him by the comandante. Still hoping to persuade the commander, he told him that he could not take the girls because he had been married by the Catholic Church. To this, the commander said, "Don't worry. If you want those girls, take them. If you have to be married, we will obligate the authorities to marry you here. Besides, your wife probably went off with some guerrilla. So take another wife. If you are afraid to talk to them, then I will call the civil patrol commander and he will take care of it. So, look, which ones do you like? Pick whoever you want." Don Jacinto was deeply offended by the commander's suggestion that he take another widow and even more so that he take the daughters of a widow. As he told me this story, he said, "I have always respected my wife and my daughters. I wanted to bring them down to save their lives. I didn't want to have relations with some poor girls. That commander was inviting me to rape someone's daughters. I worried even more for my wife and children."

When Doña Alba reached Nebaj, she too was taken to Xemamatze. After several years of eating herbs and roots, she was grateful to once again have tortillas to eat. She was given an old jacket and a petate to sleep on. "They gave us a little food for the work we had to do," she explains. "But I was always eating with fear because the soldiers were always killing people and I worried that they would never let us leave or that they were giving us food to trick us and then they would kill us. They killed ten men. They captured them and they were tied up at the neck and very swollen."[74]

In the Las Violetas re-education camp, male detainees were organized into civil patrols, and the camp itself became an urban model village. As in all army camps, re-education camps, and model villages, a large hole was dug in the earth about two meters in diameter and three meters deep. Those who did not readily embrace the army or civil patrols or who were rumored to question authority were placed in the hole as punishment. Doña Piedad's husband was placed in this hole because he wanted to work instead of patrol because his family had no food. "He was there overnight, it was terrible," she remembers. "He was filthy when they let him out because they threw garbage on him, urinated into the hole, and defecated as well."[75]

While Xemamatze no longer exists, Las Violetas is now a neighborhood on the outskirts of Nebaj. Though the model villages no longer exist in a technical or official sense, many of the structures continue. During the period of re-education, in addition to the civil patrols, the army also organized a local committee for the governance of Las Violetas. It was the committee that would decide who was to be placed in the hole of punishment at the center of the community and for how long those being punished would be held. While many local villages now elect their committees and vice-mayors, the same committee appointed by the army in 1982 still runs Las Violetas in 2002. Though the punishment hole was filled with earth in 1987 and the local committee denies it ever existed, committee members continue to reap the benefits of local power because they receive and distribute whatever aid is received in Las Violetas. Thus, committee members and their supporters have the nicest houses, running water, and other amenities, while the widows to whom the aid is directed rarely receive any assistance and do not have running water. Moreover, residents of Las Violetas continue to live in fear of the committee members, who claim continued army support. Doña Alba recalls, "Once we had a community meeting, one man said we should elect a new committee, others said no because they did not have the courage to reject the committee. They are afraid of the committee, so nothing has changed. I appreciate that you have come to ask us questions. *Tantix* (thank you)."[76]

FORCED CONCENTRATION OF MASSACRE SURVIVORS INTO ARMY-CONTROLLED MODEL VILLAGES

The re-education camps were the prelude to the third army campaign of genocide, which was the forced concentration of Maya massacre survivors into army-controlled camps, which the army called "model villages." In *Survival in Auschwitz,* Primo Levi writes of his arrival to the concentration camp: " . . . we saw a large door, and above it a sign, brightly illuminated (its memory still strikes me in my dreams): Work Gives Freedom."[77] In keeping with the Nazi fantasy of work and freedom in concentration camps, the Guatemalan army named roads within its model villages "Avenue of Development," "Avenue of Security,"[78] "National Army Avenue," "Road of the Fallen,"[79] and signposts at the entries had slogans such as: "Guatemala is peace and development,"[80] "Welcome to Saraxoch, a totally ideologically new community," "Anti-Subversive Village. Ideologically New,"[81] and "Only he who fights has the right to win. Only he who wins has the right to live."[82] Compulsory participation in re-education gatherings continued. In November of 1983, a K'iche' peasant described an army gathering:

> The army got everybody in the community together and said: "There are just two things: one is human rights and the other is Guatemala. If you're going to defend Guatemala, then that means you're from here; that means you're Guatemalans. And if you're going to defend human rights, that means you're a foreigner because that belongs to gringos and other people from out there. But we don't have to take both roads."

What all this means [to us] is that you don't talk about human rights. Because human rights belongs to "other people" from another world. . . . What the army does with these expressions is confuse people. Even though people know what human rights means—and what Guatemala means. Because in truth these are not two separate things. Those rights belong to you from the time you are little.[83]

In September of 1982, *New York Times* reporter Marlise Simons reported that Ríos Montt was carrying out a "methodical counterinsurgency program" begun when Ríos Montt imposed a state of siege in July and that included military operations of 25,000 army soldiers "aided by some 25,000 members of a newly created Civil Defense Force." Further, she wrote that the "government's new strategy . . . includes herding thousands of Indian villagers into army-controlled zones." Simon visited displaced survivors of the army massacre of Las Pacayas village, and she wrote: "Since the massacre, the army has returned 150 villagers to Las Pacayas, where they now live in rows of military tents and improvised huts. In the presence of an army captain, the Indian men repeated the official version that the 'subversives' had attacked them." Outside the surveillance of the army, several sources confirmed the massacre was committed by the army.[84]

COMMUNITIES OF POPULATIONS IN RESISTANCE

Despite ongoing army attacks and captures as well as surrender resulting from the dire conditions of survival in the mountains, thousands of Maya remained in the mountains struggling to establish some semblance of daily life. Constantly on the move, fleeing army attacks, Ixil massacre survivors sought refuge in the mountains northwest of Chajul, while in other regions CPRs were established in northern Ixcán and in the Petén. In each area, the people eventually organized themselves into the CPRs. At a structural level, to maximize safety, they organized themselves into groups of twenty-five to thirty families. Each of these groups elected delegates to represent them at regional and general assemblies of the CPR. Following the massacres in 1981 to 1982, the Guatemalan army labeled any village outside the army's model village structure and control as an "illegal village."

The army relentlessly attacked these "illegal villages" using the same counterinsurgency techniques of the 1981–82 Scorched Earth campaign: occupying villages, killing any civilians in the community, burning huts, destroying crops. And, like earlier massacres, they continued to hunt for survivors in the mountains, firing machine guns, throwing grenades, and dropping bombs. These attacks against civilians continued into the 1990s.

After the massacres, tens of thousands of survivors lived in the CPRs under army attack. They lived in near-constant movement, sometimes able to stay in a temporary village for a few months, sometimes just a few days. In groups of twenty to thirty families they traveled through the mountains always in search of safer ground. Tzalbal, Salquil Grande, Bicalama, Sumal Grande, Bicalvitz, Sacsiban, Ixtupil, Amachel, La Perla, Bachaalte, Cabá, Santa Clara, Chibatul, Chamuc, and Parramos were among the communities in which they sought temporary refuge—each the site of a village that had previously been destroyed by the army in the Scorched Earth campaign.

Don Samuel is a small, soft-spoken, and unassuming man of forty-two. He wears thick plastic glasses in a large, clear pink frame—a likely donation from a church in a local health campaign. He tells me he is happy to be able to read again. He has been helping his neighbors make lists of their financial losses during the violence: cattle, horses, chickens, turkeys, tools, houses; and the number of dead and disappeared in each family. His house in Salquil was burned in 1981. His first site of refuge was in Bachaalte with his family. "We were hidden there for almost a year," he explains. "But after the civil patrols were formed, we had to escape. We fled when they came to destroy the village." Each CPR testimony involves numerous moments of flight, survival, and reconstruction followed by an army attack setting off another round of flight, survival, and reconstruction. Don Samuel's experience is representative of the many testimonies survivors shared with me.

After fleeing Bachaalte, he recounts:

We were about sixty families. So there were many of us. We had to find a way to protect ourselves. We organized a community structure with responsables and different people responsible for being lookouts and we would dig hiding places in the earth. This was how we were able to reach Santa Clara. Still, with so many people, the army was able to find some of us even though we were all hiding. They would kill anyone they found: elderly, youth, children. They would kill whoever was there simply because they were there. Each time the army would catch up with us, some of us were unable to escape. The army would catch them and kill them.

We spent a year in Santa Clara and then nearly a year in Cabá. When we fled to Cabá, twenty families went with me and twenty stayed hidden. The army caught the ones who were hiding and killed all twenty families. This is what happened. That was in 1983. But by 1984, it was a little bit calmer. I was able to plant sugar cane and bananas in Amachel. I was displaced there. There wasn't any maize, but I was able to work the land and plant a little for my children. But then in December of 1984 the army arrived and again they cut down all my maize, cane, and bananas and again we were left with nothing. We had no harvest, no maize. We had to go looking for another place to live. These were very hard times. There was no salt, no maize. We had to eat weeds, just weeds, because there was nowhere to get any maize because everything had been destroyed by the army. But then in 1985 and 1986, things were a bit more calm and we were able to plant and harvest bananas and sugar cane. We felt a little calm then.

But then again in 1987, the army came back and it was the Scorched Earth all over again. This time they occupied Amaachel. They stayed in the village. We weren't able to work and we had to find another place. I took my family to a place called La Laguna. But every four or five days, the army would come to persecute us. We would flee and then return. We heard about how they captured eighty families in San Marcos. But those eighty families aren't alive today because they were killed by the army. We stayed in La Laguna until 1988. We had been there for a little more than a year when we had to flee the army again. I had planted some crops, but the army destroyed them. We returned to Cabá. By this time, we were some eighty families in Cabá and the army was after all of us. We had to flee and go around the entire mountain with the army behind us. We went to Amaachel. I was able to plant there. I planted four cuerdas of sugar cane, sixty cuerdas of maize, and seven cuerdas of bananas. But in 1989, the army cut all of this down and they pulled it out of the ground. We fled to Santa Clara because there was a little freedom there. In Cabá, the army was occupying the community again. We were able to reach Santa Clara but after only twenty days, the army was upon us again. This is the way it was. We were always moving from one place to the other, looking for a place without the army. The army continued to persecute us until 1990, when we became known to the public. The army lessened their offensives against us, but they still didn't stop. Beginning in 1980 until 1990, we suffered so much in the midst of all of this. All of this movement, displacing. Look what it did to us. Many people died from hunger, many died from the cold. There were women who gave birth in the mountain without food. This is what we lived. This is what we saw.[85]

At the end of 1990, the CPR issued a public declaration announcing the existence of communities that had been resisting army capture and control for more than eight years.[86] One year later, just moments after arriving at the CPR in the Ixil region in October of 1991, Christian Tomuschat witnessed an army air attack on the civilian community. Sent to Guatemala as a UN expert to investigate human rights violations, Tomuschat was the first official observer to reach the CPRs. When he presented his findings to the UN Human Rights Commission in Geneva in February of 1992, he condemned the Guatemalan army, government, and other security forces for their deliberate and continuous violation of the political, civil, cultural, social, economic, and human rights of Guatemalans.[87] In 1992, some 30,000 Maya massacre survivors were still living in the CPRs under army attacks. Though the army continued to harass and attack CPRs, Tomuschat was witness to the last army bombing in the Ixil area.

As Lucas, one CPR member told me, "They bombed us until Señor Tomuschat came to see us. He saw them bomb us. He made them stop." Lucas also told me, "El Tomuschat probably didn't know how many people were really there in the CPR. I wanted to meet him. I wanted to shake his hand. But I couldn't. A lot of us couldn't. We hid behind the trees and watched him talk to other companeros."

I asked Lucas if they were frightened, "Is that why you hid behind the trees?" "No," he responded. "We were ashamed. Our clothes were in tatters. We were practically naked. We were too embarrassed to meet such an important man when we weren't even decently covered. It is not just that we didn't have shoes. We were indecent. The rags we wore didn't even provide the most minimal coverage. It is the truth, Victoria, we were living naked in those mountains. We aren't animals. We felt ashamed to not be decent."[88]

GENOCIDE, TERROR, AND THE SACRED MILPA

In his theorizing on cultures of terror, Michael Taussig wrote that the cultural elaboration of fear was integral to controlling massive populations.[89] The loss and destruction of milpa is present in every testimony not simply because it is the principle food source of the Maya, but because maize is sacred. Nobel Prize–winning Guatemalan writer Miguel Angel Asturias wrote: "The maize impoverishes the earth and makes no one rich. Neither the boss nor the men. Sown to be eaten it is the sacred sustenance of the men who were made of maize. Sown to make money it means famine for the men who were made of maize."[90] The Maya are the "Men of Maize" and Maya origin stories begin with the birth of the Maya through maize.[91] Thus, Guatemalan army destruction of maize was a recurring ritual destruction of the Maya both physically and spiritually. This ritual destruction has new meaning under genocide law following the decisions of International Criminal Tribunal for the former Yugoslavia (ICTY) in its Rule 61 decision, which identified three new (and more expansive) categories for consideration in the interpretation of the intent requirement for genocide: "(1) the general political doctrine of the aggressor; (2) the repetition of discriminatory and destructive acts; and (3) the perpetration of acts which violate or are perceived by the aggressor as violating the foundations of the group, whether or not they constitute the enumerated acts prohibited in the genocide definition, and so long as they are part of the same pattern of conduct."[92]

As former CEH legal advisor Jan Perlin points out in her insightful work, the third category allows for the consideration of violations historically considered to be "cultural genocide," violations previously excluded from legal consideration under the definition of genocide that was limited under the genocide convention to "the construct of physical or mental destruction."[93] Thus, in the CEH's analysis, acts of cultural destruction were considered to be "signposts of the subjective intent of the attackers when they were committed together with the acts of physical destruction specifically proscribed in the Genocide Convention." In the ICTY's broadened categories of intent, "the bombing of sacred Maya lands used for religious worship . . . , the burning of huipiles . . . , the prohibition of ritual burial of the dead," and the destruction of other ritual icons "were indicative of an intent to destroy the group, as such." Perlin specifically notes that the "religious and cultural significance that the Maya attribute to the cultivation of the land, and particularly of maize" was central to the CEH's conclusion that the army committed acts of genocide.[94]

For massacre survivors, the sacred milpa not only was prominent in testimonies of community loss and destruction but was also a potent symbol of community regeneration. The endurance and reinvention of ritual belief systems is an indication of their ongoing social and cultural significance. In the case of the Maya survivors, this significance is found not only in what was lost to the violence but also in what was reconstructed in its aftermath. Just as the destruction and desecration of the milpa became a metaphor for army violation of the integrity of Maya communities, the resurrection of the milpa is a living metaphor of community rebirth.

Don Justicio, an Ixil community leader, recounted the suffering and rebirth of his community through a story of the milpa:

> In the time of the violence, a moment arrived in which the sacred milpa, which gives us life, disappeared. From so much destruction of its very roots, it disappeared. Because the maize disappeared, there was a time in which the people had to live without maize. This was a time when many people died, many children died, because the sacred maize had been exterminated. But there was an elderly man who had a buzón and even though he had to displace himself many times fleeing the army, his buzón remained untouched. The sacred maize in his buzón was untouched. A moment arrived when he was able to return to his buzón to see what was there, to see if anything remained. He found a little bit of maize. And though he was hungry, he didn't eat this little bit of maize. No, he carried it back to the communities and handful by handful, he gave it to his friends, neighbors, and compañeros. Everyone had just a little because there wasn't very much. This was how we once again began to cultivate the sacred maize. After it was planted, we had our first harvest and once again we were able to make tortillas. After so many deaths, so much sadness, we were still able to cultivate our sacred maize.[95]

Photo 1. Site of clandestine cemetery under excavation in Acul graveyard in December 1997. (Photo by Victoria Sanford.)

Photo 2. Widows, orphans, and other relatives of victims of 1978 army massacre gathered at clandestine cemetery in Panzós 1997. (Photo by Victoria Sanford.)

Photo 3. Exhumation of clandestine cemetery in Panzós in September 1997. (Photo by Victoria Sanford.)

Photo 4. Antemortem interview with widow of massacre. (Photo by Victoria Sanford.)

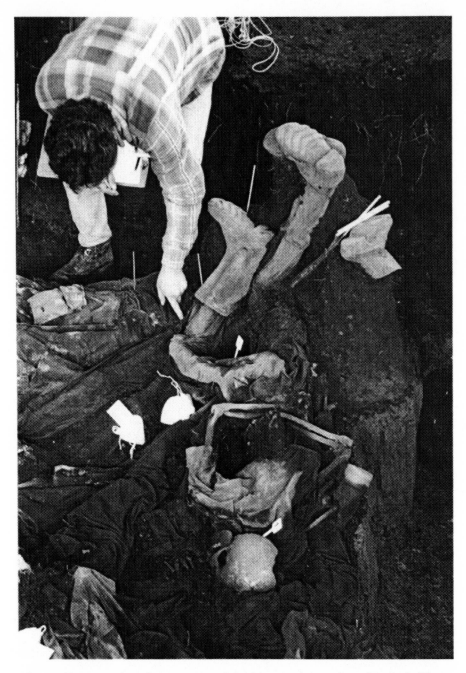

Photo 5. Forensic anthropologist examines skeletal remains being exhumed in Acul. (Photo by Victoria Sanford.)

Photo 6. Widows of victims of La Violencia in San Andrés Sajcabaja help sift dirt from graves and sort through artifacts. (Photo by Victoria Sanford.)

Photo 7. A man places candles next to the remains of his brother. (Photo by Victoria Sanford.)

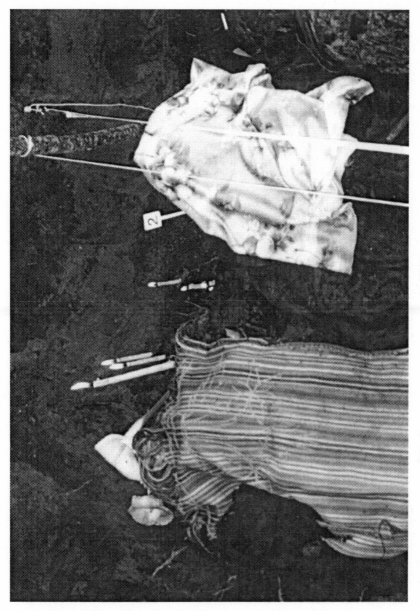

Photo 8. As remains are uncovered and identified in Acul, widows cover them with their shawls and offer candles, flowers, and prayers to the deceased. (Photo by Victoria Sanford.)

Photo 9. K'iche' priestesses perform a religious ceremony for the deceased in the plaza of San Andrés Sajcabajá while we carry out the exhumation inside the church. (Photo by Victoria Sanford.)

Photo 10. Reburial procession in Panzós in May 1998 on the twentieth anniversary of the massacre. (Photo by Victoria Sanford.)

Photo 11. Q'eqchi' Reina Indígena *(indigenous beauty queen) participating in the reburial procession. Q'eqchi' reinas indígenas have a long history of political participation in the region. (Photo by Victoria Sanford.)*

Photo 12. "Peace is constructed with democracy and justice. United we participate to build peace. CONAVIGUA."
The national Maya widows organization gathers in Nebaj on the day of the guerrilla reinsertion, March 1997. (Photo
by Victoria Sanford.)

Photo 13. Achi in Plan de Sánchez prepare sacred maize for the feast to be held the following day commemorating the victims of the Plan de Sánchez massacre. (Photo by Victoria Sanford.)

Photo 14. Local Achi gather in the Plan de Sánchez chapel built at the site of the massacre, where the remains of victims were reburied following the exhumation. The construction of this chapel is in keeping with the traditional Maya Death House. (Photo by Victoria Sanford.)

Photo 15. A Maya priest performs a religious ceremony on the anniversary of the Plan de Sánchez massacre. (Photo by Victoria Sanford.)

Photo 16. Author with friends from a widows' organization in San Andrés Sajcabajá. (Photo by Daniel Rothenberg, used with kind permission.)

Seven

FROM SURVIVOR TESTIMONIES TO THE DISCOURSE OF POWER

The army wants the people to give them information that is untrue. The only thing that matters is that the people will say whatever the army wants them to say.

—*Mateo*

INTRODUCTION

Discourse plays a significant role in the development and institutionalization of racist ideologies and in the consequent social reconstruction of power relations leading to genocide.[1] While Holocaust survivor testimonies and Latin American testimonial literature have challenged the traditional limits of oral history, the exploration of the role of survivor discourses in the reconstitution of power relations is a relatively new site of exploration.[2] After any genocide, there are always a number of different versions and sources of the story: news stories, analyses by academics representing a variety of disciplines, reports of human rights organizations, state documents, survivor testimonies and the imagination of novelists—to name but a few. Not surprisingly, opinions and experiences of the same event can greatly differ from source to source. This raises important questions about how to evaluate and weight the different voices. How does one decide which account has authority? What is at stake for all the different speakers?

The history of the debate over La Violencia is a particularly instructive example. Since the publication of *I, Rigoberta Menchú*, controversy has raged over what happened, who constitutes a believable witness, and who has authority to speak about and interpret events. In this chapter, I explore the intersection of structural relations of power with personal experiences of survival by contrasting official discourses designed to silence dissent with the truth-telling discourses of survivors. I suggest that truth-telling has power beyond the "facts" of the events.

In *Fearless Speech,* Michel Foucault traced a genealogy of truth (as a societal concept) back to the writings of Euripides and in practice in ancient Athenian democracy. He argued that truth, rather than defined by a Cartesian system of evidence, is grounded in the risk one will take to speak truth to power out of a sense of duty. Within this schema, the requisite characteristics of truth are: courage in the face of danger, a duty to speak, risk in speaking, being spoken to power, and a social or moral status from which to speak the truth.[3] In this way truth goes far beyond breaking official silence, because underlying the duty to speak the truth is the belief that there is a corrective quality to truth when it is spoken to power. Survivors who give testimony are speaking truth to power—whether the power of the army, guerrillas, local and national governments, or international community.

This act of speaking truth to power develops a dialogical relationship between truth telling and official discourses. Thus, I begin with five abbreviated life histories that offer a personal memory of surviving structural violence. The omnipresent militarization of daily life in each of the life histories is not unique, rather it is representative of the many testimonies I have taken in my field work.[4] After these personal accounts, I then draw on anthropologist Charles Hale and Guatemalan novelist Arturo Arias[5] as I introduce the work of David Stoll, sociologist Yvon Le Bot, Hector Gramajo, and Father Ricardo Falla, along with several declassified United States State Department and CIA documents, in tandem with subaltern theorist Ranajit Guha's discourse analysis.[6] This method of presentation allows the reader to consider the different conclusions that can be drawn about the causes of La Violencia, depending upon which voices are privileged. Further, it points to the urgency to include the voices of survivors in analyses of violence not simply as descriptive contextualization but as lived experiences that provide interpretation and give meaning to the very structures of violence.

Moreover, it is the voices of survivors that rupture the often polemical debates about La Violencia.

THE LIFE HISTORIES

Gaspar

> Tz'utijil who grew up on fincas and in the streets of Guatemala City. Became a Kaibil after being recruited into the Guatemalan army.[7]

My mother gave me to a finca owner when I was six. I cut coffee for several months until I could escape. I went back to my mother because when one is little, you always look for the warmth of a mother's love. I never had that. My stepfather would get home drunk and beat my mother, my little sister, and me. He was very strong. He would knock me across the room and tell us that we were garbage because we were Indians, but my mother never wanted to leave him. Instead, she would give us away to another finca.

Once I asked a finca owner for shoes. She told me that my mother told her I didn't like shoes. She threatened me a lot and beat me. They put my food on the floor inside the house where the dogs ate. I wasn't allowed to sit at the table.

I tried to kill myself because I felt that life wasn't good enough, it just wasn't worth it for me. There was a place, a lagoon of water contaminated by the plane that fumigated the cotton. I decided to bathe myself in the lagoon to see if I could die. But I wasn't lucky. Ever since then, I have thought it was bad luck and bad luck follows me. All I got was a rash.

Then, my sister and I went to live with my half-sister in Guatemala City. She told us we were Indians. She was very prejudiced because her last name was Juarez Santos. I have scars on my head from her beating me with burning sticks. She was trying to rid herself of rage. She beat us a lot. Sometimes, she would leave us tied up all day. Sometimes, she wouldn't let us in the house to sleep at night. She left us on the streets. I lived with her for three years and I tried to kill myself. I drank a toxic liquid but didn't get any results. I ran away from her.

I lived in the streets of Guatemala City and ate what I could find. I survived digging through garbage, begging, and stealing. I tried glue and paint thinner, but I didn't like it because it made me vomit. It is because of the way people look at you when you live on the streets. They never know the real feelings we have. Even living on the streets, I still felt I could be someone someday. But the people look at you and say you're lost, worthless, the scum of society. It was out of desperation that my friend Carlos put a rope around his neck. Afterward, I tried the same thing but had no luck.

Then, I went back to Mazatenango and got a job collecting garbage. I gave the money I earned to my mother to help her, but she gave it to my stepfather and he beat us. I collected garbage in the day and went to school at night. I wanted to learn and improve myself. But in the class, they laughed at me. They said I came from garbage, that garbage made me. People stopped calling me Gaspar. At school and in my neighborhood, they called me garbage man. Even the teacher called me garbage man.

When I would say my name, they would laugh at me because my surname is indigenous. I even changed my name for a while. But it made no difference, I was Indian because of my features and because that is who I am, whether or not I want to be. This created great conflict in me and I began to see a division between what is ladino and what is indigenous. I was humiliated so much that I began to hate ladinos. The hatred was so strong that I wanted a weapon. I wanted to kill my half-sister.

The army was always recruiting in the park, at the cinema, and anywhere else where young men congregated. I always got away. I was good at slipping away because I had lived on the streets. I saw that the world was made up of abusers and abused and I didn't want to be abused anymore. So, one day when I was sixteen, I let the army catch me. But they didn't really catch me, because I decided I wanted to be a soldier. I didn't want to be abused anymore.

I wanted a chance to get ahead. I saw what the soldiers did. I knew they killed people. But I wanted to see if in reality it could really be an option for me. If there would be an opportunity to get ahead, to learn to read and write. I always thought that it would be very beautiful to learn to read and write. I was always looking for a way to get ahead, to improve myself, but sometimes the doors just close and there is nowhere else to go. The army says we will learn to read and write, but when you go into the army, they teach you very little. They give you a weapon and they teach you to kill. They give you shoes because you don't have any. Many times, you join the army for a pair of shoes. When they grab you to recruit you, they say, "You don't have any shoes."

In the army, I was full of hate. I used the weapons with the hatred I had carried inside of me for a long time. Even though the hatred can be strong, you are still a human being with the spirit of your ancestors, with the spirit of peace and respect. So, inside you have great conflict. It was very difficult for me to find an internal emotional stability.

When I was recruited, there were a lot of indigenas recruited. They were beaten hard and called "stupid Indians" for not knowing how to speak Spanish. The soldiers who beat them were indigenous. The problem in the army is that no one trusts anyone else, even though most of the soldiers are indigenous.

After I was recruited, they told me that I could be a Kaibil because I was tall, fast, and smart. But I wasn't so smart. They took us to the mountains. Each of us had to carry a live dog that was tied up over our shoulders. I was thirsty. There was no water. Well, we had no water and we were given no water. But our trainer had water. He walked ahead of us on the path spilling water to remind us of our thirst. I was innocent. When we were ordered to pick up the stray dogs on the street, I thought we were going to learn how to train them, that we would have guard dogs. But when we arrived to the camp, we were ordered to kill them with our bare hands. We had to kill some chickens, too. We were ordered to butcher the chickens and dogs and put their meat and blood in a big bowl. Then, we had to eat and drink this dog and chicken meat that was in a bath of blood. Whoever vomited had to vomit into the shared bowl and get back in line to eat and drink more. We had to eat it all, including the vomit, until no one vomited.

The army kills part of your identity. They want to break you and make you a new man. A savage man. They inspired me to kill. There was a ladino recruit who said that Indians were worthless and that we didn't go to school because we didn't want to. I pushed him off a cliff. I would have enjoyed it if he had died. This is how the army creates monsters.

You become very hard in the mountains and sometimes the only thing you feel is fear. You are afraid of any man, or every man. After my first battle with the guerrilla, I decided to escape, because I wanted to improve myself and found no way to do it in the army.

Mateo

Mam Massacre survivor from Pueblo Nuevo, Ixcán. Forcibly recruited into the Guatemalan army at age fifteen.

Most of the recruits were indigenous, but there were also some ladino students. There were five instructors and they were in charge. They would hit us. Everyday they punished us. The punishment is very harsh. Sometimes they would hang us tied up very tightly to the bed. They would leave us like that for fifteen minutes. Then we would do fifty push-ups. Then, we would have to go outside and lay on the ground. We had to roll to the other side and back until we vomited. Then they would line us up and go down punching us in the stomach and knocking the air out of us. But by then it didn't hurt so much because we didn't have any food left in our stomachs.

I never said that it hurt because if you said it hurt they would hit you more. Our training was called the Tiger Course. They explained to us, "You have to complete this course to become a real man." They would say, "You have to know a lot. You can become an important officer. You can order other people. But now you have to suffer three months. If you don't obey the rules here, you can die."

There were indigenous recruits who didn't know anything. They didn't know any Spanish; they only spoke their language. The majority of recruits were indigenous. Those who didn't know Spanish had to learn. There were some who only liked to speak their language. They were separated from each other. You could be beaten for not speaking Spanish. Sometimes you got beaten just for looking at someone or something.

There were three recruits who deserted. They were caught on the border because all their hair was shaved off. They were put into an underground jail [a pit]. Each day, water and garbage was thrown on them. They weren't given anything to eat. They were in there for almost a month. They were brought into our classroom all tied up as an example of what happened when you desert. They were kept in that cell for three more months. Then they had to start training all over again.

We were taught to use weapons and practiced with live munitions. Some of the recruits died in training from bullets and others died from bombs. In the third month, they taught us how to beat campesinos and how to capture them. We practiced on each other. They gave us our machine guns. They said, "It is better than a girlfriend. The machine gun is a jewel." The truth is that it is a pure jewel.

One day, they asked us if we liked our meal. They told us we had eaten dog. I never thought that it was dog. Some people had stomachaches and others vomited. They fed us dog so that we wouldn't be afraid because it would have been impossible for us to withstand everything. I changed a lot after eating the dog. I wasn't afraid anymore. I just hated. I hated my compañeros. After three months, I was a very different person. I felt like a soldier.

After a year in the army, I went to my grandfather's village to visit. They looked at me differently. My form of speaking was different and my mannerisms had changed. The next day, I decided to go work with my grandfather. He said, "No, you have to stay here. How are you going to work? You are not one of us anymore."

In the afternoon, I met some friends. There are a lot of bars in the village. I had to go to a bar. I was overwhelmed with sadness. It is the only way the people in Guatemala can rid themselves of sadness. There you don't talk or discuss your problems. The only way is to go to the cantina and drink. I got really drunk and had to be carried to the house.

My grandfather said, "He had reason to drink, but he can't drink well." They all looked at me, but they couldn't hit me because I am a soldier. My grandfather said, "He has his reasons. Let him drink." So, they let me do whatever I wanted. And if I had hit them, they would have had to put up with it. I went to the cantina and drank with the soldiers.

When I was little, I remember the soldiers having good food. They had everything. They arrived in helicopters and airplanes and they had everything. I thought the army was good, that it was there to protect the people. My grandparents thought the same thing. But, a child is afraid of the soldiers because they have a weapon and a uniform and a very hard face. They don't look respectable. They can kick you whenever they want to. The army was very dangerous. You couldn't look a soldier in the eye. If you were watching a soldier, he would come over and say, "What are you looking at?" They would kick the children. A soldier could kill you. He could do it. They did it to some children.

Sometimes in Pueblo Nuevo on a Saturday or Sunday, the people were very frightened. They were very humble and didn't do anything. They never looked at the soldiers because if they did, the soldiers would grab them and take them to the base. I would go and hide behind an adult.

After the massacre in Pueblo Nuevo, we lived in the mountain. The army began to burn our homes and our people. They began to burn our animals. I cried because I saw our house burning. They destroyed all our crops. The corn, the beans, everything. They fired bullets. They threw grenades at my father's house. We were left with nothing. We returned to the jungle walking in a stream so we would leave no tracks for them to follow. The army killed my father in an ambush. He had gone to look for medicine because there were many sick people in our community. After the ambush, we all fled in different directions. It was two weeks before we could go back to look for my father.

I was very scared. I was nervous because I didn't know what it would be like to see my father dead. I was afraid from the moment we left. I felt like something bad was going to happen. The people were behind me, but I felt like I was being stalked. But I didn't say anything. I didn't say anything to my stepmother because she was nervous, too. When we arrived, I said, "This is my father's body."

He was in pieces and it made me very scared because I could see bits of his clothing and the things he had with him. Everything was in a path of blood. We didn't see his whole body. He was a puddle of blood. If his body had been more whole, I would have embraced my father. But all I could do was pick up the bones.

We had never seen anything like this. The people were watching to see if the army would come. So, we had to do everything in a hurry. There were frightening spirits there. There were haunted spirits there. Who knows if the spirit was devilish? I don't know. There was such fear there. There were flies and crows. There were hawks. They had been eating him. They had eaten a lot. The flies everywhere. The fear everywhere.

Many people died there. I lost my father. But really it was the children. I believe more little children died than adults. They died because of the cold and they died because they weren't well fed. The mothers didn't have any milk. So, they would give the baby water. Many died. Babies were born dead. Some were born alive, but in two weeks they would be dead. They did not have a great life. Every family lost some children. After my father was killed, I joined the guerrilla. I was a courier. I was eleven years old.

Later, when I was a soldier, I went to villages. Once I had to interrogate a woman. The woman didn't tell me anything, but she had to respect me because I was a soldier of the government and I had a gun. There was an officer behind me, watching me. I had to do it right because if you don't they beat you and sometimes they kill you. I interrogated the woman. So did some other soldiers. They beat her and I did, too. Sometimes they tell us, "Go get this person and beat him." A man was denounced by his neighbor. We beat him. He said, "I am just a campesino. I dedicate myself to working in the fields and nothing more." The man began to cry in front of us. I had to have such a face. I had to keep a tough face in front of the others because I had my orders and I was obligated to complete them. The man never said anything. The officer sent him to the base and I didn't see what happened to him after that.

The sublieutenant would ask the campesinos, "What have you been doing? What have you seen?" The campesinos would respond with their civil patrol titles. The sublieutenant would then ask them what they had seen. When they would respond that they had not seen anything, he would contradict them. He would lie and say that he had been told that subversives had been in the village. Then, the poor people would regret their answer and tell the sublieutenant, "Yes, we did see that." The army wants the people to give them information that is untrue. The only thing that matters is that the people will say whatever the army wants them to say.

Juana

Tz'utujil Widow in a village on Lake Atitlan.

My husband wasn't the first military commissioner. There was another before him and he did much harm to the village. Everyone in the village feared him because the harm was great. So they held a special meeting where the village nominated and elected my husband as military commissioner in 1983.

Before my husband was military commissioner, there were many robberies and killings—and the military commissioner led them. After so much pain and so much fear, the villagers initiated proceedings to put these men in jail for all the harm they brought us. My husband was military commissioner at this time and these men went to jail.

When my husband was military commissioner, there was no more harm: no more kidnappings, no more robberies, no more disappearances, no more rapes. The village was calm, tranquil. But, because my husband did not want to hurt the people, the men who supported the former military commissioner and the other men in jail began to threaten my husband. They complained that my husband was a bad man because he wouldn't obey the orders from the military base.

I remember one night when men came from the military base and they woke us up. It was the middle of the night. Everyone in the village was asleep. My husband got up and talked with the men. He asked them what they wanted. They said they wanted a man from the village. They wanted to take him out of his home. They wanted to take this man away with them into the night. My husband told them, "No." He said it was not permitted to wake people up in the middle of the night and take them away. My husband told them this because he did not want to be responsible for this man's life. My husband told them that it was better to wait until morning and make an appointment requesting that the man present himself to the military authorities.

So, the next morning my husband sent word to the man that he needed to present himself at the office of the military commissioner— that was my husband's office. The man presented himself, but my husband did not hand him over to the army inside the office. He did it outside in front of many villagers. The man was turned over to the army healthy, well, and with no injuries. He had to turn him over because the army had documents. The army took him away. I don't know what happened to that man, what the army did to him.

This is when problems began. The former military commissioner and the people who supported him really began to speak badly of my husband. It was like this for quite a while. "Marcos only has a few days left." "Soon, they will come for Marcos." That was my husband's name, Marcos. These men would get drunk and threaten my husband like this. In the end, these bad men got their wish.

It was a Tuesday. We had only been in bed for a short while when they broke open our door—I don't know if they did it by kicking with their feet or beating it down with their weapons. When they broke open the door, I went and asked them what they wanted. They told me they wanted my husband. My husband was in bed. I told them I would call him. But then I turned around and went back to these men to ask them why they wanted my husband. They answered that it was an army order and they wanted to talk to him. I knew something bad was going to happen. I begged them not to hurt him. I told them that my husband was an honorable man. That he wasn't rich, but that he took care of us.

The third time they demanded my husband, I went to him and advised him that he had to get up and present himself. I told him this despite feeling that they were going to take him away and hurt him.

He got up. He got dressed and as he left the place where he slept, he said to one of them, "Good evening Lt. Ruano." This was his way of letting us know who was taking him away. The man replied, "Good evening." The other man grabbed my husband's arms and they took him away. His last words were, "Goodbye Mama." That's when my mother-in-law got up and my brother-in-law, too. The three of us started to run after them, but there were two armed men who stopped us. They said,

"Stay here or we'll kill you." So we stopped, but then we went in their direction up the street and around the corner. A pick-up passed us making a lot of noise. It passed by very quickly, but we saw they had him inside. We were screaming.

For all the screaming, shouting, and noise, the entire village woke up. Someone rang the church bell. The entire village gathered. "What was the motive? Why did they take Marcos away?" Everyone asked these questions into the middle of the night. Then, at about six in the morning when the men began to go to the fields to work, they found two cadavers: my husband and his uncle. They both had terrible marks from torture. They had sequestered his uncle on Tuesday afternoon in Panajachel, then they came for my husband late that same night. From then on, things just got worse in the village.

My husband was poor, but he was honorable. He didn't want to harm anyone. He would say, "I can't be responsible. I can't turn over people in the middle of the night. Who is going to put food on the tables for the families if the men are gone?"

My husband was military commissioner for two years. When he was killed, I was twenty-five years old. Our daughters were seven, five, and three years old. I struggled for justice. I went to the capital to denounce his murder. I went to the local police and judge. Together with support from other villagers, the men who took my husband away were put in jail—but not for long. When they first got out of jail, they were humiliated. In the village, everyone ignored them. We all acted like they didn't exist. All the villagers did this.

The villagers have treated us well. They remember my husband with fondness. They appreciated him. They have tried to console us. They help us out. They bring a bit of corn, a bit of beans. Like right now, she's bringing me some *masa*.[8] To support my daughters, I wash clothes in people's houses, sometimes at the lake. I iron clothes. I make tortillas. When I work in someone's house, I bring the lunch they give me home to my daughters so they will eat better. I am lucky if I can get work three days out of the week. When I do, I work from six in the morning until six at night. I get paid ten quetzales a day.[9] It's hard to find work here.

When those men first killed my husband, I wanted justice. Then, I wanted those men judged and sent to prison for the rest of their lives so they wouldn't be able to kill more people like that, so the village could live in peace. When they killed my husband, it was a time of great violence and many people were harmed.

Now, so many years later, I look at my daughters and how difficult their lives are. Even the wood we need for the stove costs so much. It is the fault of these men. What guilt do my daughters have? Why should they suffer like this? Today my daughters are eighteen, sixteen, and fourteen years old. They all work. Not one of them was able to finish primary school. Now they will be poor all their lives. They have to work. If they don't work, there isn't enough to eat. If we stay home sitting around, we won't eat. We all have to work to eat.

So, I tell you, today justice for my husband's death would be that those men who killed him have to pay money so our daughters don't suffer like this. Justice for me today would be to see my daughters in school and those men paying for it.

Alejandro

Ixil Survivor of Salquil massacre, former CPR leader, current Maya rights organizer.

Before 1979, our people had livestock. We had the means to produce food and eat. We even sold some of what we produced. It isn't that we were rich, but we weren't so poor either. Still, we all had to travel to the fincas to earn enough money to keep our crops growing and feed our families.

In my case, well, I grew up on the fincas. I was very little when I began to work because my father was very poor and my mother was very poor. So, we had to work on the fincas. After awhile, the people began to organize a community project, a cooperative. In this way, small groups of people were able to produce enough to eat and to sell a little. There was milpa, other crops for sale, and even livestock projects. Various types of cooperative projects were begun. Life was a little better.

But after the cooperatives began to produce, that is when the repression began. From the beginning, they began by singling out our leaders. They sequestered the Catholic leaders and the cooperative presidents. Some of the catechists were kidnapped by the army. After that, the people were frightened because people were being disappeared. That's when people started to leave their houses out of fear. But they didn't leave their houses just once. They would leave when the army was coming. They would flee to the mountain. When the army had left, they would return to their homes. In the beginning, the army just stole our animals or killed them.

But it didn't take long before the army began to destroy our houses. They burned them—just like that! They did this because when your house is burned down, you have nowhere to live. This was the army's idea. But even though they had burned our houses, and the people had seen them do this, the people didn't give themselves up to the army. On the contrary, it gave us more strength because we didn't agree with the army burning our houses. But the army didn't give up these ideas. They began to steal and burn our harvest. They robbed everything they could carry. If they couldn't carry it, they burned it. They burned our milpa because they thought that if they destroyed our food, then we would have to give ourselves up [to the army]. But we didn't surrender. And that is when the army began to apply its Scorched Earth campaign. You see, it didn't all happen at once, it was done in phases. During the Scorched Earth, when they burned our houses and crops, milpa this high [about one meter], they would even machete it to leave us with nothing.

After they had burned everything and we were in the mountains, they pursued us there. They attacked us with helicopters and planes. Army infantries, sometimes two or three battalions, would hunt for us. We could see what they did. They shot people and killed them. They saw no difference between the guerrilla and the [civilian] populations. They burned temporary shelters we built in the mountains—sometimes with children inside them. That is why the people didn't give themselves up. We saw what the army had done and what they were doing. We didn't give ourselves up because we knew what they would do to us. We thought that after everything was burned, they would leave us in peace. But they never did. It seemed like it would never end.

But in 1983 or '84, they changed their strategy of war. They began to do the "levantamiento del venado."[10] That is what they call it when one group [of people] is here and another group [of people] is over there. The soldiers began to fire into the mountain, without seeing anything, without knowing anything. Their objective is to make the people run and fall into the hands of soldiers. Those [soldiers] who are above fire and those [soldiers] who are here make no noise. That way the fleeing people run right into the "coyote" [soldiers] who are below. This is how they caught a lot of people. But even though they did this, they weren't able to terminate the people.

We suffered great hunger. From 1981 to 1990, each year there was more suffering. As I told you, I am from Salquil. I kept fleeing the army. Little by little, farther and farther away. Until I arrived to the place I live now. I am a member of the CPR of Cabá, the Communities of Populations in Resistance. My family is in Cabá right now. So, the flight we took wasn't one single journey to where we live now in Cabá. We made the trip fleeing here and there to anywhere we thought the army wouldn't arrive. We would stay wherever we were for awhile. Sometimes we stayed a few weeks or a few months. A year, sometimes a year and a half before the army arrived. We would flee again with the army in pursuit. Between 1981 and 1987, we fled little by little to Cabá. We would get there and stay until the army arrived. When they left, we would go back. Since 1990, we have stayed in Cabá. Where I live now, I have been there almost ten years. In these years, all our people have suffered greatly.

In 1984 and 1985, a time came when our people had no clothes. Some covered themselves with bits of plastic. With bits of fabric of whatever color or type, our women tried to cover themselves because there was no clothing. Everything had rotted and worn out. We didn't have any salt and salt is a principal food of the people. But it was disappearing. The few who had salt were buying it at thirty-two quetzals per pound. Salt cost thirty-two quetzals per pound in 1985. Of course, our people don't have money to buy salt at thirty-two quetzals per pound, so we no longer had salt. We ate weeds, roots, a bit of tortilla if we could get it. That was it . . . without salt. That is why a lot of our people died in the mountains. They died for lack of food. Little by little, malnutrition took over and people died.

Many of our elderly died. Everyone died, men, like me, died of hunger. The women seemed to survive it better. Lots of men died because men eat more food than women. When the time came when there was no food, the women resisted better because they are accustomed to eating less. But the men perished. When there was no more food, men lost their valor to hunger and they died. All these sufferings were painful to witness and to survive. Many of our people could no longer tolerate the situation. So they gave themselves up to the army. They had to surrender because there was no food. Those who resisted the hunger are those in the CPRs today. Many of the people in the CPR were living in temporary camps in the mountain. In 1984, I began traveling from camp to camp, moving groups of people to safer places.

When the repression began I abandoned my house and my family to lead my people against the repression. I have spent the last sixteen or seventeen years working for my people, working so they don't die. In the mountains, I was a CPR leader. I still work with my people because the truth is that the struggle has not ended. We have to continue to struggle and we need to be organized. The peace accords have been signed, but we have to wait to see what the results will be. We have to struggle for the peace accords to be more than words on paper. They signed the papers, but what are they doing now? That is why I work with my people in [the Maya group] Maya-Majawil where I have been since 1992. I left the CPR in 1992 and went to the capital because alone as the CPR, we are like a little thorn, nothing more. Our people need a presence at the national level. We need to have strength and courage to confront the politics of the government.

Our people have suffered. I witnessed the death of many brothers from hunger. I found them dead on the paths from hunger. Children died from hunger. Children died in the mountains from the cold and the rain without shelter, without clothing, fleeing the army. The elderly died because they lacked the strength to run. The army would find them sitting on a rock or under a tree and kill them. Many of our brothers drowned in rivers trying to flee the army.

I remember in 1982, near the end of the year, our population was trying to cross the Cotzal River, which is close to the CPR. Crossing the river, the current carried away two women. I watched thinking, "What can I do?" I was powerless. They were crossing the river and the current must have knocked them off balance. We were all weak and hungry. One woman carried a child in her arms and another on her back. The other woman had a baby on her back. The river carried all five of them away. I saw it happen, but what could I do? How am I going to stop the river's current? It gave me great sorrow to watch these women and children die. I always think of those women trying to save their children. I continue to struggle because of what I have suffered and the suffering I have witnessed.

We still aren't free because we don't have the means to live or give our children a life. There have been no solutions for our needs. I have a wife and six children. They are sad when I leave. But I go because my family isn't the only family with these problems. All our people have these problems. Five times I survived an army circle of soldiers firing upon us in all directions. For the grace of God, nothing happened to me. I was able to escape. My only injury is the loss of my hearing in this ear from the explosion of a bomb. Sometimes I hear ringing in that ear.

Sometimes I feel dizzy and beaten down from so many travels. I walk from village to village. Where I go, there aren't roads. Yesterday, I went to a community and had a meeting with 200 people. They cried as they talked about what they had suffered and what they suffer today. So even if I am dizzy and tired, as long as I am alive, I will continue to struggle.

I told you I have six sons, but they aren't all mine. The army killed their father. They captured him on a path and stabbed him to death. My first wife was killed by the army in the mountains. So, my three children didn't have a mother. I married Maria with the three children she already had. Those children never did anything to deserve to be orphans. The army did that to them.

Esperanza

> Q'anjob'al survivor of La Violencia in a Huehuetenango village and former guerrilla combatant. She joined the EGP when she was fifteen years old.[11]

I found them in the mountain. I found the commander and I told him that if they would accept me I wanted to join their forces. I told him I wanted to fight the army. I told him I had seen the horrible things they did to people in my village, to unarmed people. I told him I wanted to go into combat. I told him it wasn't fair to die defenseless. That it was better to be armed and prepared and die in combat. They accepted me. That same afternoon, I joined the forces of the Guerrilla Army of the Poor and they gave me a weapon. I began my training.

Everything went along fine. But the truth is that, after about eight days, I was finding it pretty difficult. In my house, I had hardly ever worked. My sisters and I were the smallest, so we had always been pampered. We were peasants, but we always had enough to eat because my father had a lot of land. In my house, there was always a lot of food at mealtimes and we had enough water to bathe everyday. But in the EGP, a lot of times there wasn't any water for bathing. The truth is this was my biggest desperation, that I couldn't bathe. Sometimes we didn't even have water to drink. I even told them that I felt desperate for water—for water to drink and water to bathe in.

Two or three days had passed and there was no water for bathing, there wasn't even water to drink. I felt truly desperate. I wanted to bathe. At first it seems extremely difficult—you're very hungry, you haven't gotten any sleep, you walk all night long in darkness, you trip, you fall, you get wet, and you just keep going, going, going. You see, we had to walk at night so the army could not easily locate us. In the beginning, I really regretted my decision. But, I just kept thinking, "I'll see if I can make it through today and maybe I will leave tomorrow."

And, so this is how it was and the days began to pass. I started to get used to not bathing everyday. Every two or three days, we would organize into squads of ten combatants to bathe. We would go to the water in squads of two. One squad would bathe while the other stood guard. If the army arrived, the squad standing guard would engage in combat while those bathing got dressed and withdrew. Some days we had no food, other days we had no water, some days we had neither. But some days, we had both.

I had been in the EGP for about one month when I realized we were walking through mountains very close to my village. I thought it would be very easy to walk back there alone. As I walked I thought how one month earlier, I would have run back to my house. But the day I walked near my village in the EGP platoon, I felt proud of what I had endured and the strength I had found in myself. I thought to myself, "Tomorrow there might not be food, there might not be water," and I laughed because I realized I hadn't bathed for two days. I chose not to go home. After a month, I liked being a combatant.

It was after this first month that I began to receive military training. The training was very difficult. We had to crawl through the ground on our stomachs. In the mountain, there were lots of stickers and rocks and mud. We had to crawl through like any other soldier in military training. We had to crawl across the ground, walk across ropes, and jump very high.

For me this was all a great challenge. Because of my inheritance of being so *chaparrita*,[12] there were times when things were simply out of my reach. This always put me behind the men because they are always taller than I, so it was easy for them. But the best thing is that it was in training that I discovered that I really loved being a combatant. I loved having a weapon at my disposal and I learned how to use it well. I couldn't jump as high as the men, but I could shoot as well or better than most of them.

So it was in this month of training that the commanders asked me what I wanted to do when I was finished, if I wanted to be a combatant or an organizer. There was also a collective where uniforms were made for combatants. They asked me if I would like to work there in the sewing workshop. They told me there was also a workshop where explosives were assembled. They asked me what I preferred to do. I told them straight out, "I would like to be a combatant."

Our first action was to ambush a jeep of judiciales—these are different from the army and the police. They are the squadrons, the ones that disappear and kill people. Anyway, these judiciales always had very good weapons. We had been informed that they were transporting weapons. So, we ambushed them with a Claymore bomb that we had actually made ourselves. This was my first experience. So, when the car passed by, I didn't know what would really happen. I had never been so close to the military. The judiciales passed by and the bomb exploded. Actually, right after the explosion, I stood there frozen, half-stupid. With a big explosion like that, one feels somewhat absurd immediately afterwards.

We took their arms away and quickly withdrew from the area because almost immediately after the explosion, a helicopter arrived. It was a very bare area. There was almost no vegetation. This was my first close call. We had been running as fast as we could for about ten minutes when I felt I couldn't go on any longer. I felt dizzy. I felt like I was about to suffocate. I just couldn't breathe anymore. But then, I just calmed myself. I took some deep breaths. I told myself that my body was functioning normally and I continued to run. We ran and ran. We all escaped the army. I learned a lot, especially about weapons. I learned how to handle them all. This was my job in the guerrilla for one year.

My next job was with the National Direction,[13] which is always located in very secure areas, in places that it would be difficult for the army to find. It was not the grand physical sacrifice I was used to, but there were many new rules to learn. The security was very tight. The arms were very good, very lightweight. But, we were very heavily armed. Sometimes, I almost couldn't tolerate it because I am so small and I was carrying a mountain of weaponry. I carried an M–16 with 300 rounds of fire, a 380 with 50 rounds of fire, two grenades and a dagger. And all this was around my waist. I was really full of weapons. But, I loved it. I was enchanted.

Still, I started to think that what I really wanted to do was to directly engage in combat with the army. I wanted to see if I was afraid of the army. I wanted to see how brave I was. I asked for authorization. In 1986, I joined the military unit. I was very happy because I was going to go into combat with the army.

We attacked the army base in San Lucas on December 31. We were eighty combatants. They were 800 to 1,000 soldiers. So, we were few in comparison to them. We had been spying on them for days. Every afternoon at one, they went down to the river to bathe. So, we went down to the river and we set up an ambush on the shore of the river. Because it was the 31st of December, the soldiers started to play soccer at ten in the morning and they played until one in the afternoon. So, we knew that when they finished playing, they would come down to the river to bathe. But, at two in the afternoon, they finished playing and then returned to the barracks. We had been there since six in the morning. We hadn't eaten and we were thirsty. We couldn't move from our positions because they might see us. We had used all kinds of plants and weeds for camouflage and they tickled and itched. We were all feeling sad because they weren't coming out. Then, at four in the afternoon, we can hear everyone shouting inside the base and the first platoon comes out and heads straight down to the river.

The *compañeros* positioned closest to me were four women and some other compañeros from the capital—these are people who suffer a lot and take a long time learning to survive in the mountain. I still didn't have much experience in this type of situation, either. I saw that really we were not ready to directly combat the army when the soldiers were right in front of us. I had never before seen a Kaibil. He was four meters in front of me. He was armed and I was armed. I thought, "I am going to die here." And, I began to tremble with fear. There was another compañero who was supposed to fire first. And, I thought, "This Kaibil is going to be on top of me before he fires." And the Kaibil was actively looking all around himself, checking everything out. He didn't see anything. We were all around and he was looking, but saw nothing. When he was only three meters in front of me, the compañero began to fire and I also began to fire. The attack had begun. He was the first soldier we wasted.

Then, the entire army force came out. While the army was positioning itself, we were gathering the weapons from all the soldiers we had killed. Then, the soldiers began to fire heavy weapons. So, we withdrew to protect ourselves. We were three, one man and two women. We were ordered to advance, fire, and take the weapons away from the fallen soldiers. At first, I didn't want to do this. There were bullets flying everywhere and I knew that if I stood up or moved forward on the ground, any hidden soldier would fire on me. Then, I thought, "Well, if I am going to die anyway," and I said to the other woman, "Let's go. Advance with me so I'm not alone." Then the man said, "Let's go. the three of us go together. If we die, we die together." So, we moved forward and we took the machine gun away from the dead soldier. But it was very difficult to get his munitions because he had his belt very tightly fastened. We kept ours tightly fastened, too. You have to keep it tight to hold all the weight. But, he even had little lassos on his belt. To make it worse, he was full of machine gun fire and it was all very hard to remove. Everything was full of bullet fragments. There were three dead soldiers there, but we were only able to remove weapons from one because another army platoon came upon us and our unit was almost wiped out. We had four injured and one dead. On top of that, a lot of our weapons weren't working.

By this time, I had fired 250 rounds of munitions from my M–16. I had 400 rounds altogether. I was afraid and I was trembling, but when I started to fire, I forgot that I could die. I forgot about everything. I just kept fighting. All I thought about was how to continue firing until I heard the order to withdraw. We continued to fire. Some of us carried the injured while others protected us.

There were dead guerrilla combatants, too. We were able to remove them from the site. We buried them. We never left injured and dead combatants behind. The army did this. They would just leave their dead soldiers wherever they fell. The only thing the army did was remove their weapons. We had more respect for our compañeros. We removed them from the battle site. If the dead combatant had a better uniform than one of us, then we switched uniforms. We took the best for the living because all combatants always needed uniforms. It was really a desperate situation. Can you imagine removing your dead friend's clothes before the burial? In the beginning, one really doesn't know how to adjust to this kind of life, plus it was very sad; it gave me great sadness to see the dead compañeros, friends I had been living with for quite some time. It was very sad.

But, one gets stronger. You get used to seeing dead and injured all the time. It begins to feel normal. It is normal. You see a dead compañera and you say, "Well, she was lucky. She is no longer suffering. Now, she is resting." And each one of us knew that the next day it could be any one of us. We were all conscious that death could strike us at any moment.

So, these were my experiences in combat. This is how it was for me. As a woman combatant, in the beginning I really felt that I was out of place. But, I began to believe that women have every capacity that men have. Even more, I put forth a great deal of effort to be a good combatant and I succeeded in this. The only thing I really wanted was to not fall behind the men. I wanted to always be at their side, at the same level as them, to demonstrate that a woman could be just as good a combatant as a man.

In my village, men would always say, "I am the man and I can do everything. You can't do anything. The only thing you can do is have children." So, in the mountains, everything is different because everyone knows that everyone is capable of doing whatever a man does. I think that this is really psychological work for the men—that they have to look at the compañeras as their equals, that they can't discriminate against them. This is one of the things we learn—that everyone has equal value, men and women, indigenous and ladino, that no one is behind anyone else. I want my daughter to understand this, that she is on an equal plane with men.

Of course, all of this was difficult when I came to Mexico to live with my parents. My opinions are now different from theirs. I would say, "Women's freedom is the same as men's." And my mother would say, "No, my daughter. You have to let the man run the home. He is the one to give orders. He is the boss of the family." There was an entire year of these conversations. It was very hard, especially with my brother. He would say, "I am the boss of my house and my woman will do whatever I tell her. I'll make her do it." And I would tell them that he had to respect her as his partner, that he couldn't hit her. This was all very trying, but we are a very united family and we stick together. So, in the end, this is all part of our own personal liberation. I think we continue to liberate ourselves with these discussions even when they are very difficult. We learn from one another.

ON REPRESENTATIONS OF RESISTANCE

These are a selection of voices from Guatemala. Yet they are voices that are rarely heard in public discussion of La Violencia. Rather, the public sphere is dominated by academics, journalists, policy analysts, and government officials who interpret the experience of survivors and combatants for the rest of the world. In his critique of David Stoll's *Between Two Armies in the Ixil Towns of Guatemala*, Charles Hale points out that, "Only rarely in the more than 300 pages of analysis focused on the question of Ixil consciousness do we actually hear Ixil voices."[14] Commenting on Hale's article, Guatemalan novelist and social critic Arturo Arias succinctly states that one of the problems with Stoll's presentation is an issue found in both Stoll's work as well as that of other academics, that is, the "First World scholar speaking in the name of the subaltern subject."[15] These same criticisms about the lack of Ixil voices in Stoll's work can also be made of Yvon Le Bot's *La Guerra en Tierras Mayas*.

In *Between Two Armies*, David Stoll argues (1) that guerrillas provoked army repression and (2) that Ixil support for the guerrilla was the result of "dual violence," not a "function of preexisting grievances, of con-sciousness-raising or ideological mobilization."[16] Stoll, a former journal-ist and self-described "debunker,"[17] assumes La Violencia has only two sides: the guerrilla and the army. Through this binary lens, he concludes that Ixiles "are best understood as determined neutralists."[18] In *La Guerra en Tierras Mayas,* Yvon Le Bot, a polemical, anti-Marxist *indigenista,*[19] maintains that Ixiles are "famous for being rebels" and that the Ixiles are "faithful to this tradition" of rebelliousness.[20] Despite differing concep-tions of the "neutral" or "rebellious" political "nature" of the Ixiles, Le Bot concurs with Stoll that it is the fault of the guerrilla that the army com-mitted massacres in Maya communities throughout Guatemala. Specifi-cally, Le Bot blames the armed struggle of the Guerrilla Army of the Poor for "provoking a blood bath."[21]

In a 1994 interview, a high-ranking army official (who in 1982 com-manded a platoon responsible for the Ixcán massacres, including the mas-sacre of Mateo's village Pueblo Nuevo) told me that David Stoll's book was "the truth."[22] This officer who had ordered and participated in dozens of massacres said, "The Indian problem. Who can tell us what to do about it? They are ignorant. They are dirty. They don't even speak Spanish. We made some mistakes, but we had to terminate the guerrilla." Thus, Stoll and Le Bot, like the army official, also argue that if the guer-rilla had not made the Maya appear "subversive," then the army would not have massacred them—at best, a dubious conclusion with no evi-dence to support it. Moreover, whether understanding the Ixiles through the compartmentalization of labeling an Ixil state of "being" as in Stoll's "neutrality," Le Bot's "rebelliousness," or the army officer's "ignorance," all fall within this schema of guerrilla provocation of army massacres.

After reviewing a draft section of my chapter on the phenomenology of terror, a colleague recommended explaining village alliances with the army or guerrilla. Were those villages allied with the guerrilla more likely to be destroyed? This may seem a logical question, and probably is. How-ever, it implies the possibility of a seamless representation of alliances—that neat, clean lines can be drawn between those villages that supported the guerrilla and those that supported the army, and perhaps even those that supported neither. Indeed, it divides the cosmology of rural Maya communities into support for one of the two armed forces with little room for other alliances. Moreover, it seeks some plausible causality to the horror of 626 known massacres. Questions about village alliances, like assertions of guerrilla provocation, conflate and fail to draw distinctions between culpability, responsibility, and representation, on the one hand and political belief and action on the other.[23] Nonetheless, considering this question about alliances reveals an army that massacred and destroyed individuals, families, neighborhoods, and entire villages under the auspices of destroying "subversives." These "subversives" were identified and located by conflating political and ethnic identities, thereby categorizing Ixiles and other Maya groups as "subversive." Therefore, raising the question about village alliances reinforces the need for a nuanced understanding of local identities.

Let's consider Mateo's testimony. As previously mentioned, Mateo is Mam-Maya and a survivor of the Pueblo Nuevo, Ixcán massacre. By the time he reached fourteen years of age, he had survived a massacre, buried his father in the mountains, joined the guerrilla and fought with them in the mountains for one year, and spent two years in a refugee camp in Mexico. Just before his fifteenth birthday, within one month of his return to Guatemala, he was forcibly recruited into the Guatemalan army, where he was a soldier following orders from superiors for more than one year.[24] Recall, for a moment, Mateo's soldiering experience, after which he concluded: "The army wants the people to give information that is untrue. The only thing that matters is that the people will say whatever the army wants them to say."[25] After witnessing the testimonies presented in previous chapters, it should not be difficult for readers to understand and, most likely, agree with Mateo's assessment and also comprehend why Maya peasants might acquiesce to coercive exhortations to parrot army claims. Still, one wonders how it is that scholars of Guatemala, such as Stoll and Le Bot, arrive at arguments quite similar to those of the army.

Postulations about Maya peasant guilt based on village association with the guerrilla and guerrilla responsibility for army violence against unarmed civilians support the intentionality claimed by the army that massacres of unarmed men, women, children, and elderly were not the killing of civilians but rather the "scorching" of "communists." By placing the burden of responsibility for army massacres upon the guerrilla, both Le Bot and Stoll validate army propaganda, which claims firstly that only communists and subversives were killed in the Scorched Earth campaign and secondly that the Maya were (or at least appeared to be) subversive and/or communist and that is why they were killed. These arguments are particularly dangerous because (1) they fail to contest army assertions of the military's "right" to kill communists when, at a minimum, under international human rights law, no government (or army) has the right to eliminate human beings based on political affiliation; (2) by arguing guerrilla provocation, they also argue that guerrilla presence made the Maya appear "subversive" to the army, and thereby justify army massacres within the army's own logic of war; and (3) they fail to recognize the deliberate conflation made by the Guatemalan army (and the CIA) in which political affiliation and ethnicity became one and the same. Stoll and Le Bot neatly divide the political history of Guatemala into one of army soldiers and guerrilla combatants. Much in the way they ascribe political autonomy to the Maya in the binary world of armies and guerrillas, both Stoll and Le Bot represent themselves as "objective" scholars in that they contend that their analyses of guerrilla responsibility should not be equated with support for the army.

Here, Ranajit Guha's discussion of primary, secondary, and tertiary discourses in "The Prose of Counterinsurgency" is useful for understanding how scholars such as Stoll and Le Bot produce seemingly unbiased scholarly research that ultimately validates official claims used to justify the Guatemalan army's Scorched Earth campaign. Guha defines primary discourse as "official in the broad sense of the term . . . meant primarily for administrative use—for the information of the government, for action on its part, and for the determination of its policy."[26]

One example of primary discourse is the previously mentioned October 5, 1981, U.S. Department of State memorandum classified as "secret."[27] This memo acknowledges a "recent meeting between US General Walters and General Lucas García" (Guatemalan dictator and president at the time) and points out that General Lucas believes that "the repression is working and that the guerrilla threat will be successfully routed."[28] The memo continues, "Historically, of course, we cannot argue that repression always 'fails' nor can Lucas argue that it always 'succeeds.' Recent history is replete with examples where repression has been 'successful' in *exorcising* guerrilla threats to a regime's survival. . . ." Argentina and Uruguay are cited as "recent" examples of success.[29] The memo also points out that "during the 1960s and 1970s a policy of repression succeeded in routing the guerrilla threat" in Guatemala.[30]

As the State Department was circulating its memo on the Guatemalan government's "policy of repression" aimed at the "extermination of the guerrillas, their supporters and sympathizers," with its religious overtones in the conceptual description of "successful" repression expressing itself as an "exorcising," international human rights groups were documenting assassinations and massacres. In September 1981, the month preceding the State Department memorandum, human rights groups documented 168 people killed in army massacres in thirteen Maya communities. In October of 1981, more than 132 people were recorded as being killed in army massacres in another thirteen communities. The number of deaths was unknown in several of the massacres, meaning that the real numbers of people killed could be higher than the actual numbers reported.[31]

* * *

Let's return to the question of how one would determine the alliances of a village. The sublieutenant had one way that reflected a military strategy, that is, just as Mateo carried out his orders, the sublieutenant carried out his. Despite all but one paragraph being marked out with heavy black ink, a declassified three-page *top secret* CIA document reveals CIA knowledge of and communication with the regime of General Lucas García about the planned destruction of Maya villages. The disclosed paragraph in the February 5, 1982, document states that "the Ixil Triangle has the largest concentration of guerrillas and sympathizers in the country." It further states that General Lucas García has "acknowledged that because most Indians in the area support the guerrillas it probably will be necessary to destroy a number of villages."[32]

The other previously cited declassified CIA document from late February 1982 states that in mid-February 1982, the Guatemalan army had reinforced its existing forces and launched a "sweep operation in the Ixil Triangle. The commanding officers of the units involved have been instructed to destroy all towns and villages which are cooperating with the Guerrilla Army of the Poor (EGP) and eliminate all sources of resistance."[33] Recall the CIA "COMMENT" that "[t]he well documented belief by the army that the entire Ixil Indian population is pro-EGP has created a situation in which the army can be expected to give no quarter to combatants and non-combatants alike."[34] This again reaffirms that the entire Ixil population was the military objective regardless of any real or perceived relationship to the EGP.

It is important to note that in the month of January, prior to the writing of both of these CIA documents, a minimum of 399 civilians had been killed in army massacres and operations in twenty-four different Maya communities in seven different departments. In two reported massacres, the number of victims was unknown. One half of these communities were in the department of El Quiché and six of the communities were in the Ixil area. All of this occurred before the army began its "sweep operation" so cynically, but aptly, described in the CIA documents. In the month of February, at least 327 civilian men, women, children, and elderly were killed in army massacres in twenty-two different Maya communities.[35] The number of victims in four of the massacres remains unknown.

At minimum, this information on massacres, combined with declassified U.S. government documents, shows that village alliances were not the primary factor "triggering" army massacres (and also that systematic massacres began earlier than the CIA is reporting). If anything, CIA documents, despite their convoluted language and censored presentation, acknowledge Guatemalan army massacres of civilians and also concur with the Guatemalan army that all Ixiles are "pro-EGP." In so doing, they excuse the army for the destruction of the social, political, and materiel culture of the Maya in general, and the Ixiles in particular. The destruction was so great and so complete that it could have only been realized through detailed planning by intellectual authors and extreme discipline throughout the regimented structure of the army, from the military officers giving the orders to the soldiers and civil patrollers first carrying out the massacres and later pursuing survivors. Thus, as official sources of classified information directly implicated in administrative policy making, the above-cited U.S. government documents, like other government documents, including those for both internal and external consumption, are encompassed in Guha's primary discourse.

For Guha, secondary discourse is the recovery of primary discourse that is classified as "history" simply by virtue of the passage of time. In the process, primary discourse also becomes the data of secondary discourse without regard to its highly partial origins. Thus, secondary discourse is the transformation of the raw administrative documents of primary discourse into an apparently "new" history.[36] Most writers of secondary discourse on counterinsurgency are former military or administrative officials.[37] An example of secondary discourse would be Guatemalan General Hector Gramajo's *De la guerra . . . a la guerra—La difícil transición política en Guatemala* in which Gramajo sought to redefine La Violencia, as well as his own role in it, through the production of a self-proclaimed "objective" historical analysis that used the fight against "subversion" to justify the army's Scorched Earth campaign and obfuscate the genocide. Gramajo received a Master's degree from Harvard's Kennedy School and, at graduation, spat upon the U.S. attorney who served him a summons and complaint for a civil lawsuit filed against him for torture and other crimes against humanity.[38] Gramajo likes to think of himself as an intellectual.[39] Guha notes that these types of official authors are positioned "as observers [who are] separated clinically from the site and subject of diagnosis [and] are supposed to have found for their discourse a niche in that realm of perfect neutrality—the realm of History."[40] The product of this recovery and transformation of primary discourse through the production of secondary discourse is that "texts are not the record of observations uncontaminated by bias, judgment and opinion. On the contrary, they speak of total complicity."[41] Certainly, General Gramajo sought to redefine both La Violencia, as well as his role in it, through the production of his "objective" historical analysis. Still, there are few scholars who would consider Gramajo's work to be anything other than exactly what it is: a book by a retired military officer who is implicated in the very violence about which he is writing.

"The discourse of history, hardly distinguished from policy, ends up by absorbing the concerns and objectives of the latter."[42] Thus, Guha determines that because of "this affinity with policy, historiography reveals its character as a form of *colonialist knowledge*" because historiography, like political science and political economy, "adapted itself to the relations of power."[43] This adaptation helps explain analytic dependencies for explanation of counterinsurgency on "causes" and "reforms," which for Guha are "no more than a structural requirement for this continuum providing it respectively with context and perspective."[44] Within the context and perspective of causes and reforms, history can register events "as datum in the life-history of the Empire" and simultaneously "do nothing to illuminate that consciousness which is called insurgency."[45] Through definition of the contents and character of primary and secondary discourses, Guha concludes that "the rebel has no place in this history as the subject of rebellion."[46]

This somewhat lengthy discussion of Guha's primary and secondary discourses is necessary to understand tertiary discourse and its relationship to the arguments of Le Bot and Stoll. Tertiary discourse is the work of independent, nonofficial writers with no "professional obligation or constraint to represent the standpoint of the government." Still, Guha notes there are instances of tertiary discourse "reverting to that state of crude identification with the regime so characteristic of primary discourse."[47] However, within tertiary discourse, one also finds liberal and left idioms of historiography, which

Guha finds to be the "most influential and prolific of all the many varieties of tertiary discourse," particularly because in both the liberal and left tradition, "the literature is distinguished by its effort to break away from the code of counterinsurgency."[48]

It is within this category of the left and liberal tradition that we can place the tertiary discourse of Yvon Le Bot (indigenista) and David Stoll (liberal). Even the work of Ricardo Falla can be included in this category of discourse. While differing in ideological and spiritual orientation, there is "much else that is common between them."[49] While providing extraordinary documentation about the army massacres of more than 700 people in Ixcán, Falla never adequately addresses the presence of the guerrilla or the relationship of the guerrilla to communities in flight. Both Stoll and Le Bot effectively separate the Ixiles from the guerrilla by placing blame on the guerrilla for provoking the massacres and, thus, negating any identity the Ixiles may have had with the insurgency and basing conscious participation in rebellion on "*an ideal rather than real historical personality of the insurgent.*"[50] Certainly, homogenization of one-dimensional readings of both the Ixiles and the insurgents negate the complicated, varied, and overlapping identities of each. "From a refusal to acknowledge the insurgent as the subject of his own history," those writing history effectively deny a "will" to those who may sympathize, support, or join rebel movements and instead represent them as instruments of some other will.[51] For Falla, the Maya were crushed by the will of the state. For Le Bot, the guerrilla triggered the wrath of the state against the Maya. For Stoll, it was external dual violence triggered by the guerrilla and the left, not individual or community will, that forced Ixiles to participate with the guerrilla or army. These types of arguments have been repeated by others.[52]

Whatever purposes they may have had in their analytic attempts to "exonerate" the Maya from "responsibility" for being killed by the army, each of their historical appropriations "leads to the mediation of the insurgent's consciousness by the historian's—that is of a past consciousness by one conditioned by the present" thereby making "the task of representation even more complicated than usual."[53] As evidenced by the resonance with the army officer's official discourse, the tertiary discourse of Le Bot and Stoll is revealed as little more than a refined reproduction of primary and secondary, or official, discourse. This, in turn, reveals a serious evidentiary weakness in Stoll and Le Bot's assertions that the guerrilla provoked the massacres and also challenges their one-dimensional representations of the Ixiles as "neutral" or "rebellious," respectively. Though seemingly incidental to their analyses, these racist one-dimensional representations of the Ixiles are central to the architecture of their overall argument, which is that politics and history happen to the Maya. That is to say that both the appearance and actual political being of the Maya are determined by external forces. The testimonies in this chapter and elsewhere in this book indicate otherwise.[54]

Stoll and Le Bot's vision of guerrilla provocation, like questions about village alliances, conflate and fail to draw distinctions between culpability, responsibility, and representation, on the one hand, and political belief and action, on the other. This problem is no doubt compounded by tertiary discourse that claims to speak for the Maya while at the same time parroting army explanations and justifications for atrocities committed.[55]

As army soldiers lined up the sons and nephews of the elders of Acul in front of the grave they had forced the elders to dig, the soldiers said to the elders, "This is what happens when you let your children help the subversives."[56] When David Stoll and Yvon Le Bot blame the guerrilla for provoking army massacres, they are repeating the primary and secondary discourses of the army. They are recovering and transforming the official history of the army, not the lived experiences of massacre survivors.

When army soldiers arrived to Mateo's village in Ixcán to round up adult men and shoot them in public spaces, the soldiers would shout at the peasants, "*Es la ley*" (It is the law). At the time, Mateo was a monolingual Mam speaker. It was not until he learned Spanish that he discovered that "la ley" did not mean the army's right to kill civilians. Here, as in other instances, the official discourse conflates the real and the imagined. When he learned Spanish, Mateo knew that the soldiers were lying—in the sense that law does not mean the right of the army to kill civilians—and telling the truth—in the sense that in the absence of rule of law, guns become the law. It is ironic that, like the soldiers doing the killing and the officers planning and ordering it, Stoll and Le Bot unwittingly participate in what George Orwell referred to as the "Ministry of Truth," the place where "all history is palimpsest, scraped clean and reinscribed exactly as often as necessary."[57]

The recovery and transformation of official discourse also negates one of the central themes of all testimonies—that of agency. Despite living memory of terror, despite fear and threats, massacre survivors come forward to talk, to remember, and to share. Through their testimonies, they express fear, sadness, shame, anger, hope, and resolve. In the process of giving and witnessing testimony, survivors create new public spaces for discourse and practice—the essence of human agency. When anthropologists, sociologists, and historians fail to consider the Maya as actors in their own history, they commit a discursive silencing of human agency that has serious historiographic impact. Through their tertiary discourse, David Stoll and Yvon Le Bot compound the terror of La Violencia by not taking into account the voices of the survivors. When Stoll and Le Bot claim the guerrilla provoked the army massacres, they nullify army responsibility for atrocities and, in so doing, they also negate the diverse human agency of the Maya expressed in the testimonies of Gaspar, Mateo, Juana, Alejandro, Esperanza, and others. Thus, they compound the political, social, cultural, physical, and materiel violence with discursive violence.

Between September 1997 and May 1998, the Commission for Historical Clarification (Comisión para el Esclarecimiento Histórico—CEH) made site visits to some 2,000 communities, gathered 500 collective testimonies, 7,338 individual testimonies and met with more than 20,000 people—more than 1,000 of whom were military commissioners, guerrilla combatants, politicians, union leaders, and intellectuals and were current or former members of the army, the civil patrols, and civil society organizations.[58] Additionally, archival documentation from human rights groups, affected communities, and the U.S. State Department (which provided declassified State Department and CIA documents following a congressional order) provided significant background and statistical data to contextualize the thousands of testimonies collected by the CEH. The primary, secondary, and tertiary discourses reviewed by the CEH were likewise contextualized by the testimonies. As a result, though the actual CEH report can itself be considered new primary discourse because of its nationally and internationally sanctioned official production, it also breaks from the primary discourse of the United States and Guatemalan governments in that it sought to problematize La Violencia from the perspective of survivors rather than the state.

As a result of this comprehensive investigation, the CEH concluded that "phenomena such as structural injustice, the closing of political spaces, racism, the deepening institutionalization of exclusion and anti-democratic practices, as well as the refusal to promote substantive reforms which could have reduced structural conflicts, constituted the factors which, in a profound sense, determined the origin and subsequent explosion of the armed conflict."[59]

Moreover, the CEH attributed the extreme escalation of violence to: "a vicious circle in which social injustice provokes protest and political instability which permanently had only two responses [from the state]: repression or a military coup. In response to movements proposing economic, political, social or cultural redress, the state increasingly turned to violence and terror to maintain social control. In this sense, political violence was a direct expression of structural violence within the society."[60]

Far from a binary representation of Guatemalan political history and in direct contradiction to the theses presented by Stoll and Le Bot, the CEH found that "a profound explanation of the Guatemalan armed conflict cannot be reduced to a logic of two actors."[61] It further stated: "This interpretation neither explains nor establishes the foundations of the persistent and significant participation of political parties and economic forces in the genesis, development and perpetuation of La Violencia; nor does it explain the repeated organizational efforts and constant mobilization of sectors of the population that struggled to achieve economic, political and cultural redress."[62]

No doubt, the CEH had tremendous resources and a large team of experienced and highly skilled researchers that academics in the field can only dream about (or experience as part of a larger institutional project via participation in these types of commissions). Nonetheless, even without the resources of a truth commission, academic researchers can avoid the pitfalls of "the prose of counterinsurgency" if they heed the words of Guha, Arias, Hale, and others who posit that history can best be problematized by those who have lived it, not by those who have imposed it. This, after all, is among the greatest contributions anthropology can make to understanding social problems—the presentation of testimonies, life histories, and ethnographies of violence.

Eight

THE POWER EFFECTS OF DECLARING THE TRUTH

We will never forget. What happened here is written in our hearts.

—*Pablo*

Witnessing is necessary not simply to reconstruct the past but as an active part of community recovery, the regeneration of agency, and to a political project for seeking redress through the accretion of truth.[1] Local community initiatives for land rights, literacy, access to health care, education, and justice met with state repression but were not silenced by La Violencia. Rather, these initiatives were held in suspension until the community could reconstruct local memory in a public space. Reburial following exhumation did not draw a process to an end; it provided space for the redeployment of these local initiatives and it reinvigorated community mobilization for social justice—both of which had been suspended by fear. Just as institutional forgetting could not end community desires for justice, forgetting could not end fear.

As we carried out the 1994 exhumation in Plan de Sánchez, fear was palpable—not only at the exhumation site but throughout Guatemala. We listened to radio news of halting progress in the peace negotiations between the army and URNG (Unión Revolucionaria Nacional Guatemalteca—Guatemalan National Revolutionary Union) as well as the daily reports of human rights violations and struggles for redress. Sometimes, we concluded, "The army is in charge today." Other days, we sighed with relief as we collectively agreed, "The civilian government has a chance today." These near daily proclamations about who held the balance of power in Guatemala were not isolated discussions about distant political maneuvering in the capital. Our conclusions represented the sum of our collective analysis of Guatemala's halting transition from military rule and the role of local mobilizations for truth in relation to larger national efforts to come to terms with Guatemala's officially silenced past.

Fear and the desire for justice both emanated from the same past, and one never knew whether fear or the desire for justice would weigh in more heavily on a given day. Anthropologist Veena Das has suggested that " . . . if one's way of being-with-others was brutally injured, then the past enters the present not necessarily as traumatic memory but as poisonous knowledge."[2] It was the unpredictability of this "poisonous knowledge" that shaped each day for individuals, communities, and the nation. Genocide resting fitfully in the collective unconscious was an officially silenced national trauma reverberating throughout the society. Das's theorizing of "poisonous knowledge" is useful to contemplate this individual and collective experience because it advances understanding of trauma and memory. Psychologist Pierre Janet wrote that memory "is an action," but that when an individual is unable to liquidate an experience through the action of recounting it, the experience is retained as a "fixed idea," lacking incorporation into "the chapters of our personal history."[3] The experience, then, "cannot be said to have a 'memory' . . . it is only for convenience that we speak of it as 'traumatic memory.'"[4] Further, Janet believed that the successful assimilation or liquidation of traumatic experience produces a "feeling of triumph."[5]

My work in Plan de Sánchez since 1994 indicates that collective recovery of community memory of experiences of extreme violence can begin to break through fear and create new public spaces for community mobilization—perhaps by recasting this individual "poisonous knowledge," when collectively enacted and remembered, as a discourse of empowerment for the individual, community, and nation. Further, I suggest that these discourses are often local appropriations and reformulations of global human rights discourse.[6] In the following testimonies of Plan de Sánchez massacre survivors, Pablo tells of his forced recruitment as a child and Juan Manuel Geronimo recounts the militarization of his community. Each testimony offers a lens through which to understand survival of La Violencia and contemporary efforts for redress.

COMING OF AGE IN LA VIOLENCIA: PABLO'S TESTIMONY

First they organized the military commissioners, one or two in every community. Then they organized us—the poor peasants—as patrollers. They told us that every eight days, we had to patrol. So, as more days passed, everything got even more complicated. Some of us weren't patrolling because we are very poor and needed to work because we had so much poverty. Then they accused us of being guerrillas. The army really believed these accusations against us were true. So it became even more complicated, more and more. The judiciales became even more organized, the death squads is what we call them. They started killing people. If you went to the market to buy or sell, they killed you. People carrying their load of wood on their back to sell—they killed them right on the path. The squads traveled in groups and they kept vigilance on every path. They would just grab and kill anyone. They didn't even ask questions anymore. They grabbed people as if they were no more than dogs. That's where all this began.

It was on the fifteenth of September when I was working in the bean field with my aunt in San Miguel Chicaj when we heard that everything was very difficult in Rabinal, that it was no longer possible to travel through Rabinal to Plan de Sánchez. So what we did is that we just stayed in San Miguel working with my aunt. She fed us and took care of us. So, it was on this day of the fiesta of September 15 that everything fell apart. The judiciales were already well-organized and prepared. At five in the afternoon, they began to kill people.[7] First, they invited everyone to attend the fiesta. They charged people for entering. The people didn't know what was going to happen to them. My brother and I didn't go in. They told us we could go in for free, that they wouldn't charge us. But I could see inside. I saw their red bandanas, white shirts, and black jackets—all army style. They insisted that we go in, but I didn't want to. Plus, my brother had been drinking beer and he was drunk. Thanks to God, the bus arrived and my brother was drunk, so I helped him get in the bus and we went home. Look, if my brother hadn't been drunk, we would have fallen into the trap in San Miguel. My uncle was there. He survived because he threw himself in a gutter and pretended he was dead. He came into the house crying, "Oh my God. Oh my God!"

After that, my mother heard about the killing in San Miguel. My mother was still alive that year. She came to get us. But we couldn't go through Rabinal. There was no longer the possibility of traveling through the center. We couldn't take a bus, we came back by foot. When we reached the entrance to Rabinal, we turned to take a path through the mountains around Rabinal. As we turned, we saw four judiciales with guns and the same style—red bandanna and black jackets. We crouched down and kept moving. If we stopped to look at them, they might see us and shoot. "Dios, Dios, Dios," we passed by them praying to God that nothing would happen to us. Somehow we were saved and we got home. When my father saw us, he began to cry, he thought we were dead. We all cried.

A few days later, we were summoned by the military commissioner. We presented ourselves to the patrol commander and he put us in charge of patrolling at night with the patrollers. Because we were obedient, we were just kids, he gave us sticks and rope to make road blocks to catch people. Then a commissioner who had recently left the military base said he was going to organize a company of kids and youth to go to the villages and hide in the cliffs to see who did not patrol. I was just listening. I was just a kid of fourteen and didn't think much about it.

So that was how it was at the end of 1981. There were two men who worked for the army base. They told us their work was to *"orejón"* [spy]. They would hear a bad word about someone and arrive to investigate the poor people here. They said everyday new squads were being organized. Our job was to watch over the house where the *orejas* [spies] slept at night.[8] They would be inside sleeping and we would be outside with our sticks. If we didn't obey them, they would accuse us and we would be killed. They said, "Anyone who doesn't patrol is acting like he wants to be a guerrilla." So we followed their orders.

They were killing people, but we didn't know why. Then, one day I was summoned again. They sent me to the army base. The commissioner said, "We have to take twenty-five patrollers and whoever doesn't go, well we know why." Still, I said, "But, I am underage. I am still a minor. I'm not an adult yet."[9] He ignored all that. He said, "As soon as you are called, you have to go and complete your orders. If you don't go, they will accuse you of being a guerrilla."

At that time, my whole family was still alive and they were just sitting there listening. Then my father asked, "How is that possible? My son is just a kid. He is still little. He is not an adult. What I know is that he has to be eighteen [for army service] and he isn't." But the commissioner said, "No. If he is called, he has to go." So, I went. My mother was crying. My father asked, "So, you are really going to go?" I answered, "I have to go because if I don't, they will say I am a guerrilla."

So I found myself in the army at fourteen. The first thing the base commander said to the new recruits once we were all gathered was, "Welcome to all you guerrillas. Welcome to all of you. You are all guerrillas and your parents are all guerrillas. So welcome, fucking guerrillas." The captain of the company grabbed one of the recruits by the scruff of his neck. He pulled out his bayonet and stuck it in the recruit's mouth. And this is how it was. Each day was a new punishment. They kicked us around like balls. They tied us up and mistreated us. We were just surviving. Some were crying. Others tried to flee. But there were orders to kill anyone who tried to get away. We were full of fear. We were like startled baby chicks.

I wrote to my father that everything was really screwed in the army. He wrote that he would come to visit me at the base on July 18. But he never came. A few days later, a friend of mine came to see me. He was going to Rabinal and asked if I wanted to send anything to my father. So, I gave him a letter. Then, that same friend returned a few days later. He asked me, "Do you know your father is dead? Your whole family is dead," he said. "No," I said, "I don't know that." "Your father is dead. Your whole family. Your mother. Your brothers. In Plan de Sánchez, no one is alive. The army did it. For God, I come to tell you."

I went to the sergeant of the company. I told him what had happened. "Who killed them?" he asked. "The army did it," I told him. "Who told you this?" he asked. "The people of Rabinal saw it. Everyone knows. Everyone in Rabinal knows it was the army. It happened on Sunday." He argued with me. "No, you are mistaken. Why would they have killed your father?" I asked him to help me investigate what had happened. "Why should I do that?" he said, "There is no killing here."

Then, a sublieutenant, a woman, arrived. She asked me what had happened. I told her. She helped me because women have more conscience. Still, it was fifteen days before I had any confirmation. I went to radio communications every day. Everyday, I went and pestered them until they got mad at me. But, I still went again. Finally, the brigadier called me. He told me he was an orphan, "that's why I have never hit you or mistreated you." It was true, this brigadier never beat me, never hit me, never punished me. He defended me when others wanted to punish me. It was true, the army killed my family. "Look," the brigadier said, "do you have any money? What are you going to do now?"

"What am I going to do? I want to know about my father's case," I said. "It is not just that they kill my father. What are we doing? The army says it is here to defend our families. They say that is why we are here. But the mistake is that we are here and not defending our families. No, our own compañeros are the ones who are killing our families. Here we are taking care of the army and the army is killing our parents."

I went to the colonel. I told him I was resigning from my position and was going to search for my family. "I will never again be in this army! The army killed my father, my brothers, everyone. Never! Not one more day. I am not going to stay here. I resign. Please give me a discharge," I said. "No," said the colonel, "you're not going anywhere. They will kill you if you leave." "If they kill me, they kill me," I said. I left the next morning.

When I finally got to Plan de Sánchez, it was empty. Some of the houses were burned. When I got to my house, it was still there. I found my little brother José crying inside. He was twelve. He had some birds in a cage. He was alone and there was no food. He was hungry. I had some tortillas with me. So, I killed the birds and gave him the tortillas. I told him I would be back for him.[10]

WORKING IN THE COMMUNITY: JUAN MANUEL GERÓNIMO'S TESTIMONY[11]

I was always interested in doing things for my community. I wasn't able to go to school because my father said, "If you go to study then who will work?" So, I worked. I grew to be a man of twenty-two and had never even gone to the first year of primary school. It wasn't until I was twenty-four years old in the military reserve that I completed the first year of primary school.[12] After that, I got married. I left the house of my parents because my brothers were old enough to work.

That's when I began to study. I continued primary school studies and I also began to study health promotion. I didn't study with a teacher at a school. I studied at the parish with people who knew how to read and write a little. They were catechists. I learned a lot. Still, I was only able to complete the first year of *Básico*.[13] I began the second year, but couldn't finish because of problems that came with La Violencia.

La Violencia really hit us here in Plan de Sánchez in 1981. Francisco Herrera had land here. He was threatening people about his property lines because the principle public path entering our community crossed his property. Carlos Herrera, his son, came here and went to each house threatening people for crossing their land. "It doesn't cost us anything to get rid of you," he said. "We can eliminate your whole family because we work for the security forces of the army." It was true. Carlos was an "oreja." He worked a lot for the army. He had been a judicial.

The next thing we knew, we received an order from the military commissioner to organize ourselves into a patrol. This was in July 1981. We had to go to Chipuerta to patrol because there were military commissioners there. So, there we were, patrolling far away from our homes for twenty-four hours every eight days, and they started to kidnap the poor people. They got Isidro Castro, Abelino Cabjón, Angel Capriel, and Isidro's son Marcial. They would do it at night, the patrollers with the army soldiers.

The patrollers went around with sticks. But when they went to kidnap people, they had guns. I was a catechist. One day they said, "Get your coat because the catechists are going to be the new military commissioners." They told us to be prepared to kill and kidnap. It was valuable that they had told us to prepare ourselves, because instead, we absented ourselves. I told my brothers and neighbors that it would be better not to go down the mountain to patrol. They would either kill us or order us to kill other people.

When the kidnappings happened, there were judiciales from Rabinal, and soldiers and patrollers. The patrollers are the ones who know who and where. The judiciales, the G–2 [army intelligence], would take away the poor people. So, we didn't want to patrol. We didn't go down to patrol. We stayed here in our community and that is when they began to persecute us even more. They would come by frequently to search everyone and every house. But we didn't want to show them anyone or anything.

On the contrary, every time they came, we would hide. We would go down the mountain to hide or go to some other place to work. Not once did they catch us. We organized ourselves. We did it alone in our own community. No one helped us. So we were taking care of ourselves, watching out for each other. Some would watch for the army while others worked. That's how we did it. But only we men hid. When our families were still here, what I mean to say is before the massacre, they weren't stealing things. They would arrive, enter the house, look around everywhere. But, they never robbed anything. We thought our women were safe.

In '82, everything got worse. Señor Herrera threatened us even more. He blamed us for everything. It was all lies. That path was a public path.

Not just for those of us living in Plan de Sánchez but also for the poor people from Concul, Balachín, Conculí, La Galera, Joya de Ramos, Las Ventanas. Everyone had to pass through Plan de Sánchez to get to their homes [or to Rabinal]. And everyone used this path. Francisco Herrera tried blocking the path, but the people didn't respect his fence because they had always used the path. With all the threats, people reacted by making the path anew. So the Herreras responded by bringing their animals here and letting them loose in the milpa, which was almost ready to harvest. The animals began to eat and destroy our milpa. Then Francisco and his son went house to house with guns saying, "Watch out. Whoever hits one of our animals won't do it again because we will kill them." That's what they said because they are criminals. These were the threats we were living with. Threats to our food, our families, and our lives.

The truth is that we didn't know what was happening in the rest of the country. We had heard that there were kidnappings in Panacal and Vega Santo Domingo. It was in Río Negro, where they were damming the river, that problems really started. It wasn't directly with the guerrilla. It was a struggle over rights. But that didn't matter to the army.

When they obliged us to organize the patrols, the army told us that it was their idea that each community would watch out for their own people. They said that without the PACs, the guerrilla would come and take away our women, take away our harvest, kill us, and keep our women. They said, "We aren't going to give the guerrilla the opportunity to take away your rights." But the people didn't believe the army. We hadn't seen anything like what they were describing. We just didn't believe them.

The other thing is that we already knew what the army did. I saw it. It isn't just something that I heard; right in front of me I saw them kill people—poor people trying to sell their maize, their tomatoes, whatever thing they could sell. I was walking in the plaza in Rabinal when I heard gunfire. I saw men. They had red bandannas around their necks. That's how the death squads dressed—with red bandannas, roaming around in squads. They shot a man. People began to run in every direction. Someone called the army. The soldiers arrived and made the people run off in all different directions. But I followed those men with the bandannas from far behind. I wanted to see where they were going. Then, a few blocks away, after the streets were empty because the poor people had fled for their lives, I saw those men smoking cigarettes and conversing with the same soldiers who had told the poor people to run. That happened in

1981, I don't remember which month. It wasn't the guerrilla that was killing; it was those men. They all became even angrier with those of us who saw things because we didn't hide it. On the contrary, we told people what we had seen and the people knew it was true because we had seen it with our own eyes.

We had heard that there were guerrilla, but that wasn't really incredible because there had always been guerrilla passing through this area.[14] But they were never really based here. Mostly, they were persons trying to educate the people. They were peasants, too. They would pass through communities, but they didn't carry weapons. More or less, they were like ordinary community promoters. So, they came through talking about the rights of the people. Well, the majority of people in the communities understood what they said. They would listen and say, "That's true, they have reason to say that." It was these promoters who came through the communities without weapons. Now, those who carried weapons, they never came here, never had a meeting or anything.

I was a catechist. Those of us who were catechists, we spoke of rights and respect. We spoke of this a lot. There were people who didn't understand or misunderstood. They came to listen and then went to the military commissioner to inform on us. They said we were organizing for the Armed Forces of the Poor.[15] This was how the problems developed.

By July 1982, because the army and G–2 never found us when they came looking for us in Plan de Sánchez, they said we were guerrillas. They said that I was the commander of the guerrillas and that I was the promoter and doctor of the guerrillas, that I was in charge of the guerrillas, commanding everyone. It is true that I left the community a lot just like I do today. I would go wherever someone was sick to try to help them because I was a health promoter. I attended poor women, children, whoever was in need, but I never helped the guerrilla who carried weapons.

On Friday, July 16, soldiers came to Plan de Sánchez. They didn't do anything. They said they were just visiting. They went house to house passing out toys and dolls to the children. They still asked about us [the men of the village]. But we weren't there, so they didn't find us. Our poor families all felt content with the gifts they received. The soldiers even gave candies to the women. We didn't think anyone was going to die. So, we came down from our hiding places on Friday afternoon. We were with our families until Sunday morning.

On Sunday morning, everyone started going down to the market in Rabinal. The people from Concúl, Balamchel, Ixchel, Joya de Ramos, everyone was passing through Plan de Sánchez to go to the plaza. That same morning, the army had thrown two grenades here in Plan de Sánchez. But it was already very serious because each day a plane would fly overhead dropping bombs in the mountain. No one was killed because no one was there in the mountains. There weren't any large groups of people hiding there. The men who hid from patrolling were in small groups of two, three, or four. So those bombs didn't kill anyone. The bombs were really more a threat to us that we should return to our homes and not hide in the mountains.

We didn't go to the market with the women and children. We men hadn't been down to Rabinal since 1981. We couldn't go down because if we did, they would force us to patrol. So we never went to Rabinal. We went down to our fields to work and tend our animals.

Two days before that Sunday, I had a dream. I think that is why I am still here working in my community. In my dream, we were in a place. Father Melchor was sitting at a table and everyone in the community was meeting with the priest. But Father Melchor already had a list of everyone. He already had everything written down. This was when I arrived in my dream. "Father," I said, "Write my name down. I am going to go, too." He picked up his pen and said, "Okay," as he wrote down my name. But then when he realized he had written my name on the list, he turned around. "You, Juan," he said to me, "You are not going to go." That's what Father Melchor told me in my dream. One aunt was standing on one side of me and another aunt on the other side. They said to me, "Juan, you are not going to go because if you go, who will speak for us then?" That was my dream. At the time, I thought it meant that I was going to die. But the meaning of my dream was revealed just a few days later.[16]

HOW A VILLAGE GETS ERASED

July 18, 1982, was a Sunday—a market day for the people of Plan de Sánchez and other local villages. As villagers made the trek down to the Rabinal market, they found their path cordoned off by the military at ten in the morning. They were told that there was an army maneuver and that they would have to go back up the path. Those who lived below Plan de Sánchez were able to return to their villages. Those who were from Plan de Sánchez and those who lived in villages beyond were not so fortunate. The path leading out of Plan de Sánchez was blocked by soldiers.

Those who had been caught on the path to market in Rabinal were rounded up in a humble peasant home that used to stand where a humble chapel of scrap wood lined with tree boughs stood when I arrived in 1994. Those who had the misfortune to be in the village were rounded up by soldiers. Seven girls aged twelve to fourteen were separated from the group.

After tending his cow in the valley, twelve-year-old José returned to his home in the early afternoon. He found the house empty, with tortillas burning on his mother's wood-burning stove. He could hear family and friends screaming and crying. He could hear soldiers shouting and the pounding noise of the dozens of soldiers running through the village. Witnesses estimate that about 150 soldiers occupied the village. José fled back down the mountain with his cow.

At five in the afternoon, Juan Manuel, José, and several other men from the village who had been working with their animals down in the valley below Plan de Sánchez heard two large mortar explosions. Machine gun fire, grenade explosions, and the screams of their families echoed down the valley for the next six hours. Fearing they might encounter soldiers leaving their village, the men stayed down in the valley, huddled in the cold with their animals until dawn.

At four in the morning, Don Erazmo could bear the wait no longer. He returned to the smoldering village. The army was gone. The simple door to his one-room house had been kicked in and everything inside was smashed. His wife, his eight children, and his eighty-eight-year-old mother were missing. Passing other houses just as broken and empty, he ventured out on the path. Smoke was rising across the village from a house near the path leading out of Plan de Sánchez. As he neared the house, he came upon the naked, crucified bodies of the seven young teenage girls, who had been raped. Near the burning rubble of the house near the path, he saw bodies everywhere—but none were those of his family. So he continued on up to the source of the smoke, where he found a pile of human corpses burned beyond recognition and still smoldering. This was all that was left of the twenty-four families of Plan de Sánchez. Don Erazmo ran back to his house. Crying and praying, he waited alone until the other men from the village returned from the valley. Though many men did not return for fear that they would be ambushed by the army, by dawn about a dozen men who had been in the valley and several men from other nearby villages arrived.

While these men knew that the massacre had been committed by the army, they could think of nothing to do other than to send a delegation to the commander of the local army base in Rabinal. The army commander ordered the delegation to assemble units of civil patrol members from nearby villages and said that together these surviving villagers from Plan de Sánchez and these civil patrol members had two hours to bury the 188 people who had been massacred. The commander told them they would be bombed if they failed to meet the two-hour deadline. By two in the afternoon, the smoldering corpses had been buried in mass graves. Three young girls who survived the massacre fled to other parts of Guatemala.[17] Another girl died at a clinic in Rabinal—local people believe she was killed there with a lethal injection.

The remaining survivors in Plan de Sánchez fled the area, as did many other local villagers. They did not begin to return to Plan de Sánchez until several years later, when the army announced that villagers who returned would not be punished as long as they joined the army-controlled civil patrols.

THOSE WHO SURVIVED: JUAN MANUEL GERÓNIMO'S TESTIMONY

We were about sixty meters away when the soldiers killed everyone. We heard everything. The screams of the people. There was nothing we could do to defend them. We had no weapons. Later, we buried our families. From one moment to the next, we were left senseless. What I want to say is that we could not feel anything. We couldn't think about what to do. We couldn't think about anything. I spent fifteen days running here, there, up the mountain, down the mountain. We weren't even thinking about eating. My four brothers and my nephew, all we thought about was our families.

After the massacre, everyone fled in different directions. In Plan de Sánchez, the soldiers and patrollers stole our animals. They had no shame. They killed and burned everything. What they couldn't eat, they put in a big fire. We watched them from a distance. What they couldn't steal, they destroyed.

We hid in the mountains. The army continued to massacre villages. In the end, we were about forty families trying to survive in the mountains. They were survivors from Río Negro, Chitucán, Mangales, Canchún, and other places. I did everything I could to organize the families. We looked for food and hid from the army. Once, in 1984, the army gathered all the PACs from Concul, Xesiban, Las Ventanas, Chipuerta, and Pichec. They spread out all over the mountain looking for us. They practically passed right through us, they were so close to us. For the grace of our God, they just went on looking. They never saw us and never heard us.

We were like refugees. There weren't any whole families. Mostly women with their two or three children. Sometimes, there was an elderly man or woman, sometimes a single woman. It was rare for there to be a man with his family. The men from my community, we took responsibility for these people. We never had them all together, that would be too dangerous. We broke them up into groups and each would lead a group, help them hide, help them find food. We were left defenseless in the mountains.

The guerrillas passed by a few times and told us what was happening in other communities. There were some men who joined the guerrilla, but they had no weapons. I think they recovered three weapons in Cubulco and got some more when they occupied Xococ. But after 1982, the guerrillas were gone. They were very interested in rescuing the survivors, but they couldn't do it. They didn't have the strength. They didn't have the weapons. After our families were killed, they lost confidence, and the people lost trust. They no longer collaborated with the guerrilla because to collaborate is to give them food when they come through. But we didn't have any food and we had lost our families.

So we had to defend ourselves. We had no weapons. We had no food. We were struggling to survive however we could. Wild fruits, seeds, roots—we ate whatever we could find. We tried to grow maize in hidden places. We didn't even have a shack to live in. Forget it! We tied plastic to the trees to try to cover ourselves from the rain. We lived in great poverty.

A lot of people became ill. There was a nun who tried to help us. I had studied with her. If someone was very ill, I would do whatever I could to get the sick person to her to be cured. There were some other women and children who just couldn't survive anymore in the mountains. I walked them to Guatemala City using the Camino Antiguo.[18] Fear is what kept us in the mountains. We stayed in the mountains until 1984, when the army offered amnesty.

But when they gave us amnesty, we were once again obligated to join the civil patrols. We had nothing. We had no animals, no house. We had no food. We weren't allowed to live in Plan de Sánchez. They gave us permission to grow maize here. They gave us a document that said we had amnesty and the right to work. We had to present this document whenever we were stopped—which was always, because they were always watching what everyone did.

The army didn't want to give us a place to live. They didn't want to give us permission to return to Plan de Sánchez. But what could we do without a place to live—we couldn't live. So, in 1985, we organized ourselves. We were eighteen families. These families were our new families. The women and children we brought with us were like us. They had lost their families. They aren't from Plan de Sánchez, they are from other places. My poor wife, the one I have now, she is a widow from the massacre in Chitucán. She had two little boys—one was three years old and the other one was five. They were in the group I was protecting in the mountains. So, that is how we returned to Plan de Sánchez with families. We are a community of widows, widowers, and orphans.

The army made us organize ourselves to patrol. But we didn't patrol here in Plan de Sánchez. We had to go to Cuxumabá. For four and a half years, we patrolled for twenty-four hours every eight days. They didn't give us any weapons. They ordered us to patrol, so we just walked around without incident.

The army sent an educator. The educator travels with the soldiers and meets with the PACs. The educators are professionals. Their job is to tell us not to involve ourselves with the guerrillas. What guerrillas? There were no guerrillas here. When we patrolled, we never saw anything. We never saw anyone with weapons, except for the soldiers.

We were all patrollers. If you arrived just ten minutes late for your patrol, they would punish you. They would put you in a hole with dirty water for twenty-four hours. After I lost my sons, lost my family, somehow it gave me a lot of courage. I always responded to whatever injustice the patrollers were doing. I told the patrol chief that it wasn't possible to do this to a human being. That it was wrong to enslave people in this way. He would order someone into this dirty hole of water. Then they would cover the hole with wood planks. The water rose above the poor man's shoulders. He would order that no one could give the poor man any food or water. But, I always gave them food. I told the other brothers in the patrols that if someone was in that hole, they should give them food. When the poor men would be released from the hole, their skin would be covered with welts from the filth of the water.

I had a lot of problems with this patrol chief. First he tried to win me over. But I refused to take his side. Even with his threats, I wouldn't join him and I wouldn't back down. He ordered me into the hole. He did this because I was very opinionated. I refused to go into the hole. He tried to attack me with his machete. I didn't carry a machete with me, then. I just responded to him with words. I told him that he was an opportunist who took advantage of our tragedies for his own personal gain. He was abusing people and ordering the abuse of people simply because he wanted to do it. He didn't have orders to do it. It was pure abuse. I told him that we didn't deserve this slavery. I told him to think about what he was doing before he hit me with his machete. When he realized that I wasn't going to back down, he just stopped bothering us.

In the midst of all this slavery, we started to organize projects for our communities. We went to the army base and presented a request to the commander. Six of us went together to ask that we be reassigned as patrollers to our own community to protect our own families. We didn't want to patrol at all. We asked in this way so that our families wouldn't be abandoned and so we would have more freedom. He gave us permission. This was in 1988. We still had a local chief, commander, sergeant, and corporal, but the structure was never activated. We were just ordered to patrol. These local commanders were from Cuxajón. They were united with us. We had all suffered patrolling under the PAC [civil patrols] of Chipuerta, that's were there was slavery. In Chipuerta, they obligated us [the men of Plan de Sánchez and Cuxajón] to build a bridge, a community center, and a building for the PAC commanders. That's why we needed to be independent from Chipuerta. We didn't want to be enslaved and we didn't want to hurt people.

The PACs were organized by the army. The army activated them in a very bad way. The PACs did bad things. The army organized the PACs so that it would be the people from the villages who killed the people in the villages. The army gave the orders and the people carried them out. That was the army's strategy; that the people would do bad things to their own communities. The army was like Pilate, who didn't want to be responsible for the death of Jesús; he wanted the people to be responsible. The army had the same idea. But with the passage of time, in some places, the people in the PACs began to change their ideas and modify their behavior. They stopped doing the bad things they had done before. Still, not everyone changed. Those in Xococ never changed.

"WHAT IS WRITTEN IN OUR HEARTS"

Like human rights ombudsman Jorge Mario García La Guardia, the forensic team, and human rights groups, the people of Plan de Sánchez had also learned how to negotiate daily life despite ongoing threats from the army. Unlike nationally and internationally known human rights leaders, this negotiation was most often done in isolation, where community unity was the greatest protection. As Juan Manuel chronicled in his testimony, the army and PACs continued to threaten the community after the villagers returned to Plan de Sánchez.

After taking refuge in the capital and other parts of Guatemala, Pablo and José returned to Plan de Sánchez in 1984. Shortly after their arrival, a platoon of soldiers passed through Plan de Sánchez and ordered the men to attend a meeting in Chipuerta. Pablo describes the meeting:

The army official said, "Welcome to all of you. I have called you here to ask you some questions. Do you deserve to have what happened in Plan de Sánchez happen again? Who of you here behaves like shit? Who of you here doesn't want to collaborate?" That's how he began. Then, he took off his jacket. He took off his machine gun. He took off his belt and threw it down in front of the people. "Who is opposed?" he shouted and he picked up his machine gun and pointed it at all the patrollers. "Who is it here who doesn't want to collaborate?" he said. "Whoever doesn't want to collaborate, I will finish him off right here with this," he said with his machine gun pointing out at the people. "Look here, what happened in Plan de Sánchez, please, no one is going to complain about it because whoever complains," he said holding up his machine gun, "this is what you get." By then he was really red in the face. He said, "Forget about everything that has happened. Your mothers, your fathers are dead. Leave it at that. Forget it."

"Watch out!" he said, "If you start complaining. . . ." Then, he was right in front of me. He looked at me and said, "Do you hear me?" "Yes," I said. And then I guess because I was already conquered by death and I felt no fear, I thought, "If they kill me, they kill me. But they are going to kill me for the truth." I looked up at him and said, "Excuse me sir, pardon my question. In my case, I was in the army in Jutiapa and the army killed my father. So, why do you say now we have peace and should forget everything that has happened? Why has all this happened? Why did the army kill my father?"

The official shouted at me, "Shut your mouth!" But I said, "You can forget, but we are the ones in pain. We will never forget. What happened is written in our hearts. What would you do if they killed your whole family? Would you be capable of forgetting it? Look sir, the truth is that I am not afraid to declare and speak the truth. I was in the army. I was told that I was there to defend the patria, the land, and the family, and the army killed my family. And this sir, I will never forget. Maybe you can forget it happened, but we can't."

He shouted at the patrollers, "And is this true? Is that what happened in Plan de Sánchez?" All the patrollers were looking at the ground. He was expecting everyone to say "No," that everyone would agree with him. Someone in the group softly said, "Yes, it is true." And others started to nod in agreement and say, "Yes, it is true. It is true." The official was still holding the machine gun, but he grabbed his jacket and belt and the rest of his things. He didn't say anything to us. He said, to another officer, "Bring in the specialist to explain to this kid." Then, he left.

The specialist was one of these people from civilian affairs who just said the same things that official had said, but in a softer voice. "We have to forget everything. What you said is true, but we can't bring back the dead. There is nothing to be done. We are with you now and you are with us," he said. After the meeting, lots of people congratulated me. They thanked me. They said, "You are really aggressive. You declared the truth. We will never forget your courage." The patrols came through a few days later. They just kept walking around. They were always coming back and walking through here.

They did that when you were here during the exhumation. They came at night. They wanted to know what was in the house where the *forenses* kept their tools. I told them we had had loaned the house to people to store their belongings. That was the army's revenge against us—to send a platoon here. One of the soldiers came over to ask me questions. They asked me for a place to spend the night. I told them that we never refuse shelter to anyone and told them they could sleep in the corridor outside. "What about that house?" he asked. I told him there was no space there.

But, I didn't like that I couldn't see them, that I didn't know who they were. So, I poured some gasoline on some wood, which quickly gave me a large flame. Then, I offered them the warmth of the burning wood so that I could see their faces. What did they do? They hid their faces, but because the flame was so hot! When the sun rose, they got up and stayed about two hours. They said they wanted to buy some food. But we didn't have enough to sell. So, I gave them each a tortilla. They left. But, instead of taking the main road, they went to the path that leads to Juan Manuel's house. They were going there to investigate him. They were separating so they could surround his house. So, I went after them. I said, "Excuse me, I think you have lost your way. The path out of the village is up there. This path doesn't go anywhere." Then, they left.[19]

Army visits were not limited to the houses in Plan de Sánchez. During the second month of the exhumation, we began to hear commentaries about the army's *"auto-limpieza"*—self-cleaning. The lieutenant who had led the Plan de Sánchez massacre and two local soldiers from Rabinal who had participated in the killing were found dead in their beds with a single bullet through their heads. Rumors circulated that the army had eliminated the possibility of these material authors identifying the officials who gave them the orders to massacre—thus also eliminating the possibility of material authors fingering the intellectual authors of genocide.

As Pablo recounted the military threats they had received during the exhumation, I remembered giving a leader from another community a ride to Plan de Sánchez. He had never before been there and wanted to surprise his friends. When we reached his friend's house, he looked at me smiling and said, "Look how smart he is," as he pointed to the exterior wall. "He is smarter than they are. When the soldiers come, they think they have the wrong house." He was pointing to framed photographs of soldiers that adorned the wall at the entrance to the house.

THE BURIAL

On July 4, 1994, as everyone prepared for national human rights ombudsman Jorge Mario García La Guardía's visit, Juan Manuel, Pablo, Erazmo, and José asked several of us if we had time to meet with them. They appeared concerned. They explained to us that the mayor of Rabinal was scheduled to visit the site that same day. They asked us if we would help them present a petition to the mayor because they felt our presence would affect the mayor's response. The community had decided that when the remains of their loved ones were returned, they did not want them buried in the cemetery in Rabinal. They wanted the location of the clandestine cemetery declared a legal cemetery. They wanted the proper religious burial in Plan de Sánchez. Juan Manuel explained, "We want them to rest here because this is where their blood spilled, this is where they suffered, so their spirits are here. We don't want to leave them abandoned. We can't bury them anywhere else. We are prepared to sacrifice this land." The owner of the land was in agreement with this plan and was willing to sign a document releasing his property rights.

We agreed to assist the community in whatever way we could. We said that we imagined the mayor would have no problem with their plan because there was no dispute regarding land ownership and everyone was in agreement. "Everyone except the mayor," they responded. They had been to the Rabinal cemetery, the mayor, the health center, and the public ministry. "They always meet with us," explained Juan Manuel, "and they always listen to us. But then they say, 'It's not possible to have a cemetery there. It will affect the health of everyone in the community. It isn't sanitary. There are microbes that can kill people.'" Incredulously, Juan Manuel said, "How is that going to affect our health? They were buried here for twelve years. No one ever died from microbes."[20]

So when the mayor arrived with two armed guards, we all stopped our work to greet him. Then Juan Manuel gave a speech for the community. He thanked the mayor for his support and for coming to visit. Then he explained to the mayor that the community wanted to bury their loved ones in Plan de Sánchez and that the owner of the land was in agreement. He publicly requested the mayor's support for their petition. The mayor glanced around at the community members and then at each of us. He said, "Of course I will help you in any way I can." Juan Manuel thanked him and said, "Then, we have your word here before the public that we can have a legal cemetery here in Plan de Sánchez?" "I give my word," the mayor firmly responded.

Of course, his word was less steady when Juan Manuel returned to the mayor's office for the paperwork. Again, he was sent from the mayor's office to the cemetery, to the public ministry, and to the health center. Again, they all discussed microbes and claimed a cemetery in the community would be a health hazard. "I told them we had worked in the exhumation and no one died from microbes. In twelve years, no one died with the clandestine cemetery there," recounted Juan Manuel. "Finally, I told them, and this is the truth, I told them that if they didn't stop sending me from one office to the other and if no one had the courage to sign the legal documents, then we were just going to do it anyway. I told them that we were prepared to carry out the idea we had, which was a legal cemetery in Plan de Sánchez." With satisfaction, he told me, "In the end, they signed the papers and everyone who had watched me being pushed from office to office saw that really, if we stand together, there are possibilities. And, thanks to all the international brothers and sisters who came here to take our declarations, everyone saw that it is possible to speak the truth."

In October 1994, the plaza of Rabinal filled with thousands of Achí from outlying villages and Rabinal to witness the burial procession. After a mass inside the church, the crowd in the plaza listened to the words of the survivors from Plan de Sánchez, which were amplified throughout the community. Juan Manuel remembered that moment:

> After the exhumation, people had been congratulating me. They would say, "Congratulations Juan. You really have balls to declare the truth." But then they would tell me to be careful because everyone knew who I was and there were people who didn't like what I did. I was thinking about this as we carried the coffins to the church. After mass, when I was standing there in front of everyone, I just wasn't afraid. I told the whole truth. I said that the army should be ashamed. "How shameful for them to say that my wife with a baby on her back was a guerrilla. They dragged her out of my house and killed her. Shameful! They opened the abdomens of pregnant women. And then they said that they killed guerrillas. Shameful!" I said. I talked about the people in Rabinal who had collaborated with the army and how they walked through the streets with no shame for the killings they had done. In this moment, I had no fear. I declared the truth.
>
> Afterwards, a *licenciado*[21] told me, "What a shame that you are a poor peasant and not a professional. If you were a professional, there would really be change here." I thought to myself, "I may be a sad peasant who can only half-speak, but I wasn't afraid and I spoke the truth." The entire pueblo was there. The park was completely full. Everyone was listening to what I was saying and I didn't feel embarrassed. I knew that afterwards maybe they would be waiting for me in the street somewhere and that that might be my luck. I said, "Believe me, the guilty think that with just one finger they can cover the sun. But with what they have done here, they simply can't."[22]

Juan Manuel's public speaking of truth before his community is a transformation of "poisonous knowledge" into a collective discourse of empowerment. And truth, as Italian theorist Giorgio Agamben suggests, "cannot be shown except by showing the false, which is not, however, cut-off and cast aside somewhere else."[23] Indeed, for Agamben, truth can only be revealed by "giving space or a place to non-truth—that is, a taking place of the false, as an innermost impropriety."[24] More than ten years after the massacre, the public events of exhumations, processions, and re-burials, like the legal cases against perpetrators, represent a public performance of the accretion of truth, and thus, the accretion of power. The effects of this power are experienced in the everyday life of the community and directly challenge the spectral presence of the state (the state's production of truth) by establishing a new domain in which "the practice of true and false can be made at once ordered and pertinent."[25]

Following Juan Manuel's speech, the survivors of Plan de Sánchez carried the decorated coffins of their loved ones in a procession throughout Rabinal, then three and one-half hours up the mountain to Plan de Sánchez, where they reburied the remains of their loved ones at the site of the massacre and clandestine cemetery. Later, a Maya death house (or *capilla*—chapel) was built on the site with marble plaques chronicling the Plan de Sánchez massacre. Residents of the village regularly visit the capilla to pray with their ancestors. Each year a public commemoration with a Catholic mass and Maya costumbre mark the anniversary of the massacre. Also, since the exhumation, many new community projects were started in Rabinal, including a community healing project and an orphans and widows organization.

In Plan de Sánchez, the local development of these political and social practices began with the community organizing and "standing up"[26] to request an exhumation and ultimately succeeded not only in the exhumation but also in the retaking of public spaces—the municipal plaza, the church, the clandestine cemetery. As a community, survivors challenged these public spaces as mere reminders of Maya loss and remade them into sites of popular memory contesting official state stories. Far from eroding agency, these appropriations, reworkings, and enactments of global rights discourses created "a framework within which people [were able to] develop and exercise agency."[27] Further, these same survivors, widowers, and widows seized the space they had created not only to publicly adjudicate collective memory but also to move forward with legal proceedings against intellectual and material authors of the massacre.

The exhumation was transforming what Michael Taussig refers to as a "space of death"[28] and all its silences, inscribing it with truth and reclaiming it as a public space affirming the rights of the dead and living. Moreover, this transformation was possible because, as Foucault observed, "truth is a thing of the world: it is produced only by virtue of multiple forms of constraint. And it has regular effects of power."[29]

EXCAVATIONS OF THE HEART

Healing Fragmented Communities

The people that walked in darkness have seen a great light. They walk in lands of
shadows but a light has shone forth.

—*Isaiah 9:1–2*

"TO FEEL GOOD IN THE HEART"

In Plan de Sánchez, we were excavating eighteen mass graves. This meant
we were unearthing a tremendous number of artifacts and clothing associated with each skeleton. On one occasion, local villagers sorted through artifacts found in a grave of burned skeletons. The bones were so badly
burned and contorted from the fire that though we could count that there
had been at least sixteen victims, we had no complete skeletons and were
unable to associate any of the artifacts with individual skeletons. Survivors
asked us if they could examine the artifacts. We laid them out above the
grave in an orderly and respectful manner on top of flattened paper bags.
Then the survivors surrounded the artifacts spread out before them. With
great tenderness, they began to look through burned bits of clothing,
necklace beads, and half-melted plastic shoes, trying to recognize something of their relatives who had been killed in the massacre. A few of the
men recognized their wives' wedding necklaces and asked us if it might be

possible for them to have the necklaces after the investigation was completed. There was no dissension in the community about which necklaces had belonged to which wives. Those who couldn't find the necklaces of their wives, sisters, and daughters asked if they might be able to have some of the stray beads because "surely some of those beads must have fallen from our relatives' necklaces." Then, they said something I was to hear repeated in every other exhumation in which I have participated, *"Si no tiene dueño, entonces es mío"* (if it doesn't have an owner, then it is mine).

In Panzós, in the late evening after the church mass and public gathering, we moved the boxed remains to the community center. We placed the bones in small coffins and the artifacts on top of the closed coffins. We had only been able to name two of the thirty-five skeletons exhumed based on positive scientific identification. Because the greatest desire of family members is to carry the remains of their loved ones in the burial procession, we give them an opportunity to look at the artifacts to fulfill their desire to identify their lost loved one—*"para sentir bien en el corazón,"* to feel good in the heart (what we might call closure). Though not considered positive scientific identifications, when a survivor recognizes artifacts, we mark the coffin so that they may carry it in the burial procession. Sometimes, there is nothing concrete in the identification, but other times it is emotionally overwhelming. One elderly man had passed nearly half of the coffins. He passed those with women's clothing and stopped at each that had men's boots. He would pick up the boots and swiftly review the instep. In front of one of the coffins, as those in line pushed forward to look at the next set of artifacts, he remained frozen in place, gripping the heel of a plastic boot. I walked over to him. He said, "This is my son. These are his boots. Look here. See that stitching? That is my stitching. I sewed his boot together the morning before he was killed. This is my son." As other survivors reached the end of the row of coffins without immediately recognizing anything, they would return and start over. During the second round, they began to stand by different coffins. When I approached them to find out what they had identified, each said, *"Si no tiene dueño, entonces es mío."*

THE WIDOWS OF XOCOC

Every day I spent in Plan de Sánchez, campesinos from other villages— elderly women, elderly men, young women and men, children, entire families—came to witness the excavation of the graves. First, they would watch from a distance. As the morning wore on, they would move closer and closer. Whether alone or a part of a group, they were silent, occasionally whispering to one another. Usually after lunch, they would move right up to the edge of the grave, positioning themselves close to me and other working forensic team members. Usually, it was a woman crouched down as close as she could get without actually entering the grave. After a deep breath and brief pause, she would say, "You know, we need an exhumation, too. We also suffered a massacre." I would always ask how many people died and the response was always the same: *"Casi todos,"* nearly everyone. Sometimes they meant all the men in their family. Sometimes they meant all the women. Sometimes, they meant nearly everyone in their village had been killed.

Just one week after I began working with the forensic team in Plan de Sánchez, a delegation of some forty women and one elderly man arrived to our work site in the late morning of June 28. Doña Soledad appeared to be the leader of the group, though her father, the elderly Don Miguel, was treated with great deference by all the women. They came from Xococ, a village on the other side of the mountain, in the valley, much closer to Rabinal than Plan de Sánchez. They came to report that on June 26 Xococ civil patrollers had damaged several sites of clandestine cemeteries in their village. Doña Soledad feared the civil patrol had removed the bones in an effort to destroy any evidence that might subsequently be uncovered should an exhumation take place in Xococ in the future. This delegation had walked six hours to request our intervention. They wanted the forensic team to determine if the bones of their loved ones had been taken. And they specifically wanted the judge to place an official sign, like the one we had in Plan de Sánchez, over each of the graves in Xococ. Over our work site stood a hand-painted sign on a rusting piece of metal that read: "Do Not Touch. Site of Legal Investigation By Order of the Justice of the Peace Under Protection of the National Police."

That same morning, I accompanied several members of the forensic team, the local justice of the peace, and the Xococ delegation to Xococ to survey the grave sites. Plants used by survivors to mark the graves had been cleared and the superficial layer of earth (ranging from one to two inches) had been dug and loosened. At one grave, fragments of a human rib were found mixed in the top soil. It was, however, determined that while the graves had been disturbed, the skeletons had not been removed.

The women were relieved to learn that the skeletons were still in the graves. They reiterated to the judge the need for an official "Do Not

Touch" sign. The judge explained that these signs were issued by the court after an exhumation had been approved. He also commented on the conspicuous absence of men from the village. The women explained that the men were absent because of the civil patrol. Doña Soledad said, "Some of the men want the graves exhumed, but the military commissioner does not. So none of the patrollers are here. The thing is that those who don't oppose the exhumation are afraid of those who do."[1]

The women wanted a speedy exhumation for fear of the civil patrol stealing the bones of their dead sons and husbands. We recommended that they might be able to speed up the bureaucratic process by personally petitioning the national human rights ombudsman, Jorge Mario García La Guardía, who would be making a site visit to Plan de Sánchez the following Monday.

Two vans full of national Guatemalan press accompanied García La Guardía to Plan de Sánchez that Monday. He was greeted by the villagers of Plan de Sánchez and those from surrounding communities, the forensic team, and the delegation from Xococ. Before the national print, television, and radio reporters, these bold women from Xococ denounced the 1981 massacre of their sons and husbands and the recent actions of the civil patrol. They presented their personal petition to the ombudsman, who publicly promised to move the paperwork as quickly as possible. He also reproached the civil patrol for disturbing the graves. The women of Xococ were satisfied and thanked García La Guardía for listening to their petition.

I was fascinated by the independence and courage displayed by these women, who lived in what was widely regarded throughout the region as the most militarized community in Rabinal. In Xococ, the PAC (Patrullas Autodefensa Civil—Civil Patrol) had always been armed with Winchester rifles. Particularly interesting to me was this very public expression of the fragmented social relations of a community. On the one hand, the consent and coercion of the army's hegemonic control of Xococ was manifested by the continuation of an armed civil patrol in which all men in the community participated at a time when most communities in Rabinal had simply stopped patrolling, either by intentional noncompliance, passive resistance, or incremental neglect. On the other hand, a significant number of women from Xococ had seized, if not created, a public space from which to assert their demands for justice. When I mentioned my interest in interviewing the Xococ widows to Doña Soledad, she enthusiastically supported the idea. She invited me to visit Xococ. She told me that I could go any day. "Just go to the village plaza and use the megaphone," she said. "Say, '*Que vengan las viudas,*'" (Widows come here). She assured me that they would all respond.[2]

When I spoke with Father Luís in Rabinal later that same Monday, he told me that he did not believe that Doña Soledad was sincere. "This story of the widows of Xococ is some kind of trick to sabotage the work of the forensic team. Most likely, it is an army plot," he said. "Her father, Don Miguel, is with the army. He cannot be trusted. He is a leader of the civil patrol and he likes it. He opposes the guerrilla." Father Luís went on to explain that these organized visits to Plan de Sánchez had to be part of an army trap for the forensic team; that in the past there had been some armed confrontations between the army and guerrilla in Xococ. He was convinced that the pressure to exhume quickly in Xococ was a plot to trick the forensic team into exhuming civilians killed by the guerrilla or guerrilla combatants killed in battle—either of which would have supported army claims of armed confrontations with the guerrilla rather than massacres of unarmed civilians. "Moreover," Father Luís reminded me, "the civil patrol from Xococ committed the massacre in Río Negro. This is a trap. Believe me. I know these people."

For the priest's interpretation of these events to be correct, the Xococ civil patrol, as well as the many women who traveled to Plan de Sánchez and accompanied us in our survey work in Xococ, would have all had to have been in collusion with the army in the orchestration of a huge lie to the forensic team, the local judge, the human rights ombudsman, and the villagers of Plan de Sánchez and other Rabinal communities.

"QUE VENGAN LAS VIUDAS"

While I was not convinced of the priest's interpretation, it was present in my thoughts ten days later as Kathleen Dill and I prepared to visit Xococ to interview the widows. Initially, we had scheduled our trip for that day in order to go with the judge and departmental human rights ombudsman, who already had arranged a visit. Our plans were cut short when the ombudsman failed to arrive with his vehicle. Kathleen and I went to the Rabinal plaza and hired a driver with a vehicle. The justice of the peace declined our offer to accompany us in the vehicle because he deemed it unsafe to travel to Xococ without benefit of the ombudsman's armed security guard.

Forensic team members were divided about our plans. One told us not to go. He said, "Look, they think gringas are stealing their babies for organs all over the country. The patrollers there will use that as their excuse to hang you. Don't go."[3] Another said, "No, they should go. They know what they're getting into." Then they all began to give us conflicting suggestions about how to ensure our security. "Go alone." "Go as part of a group." "Act like tourists." "Don't act like tourists."

We were relieved to discover that July 14 was the day of the livestock fair in Xococ. We decided to take advantage of the presence of the Achí from all over Rabinal who would be attending the fair. Though we knew that we would most likely be the only gringas, at least there would be people from other communities visiting. As we drove to Xococ, we invited the driver to pick up additional fares—this helped us stand out a little less when we arrived. To ensure he would not leave us stranded, we told him that we would pay him at the end of the day. We decided to take lots of photographs and act like wayward tourists. The women of Xococ had invited me and I wanted to honor their invitation.

While we were not necessarily expecting to be welcomed by everyone in Xococ, we had expected the festive atmosphere of a fair. Thus, we were taken aback when people leaving the fair ignored and avoided us. Women with whom I had waded through a river in Xococ only ten days earlier fixed their gaze upon the ground as they passed us silently. As we reached the plaza, we immediately knew their reason. Xococ was occupied by the army. Soldiers in camouflage with grenades hanging at their waists and machine guns in hand were everywhere.

Kathleen and I began to photograph horses and cows. When we reached the center of the plaza, we photographed the masked children in the dance competition. We were concerned about endangering anyone in Xococ and agreed that we would stay just long enough to show an interest in the fair (for anyone who might have been watching us) and then quietly return to Rabinal. After we had been there for about thirty minutes, Doña Soledad caught my attention and motioned for us to follow her outside of the sight and earshot of the soldiers. She invited us back to her house. She directed us to take a path through the cornfields to the back of her house. She walked home alone through the street. We met her at her back door.

IN DOÑA SOLEDAD'S HOUSE

Though it was late morning, we sat in darkness with all doors and windows closed. She told us that the soldiers had been in her village since the day of the ombudsman's visit to Plan de Sánchez when the Xococ widows had presented their petition. Her village was occupied when the delegation returned that day from Plan de Sánchez. Fearing intervention from the ombudsman, the Xococ civil patrol had gone to the local army base to request the troops in hope of discouraging the women from pursuing the exhumation. Doña Soledad was overcome with fear. She told us that local villagers were blaming her for the occupation. If she had not pursued the exhumation, the soldiers would not be in Xococ. Everyone was scared. People were saying that something was going to happen to her father, Don Miguel. They said it would be Soledad's fault for convincing him to lead the delegation. Don Miguel was one of the oldest principales in Xococ. People were saying, "If they kill Don Miguel, then the civil patrol can kill anyone."

Though the soldiers had thus far not directly threatened anyone in the community, their mere presence was enough to terrify everyone. Doña Soledad was crying, "All I wanted was my husband's bones for a proper burial. I don't want my father to die. What should I do?"

We spent more than an hour discussing her options: denouncing the occupation to the national and international press; seeking support from CONAVIGUA (Coordindora Nacional de las Viudas de Guatemala—National Coordinator of Guatemalan Widows), withdrawing the petition for the exhumation, leaving Xococ to visit relatives in Guatemala City, thinking about these options for a few days in Xococ or in Guatemala City. Knowing she had options and feeling no pressure to make any immediate decisions calmed her significantly. Then, she began to tell her story, not in the form of an interview, but as an unloading of pain to someone who seemed to understand.

In March 1981, while her husband and fourteen other men were working in their fields, a blue Toyota full of judiciales raced into Xococ. They drove through the fields rounding up the men, accusing them of being guerrillas and killing them. Local villagers quickly buried them at the sites of their deaths. Doña Soledad wanted a proper burial for her husband. After she told me this, she said, "I feel better now. If you want to interview me, you can." I told her that an interview was unnecessary. I did not want her to feel that she owed me something because I had listened to her. She asked me how to get in touch with CONAVIGUA.[4]

Later that day, I spoke with Father Luís. While he was clearly concerned about the army occupation of Xococ, he maintained his initial interpretation that still, somehow, this all had to be some kind of conspiratorial army plot.

TESTIMONY AND HEALING

For massacre and torture survivors, and other victims of extreme state terror, testimony has meaning beyond its implications for individual agency, community action, and challenging repressive state practices. Psychologists and other mental health professionals have found testimony, as a therapeutic model, to be an effective method for survivors to process and come to terms with the extreme traumas they have suffered. Though grounded in Western psychological training, which seeks to categorize individuals and all manifestations of psychological trauma into quantifiable and identifiable diagnostic concepts related to an assumed baseline of individual autonomy, experienced trauma researchers and practitioners have further sought to develop interventions that better address survivors' needs and recognize cross-cultural differences. The therapeutic testimonial model is one such intervention.[5]

Just as the landscape of contemporary anthropology is marked by debates about its theory and practice, the discipline of psychology and the mental health field have ongoing debates about the clinical efficacy and limitations of diagnostic concepts—which are the cornerstone of therapeutic practice. The realities of lived experiences of survivors have presented significant challenges and controversy regarding traditional Western models of labeling (and treating) individual survivors and their traumas. One example of this is post-traumatic stress disorder (PTSD), one of the many categories of psychiatric disorders defined and operationalized in the *Diagnostic and Statistical Manual of Mental Disorders* (DSM).[6] The DSM is the near-universal tool used in the United States for diagnosis and treatment of mental disorders. The therapeutic testimonial model challenges the core assumptions of homogenized culture underlying the very concept of universal diagnosis (and its emphasis on individual autonomy) and in particular the relevance of PTSD (which is based on symptoms and treatment of individuals) to cultures in which individual personhood is based more in the identity of community culture than in that of the individual. Still, when PTSD became a category of the DSM-III in 1980, its inclusion was significant in that it was the first time a collection of symptoms resulting from an environmental stress were specified and classified as a disorder.

As the mental health community sought to come to terms with the common collection of trauma symptoms present in vast numbers of Vietnam veterans, PTSD gained currency with both clinical researchers and practitioners. These symptoms later came to be recognized as a syndrome.[7] The timing for categorizing the trauma of Vietnam veterans as PTSD coincided with significant increases in immigration of traumatized refugee populations to the United States, Australia, New Zealand, and Europe. Patrick McGorry notes that mental health services to these refugee populations were a categorical failure in the 1970s and early 1980s due to a lack of appreciation of the unique needs of traumatized refugees.[8] Despite existing literature offering new insights to the treatment of trauma,[9] PTSD swiftly became the diagnosis of choice for identifying and addressing the traumas of war and torture survival. By the 1990s, significant studies of mental health treatment models for Bosnian, Guatemalan, Chilean, Salvadoran, and Cambodian trauma survivors offered new treatment frameworks and challenged the relevance of PTSD, as well as many standard practices in psychotherapeutic treatment. Many of these new treatment models were the direct result of researchers and mental health practitioners working directly with trauma survivors in community health programs serving affected refugee populations, or explicitly involved in the provision of mental health services through new centers established for the treatment of torture survivors. Thus, their development of new models of intervention and their research on the efficacy of these models was driven by clinical experience with the inadequacies of DSM categories and treatment.[10]

Testimony became a key tool recognized for its efficacy in healing both public and private domains.[11] Drawing on psychotherapeutic models of treatment developed in the Southern Cone during the state repression of the 1970s, therapists in the United States, Europe, Australia, and New Zealand began to set aside the "neutrality" that had always been one of the basic tenets of therapeutic practice. Argentine psychiatrist Tato Pavlovsky explained his own experience with the inevitable necessity of this shift in therapeutic practice:

> Lots of people were dying and it was impossible to be objective in this period. . . . The issue of neutrality was dead along with the dying. . . . I tried to be as neutral as possible in order to understand the nature of the more irrational conflicts that a patient might be suffering. But, given the conditions we were living through, sometimes the therapy provided the important function of helping patients with the difficult task of developing a language with which to articulate their experience of terror. In retrospect, I realize that often the therapy group provided the only space in which people could put into words the fear, the panic. It was the only space in which to speak.[12]

Likewise, North American, Australian, and European therapists learned from experience that in order to establish an effective therapeutic relationship with trauma survivors, therapists needed to take explicit positions on the side of the survivors. These included an open commitment to human rights,[13] a "partisan" position,[14] and an acknowledgment of professional responsibility for the prevention of acts of state terror by encouraging "appropriate opposing actions."[15] This shift from neutrality to partisanship reflected a growing awareness of prevalent thematic conflicts common among trauma survivors. Recurring themes included:

> fear of destroying others, such as relatives and therapists, by relating the trauma; fear of loss of control over feelings of rage, violence, and anxiety; shame and rage over the vulnerability and helplessness evoked by torture; rage and grief at the sudden and arbitrary disruption of individual, social, and political projects, and at the violation of rights; guilt and shame over surviving and being unable to save others; guilt over bringing distress on self and family and over not protecting them . . . ; fear and rage at the unpredictability of and lack of control over events; grief over the loss of significant others, through both death and exile; and loss of aspects of the self, such as trust and innocence.[16]

By transforming the therapist's role from neutral observer to partisan witness, the survivors are given the opportunity to "understand the impossible nature of the situation to which they had been exposed" and are then able to begin transferring "the burden of responsibility" to the perpetrators of violence and to the repressive structures that fomented their traumas.[17] The research experiences of the forensic team and my own fieldwork experiences reaffirm the necessity of recognizing our professional obligations as anthropologists to contribute to the prevention of human rights violations and support survivor efforts for justice by establishing solidarity with survivors of trauma.

The testimonial therapy model, as developed in the Southern Cone and now practiced in the United States, Australia, Europe, and other parts of Latin America, has much in common with the theory and practice of testimonial literature. It also resonates with the FAFG (Fundación de Antropología Forense de Guatemala—Guatemalan Forensic Anthropology Foundation) model of collecting testimonies. In each case, the testimony of survivors reflects their individual and community experiences as a part of a larger national history. In their work with Bosnian survivors of "Ethnic Cleansing," Stevan Weine and Dóri Laub write that the historical narrative of therapeutic testimony is "one dimension of the survivors' struggle to reassert their connectedness to the threatened collective entities of community, ethnicity and nationality."[18] A written record of the testimony is produced in the therapeutic process. In addition to the possibilities of catharsis and closure presented by the therapeutic model of testimony, the survivor, who plays an active therapeutic role by giving testimony, also participates in the production of the written record, which can later be used in individual and community attempts to provide evidence of human rights violations and seek justice.[19]

COMMUNITY HEALING

When Rolando Alecio completed his fieldwork as a contributing author for *Las Masacres en Rabinal*,[20] he was convinced that massacre survivors were in great need of psychotherapeutic intervention. A long-time human rights activist trained as an anthropologist and with extensive fieldwork in the Achí communities of Rabinal, Alecio was well-aware of the debates of cultural relativism in psychotherapy as well as the doubts about the relevance of the PTSD model. Seeking to learn from similar experiences with state repression in other countries, he immersed himself in trauma therapy literature from all over the world. With psychologists Olga Alicia Paz and Felipe Sartí, he founded the Equipo de Estudios Comunitarios y Acción Psicosocial (ECAP—Psycho-Social Community Studies and Action Team) to develop a pilot community healing project in Rabinal. Recognizing the cultural importance of community identity for the Achí, ECAP transformed the individual testimony model to a community model. Like the individual testimony model, ECAP's community healing project breaks the binary that counterpoises justice and healing, further challenging Western constructs of both politics and therapeutic healing.

The community-articulated support groups for widows, widowers, and orphans, which grew out of the exhumations, and other human rights activities in Rabinal became the base of ECAP's community work. Though ECAP was initiated in 1996 as a pilot project limited to only a few communities in Rabinal, the popular response was so great that by the end of the first year, ECAP was working in nineteen Rabinal communities at the request of local residents.[21]

Conscious of the instability of NGO (nongovernmental organization) funding, from the outset ECAP sought to develop community skills in mental health promotion. Indeed, when Alecio, Paz, and Sartí began the project, they did so with their own funds and made a collective commitment to go without salaries for six months.[22] "We began ECAP with our own funds and we always worked with the assumption that in six months or a year, we might not have any funding," explained Alecio. "So, we always sought to develop community-based mental health promotion so that community healing would continue even if ECAP collapsed."[23]

To these ends, ECAP community participants received training in responsible listening techniques, participatory healing techniques, and the development of community mental health safety nets. In addition to community participation in workshops and support groups addressing these themes, ECAP developed three low-literacy training publications and other educational tools for community use. ECAP's organizational philosophy resonates with Francesca Polleta's research on the United States civil rights movement, which emphasized development of local community leadership, "standing up" (speaking publicly), consensus decision making, and an emphasis on the collective process as a part of emancipation.[24]

I had the privilege of accompanying ECAP in their community work on numerous occasions, both formally and informally, from 1996 to 2002. Village support groups meet in their communities and at the ECAP office in Rabinal. Frequently, collaborative intercommunity meetings are held to share experiences and plan joint community projects. The following is a brief composite sketch of my observations of some of ECAP's healing techniques in action.

At community support groups, a near life-size drawing of an Achí man and/or woman is displayed (depending upon the gender composition of the group). The Achís represented in these drawings are seated in chairs with their bodies slumping forward and sad facial expressions. The group begins by describing how the person in the drawing is feeling. Nearly everyone comments that the person is "very sad," and some say the person is "angry." When asked by ECAP or local community facilitators why they describe the person in the drawing as sad or angry, support group participants identify the body language and facial expressions as those of "pain." When asked why the person might feel pain, sadness, or anger, the responses are profound. "She is sad because her eyes dried from crying so many tears," explained one woman. "He has pain because his heart has fallen into his stomach," said a man. "Her head hurts from being filled with so much pain for so long. She has no room for good thoughts," explained a woman. "His bones hurt because the weight of his pain pulls him to the ground," said a man.

These initial discussions in support groups provide an opening for community therapy to begin. ECAP points out that community healing reaffirms Maya community values and practices of cooperation, equilibrium, and respect. ECAP's goals of community healing include creating: (1) a space where community members can express themselves and be heard; (2) a space of trust and acceptance; and (3) a space for solidarity to nurture new relations of mutual support. Through the collective creation of this space, and with the assistance of ECAP facilitators, support groups themselves identify their existing community resources and new resources that arise out of group discussion. Additional goals of the community healing project are the development of: (1) local capacity to collectively sustain community healing; (2) a sense of belonging; (3) validation of community experiences; (4) community empowerment for local action; (5) the group's ability to put forth solutions for community problems; and (6) local skills in conflict resolution to reduce community divisions and antagonisms resulting from internal village disputes.[25]

After the exhumation, Juan Manuel Gerónimo participated as a local researcher/organizer in the archbishop's *Nunca Más* [REHMI—Proyecto Interdiocesano de Recuperación Histórico—Interdiocesene Project for the Recuperation of Historical Memory] human rights project. Now, he participates in ECAP's community healing project in Plan de Sánchez and in other communities throughout Rabinal. I asked Don Juan Manuel why he decided to dedicate a significant amount of his time to ECAP meetings and workshops. He explained: "I believe the work of REHMI needs to continue in the communities. The same people who worked in REHMI can collaborate with ECAP to help the poor people who suffered these massacres talk about what happened and how it happened. This needs to be done and it needs to be done formally so that as our children and families grow, they will have clarity about our history and so there will be a space to continue to declare the truth."[26]

In their efforts to develop safe community spaces of mutual emotional support, those who participate in community healing in Rabinal have strengthened practices of solidarity, trust, communication, participation, integration, support, and tolerance grounded in Achí community practices. ECAP's methodology and practice of community healing recognized and elaborated community experiences of traumas suffered. By creating safe collective spaces for individuals to speak and be heard, individuals and communities are able to recuperate and redefine collective identity in the aftermath of violence. It is this nascent collective identity that offers hope for the recovery of human dignity and the reconstruction of the social fabric so damaged by political violence. Like the exhumations, this process of collective recovery of psycho-social community identity also establishes the community as the conduit from the individual to the nation.

"NOW THERE IS MORE FREEDOM"

Following the public burials of massacre victims in Rabinal, survivors sought the healing of space and community by building monuments to commemorate the victims. In Plan de Sánchez, survivors requested support from the Catholic Church and NGOs to raise funds to purchase materials for the community construction of a memorial chapel at the site of their new, legal cemetery. The chapel in Plan de Sánchez was constructed in keeping with Maya religious burial practices. Massacre victims are buried under the chapel floor, making the chapel a large monumental marker and facilitating Maya religious practices of communicating with the ancestors at the altar within the chapel. A chiseled marble plaque entitled "It is not possible to cover the sun with just one finger" tells the history of the army massacre in Plan de Sánchez. Local residents frequently visit the chapel, leave flowers, light candles, and pray to the ancestors. Each year on the anniversary of the massacre, the residents of Plan de Sánchez invite friends, relatives, neighbors, government officials, the press, national and international NGOs, and all of Rabinal to participate in a religious commemoration for the victims.

In 1997, more than 500 people attended the event, where both Catholic mass and Maya costumbre were celebrated. The community provided all in attendance with an impressive feast of tamales, meat, beans, tortillas, coffee, and sodas. While Achí from Rabinal and other villages, as well as many NGO representatives, attended the commemoration, the only Rabinal ladinos attending were two elderly women. I asked them why they came to Plan de Sánchez. Doña Sonia responded, "Doña Angela is very religious. She attends every mass for the dead. La Violencia really affected her. So, now she is very religious." I asked Doña Sonia if she too was "very religious." "Not really," she responded as she drank her second beer purchased from the Plan de Sánchez *tienda*. "These people are my friends. They are human beings. I have always known that. After the massacres, I tried to help them. But, what can one widow do?"

she asked. Then she went on to explain, "When they were in the mountains, if they came to my house, I would give them food, candles, and some clothing, because they had nothing. They were wearing rags. They are my friends. They always came to my store before [La Violencia]. So I couldn't turn my back on their needs."

When I asked why other ladinos from Rabinal were absent, she said, "Some are embarrassed because they did nothing. Others are scared because of what they did. Bad people became rich from the massacres. They stole the livestock from the villages. They became rich as butchers selling the meat of the animals they stole." I asked her if these men were always bad or if the violence had made them bad. After thinking for a few minutes, she said, "I think they were always bad. What happened is that La Violencia gave them the power to do bad things with impunity. So they became worse."[27]

While much of the distance remains between the ladinos and the Achí of Rabinal, there are notable changes in the town. Windows and doors that, in the past, were locked shut in the daytime are now left open into the early evening. People no longer rush through the streets to reach their destination. At night, Achí and ladina women stroll the streets arm in arm, visiting friends and neighbors, buying an ice cream in the park; children play games and cruise the streets on their bicycles. While some might think that these changes are due simply to the passage of time, this comfortable freedom of movement is hard to find in other municipalities where truth of La Violencia remains locked in silence.

An Achí professional in Rabinal commented, "The exhumations changed the way people understand themselves in this community. Now, people are living better lives. They're not afraid to leave their homes."[28]

"Now there is more freedom," explained Don Juan Manuel. "The ex-authorities, the ex-commissioners, these people aren't threatening to us anymore. If someone declares their reality, there aren't threats like there were before the exhumation."[29]

Don Pablo described his feelings about the changes:

We are grateful for the exhumations and we are grateful to Juan Manuel for his example. He struggled for the community. Now, there is liberty. Now, our lives are a little better. Some of the fear is gone. We can walk on the paths, we can go to our fields to work without fear. We can go to Rabinal to make our purchases in the market without worries. There are still some bad people there. But now, all they have are words and their words don't hurt us.

Even though we are still very poor, we can live without fear. We are tranquil in our homes. We are grateful to all of you internationals who have taken our declarations because the government had to take account of our case, take account of what happened here.

It is our hope that what happened here never happens again and that the army officials who are responsible go to jail. Now, we go on with our lives: taking care of the land, growing our crops, and trying to give our children some schooling, trying to improve the lives of our families.

As I have said to you before, and maybe others have also told you in their testimonies, it isn't just that we heard it, it isn't just that we saw it. We lived La Violencia and it is written in our hearts. Thanks to God, we have reached an equilibrium. Perhaps now peace will come. This is my testimony. Thank you for listening.[30]

Ten

GENOCIDE AND THE "GREY ZONE" OF JUSTICE

> Cease to do evil, learn to do good; seek justice, correct oppression; defend the fatherless, plead for the widow.
>
> —*Isaiah 1:16–17*

INTRODUCTION

On October 13, 1999, a local Guatemalan court convicted three civil patrollers of murder for their participation in the 1982 army-orchestrated Río Negro massacre. While at first glance the sentence of death by lethal injection might suggest that Guatemala's newly reconstructed legal system is finally functioning, the verdict raises more questions than it answers—among them, the chilling effect this conviction will have on the collection of evidence for future prosecutions of military officials as well as the propensity of the Guatemalan state to exterminate Maya peasants for political expediency. Additionally, it further complicates the already complex and sometimes perplexing international debates about human rights, truth commissions, amnesty, justice, prosecution, rule of law, and democratization.

While there is a growing literature analyzing truth commissions, transitional justice, democratization, and rule of law, the role of nongovernmental organizations (NGOs), and their myriad supporters has been less explored. Political science literature in the 1980s and 1990s ranged from arguing against redress for past human rights violations in transitions from military regimes[1] to those who argued that past rights violations needed to be addressed in some way in order to build rule of law and strengthen democracy.[2] Legal literature in the early 1990s argued for prosecution of perpetrators to establish accountability and rule of law.[3] Literature on NGOs has tended to focus on social movements, development, and humanitarian aid,[4] but not the relationship between NGOs and rule of law or democratization—which has only recently drawn attention.[5] Whether understood as an end or a means to truth, justice, and rule of law, truth commissions are now seen as a critical step for societies experiencing the transition from military rule. Recent literature on transitional justice has begun to explore the relationship among truth, justice, reconciliation, rule of law, and democratization.[6] This chapter builds on the existing literature by bringing the role of NGOs in transitional justice into the conversation.

Through the ethnographic exploration of the trial and murder conviction of military commissioners for their participation in the massacre of Río Negro, and the exhumation of clandestine cemeteries, as well as other rural Maya human rights initiatives, this final chapter discusses contemporary debates about truth versus justice, international tribunals versus domestic prosecution, a nation's international law obligations, and the interplay of these practices and discourses at the local level as the nexus of relations between citizens and the nation state. In this way, I distinguish between vertical and lateral impunity in Guatemala in order to problematize rule of law and the role of NGOs in national and local peacebuilding initiatives. This chapter concludes this book by calling attention to the myriad ways in which rural Maya have created and seized new political spaces in Guatemala's nascent democracy and identifying Maya community human rights organizing as a nexus of engagement between Maya citizens and the nation.

THE RÍO NEGRO MASSACRE[7]

On March 13, 1982, as the army and civil patrol came close to the Achí-Maya village of Río Negro, the men fled. They abandoned their village because, just a few months earlier, seventy men from Río Negro had been massacred by the same army and civil patrol from Xococ. The women and children remained in the village because the army had only ever looked for men, not women and children. This time, however, the civil patrol gathered together these 70 women and 107 children and ordered them to hike up a nearby mountain. The women were ordered to dance with the soldiers "like you dance with the guerrilla." Forensic analysis of the remains showed that the women had been strangled, stabbed, slashed with machetes, and shot in the head. It also revealed that many of the women had received severe beatings to the genital area as evidenced by numerous fractured pelvises, including that of Marta Julia Chen Osorio, who was nine months pregnant at the time of her death. All the women and even the little girls were buried naked from the waist down. Fourteen adolescent girls who were separated from the group early on were later gang raped, then stabbed and macheted to death. The majority of children died from having their heads smashed against rocks and tree trunks.[8]

Eighteen children survived because the patrollers who had killed their families took them into servitude in slave-like conditions in Xococ. The patrollers never imagined that seventeen years later these same survivors would testify against them in a court of law. At the time of the massacre, Jesús Tec was ten years old and carrying his two-year-old brother in his arms. One of the defendants in the court case grabbed the baby by the ankles and pulled him from Jesús. "I begged him not to kill my brother," Jesús testified during the court proceeding, "but he broke his head on a rock." Jesús survived the massacre because the civil patroller who killed his baby brother took him home as a slave.

NATIONAL SECURITY IDEOLOGY

As previously mentioned, the Guatemalan army established numerous military bases and airstrips in the predominantly Maya highlands in the late 1970s and early 1980s. From these bases, the army planned and conducted raids and massacres of Maya villages. Those who survived the massacres were driven into the mountains or forcibly relocated to strategic hamlets where they were required to participate in the army-controlled civil patrols—participation that frequently involved the destruction of other villages as well as the murder of neighbors and other Maya.[9] At the same time, Guatemala received an increasing number of international condemnations for human rights violations, which reflected the Guatemalan army's shift from a strategy of selective terror in the cities to the mass terror of the Scorched Earth campaign in the countryside.[10] The army's objective in the campaign, according to one high-ranking military officer, was to "invert the guerrilla structure" (that is, to so terrorize the Maya communities that those who had or might have participated in popular opposition or armed insurrection would instead do the bidding of the military in army-controlled civil patrols).[11]

Less than one month after General Efraín Ríos Montt declared himself president of Guatemala (after a falling out with other members of the ruling junta with whom he came to power in a March 1982 coup d'état), he further institutionalized the national security state by declaring a state of siege on July 1, 1982.[12] If kidnapping, torture, assassinations, and disappearances have a chilling effect on the court system, the state of siege declared by Ríos Montt provided an affirmation of impunity for the perpetrators of gross human rights violations, a guarantee of continued terror for the rest of society, a state-fomented paralysis of the court system, and a green light to the genocide begun under Lucas García.

Rather than an outwardly focused defense of sovereign borders, the national security state is based on national security ideology.[13] The nation, state, and armed forces come to be classified as synonymous entities, meaning that a challenge to any one of them represents a threat to them all. From this perspective, the armed forces and their agents embody the primary articulation of state dominance. Thus, all challenges to the military, including (and perhaps especially) attempts to seek redress for human rights violations, are perceived as direct assaults on the nation and the state. Past, present, and future analyses of national goals and state actions, as well as the popular movements seeking to shape these goals, are viewed by this triumvirate as subversion because national security ideology is grounded in the recourse of coercion and has no room for the participation or consent of civil society. Instead, the goals of the nation are determined by the state and imposed on the citizenry.[14]

As the CEH (Comisión para el Esclarecimiento Histórico— Commission for Historical Clarification) noted in its final report, "During the armed confrontation, the State's idea of the 'internal enemy,' intrinsic to the National Security Doctrine, became increasingly inclusive."[15] In more specific terms, the state originally identified individuals who directly challenged the state (such as opposition party leaders, student leaders and unionists) as subversives. As time went on, the category of "subversive" was increasingly expansive and included all who provided services to the poor and the poor themselves, which placed the Maya as the "internal enemy" in National Security Doctrine. The needs of the state, rather than the needs of the people, determined state actions. Violations of human rights and abnegation of constitutional guarantees necessarily result when those who govern a state by force regard the reproduction of the state apparatus as the "common good." In this model, rights do not inhere in the individual. Moreover, democratic participation in government is both unnecessary and antithetical to the "common good." The military becomes the enforcer and beneficiary of the "common good," and violations of civil and political rights are among the first acts of enforcement, often in the name of order, stability, and social peace.[16] In its comprehensive investigation, the CEH found the army and related paramilitary groups responsible for 93 percent of all documented violations, 91 percent of forced disappearances, and 92 percent of arbitrary executions. The vast majority of their victims were Maya.[17]

National security ideology thus casts social peace and justice as counterplots. Justice is viewed as an individual concern whereas social peace is perceived as a collective condition having priority over justice. Order, social peace, and common good as defined by the national security state require that the exigency of justice be sacrificed. Even as the national security state begins to fail, lose control, or even self-destruct, this ideology permeates transitions from military rule so that reconciliation (used interchangeably with stability, social peace, or common good) is perceived to have higher moral or political standing than justice.[18] It is indeed ironic that post-conflict governments in transition and many architects of transitional justice have reinvented the counterplot of peace versus justice in policies and practices that privilege truth over justice rather than recognize their mutually constitutive relationship.

AMNESTY AND IMPUNITY

In transitions from military rule, national security ideology is most often expressed as favoring amnesty for the military and their agents who systematically violated human rights under military rule. Whether in Brazil, Chile, Argentina, El Salvador, South Africa, Guatemala, Uruguay, or elsewhere, the arguments favoring amnesty consistently point to amnesty as a necessity for social stability."[19]

In 1994, high-ranking officials repeatedly said that "reconciliation [read here social peace or common good] requires sacrifice." Moreover, though the army had "made mistakes" and committed "abuses," the overriding need of society was "equitable justice" [read here, prosecution of the guerrilla]. This topic of conversation inevitably concluded with the official saying, "We won the war." One army official added, "Look, whoever is most organized wins the political space and we have the most organization."[20] Given that "impunity permeated the country to such an extent that it took control of the very structure of the State, and became both a means and an end,"[21] it is not surprising that military organization, or structures of repression, reinforced impunity which in turn reinforced the military state while weakening, if not destroying, other governmental and nongovernmental institutions. This weakening of non-military institutions, or their militarization, had the effect of limiting their functioning and efficacy, which further contributed to the loss of public confidence in the legitimacy of state institutions (especially legal institutions), "since for years people lived with the certainty that it is the Army that retains effective power in Guatemala."[22]

Those within the Guatemalan army who are willing to recognize that there were "abuses" do so by drawing a definitive distinction between the past and the present within the context of the Cold War. Another official explained, "The Guatemalan army, like all armies of democratic countries, celebrates the fall of the Soviet Union and the liberation of the end of the Cold War which will bring us tranquillity because this ideological conflict had great costs."[23] To view the past through the prism of the Cold War provides both a justification for previous "abuses" as well as an explanation as to why the army should now be trusted not to repeat those "abuses"—that is, human rights violations (and genocide) are no longer necessary because the Cold War has ended and, therefore, amnesty should be granted in recognition of the historical necessities imposed upon the Guatemalan army by the Cold War.

Yet experiences in transitions from military rule around the world indicate that amnesty brings neither reconciliation nor social peace. On the contrary, Amnesty International has found that "a failure to investigate past abuses and bring those responsible to justice increases the chances of human rights violations recurring, both because torturers and killers are still at large and may once again be in a position where they have custody of prisoners or the power to kill, and because the measures necessary to prevent abuses are not identified and implemented."[24]

Indeed, the granting of various amnesties has not meant an end to impunity in Guatemala.[25] Impunity is a law of exception that permits and foments actions of the state against the citizenry.[26] It is antidemocratic in that it inverts the relationship of a state that represents and responds to the needs of the people to a people who are submitted to the whims of the state. Impunity is an exemption from punishment, which "negates the values of truth and justice and leads to the occurrence of further [human rights] violations."[27]

The extreme cruelty enacted by the Guatemalan army in rural and urban violence was "a resource used intentionally to produce and maintain a climate of terror."[28] This terror was produced and maintained not only by acts of army violence but also by systematic structural practices of impunity for perpetrators, criminalization of victims, and forced participation of civilians in the commission of atrocities.[29] Indeed, among its findings of institutional responsibility, the CEH determined that the complete absence of investigations, trials, and convictions of mid-level to high-level members of the army command indicated that human rights violations were "the result of institutional policy," not "excesses" or "errors" of low-ranking commanders acting with autonomy. This lack of accountability further reinforced institutional policies of human rights violations by "ensuring impenetrable impunity, which persisted during the whole period investigated by the CEH."[30]

Amnesties granted in Guatemala in the 1980s served to further institutionalize and legitimize impunity. First, amnesty provisions reaffirm the historical silences imposed through repression by previous regimes because amnesty is, in effect, an official negation of government/military responsibility, as well as a negation of the very violations perpetrated. Second, amnesty creates an "official story" that denies individual victims of violence, as well as their families and society in general, a forum for truth. Without truth, there is no chance of justice and accountability. Third, even after historical silence has been broken, prosecution is necessary to end impunity. Indeed, prominent among the "Recommendations of the CEH" is that the Guatemalan state must "fulfill, and demand fulfillment of, the National Reconciliation Law" and especially Article 8, which calls for the prosecution of perpetrators of "crimes of genocide, torture, and forced disappearance."[31] Significantly, the CEH urged that application of the Reconciliation Law should consider "the various degrees of authority and responsibility for the human rights violations and acts of violence, paying particular attention to those who instigated and promoted these crimes."[32]

NGOS AND TRANSITIONAL JUSTICE

In June of 1994 while working with the FAFG (Fundación de Antropología Forense de Guatemala—Guatemalan Forensic Anthropology Foundation) on the exhumation in Plan de Sánchez, we heard over the radio that the Guatemalan government and URNG (Unión Revolucionaria Nacional Guatemalteca—Guatemalan National Revolutionary Union) had signed an accord establishing a "truth commission," to be called the Commission for Historical Clarification (CEH). Our shared celebratory feeling soon dissipated as the radio broadcast that this commission would name institutional responsibility but would not name individual perpetrators of human rights violations. Earlier that week, the FAFG, local peasants, and the regional human rights ombudsman had received an ominous and anonymous threat: *"Deja los muertos en pas* [sic] *Hijos de puta"* (Leave the dead in peace sons of a whore). "How will we ever end impunity?" asked one of the forensic anthropologists.

In my twenty-four months of fieldwork in Guatemala between 1994 and 1999, and a final site visit in 2002, I had the opportunity to witness the process of truth gathering from the perspective of peasants in the villages in which I work as well as from the view of local prosecutors, government officials, UN functionaries, various national and international human rights NGOs, CEH investigators and commissioners, and my own perspective as a human rights advocate, anthropologist, and research consultant to the FAFG report on massacres to the CEH.

As detailed in chapters three and four, our investigation of the 1981 massacre in the Ixil village of Acul revealed a fifteen-year process of extreme militarization that began several years before the 1981 massacre and did not end until the signing of the peace accords in December of 1996. Indeed, the civil patrol of Acul was one of the last in the country to be disarmed.

As we came to the close of our investigation, Dr. Christian Tomuschat, the United Nations-appointed President of the CEH, made a site visit to Acul. About 400 local peasants were there to greet him and all waited patiently for him to hear their stories—spoken publicly for the first time. As Don Sebastián, a respected elder of the community who lost his entire family to La Violencia, began to tell Dr. Tomuschat how the violence began in Acul, Dr. Tomuschat silenced him with a wave of his hand and said, "No, I only want to know about the massacre."

As I have emphasized in previous chapters, the massacre, in which thirty-five people were killed, is not a discrete event that explains what happened in Acul. It is, like hundreds of other massacres, one of many acts of extreme violence in a chain of events that together fomented a state of terror in which it was possible for a government to burn 626 villages off the map, internally displace 1,500,000 people, send another 150,000 into refuge, and leave more than 200,000 dead or disappeared.[33]

Limiting data collection to only the massacre provides no insight to understanding La Violencia. Further, if we fail to understand the context of La Violencia from the lived experiences of massacre survivors, then we are likely to fail to understand the contemporary context of transitional justice in which they live. Fortunately, the CEH did not limit its investigation or its report to discrete incidents of human rights violations. Instead, it produced one of the most comprehensive truth commission reports giving local, regional, national, and international context to extensively documented violations of human rights in rural and urban areas. Human rights NGOs (like the FAFG), in collaboration with massacre survivors and local peace-building initiatives, had much to do with the success of the CEH.

TRUTH COMMISSIONS

While Brazil, Uruguay, and Paraguay produced *"Nunca Más"* (Never Again) reports about human rights abuses under military regimes, these reports were sponsored and produced by church and human rights organizations—and thus seen as alternative or oppositional interpretations. Additionally, their mandates and recommendations were neither official nor legally binding. Presidential sponsorship of the Argentine and Chilean commissions, United Nations sponsorship of the Salvadoran commission, and heavy involvement of the United Nations and the international community in staffing and funding Guatemala's "independent" commission lend an official stamp to the "truths" produced.

The report of the Argentine National Commission on the Disappeared, which documented close to 9,000 cases of disappeared individuals, became a national bestseller. While the names of perpetrators were not made public in the report, a list of names was given to the president with the intention that legal action be taken in the future. Whether from the office of the president or the commission itself, the names were leaked to the press and the entire list was published in Argentine newspapers. Some military officers were brought to court for trial.[34] While amnesties were eventually regranted, the convictions were significant for at least three major reasons: (1) They reaffirmed the veracity of victim and survivor testimonies of human rights violations, (2) they passed judgment on the military dictatorship, and (3) they contributed to the army's subordination to the constitution resulting from the army's loss of power and prestige during the trials.[35] Moreover, in March 2001, a federal judge overturned two laws granting immunity to some 400 military officers and opened the way for renewed prosecution efforts.[36]

In Chile, the National Commission for Truth and Reconciliation identified military and government branches responsible for human rights violations but did not name individual perpetrators. However, all evidence of criminal action, including perpetrator names, was submitted to Chilean courts for possible legal action. Many of the recommendations of the commission were formally accepted, and the National Corporation for Reparation and Reconciliation was founded to disburse reparations to the survivors of the disappeared and assassinated.[37] Since the Truth Commission issued its report, seventy military officers have been convicted for human rights violations. While the Chilean government argued against the extradition of former dictator General Augusto Pinochet to Spain, it appears that Chilean courts are trying to prosecute him for at least some of his crimes.[38]

The Salvadoran Truth Commission sought to investigate all "serious acts of violence" that occurred between 1980 and 1991 and caused an impact on society, necessitating that the "public should know the truth." The commission received more than 22,000 denunciations of grave human rights violations, 7,000 of which were made directly to the commission. The Salvadoran commission offered a new vision of the work of truth commissions by naming the perpetrators of these violations. Among those named were prominent guerrilla leader Joaquín Villalobos and a member of the Salvadoran Supreme Court.[39]

The Guatemalan Peace Accord for the establishment of the CEH was being negotiated shortly after the release of the Salvadoran Truth Commission's report. The parties agreed that institutional responsibility would be assigned for human rights violations, but individual perpetrators would not be named. Though envisioned as an independent commission, the majority of investigative staff moved from the United Nations Guatemalan Mission (Misión Naciones Unidas de Guatemala—MINUGUA) offices to the CEH. Indeed, many of the MINUGUA staff had previously worked on the UN Mission in El Salvador (ONUSAL) and also for the Salvadoran Truth Commission. Still, unlike the Salvadoran commission, the CEH included a significant number of Guatemalan nationals on its staff, many of whom formerly worked with human rights NGOs. While it has been suggested that truth commissions are more successful when staffed by internationals,[40] the experience of the CEH and the FAFG suggests that a combination of internationals and nationals works extremely well. In the Guatemalan case, the presence of internationals was important to the security of the nationals and also to demonstrate the international visibility of the work of the FAFG and the CEH. Still, when internationals arrive to conduct sensitive human rights research, it is critical to local involvement that nationals are included in the project because everyone knows that when the going gets tough, internationals have passports to get going. The presence of fellow citizens encourages potential participants (and especially local officials) to come forward. As one local leader explained, "If they haven't killed him for doing his work, they probably won't kill me for talking to him. That's how we decided to participate."[41]

In spite of their differing approaches, each of these commissions benefited from being official and they all shared a belief in the moral obligation to reveal truths to heal painful pasts. Each commission envisaged its mission as an integral contribution to reconciliation following extreme state violence. Labor rights, agrarian reform, access to justice, citizen security, respect for human rights, and meaningful participation of civil society were among the expected outcomes. Indeed, these rights were included in the recommendations of the Argentine, Chilean, and Salvadoran commissions and were highlighted in the Guatemalan CEH's report as well.

In 1995, as the first president of the new South Africa, Nelson Mandela appointed the Truth and Reconciliation Commission (TRC) to investigate the crimes of apartheid and empowered the commission to grant amnesty to individual perpetrators in exchange for information. The TRC began its investigation in 1995 and published its report in 1998.[42] During the tenure of Guatemala's CEH investigation, educated Guatemalans interested in the CEH talked about the TRC as much as they did about the CEH, both lamenting and resigning themselves to what many perceived as a "weaker" truth commission in Guatemala. That TRC hearings were televised and the commissioners granted subpoena powers seemed almost a fantasy. In Guatemala, many thought the more expansive powers of the TRC would mean more justice for black South Africans. Many doubted that the CEH would be able to collect evidence, and even after evidence was collected, many doubted the political will of the CEH to assign legal categories to the violations committed by the Guatemalan state. Hearteningly, the CEH carried out a thorough and comprehensive investigation, followed by painstaking legal analysis, which concluded that "acts of genocide" had been committed by the Guatemalan army.[43]

In South Africa, amnesty was traded for truth. The risk in this trade is that institutional structures of violence become secondary while individual perpetrators, their crimes, and their victims become the focus of the atrocities of the previous regime (this is all the more true when hearings of perpetrator "confessions" are televised). While the international security ideology of authoritarian regimes casts social peace (or common good) and justice as counterplots, the current academic and policy debates about transitional justice emanating from the South African experience cast truth and justice as counterplots. Though the ANC (African National Congress) was not a military victor and apartheid ended through a negotiated agreement, the ANC was the political and moral victor. The ANC was swiftly elected by the majority and Nelson Mandela became president. In these unique circumstances, it is perhaps plausible to believe that the ANC government, despite granting amnesty to many perpetrators who maintain their positions in police and security units, can end impunity by virtue of its electoral mandate. Guatemala had no comparable democratic victory for the majority Maya who continue to be politically marginalized from the electoral process.

Despite these significant differences, it seems worthwhile to think for a moment about institutional structures of violence in South Africa. Particularly worrisome is the February 2001 confrontation between South African police and black South Africans living in the Alexandra township in Johannesburg. Police responded violently to squatters who were protesting their forced removal from their homes, which were on a "cholera-infested river."[44] Reminiscent of clashes between Palestinian youth and Israeli armed forces, the police responded with tear gas, rubber bullets, and stun grenades to the squatters who threw rocks at them. While the *New York Times* reported that the police were attempting to move the squatters to "new homes from their makeshift shacks," a report on ABC Evening News showed the removed squatters were taken to a vacant soccer field with no houses, electricity, or running water.[45]

Although the CEH did not have the sweeping powers to grant amnesty, did not hold televised public hearings, and did not name names, the CEH investigative process and report (like the Archbishop's Nunca Más report that preceded it) made a significant contribution to truth and justice. In addition to the vast participation and opening of political space for truth-telling it achieved in rural Maya communities, it is particularly significant that the CEH determined that the state had carried out genocidal acts and recommended administrative procedures against those responsible. Defining the massacres as genocidal acts wed truth with justice by emphasizing both the primary role of state institutional structures of violence and the state's international legal obligation to prosecute responsible parties.

JUSTICE AND TRUTH

Prosecution as an obstacle to democracy, the need for amnesty to achieve reconciliation, South Africa's dysfunctional legal system, the ability of highly skilled operatives to conceal their crimes, the economic cost of political trials, and the infinite time ("literally hundreds of years") for trial preparations and proceedings are among Paul van Zyl's arguments for opposing prosecution and supporting amnesty in exchange for truth. A co-founder of the International Center on Transitional Justice, van Zyl argues that the TRC represents a "third way," a "middle path between an uncompromising insistence on prosecution on the one hand and a defeatist acceptance of amnesty and impunity on the other."[46] Citing the Chilean transition, van Zyl supports amnesty as the only option in a transition in which "the former government maintained considerable power during regime change" and concludes that a country's decision regarding amnesty "has as much to do with power as it does with principle."[47]

Though somewhat similar in approach, Chilean Truth Commissioner José Zalaquett does not take such an extreme position. Zalaquett argues for the supremacy of forgiveness and reconciliation.[48] He is particularly concerned with decisions about who will be prosecuted. Will the least powerful perpetrators be scapegoats for the rest? And, particularly, he is concerned for the culprits themselves: how their culpability is determined, what happens to those who obeyed orders under duress, and who makes these decisions. Further, Zalaquett is " . . . bothered by any imperialism by those fortunate enough to be righteous about the rest" because "the law can only demand from the common citizen to be a lawabider, not to be a hero."[49] Still, Zalaquett believes that "those responsible for the worst crimes" should be punished, if possible. Significantly, he is certain that "the answer is clear when it comes to a grave breach of the Geneva Conventions such as genocide."[50]

An even more nuanced position in the direction of truth and justice comes from Juan Méndez, former director of Human Rights Watch and current director of the Center for Civil and Human Rights at the University of Notre Dame. Méndez asks, "Who should be prosecuted?" His answer: "those with the highest level of responsibility for the most outrageous crimes. The successful prosecutions are those which focus on top officials."[51] Mendez also challenges those who argue that trading amnesty for truth allows for more complete disclosure because the "truth does not necessarily emerge from a commission or exercise in truth-telling." Significantly, Méndez finds the separation of truth and justice to be "misguided" because " . . . prosecutions provide a measure of truth that is more complete and more undeniable than that which is achievable through a truth commission."[52]

Aryeh Neier directly addressed these issues with Zalaquett and Méndez at the 1994 "Justice in Transition" conference at the Institute for Democracy in South Africa. On the question of punishment, prosecution, and justice, Neier said, "The debate has often been whether truth should be the aim of accountability or whether justice should be the aim of accountability. I would argue that in the case of the most severe abuses it is necessary to provide justice. I would go further and say that in some circumstances it is only justice that can be an appropriate acknowledgment of the past."[53] Neier, former director of Human Rights Watch and current president of the Open Society Institute, went on to conclude that the framework that considers amnesty, reconciliation, and social peace as mutually dependent is an "approach of utilitarian calculus" that is "illegitimate." He offered instead an "accounting approach." He explained, "It seems to me that the concern for the victim is in fact the concern to uphold the rule of law. This demands that we do not sacrifice the victim on behalf of larger concerns. . . . I believe these to be the same concern because upholding the rule of law means that society as a whole will protect the victims."[54]

Amnesty, with or without truth, provides for neither justice nor true reconciliation because there is no accountability and the state cannot truly pardon those responsible for human rights violations. The power to grant a meaningful pardon inheres not to the state, but to the victims, survivors, and their families. This power to pardon or forgive can only be exercised with the knowledge that all of society is empowered with truth derived officially and resulting in legal sanctions against perpetrators. For independent Spanish prosecutor Baltasar Garzón, pardon and forgiveness are not the first step. For Garzón, it is only after justice and punishment that forgiveness can be considered.[55] Returning to Neier, pardon or forgiveness is not the goal of truth and should not be the goal of reconciliation. Rather, creating a forum for truth and official acknowledgment of the past is necessary to (1) validate the humanity and dignity of victims and survivors of human rights violations; (2) constitute and enact the rule of law and thereby demonstrate that all citizens are subject to and protected by the same laws; and (3) to deter future abuses.[56]

Neier is not alone in this assessment. In his work on justice and rule of law in postsocialist Europe, John Borneman concurs with the need for rule of law and retributive justice. He writes, "If the principles of the rule of law are not invoked and ritually reaffirmed, a society will be confronted with a potentially endless cycle of violent retaliations."[57] Moreover, the legal establishment of victimizer accountability and victim/survivor rights to redress are not simply for the settling of accounts. It is in this dual process that the political community is constituted as a moral community.[58]

THE RÍO NEGRO PROSECUTION[59]

The establishment of victimizer accountability for the Río Negro massacre is a case study of the mutual constitution of a new political and moral community in Guatemala. The Río Negro case was initiated in 1993 when massacre survivors, including Jesús Tec, denounced the massacre to authorities in Salamá, the departmental capital of Baja Verapaz. The survivors asked for an investigation of the civil patrollers from Xococ, the platoon of forty soldiers from the Rabinal army base, and the intellectual authors of the violence. In 1993, the FAFG was named as the court investigator and carried out an exhumation of the clandestine cemetery containing the remains of the 177 Río Negro massacre victims. Of the more than 120 forensic exhumations of massacres carried out to date, the Río Negro case is the first to reach trial. The October 13, 1999, verdict was the second time the three military commissioners from Xococ were found guilty in this case; the first conviction was nullified on procedural grounds earlier that same year.

During the court proceedings, prosecutors called military officers to the witness stand. One witness was General Benedicto Lucas García, who served as army chief of staff during the reign of his brother, General Romeo Lucas García (1978–1982), who ushered in the epoch known as La Violencia. Credited with designing the "Scorched Earth" campaign and trained by the U.S. army School of the Americas in combat intelligence and high military command, Benedicto testified that the civil patrols were his idea and that he had personally reviewed the patrols in Salamá in 1981. (This would be the same year that the U.S. State Department document classified as "secret" stated that General Romeo Lucas García believed that "the policy of repression" was "working.")[60] Entering the courtroom as the grand populist, Benedicto waved and shook hands with everyone including the prosecutors, the defense, the judges, and the defendants. When asked about the Río Negro massacre, he pled ignorance. When asked if he had ordered it, he gasped as if in shock and said, "That, that . . . would be . . . a crime against humanity."[61]

Another witness was General Otto Erick Ponce, previously a commander of the Rabinal army base and vice-minister of defense in 1994—the same year that, as we entered our fourth month of the exhumation in Plan de Sánchez, the army gathered 2,000 local Achí peasants from nineteen villages in a meeting at the Rabinal army base and declared: "The anthropologists, journalists, and internationals are all guerrilla. You know what happens when you collaborate with the subversives. The violence of the past will return. Leave the dead in peace." General Ponce refused to provide the court with names of ranking officers at the base and indeed denied that the civil patrols had ever existed.

Witnesses for the defense argued that the defendants "were not military commissioners," had "never been in the civil patrol," that "there had never been a civil patrol in Xococ," and that the defendants "did not even know what a civil patrol was." Further, they argued that on the day of the massacre, the defendants "had been planting trees in a reforestation project." As for the Río Negro children, they had "gone voluntarily to Xococ to live." Among the extensive evidence against the defendants were official documents with signatures of the military commissioners with their titles, and photographs of the same commissioners with other Xococ patrollers carrying army-issue weapons.

During the trial, relatives of the Río Negro victims held marches demanding justice and placed banners in front of the tribunal. These relatives filled the courtroom throughout the trial. Achí from other Rabinal communities also attended the trial—especially those hoping to have their massacre cases heard in court. Civil patrollers from Xococ demonstrated for the release of the military commissioners.

The criminal court proceeding in Salamá was marked by death threats to survivors and witnesses, a military officer defiantly raising his right hand in a salute reminiscent of Nazi Germany as he was sworn in, the relocation of defendants to prevent the possibility of a mob's breaking them out of jail, and the clearing of the courtroom on several occasions due to threats of violence.

The ambient violence that marked this trial is not unique to legal attempts to prosecute perpetrators of human rights violations in Guatemala. On October 7, as the trial in Salamá proceeded, Celvin Galindo, the prosecutor investigating the murder of Bishop Juan Gerardi, resigned and fled to the United States following numerous death threats.[62] Indeed, between March and October 1999, a second judge assigned to the Gerardi case and two key witnesses also fled the country after receiving death threats.

In 1994 when I first interviewed massacre survivors in Rabinal and asked them what they wanted from the exhumation, I was told collectively by twenty-four widowers that they wanted "revenge." In 1998, after much community reflection on collective trauma, healing, and truth, the same Achí told me they wanted the intellectual authors to be punished, but not their neighbors who participated in the massacres. They did not want their neighbors to go to jail because "jailing my neighbor will only create more widows and orphans. More widows and orphans will not help anyone."

As the court proceedings dragged on in 1999 with the defendants sitting in silence, intellectual authors mocking the legal process, and other local perpetrators threatening survivors and witnesses, Río Negro survivors did not express the generosity of forgiveness. All demanded the dismantling of impunity in which the local perpetrators had lived and many requested application of the death penalty. Still, at the close of the trial, when survivor and human rights activist Jesús Tec once again spoke before the court, he said, "I am not asking for the death penalty. I am asking for justice. I am not prepared to decide. You decide." As one international observer explained, "He didn't want the death penalty, but he couldn't oppose it. The community would hate him if he had."[63] Taking into account the violence of the accused, the magnitude of the crime, and the opinion of the survivors, the prosecutor, who is personally opposed to the death penalty, requested this maximum sentence. Despite the volatile and tense atmosphere in Salamá and elsewhere, the three judges in the Río Negro trial distinguished the court proceeding by demonstrating objectivity and equanimity in their efforts to discover the truth about the massacre. The military commissioners were found guilty and sentenced to death. Today, they remain jailed with appeals pending. The hundreds of other massacre cases await hearings in the Guatemalan court system. Still, the Río Negro conviction has given many Guatemalans the hope that justice, which has generally been a privilege of the powerful, may now be within the reach of the poor and the indigenous.

THE "GREY ZONE"

Still, the image of justice emerging from this verdict is skewed, regardless of one's moral position on the death penalty. The massacre was committed by civil patrollers from the neighboring village of Xococ under army order. As extensively outlined in previous chapters, the civil patrols themselves constituted an integral part of the army's counterinsurgency campaign. Patrollers were often forced to torture, assassinate, and massacre innocent people under army order. Those civil patrollers who refused to comply were always tortured and often killed. It is within this context that civil patrollers from Xococ committed the Río Negro massacre, one of the 626 known massacres committed by the Guatemalan army in the early 1980s.[64]

Arguing against those who might believe in a fundamental essence of brutality in human beings, Holocaust survivor Primo Levi wrote that "the only conclusion to be drawn is that in the face of driving necessity and physical disabilities, many social habits and instincts are reduced to silence."[65]

Writing about the Jewish prominents who violated their own within the German Lager, Levi wrote:

> . . . if one offers a position of privilege to a few individuals in a state of slavery, exacting in exchange the betrayal of a natural solidarity with their comrades, there will certainly be someone who will accept. . . . the more power he is given, the more he will be consequently hateful and hated. . . . he will be cruel and tyrannical, because he will understand that if he is not sufficiently so, someone else, judged more suitable, will take over his post. Moreover, his capacity for hatred, unfulfilled in the direction of the oppressors, will double back, beyond all reason, on the oppressed; and he will only be satisfied when he has unloaded on to his underlings the injury received from above.[66]

Indeed, the victims of the Xococ civil patrol were not limited to Río Negro, just as Xococ was not the only civil patrol to commit crimes against humanity. In a 1983 armed confrontation between the guerrilla and the Xococ patrollers, twenty-six insurgents were killed. Ten of the dead insurgents were from Xococ. The same day as the guerrilla attack, the families of the ten dead Xococ insurgents and several other Xococ widows were taken from their homes and tortured. The widows of the dead men were held in a house converted into a jail and gang raped by military commissioners and patrollers for several weeks until local clergy were able to convince the army commander to stop this violence against the widows.[67]

In its comprehensive investigation, the CEH found that 18 percent of human rights violations were committed by civil patrols. Further, it noted that 85 percent of those violations committed by patrollers were carried out under army order.[68] It is not insignificant that the CEH found that one out of every ten human rights violations was carried out by a military commissioner and that while these commissioners often led patrollers in acts of violence, 87 percent of the violations committed by commissioners were in collusion with the army.[69]

In 1995, there were 2,643 civil patrols organized and led by the army. In August of 1996, when the demobilization of civil patrols was begun, there were some 270,906 mostly Maya peasants registered in civil patrols.[70] This is significantly less than the one million men who were organized into civil patrols in 1981—one year before the Río Negro massacre. Taking into account the population at the time and adjusting for gender and excluding children and elderly, this means that in 1981, one out of every two adult men in Guatemala were militarized into the army-led civil patrols.[71]

Like recent genocides in other parts of the world, the systematic incorporation of civilians in murderous army operations complicates prosecution of perpetrators in many ways because it shifts a seemingly black and white act of wrong into what Primo Levi called the "grey zone." One lesson of the recent conviction and sentencing of the patrollers in Guatemala is that if civilians evade certain death under military regimes by acquiescing to army orders to commit acts of violence, the democratic state that follows will kill them, albeit through a civilian court, for following the orders of the previous regime.

This is not to suggest that civilians who participated in crimes against humanity should not be tried for their crimes. Indeed, the February 23, 2001, United Nations war crimes tribunal ruling against three former Bosnian Serb soldiers noted that while the soldiers were not the intellectual authors or leaders behind the war crimes, those "leaders would be rendered powerless if ordinary people refuse to carry out criminal activities in the course of war." The judge added that "lawless opportunists should expect no mercy, no matter how low their position in the chain of command may be."[72] The importance and validity of the UN tribunal's ruling notwithstanding, the point here is that to focus on the least powerful perpetrators in the Guatemalan military regime ultimately protects the intellectual authors and introduces the need for justice to reflect the nuanced cultural and political specificity of the crimes being tried. This is the type of scapegoating prosecution that concerns former Chilean truth commissioner Zalaquett. In this case, it goes far beyond scapegoating. In this sense, the murder conviction of the Achí-Maya military commissioners for participating in the massacre of Achí-Maya women and children is a Machiavellian judgment that ultimately protects the army and the intellectual authors of what the CEH described in legal terms as genocidal acts of the army. What civil patroller will now come forward as a material witness to identify army perpetrators of any of the other 625 known massacres in light of the Río Negro precedent?

JUSTICE AFTER GENOCIDE?

Despite their different perspectives on the relationship between truth and justice, Zalaquett, Méndez, and Neier are all clear that genocide requires prosecution, and each argues for prioritizing the high-ranking officials, the intellectual architects, and those who gave the orders. The question then arises as to what to do with the middle-level officers and, in the case of Guatemala, the forcibly recruited soldiers, army-controlled civil patrols, and army-appointed military commissioners. In this case, in order to attempt to locate justice or at least explore it, it is perhaps necessary to step back from the tribunal judge's righteous condemnation of soldiers following orders and also from Zalaquett's condemnation of the righteous who find themselves passing judgment over what Holocaust historian Daniel Goldhagen has termed "ordinary" citizens who become "willing executioners."[73] I suggest a way to do this is to cast our view away from the vertical impunity of the state's repressive apparatus and refocus on the expression of this structure of impunity at the local level. One might call it lateral impunity—that is, local expression of structures of impunity, both formal and informal, borne out of the national vertical structure of impunity. Moreover, this local structure of impunity can take on a life of its own with lateral impunity continuing long after the vertical structure of state repression and the impunity it fomented withdraws from the area, falls into remission, or crumbles. Thus, victimizers from La Violencia, such as the condemned military commissioners, can redeploy the local power they secured through previous alliances with the army even after the army formally withdraws.

For many human rights advocates, including some involved in the court proceedings, the trial of the civil patrollers was morally and ethically unsettling. Fernando Moscoso, who led the Río Negro exhumation, was the forensic witness for the prosecution. Moscoso, a devout Catholic who personally opposes the death penalty under all circumstances, gave compelling testimony when explaining the evidence gathered in the exhumation of massacre victims. The experience left him with deep moral conflicts over the role of his testimony in the trial. "I worked in the exhumations all these years because I believe in the value of human life; I didn't work to increase the number of dead," he explained. "These men are guilty. They took advantage of the violence in their community for their own personal gain. They should probably be punished, but this exhumation, like other exhumations we did, provides evidence against the army. It is the architects of genocide and those who gave the orders who should have been on trial."[74]

In my experience, survivors have always expressed at least three key reasons for wanting an exhumation: (1) for the truth to be known; (2) to have proper burials and accompanying rituals for their deceased loved ones; and (3) for justice (and sometimes revenge). When I have asked what justice means, I have been told: "We want the people who did this punished" and "the army should be punished." Though neither army officials nor soldiers who participated in the massacre were included in the Río Negro charges, it was hoped by many massacre survivors in Rabinal that, in the course of the trial, evidence against the army would somehow lead to charges against those who gave orders and the intellectual authors, if not during the Río Negro trial, at least for some trial in the future. This seems also to have been in the minds of the prosecutors who subpoenaed army officials to testify.

As previously mentioned, the desire for local justice appeared to increase as the trial proceeded. Having explored these issues of truth, memory, justice, and healing in Rabinal communities (including Río Negro and Xococ) since 1994, I believe this publicly expressed desire for local justice is located in collective and individual memory of experiences during La Violencia that reflected the vulnerability of communities to the violence of both the army and the civil patrols. At the local level, during and after La Violencia, inter and intracommunity problems and injustices were as often traced to the impunity of military commissioners as they were to army orders. While massacres and other gross violations of human rights in Maya communities were systematically carried out by the army and civil patrollers under order of the army high command, many of the daily injustices suffered by massacre survivors were enacted by civil patrollers and especially by military commissioners who acted with impunity at the local level based on the real or perceived support of the army officials who appointed them. Military commissioners used their ill-gotten power to steal the lands of neighbors, rob livestock, extort money, rape women, and commit other crimes.

So, while international and national investigators of human rights violations may correctly categorize military commissioners or civil patrol chiefs as low on the national structure of accountability and the vertical pole of impunity, they were often as feared in their own communities as the army officials. Moreover, the case of the Xococ patrollers raping women from their community until the local commander ordered them to stop is not unique.[75] After the massacres, as time wore on in rural communities and military presence dwindled, military commissioners continued to threaten and harm members of their own communities to maintain and increase their own local power and wealth. Because the civil patrol in Xococ was still armed long after most patrols had organized themselves to disarm and dissociate themselves from the army, other Rabinal communities continued to fear the armed residents of Xococ and especially the military commissioners. This is why local human rights leaders in Rabinal who are themselves massacre survivors mobilized their communities to march in favor of prosecuting the three Xococ civil patrol commissioners on trial. While the trial of the patrollers was not bringing high-ranking officers to justice, it was bringing justice to Rabinal by removing the most powerful local members of the local apparatus of repression. The prosecution of the patrollers might have a chilling effect at the national level on other patrollers coming forward to name army officials who gave them orders. However, from a local perspective this prosecution may also serve to decrease lateral impunity in other communities: Military commissioners fearing prosecution may now think twice before threatening or abusing their neighbors. From a local perspective, this probably fits into Neier's category of circumstances in which only prosecution can be an "appropriate acknowledgement of the past."[76] While army officials fear they may be tried for genocide, military commissioners now know they can be tried and convicted for murder and that the army will do nothing to stop the convictions. Indeed, after sitting silently through the court proceedings, the day after their sentencing, the military commissioners spoke for the first time: "We were only following orders."[77]

CONCLUSION: JUSTICE AND DEMOCRACY AFTER GENOCIDE

In the 1980s, the Guatemalan state massacred Maya communities in the name of anticommunism. While the prosecution of low-ranking military commissioners addresses local structures of impunity, if the Guatemalan state is serious about constructing rule of law, it must begin to prosecute the intellectual authors who continue to live with impunity in Guatemala. In so doing, the Guatemalan state would take a large step toward constructing a viable democracy by demonstrating that the rule of law extends to the powerful as well as to the poor.

At the national level, the FAFG continues to carry out exhumations throughout Guatemala. Human rights NGOs continue to demand accountability and push forward with legal cases against perpetrators of past human rights violations. At the local level, community leaders continue to organize their families, friends, and neighbors in the pursuit of justice. Rabinal activists and community leaders have appropriated national and international human rights discourses and resources to enhance their own community agenda for justice, rather than have that agenda shaped by external actors.

Community mobilization around truth, memory, and prosecution has opened political and social space that, in turn, has initiated the process of resolution and reconciliation of the armed conflict within Rabinal. This political opening and unfolding of public space generates a meaningful peace process from the individual, to the community, to the nation. In Rabinal, these local mobilizations were strengthened and new political space reinforced by the exhumation of clandestine cemeteries, the official truth-telling processes of the REHMI (Proyecto Interdiocesano de Recuperación Histórico—Interdiocesene Project for the Recuperation of Historical Memory) and the CEH, the prosecution of the civil patrollers, and ongoing, if sometimes contradictory, involvement of national and international human rights NGOs.

It is not insignificant that several civil patrollers from Xococ who participated in the Río Negro massacre have approached several NGOs requesting arbitration and a public meeting. These patrollers know that everyone else in Rabinal knows of the crimes they committed in Río Negro and elsewhere. They would like to publicly confess their crimes and have the community pass judgment. This would allow them to make amends for their crimes and be reintegrated into the larger Rabinal community. Revealing and reflecting upon the true responsibilities and motivations of La Violencia has allowed for public recognition of local structures of violence and lateral impunity, which has opened the way to community reconciliation and healing. Each of these discrete actions are the very building blocks for the establishment of rule of law, without which there can be no democracy. Strengthening civil society and establishing rule of law are key among the indicators to be measured when evaluating the success of Guatemala's peace process and democratic transition. Recognition of the collective trauma of state genocide, community healing, and local participation in legal efforts to institutionalize truth and bring perpetrators to justice are vital elements of Guatemala's transition from military rule. In addition, local communities in tandem with NGOs are integral and mutually constituted components of this process, which strengthens the linkages between rural Maya citizens and the Guatemalan nation-state.

An Achí woman who survived an attack by the Xococ civil patrol in her village of Santo Domingo told me, "I complain to God and pray that one day the guilty will pay for what they did." An Achí man from another village who accompanied me later commented, "She isn't demanding that they ask forgiveness. *Perdón* (forgiveness) is not in our *lingüística*. This idea of forgiveness comes from the NGOs." He went on, "The guilty can say, 'We did these bad things under someone else's order, forgive me.' But this perdón has no meaning for me because there is no perdón in Achí."

Where we might use "forgive" in English or "perdón" or *"disculpe"* in Spanish, the Achí say *"Cuyu la lumac,"* which in Spanish is translated as *"Aguántame un poco,"* in English roughly "tolerate me a little." Perhaps if the intellectual authors of massacres and other crimes against humanity as well as those who perpetuated lateral impunity in local communities are brought to justice, the survivors will again find the generosity and strength to tolerate the remaining guilty among them.[78]

NOTES

PROLOGUE

1. The December 1996 signing of the peace accords brought an official end to the war (often referred to as the internal armed conflict) between the Guatemalan army and guerrilla forces that began in 1962.
2. A total of 2,500 URNG combatants were demobilized to five different UN-protected camps throughout the country.
3. "Corte" is the name of the woven red, yellow, black, and white fabric that is wrapped around the waist of Ixil Maya women to form an ankle-length skirt. "Huipil" is the name of the colorful, woven, and embroidered blouses worn by Maya women.
4. See David Stoll, *Between Two Armies in the Ixil Towns of Guatemala* (New York: Columbia University Press, 1993).
5. "Compañero" is a commonly used term for a friend, companion, or comrade.
6. "Responsable" (person in charge) refers to the local leader of the EGP (Ejército Guerrillero de los Pobres—Guerrilla Army of the Poor).
7. All names used in this book are pseudonyms except for those of public figures. Any other exceptions are noted. "Don" is a title of courtesy and respect used to address adult men in Maya communities. I use this title throughout the book.
8. "Palo" is a generic word for tree trunks small and large, as well as the poles of wood, bush, and tree branches used in construction.
9. The word "gringo/a" is used, often contemptuously, to refer to North Americans from the United States. It can also be used as a term of endearment or to connote innocence or in-experience with life in rural communities. Thus, it is used to explain why the gringa does-n't know she has a coyote, can't cross the river or scale the cliff very quickly, makes tortillas like a child, and can't wring the water out of her jeans or towels when hand washing in the river but can four-wheel drive. For an interesting analysis of gringas in Guatemala, see Diane Nelson, *A Finger in the Wound* (Berkeley: University of California Press, 1999).
10. In Carolyn Forché, ed., *Against Forgetting: Twentieth Century Poetry of Witness* (New York: W.W. Norton, 1993), 616.

INTRODUCTION

1. I gratefully acknowledge Marguerite Feitlowitz for taking the time to help me process my experiences and sharing her wisdom. I also thank Fernando Moscoso, Freddy Peccerelli, Asale Angel-Ajani, Shannon Speed, Lotti Silber, Julia Lieblich, and Carolyn Nordstrom for many thoughtful conversations about the personal intensity of conducting field research on violence.
2. Mahmood Mamdani, *When Victims Become Killers: Colonialism, Nativism, and the Genocide in Rwanda* (Princeton: Princeton University Press, 2001), 228–229. Italics in original. For more on genocide in Rwanda, see also Phillip Gourevitch, *"We Wish to Inform You that Tomorrow We Will Be Killed With Our Families"—Stories from Rwanda* (New York: Farrar,

Strauss & Giroux, 1999) and Elizabeth Neuffer, *The Key to My Neighbor's House: Seeking Justice in Bosnia and Rwanda* (New York: Picador USA, 2001).

3. Carol Smith, *Guatemalan Indians and the State, 1540 to 1988* (Austin: University of Texas Press, 1990); Robert Carmack, *Harvest of Violence: The Maya Indians and the Guatemalan Crisis* (Norman: University of Oklahoma Press, 1988); Kay Warren, *The Violence Within: Cultural and Political Opposition in Divided Nations* (Boulder: Westview Press, 1993); Ricardo Falla, *Masacres de la Selva* (Guatemala City: Editorial Universitario, 1992); Beatriz Manz, *Refugees of a Hidden War—The Aftermath of Counterinsurgency in Guatemala* (Albany: State University of New York Press, 1988); George Lovell, *A Beauty the Hurts—Life and Death in Guatemala* (Austin: University of Texas Press, 2000); Clark Taylor, *Return of Guatemala's Refugees—Reweaving the Torn* (Philadelphia: Temple University Press, 1998).

4. Commission for Historical Clarification (CEH), *Guatemala Memory of Silence—Conclusions and Recommendations* (Guatemala City: CEH, 1999); CEH, *Guatemala Memoria del Silencio*, vols.1–12 (Guatemala City: CEH, 1999).

5. In 1990, I traveled to Guatemala with immigration lawyer Phyllis Beech to meet with the rural families of Maya refugees living in the United States.

6. Others have also noted the use of the terms "La Situación" and "La Violencia." See Linda Green, *Fear as a Way of Life—Mayan Widows in Rural Guatemala* (New York: Columbia University Press, 1999); and David Stoll, *Between Two Armies in the Ixil Towns of Guatemala* (New York: Columbia University Press, 1994).

7. See, for example, Stanley Tambiah, *Leveling Crowds—Ethnonationalist Conflicts and Collective Violence in South Asia* (Berkeley: University of California Press, 1996); Liisa Malkki, *Purity and Exile: Violence, Memory, and the National Cosmology Among Hutu Refugee* (Chicago: University of Chicago Press, 1995); Carolyn Nordstrom, *A Different Kind of War Story* (Philadelphia: University of Pennsylvania Press, 1997); Allan Feldman, *Formations of Violence: The Narrative of the Body and Political Terror in Northern Ireland* (Chicago: University of Chicago Press, 1991); E. Valentine Daniel, *Charred Lullabies: Chapters in an Anthropography of Violence,* (Princeton: Princeton University Press, 1996); Ranajit Guha, "Discipline and Mobilize," in Partha Chatterjee and Gyandra Pandey, eds., *Subaltern Studies VII* (Delhi: Oxford University Press, 1992); Michel Foucault, *Discipline and Punish—The Birth of the Prison* (New York: Vintage Press, 1979); Michael Taussig, *Shamanism, Colonialism and the Wild Man: A Study in Terror and Healing* (Chicago: University of Chicago Press, 1987).

8. Until 1997 the FAFG was known as the EAFG (Equipo de Antropologia Forense de Guatemala—Guatemalan Forensic Anthropology Team). In 1997, the organization received its official status as an independent NGO from the Guatemalan government, which bestows the title of "foundation" on officially recognized NGOs. Thus, the EAFG became legally known as the FAFG (Fundación de Antropologia Forense de Guatemala—Guatemalan Forensic Anthropological Foundation). For simplicity's sake, I use the FAFG acronym throughout the book.

9. The spelling of names of Maya languages follows the alphabet proposed by the Academia de Las Lenguas Mayas de Guatemala, which was made official by the Guatemalan government in 1987. For more on Maya language activism, see Edward Fischer and McKenna Brown, eds., *Maya Cultural Activism in Guatemala* (Austin: University of Texas Press, 1996).

10. I thank John Watanabe for insisting that I consider this important point.

11. Special thanks to Bill Durham for supporting my sociocultural engagement with forensic anthropology and challenging me to think about this relationship.

12. I gratefully acknowledge Carolyn Forché for pointing out that language is evidence and helping me to think about the relationship between language and genocide in her poetry reading and in a workshop I moderated at the Postwar Symposium, which was lovingly organized by Roberta Culbertson and hosted by the Institute on Violence and Survival, Virginia Foundation for the Humanities, February 28–March 3, 2002.

13. Among those who have most eloquently written of "limit events," see Dominick LaCapra, *History and Memory after Auschwitz* (Ithaca: Cornell University Press,1998); and Primo Levi, *The Drowned and the Saved* (New York: Vintage, 1988).

14. I conducted an extensive survey on the political, social, economic, cultural, and psychological impact of massacres in two villages. One village was surveyed eight months before an exhumation of a clandestine cemetery and one village was surveyed three years after an exhumation. Surveys conducted prior to an exhumation revealed a citizenry largely unaware of the political and legal institutions of the state and its representatives, except for the army and its generals. After the exhumation, the majority of individuals, including monolingual Maya women, had knowledge of the legal system from the local justice of the peace to larger regional courts, the human rights ombudsmen, and elected officials. Additionally, individuals had a more nuanced understanding of different types of remedies available through elected officials, the courts, the media, etc. Data from testimonies, interviews, and surveys were collected before, during, and after exhumations over a four-year period, with a final follow-up visit in 2002 as I completed the final manuscript for this book. My first visit to rural Guatemala was in January of 1990. Formal field research began during the summer of 1994, continued in summer of 1995, spring 1996, fall 1996–fall 1997, and concluded in summer 1998 with a follow-up visit during summer 2002.

15. The CEH (Comisión para el Esclarecimiento Histórico) was established by the peace accords, which were brokered by the United Nations and formally signed by the Guatemalan government and URNG in December 1996.

16. CEH, *Memoria del Silencio,* 5:61.

17. Jan Perlin, "The Guatemalan Historical Clarification Commission finds Genocide," *ILSA Journal of International and Comparative Law: International Practitioner's Handbook* 6, no.2 (spring 2000): 411.

18. Mark Gibney and David Warner, "What Does It Mean to Say I'm Sorry? President Clinton's Apology to Guatemala and Its Significance for International and Domestic Law," *Denver Journal of International Law and Policy* 28 no.2 (2000): 223. Gibney and Warner also note that Clinton reiterated his apology at the end of the summit meeting: "[W]hat I apologized for has nothing to do with the fact that there was a difference between the policy of the administration and the Congress in previous years, going back for decades, and including administrations of both parties. It is that the policy of the Executive Branch was wrong. And what we're doing here is in the open, it's not a secret" (223). For an exploration of U.S. obligations under international law, see Anna M. Haughton, "United States Accountability for Intervention in the Western Hemisphere and Compulsory Compliance with the International Court of Justice," *The New England Journal of International and Comparative Law* 8 (2002).

19. See Victoria Sanford, "Between Rigoberta Menchú and La Violencia: Deconstructing David Stoll's History of Guatemala," *Latin American Perspectives* 109, vol. 26, no. 6 (November 1999): 38–46.

20. These research assistants, like many others, came forward to offer their support for this research project with the hope that their efforts would contribute to improved national and international understandings of La Violencia. Most also requested that their contribution not be acknowledged by name due to ongoing fear of retribution.

21. I am especially grateful to Terry Karl for helping me think about the relationship between the state, rule of law, and exhumations, for generously sharing her many insights on democratization and transitions from authoritarian regimes, and for supporting numerous human rights leaders over the years. See Terry Lynn Karl and Philippe Schmitter, "What Democracy Is . . . and Is Not," in Marc Plattner and Larry Diamond, eds., *The Global Resurgence of Democracy* (Washington, D.C.: Johns Hopkins Press, 1993); and "Democratization around the Globe: Opportunities and Risks," in Michael Klare and Daniel Thomas, eds., *World Security: Challenges for a New Century* (New York: St. Martin's Press,

1994). See also Guillermo O'Donnell and Philippe Schmitter, *Transitions from Authoritarian Rule: Tentative Conclusions about Uncertain Democracies* (Baltimore: Johns Hopkins University Press, 1986).

22. John Borneman provides a compelling ethnography with keen analysis about justice in *Settling Accounts: Violence, Justice and Accountability in Postsocialist Europe* (Princeton: Princeton University, 1997).

23. Dominick LaCapra, *Writing History, Writing Trauma* (Baltimore: Johns Hopkins University Press, 2001), 78. LaCapra also suggests that for the study of trauma, it is essential for the researcher to acknowledge this transference because failure to do so has serious, and perhaps unintended, consequences in one's continued research and analysis.

24. While I am firmly opposed to outsiders who enter communities with their own agenda for "improvement," I do believe that anthropologists and others who carry out research in foreign locales have an obligation to assist, to the best of their ability, the community in ways the community may request. Over the years, I have assisted the FAFG in research, community preparation for exhumations and participation in those exhumations, as well as fundraising efforts. I developed a *Directory of 145 Non-Governmental Organizations in Guatemala* (San Francisco: Shaler Adams, 1997) for distribution to foundations and others interested in funding projects in Latin America as well as a *Guía de Fundaciones Norteamericanos*—Guide to North American Foundations (San Francisco: Shaler Adams, 1997) in Spanish for distribution to NGOs in Guatemala. I have helped facilitate contacts between local community projects and potential funders. I have also organized numerous speaking tours for human rights leaders from Guatemala and El Salvador.

25. I gratefully acknowledge Purnima Mankekar for many thoughtful conversations on the subject of agency.

26. Veena Das, conversation with author at School of American Research seminar, Santa Fé, April 22, 2001.

27. "Bare Life" is the life that is left by the state of exception. See Giorgio Agamben, *Homo Sacer—Sovereign Power and Bare Life* (Stanford: Stanford University Press, 1998). See also, Walter Benjamin, *Illuminations* (New York: Schocken Books, 1978).

28. Victoria Sanford, "Buried Secrets: Truth and Human Rights in Guatemala" (Ph.D. diss., Stanford University, 2000).

29. Theodore Downing and Gilbert Kushner, *Human Rights and Anthropologists* (Cambridge: Cultural Survival, 1988).

30. Paul Magnarella, "Anthropology, Human Rights and Justice," *International Journal of Anthropology* 9, no.1 (1993): 7.

31. Stoll, *Between Two Armies*; Green, *Fear as a Way of Life*, 55.

32. Judith Zur, *Violent Memories—Mayan War Widows in Guatemala* (Boulder: Westview Press, 1998), 172.

33. Warren, *The Violence Within*, 49–50.

34. Michael Taussig, "Culture of Terror—Space of Death: Roger Casement's Putumayo Report and the Explanation of Torture," *Comparative Studies of Society and History* 26 (1984): 482.

35. Nordstrom, *A Different Kind*, 13.

36. Daniel, *Charred Lullabies*, 9.

37. Primo Levi, *Survival in Auschwitz* (New York: Simon and Schuster, 1958), 117.

38. Yazir Henry, "A Space Where Healing Begins" (paper presented at South African Truth and Reconciliation Commission Conference: Commissioning the Past, Johannesburg, South Africa, June 14, 1999), 6. I also thank Yazir and the West Cape Action Heritage Tours Team (especially Thabo) for many thoughtful conversations about survival and healing. In other anthropological research on violence, see Begoña Arextaga, *Shattering Silence—Women, Nationalism and Political Subjectivity in Northern Ireland* (Princeton: Princeton University Press, 1997). She suggests that "narratives of violence mediated and constructed the experience of actual violence" in Northern Ireland (74). Allen Feldman asserts that

there are "two passageways into the political culture of violence in Northern Ireland; categories of the body and categories of performance" (*Formations*, 99). For more gendered perspectives on violence, see also Irina Carlota Silber, "A Spectral Reconciliation: Rebuilding Post-War El Salvador" (Ph.D. diss., New York University, 2000); and Shannon Speed, "Global Discourses on the Local Terrain: Grounding Human Rights in Chiapas, Mexico" (Ph.D. diss., University of California at Davis, 2002); and Rosalva Aida Hernandez Castillo *La Otra Palabra—mujeres y violencia en Chiapas, antes y después de Acteal* (Mexico City: Pangea Editores, 1998).

39. Taussig, *Shamanism*, 1987; Nancy Scheper-Hughes, *Death without Weeping—The Violence of Every-Day Life in Brazil* (Berkeley: University of California Press, 1992); Warren, *The Violence Within*, 1993.

40. Primo Levi, *The Reawakening* (New York: Touchstone Press, 1965), 228.

41. Marguerite Feitlowitz, *A Lexicon of Terror—Argentina and the Legacies of Torture* (New York: Oxford University Press, 1998), 50.

42. Elaine Scarry, *The Body in Pain: The Making and Unmaking of the World* (Oxford: Oxford University Press, 1985), 50.

43. See especially Ranajit Guha, "The Small Voice of History," in Shahid Amin and Dipesh Chakrabarty, eds., *Subaltern Studies IX* (Delhi: Oxford University Press, 1996); Gyanendra Pandey, "The Colonial Construction of 'Communalism': British Writings on Banaras in the Nineteenth Century," in Ranajit Guha, ed., *Subaltern Studies VI* (Delhi: Oxford University Press, 1992); Shahid Amin, *Event, Metaphor, Memory—Chauri Chaura 1922–1992* (Berkeley: University of California Press, 1995); Akhil Gupta, *Postcolonial Developments* (Durham: Duke University Press, 1998); Purnima Mankekar, *Screening Culture, Viewing Politics: An Ethnography of Television, Womanhood, and Nation in Postcolonial India* (Durham: Duke University Press, 1999).

44. For historical and contemporary discussion, see John Beverly and Marc Zimmerman, *Literature and Politics in the Central American Revolutions* (Austin: University of Texas Press, 1990); Georg Gugelberg, *The Real Thing—Testimonial Discourse in Latin America* (Durham: Duke University Press, 1996); Carol Smith, "Why Write an Exposé of Rigoberta Menchú?" *Latin American Perspectives* 109, vol. 26, no. 6 (November 1999): 15–28.

45. David Stoll, *Rigoberta Menchú and the Story of All Poor Guatemalans* (Boulder: Westview Press, 1998).

46. "Doña" is a title of courtesy and respect used to address adult women in Maya communities.

47. Ranajit Guha, "The Prose of Counterinsurgency," in Ranajit Guha and Gayatri Chakravorty Spivak, eds., *Selected Subaltern Studies* (New York: Oxford University Press, 1988).

48. Oficina de Derechos Humanos del Arzobispado de Guatemala (ODHA), *Guatemala-Nunca Más, vols. 1–4, Informé Proyecto Interdiocesano de Recupaeración de la Memoria Histórica (REHMI)* (Guatemala City: ODHA, 1998); CEH, *Memoria del Silencio*, 1999.

CHAPTER ONE

1. Fundación de Antropología Forense de Guatemala (Guatemalan Forensic Anthropology Foundation—FAFG), *Las Masacres de Rabinal* (Guatemala City: FAFG, 1995), 19.

2. Dr. Clyde Snow is internationally renowned as the leading expert and founder of the field of forensic anthropology. It was through Dr. Snow's tireless efforts that both the Argentine and Guatemalan forensic teams were established. Dr. Snow serves as an expert research consultant for international war tribunals and United Nations investigations. For background on forensics and the law in Guatemala prior to the FAFG, see Americas Watch, *Guatemala: Getting Away with Murder* (New York: Americas Watch, 1990).

3. Trinh Minh-ha, *Framer Framed* (New York: Routledge, 1992), 13.

4. Indeed, Fernando Moscoso wrote his thesis at the Universidad de San Carlos in Guatemala on this process. His thesis, "La Antropología Forense en Guatemala" (University of San

Carlos, Guatemala City, 1998), is considered the blueprint for training forensic anthropologists. This section draws from "Strengthening the Peace Process in Guatemala—A Proposal of the Guatemalan Forensic Anthropology Foundation to the Open Society Institute," grant proposal, Victoria Sanford, 1998. See also FAFG, *Informe de la Fundación de Antropología Forense de Guatemala: Cuatro Casos Paradigmaticos por la Comisión para el Esclarecimiento Historico de Guatemala* (Guatemala City: Editorial Serviprensa, 2000).

5. For more on forensic anthropology and forensic osteology, see Kathleen J. Reichs, ed., *Forensic Osteology: Advances in the Identification of Human Remains* (Springfield, IL: Charles C. Thomas, 1998); Myriam Nafte, *Flesh and Bone: An Introduction to Forensic Anthropology* (Durham: Carolina Academic Press, 2000); Eric Stover, *Unquiet Graves: The Search for the Disappeared in Iraqi Kurdistan* (New York: Middle East Watch and Physicians for Human Rights, 1992).

6. The antemortem interviews, archival research, testimony collection, and the actual excavations are conducted by FAFG staff, expert consultants, volunteers, and interns. All phases of the exhumation include the participation of expert consultants and trained volunteers invited from national and international universities. To complete the excavation, the FAFG uses an extensive supply of tools ranging from picks, axes, shovels, sifting equipment, and other excavation tools to tape measures and compasses for the elaboration of maps. Additionally, the FAFG uses the necessary camera equipment to document this phase. Given the isolated rural locations of many investigations, the FAFG has developed the necessary experience and equipment to establish provisional camps for the duration of this phase. Because of previous investigations in caves and wells, the FAFG also has the training and equipment to scale deep caves.

7. Today, the FAFG has its own very large laboratory, and, with the new court system, the FAFG's lab locations are no longer determined by the whims of a judge. The FAFG has legal custody of the evidence throughout the investigation. The forensic anthropologists at the FAFG lab utilize technologically advanced equipment for slicing and analyzing bones, a microscope for examination of tissue and the calculation of age, as well as other precision instruments and necessary lab furniture.

8. The FAFG has had the good fortune of working with Dr. Mary-Clair King, who has provided similar collaboration to projects in Argentina, El Salvador, Ethiopia, Rwanda, Bosnia, and Croatia. Dr. Michelle Harvey, who collaborates with Dr. King, has also provided the FAFG with this technical support *pro bono*.

9. FAFG, *Las Masacres*, 1995; and FAFG, *Nada Podrá contra la vida—Investigación sobre tres masacres en Rabinal* (Guatemala City: FAFG, 1995). The reports on each exhumation are presented in hard copy and on diskette (which includes digital photos) to the human rights ombudsman, local prosecutors, the attorney general, relevant nongovernmental organizations, community members, and other interested parties.

10. The human rights ombudsman (Procaduría de Derechos Humanos—PDH) was created to investigate human rights violations under Article 30 of the 1985 constitution. The Guatemalan Congress appoints the national PDH. Each department has a regional PDH.

11. In the new legal system, it is the prosecutor, not the judge or court, that initiates the exhumation. Now, an individual can go directly to the prosecutor to request an investigation. The PDH continues to play an important role assisting individuals in the filing of their claims with the prosecutor or directly filing claims on behalf of the PDH.

12. Other popular human rights organizations, such as CERJ (Consejo de Etnías Runujel Junam—Council of Ethnic Groups—"We Are All Equal") and FAMDEGUA (Familiares de los Desaparecidos de Guatemala—Families of the Disappeared of Guatemala) have also provided assistance to communities filing legal requests for exhumations and provided resources for food during the exhumations and materials for reburial. The ODHA has also conducted exhumations.

13. Military commissioners (comisionados militares) were the army-appointed leaders of the PACs (civil patrols), which were the army-controlled units of local men forcibly recruited

and compelled under threat to patrol for the army. For more on PACs, see chapters three, six, and eight. For critical analyses on the PACs and forced recruitment, see also Miguel Angel Aguilar, *El Servicio Militar: Obligatorio o Voluntario?* (Notre Dame: University of Notre Dame Press, 1992); Americas Watch, (hereafter AW) *Messengers of Death—Human Rights in Guatemala* (New York: Americas Watch, 1990); AW, *Civil Patrols in Guatemala* (New York: AW, 1986); AW, *Persecuting Human Rights Monitors: the CERJ in Guatemala* (New York: AW, 1989); AW, *Guatemala—A Nation of Prisoners* (New York: AW, 1984).

14. The Maya are not alone in reverence for spilled blood. Hassidic Jews also bury belongings and spilled blood of the deceased. For more on Maya burial and other religious practices, see Patricia Mcanany, *Living with the Ancestors: Kinship and Kingship in Ancient Maya Society* (Austin: University of Texas Press, 1995); Benjamin Colby and Pierre van den Berghe, *Ixil Country: A Plural Society in Highland Guatemala* (Berkeley: University of California Press, 1969); B. N. Colby and L. Colby, *The Daykeeper: The Life and Discourse of an Ixil Diviner* (Cambridge: Harvard University Press, 1981); June Nash, *In the Eyes of the Ancestors—Beliefs and Behavior in a Maya Community* (New Haven: Yale University Press, 1970); Maude Oakes, *Two Crosses of Todos Santos* (Princeton: Princeton University Press, 1951); Jean Piel, *Sajcabajá—Muerte y resurrección de un pueblo de Guatemala 1500–1970* (Mexico City: CEMCA, 1989); Sheldon Annis, *God and Production in a Guatemalan Town* (Austin: University of Texas Press, 1987); "Popol Vuh," trans. Dennis Tedlock, in *Popol Vuh—The Definitive Edition of the Mayan Book of the Dawn of Life and the Glories of Gods and Kings* (New York: Simon and Schuster, 1985); Barbara Tedlock, *Time and the Highland Maya* (Albuquerque: University of New Mexico Press, 1982); John Watanabe, *Maya Saints and Souls in a Changing World* (Austin: University of Texas Press, 1992); Victor Montejo, *The Bird Who Cleans the World* (Willimantic: Curbstone Press, 1992).

15. E-mail communication with Patricia Macanany, April 16, 2002.

16. "Leña" is firewood.

17. Michel Foucault, *Power/Knowledge: Selected Writings and Other Interviews 1972–1977,* Colin Gordon, ed. (New York: Pantheon Books, 1980), 131.

18. Collaboration in the labor of the exhumation had much to do in determining inclusion of outsiders in community and forensic team activities. Researchers, journalists, and others who voluntarily helped with labor, transportation, running messages, etc., had their gestures reciprocated by forensic team and community members in the form of interviews, explanations of the process of the exhumation, introduction to community members, procurement of translators, inclusion in community meals, and invitations to relax with the team in the evening, etc. These were not practices of exclusion. They were a response to the many NGOs and journalists, both national and international, who would arrive to Plan de Sánchez with no prior warning and expect forensic team and community members to drop whatever they were doing to accommodate NGO/journalist needs ranging from organizing interviews, food, or accommodations. Several NGOs arrived with groups of internationals and claimed that they were sponsoring the exhumations—when in fact, they had nothing to do with the FAFG or the community and were simply using the exhumation as a fundraising tool. Forensic team and community members referred to the people as "zopilotes"—buzzards who feed off the dead.

Moreover, many NGOs and journalists did give notice of their intentions because they didn't want to interrupt the work and hoped their needs could be integrated into the ongoing activities. These NGOs would collaborate with the exhumation, providing support, both emotional and financial, to the community; individuals would help out with the physical labor of the excavation. The individual journalists, both national and international, provided transportation to the team and community members and made unsolicited personal contributions to the community coffers for the burial celebration the survivors were planning when the remains were returned. These journalists always made a point of explaining that to make a personal contribution was not a violation of "objectivity" but rather a recognition of their individual humanity and desire to contribute something to the community. A driver of the vehicle loaned to the team by the PDH worked in the exhumation doing heavy digging everyday. He was not expected, nor was it in his job description, to do anything beyond drive and maintain the vehicle. From his first day at the site, he volunteered his labor.

19.   Plan de Sánchez, collective interview, 25 July 1994. All interviews are author's unless otherwise noted.

20.   Personal communication with FAFG president Fredy Pecerrelli, February 24, 2002, and with former FAFG president Fernando Moscoso, February 28, 2002.

21.   FAFG, "Plan de Sanchéz Caso 319–93, 5TO," exhumation file (1997).

22.   Rabinal testimony no. 7–3, 18 July 1994. All testimonies cited are author's unless otherwise noted.

23.   Rabinal testimony nos. 7–3, 27 July 1994; 7–5, 20 July 1994; 7–3, 18 July 1994; 7–2, 27 July 1994; 7–1, 18 July 1994; 7–1, 27 July 1994; Plan de Sánchez, collective interview, 25 July 1994.

24.   Patricia Macanany, conversation with author, Cambridge, MA, April 12, 2000.

CHAPTER TWO

1.   This chapter builds on previously published pieces on Guatemalan women in general and Maya women in particular. See Victoria Sanford, "Between Rigoberta Menchú and La Violencia: Deconstructing David Stoll's History of Guatemala," *Latin American Perspectives* 109, vol. 26, no.6 (November 1999): 38–46; Victoria Sanford, "From *I, Rigoberta* to the Commissioning of Truth: Maya Women and the Reshaping of Guatemalan History," *Cultural Critique* 47 (winter 2001): 16–53; Victoria Sanford, "The Silencing of Maya Women from Mamá Maquín to Rigoberta Menchú," *Social Justice* 27, no. 1 (June 2000): 128–156; Victoria Sanford, *Mothers, Widows and Guerrilleras: Anonymous Conversations with Survivors of State Terror* (Uppsala: Life and Peace Institute, 1997). For more on Guatemalan women and their testimonies, see also Margaret Hooks, *Guatemalan Women Speak* (London: Catholic Institute for International Relations, 1991); and Ayuda de la Iglesia Norwega, *Por favor, Nunca Más: Testimonios de mujeres, víctimas del conflicto armado en Guatemala* (Guatemala City: Ayuda de la Iglesia Norwega, 1997).

2.   Paul Ricoeur, *Husserl—An Analysis of His Phenomenology* (Evanston: Northwestern University Press, 1967), 211.

3.   Marguerite Feitlowitz, *A Lexicon of Terror—Argentina and the Legacies of Torture* (New York: Oxford University Press, 1998): 77–83, 104.

4.   Elaine Scarry, *The Body in Pain: The Making and Unmaking of the World* (Oxford: Oxford University Press, 1985): 50.

5.   Sanford, *Mothers, Widows and Guerrilleras*, 12–13.

6.   Ranajit Guha, "The Small Voice of History," in Shahid Amin and Dipesh Chakrabarty, eds., *Subaltern Studies X* (Delhi: Oxford University Press, 1996): 11. Guha is referring to the women who participated in the Telangana movement (1946–51) in India.

7.   Elizabeth Burgos Debray, *I, Rigoberta Menchú—An Indian Woman in Guatemala* (London: Verso, 1984). For a compelling testimony from the founder of the Mothers of the Disappeared in El Salvador, see Maria Teresa Tula, *Hear My Testimony* (Boston: South End Press, 1994). From a peasant union leader in Honduras, see Elvia Alvarado, *Don't Be Afraid Gringo. A Honduran Woman Speaks from the Heart* (San Francisco: Institute for Food and Development Study, 1987).

8.   "Campesino" is the term for peasant. "Campesina" is the term for peasant woman.

9.   CEH, *Memory of Silence—Online Report,* 1999. Available at shr.aaas.org/guatemala/ceh/report/english/toc.html.

10.   Guha, *Small Voice,* 11.

11. Sanford, *Mothers,* and Sanford, "Buried Secrets: Truth and Human Rights in Guatemala" (Ph.D. diss., Stanford University, 2000).

12. For more on the history of the reinas indigenas, see Ramon Gonzalez-Ponciano, "Esas sangres no están limpias," in *El Racismo, el Estado y la Nación en Guatemala 1944–1997* (Tuxtla Gutierrez, Mexico: Centro de Estudios de Mexico and Centroamérica, 1998).

13. "Ladino" is a term used in Guatemala to refer to non-Maya. While often compared to the Mexican usage of the word *mestizo,* which has been historically used to label the hybrid identity of Spanish and indigenous, the Guatemalan term "ladino" is most commonly used to refer to all non-Maya. For an interesting discussion of the history of this term and ladino identity, see Greg Grandin, *The Blood of Guatemala—A History of Race and Nation* (Durham: Duke University Press, 2000); and Marta Casaus-Arzú, *Guatemala: Lineaje y Racismo* (San José, Costa Rica: FLACSO, 1992).

14. *El Gráfico,* Guatemala City, 26 July 1978, 7. In Sanford, "Buried Secrets," 158, and Sanford, "From *I, Rigoberta,*" 19, I wrote: "this was, perhaps, as much a message to the army investigators as it was to the public at-large. Testimony Number 30,478 was given to a REHMI investigator by someone who knew Amalía Pop. Her name is among the thousands listed in chapter 2, 'The Dead,' of Volume 4, 'Victims of the Conflict.' [*Nunca Más,* ODHA] She was killed in August of 1983 in Cobán—roughly the same time Rigoberta's book was published. Perhaps Amalía Pop is not Amalía Eróndina Coy Pop. Maybe Amalía Eróndina Coy Pop beat the odds that were stacked against anyone who challenged the Guatemalan army. It is a possibility, but not a probability. If Amalía Eróndina Coy Pop escaped the terror that violently took the lives of so many, wherever she is today, she knows she is lucky." Thanks to Betsy Konefal's diligent search for Amalía Eróndina Coy Pop in Alta Verapaz, I can now report that Amalía Eróndina Coy Pop is not the Amalía Pop reported in "The Dead." Amalía Eróndina Coy Pop is alive and well.

15. The participation of women in protest is indeed a widespread, if insufficiently documented, phenomenon. On the key role of beauticians as community leaders during the civil rights movement in the United States, see Francesca Polletta, "Outsiders in Social Protest" paper presented at the American Sociological Association, January 5, 1999; and, her *Freedom is an Endless Meeting: Experiments in Participatory Democracy from Pre-War Pacifism to the Present* (forthcoming). On women in the Sandinista revolution, see Margaret Randall, *Sandino's Daughters. Testimonies of Nicaraguan Women in Struggle* (Vancouver: New Star Books, Ltd., 1981); on peasant women taking up arms in the Telengana uprising in India, see Vasantha Kannibiran and K. Lalita, "That Magic Time," in Kumkum Sangari and Suresh Vaid, eds., *Recasting Women* (New Brunswick: Rutgers University Press, 1990); on African women in prison, see Asale Angel-Ajani, *Negotiating Small Truths* (forthcoming); on post-revolutionary women activists in El Salvador, see Irina Carlota Silber, *A Spectral Reconciliation: Rebuilding Post-War El Salvador* (Ph.D. diss., New York University, 2000) ; and Lynn Stephen, *Women and Social Movements in Latin America* (Austin: University of Texas Press, 1994); on the role of indigenous women in the Chiapas uprising, see Rosalva Aida Hernandez, *La otra palabra-mujeres y Violencia en Chiapas, antes y después de Acteal* (Mexico City: Pangea Editores, 1998); and Shannon Speed, *Global Discourses on the Local Terrain: Grounding Human Rights in Chiapas, Mexico* (Ph.D. diss., University of California, Davis, 2002). See also Marjorie Agosin, *Surviving Beyond Fear: Women, Children and Human Rights in Latin America* (Fredonia: White Pine Press, 1993); Sonia Alvarez, *Engendering Democracy in Brazil: Women's Movements in Transitional Politics* (Princeton: Princeton University Press, 1990); Jane Jaquette, ed., *The Women's Movement in Latin America: Participation and Democracy* (Boulder: Westview Press, 1994); Elizabeth Jelin, *Women and Social Change in Latin America* (London: Zed Press, 1990).

16. *Guatemala News and Information Bureau* (hereafter GNIB) 4, no.2 (March/April 1983): 9.

17. Nancy Caro Hollander, *Love in a Time of Hate—Liberation Psychology in Latin America* (New Brunswick: Rutgers University Press, 1997), 95. See also Ximena Bunster-Burotto,

"Women and Torture in Latin America," in *Women and Change in Latin America,* June Nash and Helen Safa, eds. (South Hadley, MA: Bergin and Garvey, 1985).

18. Hollander, *Love in a Time of Hate,* 95.

19. Rene Jara and Hernan Vidal, eds., *Testimonio y Literatura* (Minneapolis: Monographic Series of the Society for the Study of Contemporary Hispanic and Lusophone Revolutionary Literatures, no. 3, 1986): 3; John Beverly and Marc Zimmerman, *Literature and Politics in the Central American Revolutions* (Austin: University of Texas Press, 1990), 175 and 36.

20. Construction of this bridge began in 1860, the same year that local and regional officials implemented labor drafts upon Maya communities, which obligated local Maya to work on coffee plantations. For more on Panzós, see Sanford, "Buried Secrets," 45–50. For an in-depth analysis of the usurpation of Maya lands and forced labor in the late nineteenth century, see Julio Castellano Cambranes, ed., *550 Años de Lucha por la Tierra,* vols.1–2. (Guatemala City: FLACSO, 1992). See also Severo Martínez Peláez, *La Patria del Criollo: Ensayo de interpretación de la realidad colonial guatemalteca* (San Jose, Costa Rica: Editorial Universitario Centroamericano, 1979); and Martínez Peláez, *Motines del Indios—La Violencia Colonial en Centroamerica y Chiapas* (Puebla, Mexico: Cuadernos de la Casa Presno, 1985).

21. Engineer requested anonymity. Interview with author, Guatemala City, July 12, 1997.

22. *Libro de Actas de Panzós,* vol. 18 (1964): 432–444.

23. Former Panzós functionary requested anonymity. Interview with author, September 7, 1997; and Panzós testimony no. 1, 2 October 1997.

24. Panzós testimony no. 2, 6 September 1997.

25. *GNIB* (1981): 8.

26. *GNIB* (1983): 9.

27. Dictator Jorge Ubico (1931–1944) had a very paternalistic, near-royal self-image. Ubico believed that the Maya should be conscripted into the Guatemalan army, where they would be trained to leave their "primitive" ways behind. Through the complicated Decree 1995, he legally granted free access to Maya labor as the right of large landholders. See Jim Handy, *Gift of the Devil—A History of Guatemala* (Boston: South End Press, 1984); Castellano Cambranes, *550 Años de Lucha por la Tierra.*

28. CEH, Staff interview (1997): internal document D231.

29. For more on the Democratic Spring, the Arbenz government, land reform, and U.S. intervention, see Rafael Menjivar, *Reforma Agraria: Guatemala, Bolivia, Cuba* (San Salvador: Editorial Universitaria de El Salvador, 1969); Roger Williams, *States and Social Evolution—Coffee and the Rise of National Governments in Central America* (Chapel Hill: University of North Carolina Press, 1994); Castellano Cambranes, ed., *550 Años de Lucha por la Tierra;* Jim Handy, *Revolution in the Countryside: Rural Conflict and Agrarian Reform in Guatemala, 1944–1954* (Chapel Hill: University of North Carolina Press, 1994); David McCreery, *Rural Guatemala, 1760–1940* (Stanford: Stanford University Press, 1994); Piero Gleijeses, *Shattered Hope—The Guatemalan Revolution and the United States, 1944–1954* (Princeton: Princeton University Press, 1991); Jesús García Añoveros, *La Reforma Agraria de Arbenz en Guatemala* (Madrid: Ediciones Cultura Hispana, Instituto de Cooperación Iberoamericano, 1987); Richard Immerman, *The CIA in Guatemala: The Foreign Policy of Intervention* (Austin: University of Texas Press, 1982); Nick Cullather, *Secret History: The CIA's Classified Account of its Operations in Guatemala, 1952–1954* (Stanford: Stanford University Press, 1999). Specifically on Panzós, see *Libro de Actas de Panzós* no. 3, 1944: 83–87. On the department of Alta Verapaz, see Richard Wilson's ethnography, *Maya Resurgence in Guatemala* (Oklahoma City: University of Oklahoma Press, 1995).

30. CEH, Staff interview, internal document D231.

31. Arbenz was forced into exile. See Gleijeses, *Shattered Hope;* Cullather, *Secret History.*

32. "Mama Maquín" was organized in 1990 by refugee women to unite Guatemalan women across ethnic, language, and refugee camp boundaries in Mexico. They were demanding

women's participation in daily camp life decision-making and their planned return to Guatemala. The organization became the space through which women could assert their needs and their goals for themselves as well as their communities. Deborah Billings offers a powerful ethnography of Guatemalan refugee women in "Identities, Consciousness and Organizing in Exile: Guatemalan Refugee Women in the Camps of Southern Mexico" (Ph.D. diss., University of Michigan, 1995). For more on land struggles in Guatemala, see Episcopado Guatemalteco (hereafter EG), *El Clamor por la Tierra—Carta Pastoral Colectiva del Epioscopado Guatemalteco* (Guatemala City: EG, 1988). For more on rural movements in Central America, see Marc Edelman, *Peasants Against Globalization: Rural Social Movements in Costa Rica* (Stanford: Stanford University Press, 1999); Philippe Bourgois, *Ethnicity at Work: Divided Labor on a Central American Banana Plantation* (Baltimore: Johns Hopkins University Press, 1989); Charles Hale, *Resistance and Contradiction—Miskitu Indians and the Nicaraguan State* (Stanford: Stanford University Press, 1994); Jeffrey Gould, *To Die this Way—Nicaraguan Indians and the Myth of Mestizaje, 1880–1965* (Durham: Duke University Press, 1998), and Jeffrey Gould, *To Lead as Equals—Rural Protest and Political Consciousness in Chinandega, Nicaragua, 1912–1979* (Chapel Hill: University of North Carolina Press, 1990); William Durham, *Scarcity and Survival in Central America: Ecological Orginis of the Soccer War* (Stanford: Stanford University Press, 1979).

33.   Julia Lieblich, "Pieces of Bone," *AGNI* 47 (1998): 5. Lieblich's piece is one of the most thoughtful and compelling meditations written about what it means to survive torture and be re-traumatized by officials casting doubt on survivor credibility.

34.   Lieblich, "Pieces," 5–6.

35.   Lieblich, "Pieces," 5–6.

36.   Army officer requested anonymity and requested that I not identify the location or exact date of our interview. Interview with author, Guatemala, July 1994.

37.   Lieblich, "Pieces," 5–6.

38.   Lieblich, "Pieces," 9.

39.   David Stoll, *Rigoberta Menchú and the Story of All Poor Guatemalans* (Boulder: Westview Press, 1998): 12, 282.

40.   Stoll, *Rigoberta Menchú,* 10–11; and "To Whom Should We Listen? Human Rights Activism in Two Guatemalan Land Disputes" in Richard Wilson, ed., *Human Rights: Culture and Context—Anthropological Perspectives* (London: Pluto Press, 1997): 187–188.

41.   United States government, Department of State. "Secret Memorandum Guatemala: Human Rights Analysis," November 3, 1982, 2. Declassified January 1998.

42.   Stoll, *Rigoberta Menchú,* 48.

43.   Allan Nairn, "Behind the Death Squads," *The New Republic* (April 11, 1984): 21. Nairn's analysis of the U.S. role in developing paramilitary organizations throughout Central America is further confirmed by the following declassified CIA and U.S. State Department documents: United States Embassy in Guatemala Memoranda to the Secretary of State on September 15, 1962; March 13, 1963; and January 23, 1964. See also Memorandum of the Special Group September 25, 1963; Telegram from U.S. Embassy in Guatemala to the State Department January 5, 1966; Public Safety Division U.S. AID/Guatemala, "Operational Rescue of Terrorist Kidnapping and Guatemala Police Activity to Counter," December 1965; CIA Memoranda dated March and April 1966. All declassified documents cited in this book are now available from the National Security Archive in Washington, D.C.

44.   Stoll, *Rigoberta Menchú,* 71–88.

45.   Comisión para el Esclarecimiento Histórico (CEH*), Guatemala Memoria del Silencio,* vols. 1–12 (Guatemala City: CEH, 1999), vol. 6: 173.

46.   Stoll, *Rigoberta Menchú,* 25, 32,104.

47.   Commission for Historical Clarification (CEH), *Guatemala Memory of Silence—Conclusions and Recommendations* (Guatemala City: CEH, 1999): 40–41.

48. Personal conversations with CEH and FAFG staff in May 1998. At the request of the FAFG, I developed a research methodology and led the investigation for the historical reconstruction of massacres in Panzós, Alta Verapaz and Acul, Nebaj, El Quiché. The methodology was then replicated in two additional FAFG investigations for the CEH in Chel, Chajul, El Quiché and Belen, Sacatepequez. In May and June of 1998, I wrote the historical reconstruction of the massacres in Panzós and Acul and supervised the writing of the reconstructions for Chel and Belen for the FAFG report to the CEH. See FAFG, *Informé de la Fundación de Antropología Forense de Guatemala: Cuatro Casos Paradaigmáticos Solicitados por la Comisión para el Esclarecimiento Histórico de Guatemala* (Guatemala City: FAFG, 2000).

49. See José Barnoya García, *Panzós y unas Historias* (Guatemala City: Editorial Universitaria, 1984); Tom Barry, *Guatemala. The Politics of Counterinsurgency* (Albuquerque: Inter-Hemispheric Education Resource Center, 1986); George Black, *Garrison Guatemala* (London: Zed Books, 1984); Centró de Investigaciones de Historia Social (CEIHS), *Panzós—Testimonio* (Guatemala City: CEIHS, 1979); Carlos Figueroa Ibarra, *El Recurso del Miedo—Ensayo sobre el Estado y el Terror en Guatemala* (San Jose, Costa Rica: EDUCA, 1991); Gabriel Aguilera Peralta, *Dialectica del Terror* (San Jose, Costa Rica: EDUCA, 1981).

50. Alessandro Portelli, *The Death of Luigi Trastulli and Other Stories—Form and Meaning in Oral History* (Albany: State University of New York, 1991), 69. For a compelling study of time and violence in Peru, see Billie Jean Isbell, "Time, Text and Terror," *Journal of the Steward Anthropological Society* 25, nos. 1, 2 (1997): 57–76. See also Deborah Poole and Gerardo Enrique, *Peru: Time of Fear* (London: Latin American Bureau. 1992).

51. Oficina de Derechos Humanos del Arzobispado de Guatemala (ODHA), *Guatemala—Nunca Más*, vols. 1–4, *Informé Proyecto Interdiocesano de Recupaeración de la Memoria Histórica (REHMI)* (Guatemala City: ODHA, 1998), vol. 4: 69; CEH, *Memoria*, 1999, vol. 6: 21; and FAFG, *Informé*, 57.

52. ODHA, *Nunca Más*, 69.

53. CEH, *Memoria*, 1999, vol. 6: 21.

54. At the entrance to Panzós shortly after the massacre, soldiers verbally and physically abused journalists trying to cover the massacre. They were denied entry and soldiers took away their cameras and tape recorders at gunpoint. See, *El Imparcial*, 1 June 1978:1.

55. John Beverly, "The Margin at the Center," in Georg Gugelberger, ed., *The Real Thing—Testimonial Discourse and Latin America* (Durham: Duke University Press, 1996), 37.

56. Portelli, *Death of Luigi*, 26.

57. A finquero is an owner of a large finca (plantation).

58. Eduardo Galeano, *The Book of Embraces* (New York: W.W. Norton, 1991), 11.

59. Dominick LaCapra, *History and Memory after Auschwitz* (Ithaca: Cornell University Press,1998), 11.

60. "We sing because the survivors and our dead want us to sing." The words on the pamphlet are from Mario Benedetti's poem "Por qué Cantamos" (Why We Sing). For more of Benedetti's poetry, see Mario Benedetti, *Inventario: poesia completa (1950–1985)* (Madrid: Visor, 1990).

61. Joanne Rappaport, *The Politics of Memory—Native Historical Interpretation in the Colombian Andes* (Cambridge: Cambridge University Press, 1990), 18.

62. Beverly, "The Margin," 272–273.

63. Beverly, "The Margin," 273.

64. Rosemary Jane Jolly, *Colonization, Violence and Narration in White South African Writing: André Brink, Breyten Breytenbach, and J. M. Coetzee* (Athens: Ohio State University Press, 1996), xiv.

65. Mario Moussa and Ron Scapp, "The Practical Theorizing of Michel Foucault: Politics and Counter-Discourse," *Cultural Critique* 33 (spring 1996): 93.

66. Portelli, *Death of Luigi*, 50.

67. Polletta, "Outsiders in Social Protest," 7.
68. Portelli, *Death of Luigi*, 50.
69. LaCapra, *History and Memory*, 139.
70. LaCapra, *History and Memory*, 12.
71. LaCapra, *History and Memory*, 12.
72. Guha, "Small Voice," 10.
73. CEH, *Memoria*, vol. 6: 22.
74. Guha, "Small Voice," 12.

CHAPTER THREE

1. Cultural Survival, "Counterinsurgency and the Development Pole Strategy in Guatemala," *Cultural Survival Quarterly* 12, no. 3 (1988): 11.

2. All testimonies included here were collected by the author. Archival data from Nebaj and Chajul were gathered with the assistance of FAFG team members and volunteers. I especially thank Carlota MacAllister for her fast and meticulous recording of Nebaj Death Register data. Testimonies were translated from Ixil to Spanish by "Julia." All translation from Spanish to English is mine.

3. For more on model villages and poles of development, see Cultural Survival, "Counterinsurgency and the Development Pole Strategy"; AVANSCO, *¿Dónde esta el futuro? Procesos de Reintegración en Comunidades de Retornados* (Guatemala City: Infopress Centroaméricano, 1992); George Black, *Garrison Guatemala* (London: Zed Books, 1984); Chris Krueger and Kjell Enge, *Security and Development: Conditions in the Guatemalan Highlands* (Washington, D.C.: Washington Office on Latin America, 1985); Luis Padilla, ed., *Guatemala: Polos de Desarrollo—El Caso de la Desedtructuración de las Comunidades Mayas*, vols. 1–2. (Mexico City: Editorial Praxis, 1988 and 1990); James Painter, *Guatemala: False Hope, False Freedom* (London: Catholic Institute for International Relations, 1987); Rolando Alecio, "Uncovering the Truth: Political Violence and Indigenous Organizations," in Minor Sinclair, ed., *The New Politics of Survival: Grassroots Movements in Central America* (New York: Monthly Review Press, 1995).

4. Because there are numerous testimonies from different individuals presenting a collective history of La Violencia in Acul, I have chosen to include as many of the voices as possible and to name them. Each testimony presented was corroborated by the majority of those interviewed in Acul. After being silenced in so many ways for so many years, those interviewed deserve to be named, even if only via pseudonym. I feel an ethical obligation to use active naming of individuals and not create amalgams of individual experiences or words. I have inserted a pseudonym for the speaker or speakers at the beginning of each section. Also, with the intention of maintaining the ethnographic present, I use the past tense when I describe and analyze from a historical perspective. In conversation with the Acules and when they speak, I maintain the tense they used, as well as my own. Finally, to signal to the reader a shift in place and time, I use a series of three *   *   * to indicate my analysis today.

5. "Corte"—skirt of ankle-length woven cloth wrapped several times at the waist and secured with a brightly colored, hand-woven belt.

6. "Huipil"—blouse of intricately embroidered hand woven fabric. For a thoughtful analysis on the relationship between indigenous clothing and identity, see Carol Hendrickson, *Weaving Identities: Construction of Dress and Self in a Highland Guatemalan Town* (Austin: University of Texas Press, 1995).

7. Quetzales—Guatemala monetary unit exchanged for seven quetzales to the dollar in 1997. Most peasant women I have interviewed had family incomes of less than 150 quetzales per month. A round-trip bus ticket to Guatemala City cost forty quetzales in 1997.

8. Author's interview, testimony no. 28, 16 December 1997.

9. "Principal"—elder religious leader of the community.

10. With the arrival of the forensic team, the word *forense* quickly entered the Acul vocabulary. "Are they *forenses?*" means "Are they with you? Can they be trusted?"

11. "Cédula"—the national identification card that all Guatemalans are required to carry. During La Violencia, lacking a current cédula could mean being pulled off a bus or out of a line because all who lacked cédulas were labeled guerrilla.

12. We later discovered the man with the glasses was a leader of another popular organization seeking to recuperate some of what community members lost during La Violencia.

13. Author's interview testimony no. 7, 10 December 1997

14. Bertolt Brecht, "Motto," in Carolyn Forché, ed, *Against Forgetting: Twentieth Century Poetry of Witness* (New York: W.W. Norton, 1993): 51.

15. Unless otherwise noted, testimony quoted was gathered on same day as cited in first footnote identifying author's interview

16. As was common in international and national literacy and development programs of this period, Acul women were neither the targets nor the beneficiaries of skills-building programs. Thus, gender divisions of labor within the Maya community were reconfigured and patriarchal structures strengthened by the exclusion of Maya women from these programs.

17. Libro de Defunciones de la Municipalidad de Nebaj 1982, vol. 59: 57.

18. Acul testimony no. 17, 12 December 1997.

19. Acul testimony no. 16, 11 December 1997.

20. Acul testimony no. 32, 16 December 1997.

21. Acul testimony no. 15, 11 December 1997.

22. "Buzones"—Large, hidden storage pits dug in the earth.

23. Acul testimony no. 37, 17 December 1997.

24. Acul testimony no. 8, 10 December 1997.

25. Acul testimony no. 23, 13 December 1997.

26. Acul testimony no. 20, 12 December 1997.

27. Acul testimony no. 12, 11 December 1997.

28. Acul testimony no. 24, 15 December 1997.

29. Acul testimony no. 8, 10 December 1997.

30. Acul testimony no. 7, 10 December 1997.

31. "Faja"—woven belt of brightly colored cloth.

32. Literally, "oreja" means ear. It is also a colloquial expression used for spy, spies, and spying.

33. Acul testimony no. 3, 10 December 1997.

34. Libros de Defunciones de la Municipalidad de Nebaj 1977 to 1982, vols. 56–59.

35. Acul testimony no. 8, 10 December 1997.

36. In its final report, the CEH listed the Acul massacre date as April 22, 1982, which is most likely a typographical error. A 1983 article reports the massacre as April 20, 1982 (See Allan Nairn, "The Guns of Guatemala," *The New Republic*, [April 11, 1983]: 17), based on interviews conducted in 1983 with a survivor in an army relocation camp. Yet, all survivors interviewed during the FAFG investigation reported being in the mountains for at least two years prior to surrendering to the army. For the FAFG investigation, I interviewed forty-three massacre survivors and Carlota MacAllister interviewed thirteen. Our testimonies, gathered during the FAFG exhumation, consistently noted the date as April 1981, April 21, 1981, or 1981. Acul massacre survivors also consistently said it happened the year before the massacre in Chel (April 3, 1982), and Chel massacre survivors consistently reported the date of the Chel massacre as taking place one year after the Acul massacre, offering 1982, April 1982 and April 3, 1982, as the date of the Chel massacre. Doña Magdalena reported her husband and son's assassination by the EGP as having happened on April 12, 1981 and said that this took place the same year as the massacre (Acul testimony no. 3, 10 December 1997). Further, the April 1981 date of the EGP assassination was a marker of time also consistently used by other members of the community as taking

place the same year as the Acul massacre. Significantly, testimonies consistently dated the Acul massacre as having occurred one week after the massacre in neighboring Cocop. The Cocop massacre is one of the few massacres recorded in the Nebaj Death Register (April 15, 1981) and notes the "assassination" of sixty-four men, women, and children—thus corroborating survivor testimonies of the 1981 massacre date. The human rights group GAM (Mutual Support Group) also reports the Acul massacre date as April 1981 (Grupo de Apoyo Mutuo [GAM], *Quitar el agua al pez* [Guatemala City: GAM, 1996]; 53). *Nunca Más* reports the Acul massacre date as 1980 and 1982 but is based on interviews with only three witnesses (Oficina de Derechos Humanos del Arzobispado de Guatemala [ODHA], *Guatemala—Nunca Más, vols. 1–4, Informé Proyecto Interdiocesano de Recupaeración de la Memoria Histórica [REHMI]* [Guatemala City: ODHA, 1998]: vol. 1, 53). These conflicting dates again raise the issue of the confusing puzzle created by genocide and indicate that the puzzle can best be reconstructed by collecting, comparing, and contrasting as much testimonial and archival information as possible. Based on the consistency of the dozens of testimonies of Acul and Chel massacre survivors, death register evidence and the recreation of a calendar of progressive army violence against Nebaj communities, I believe the April 21, 1981, date of the Acul massacre to be a positive date, not a probable date. The FAFG final reports to the CEH in 1998 and FAFG final reports to the Nebaj prosecutor in 1998 as well as the FAFG published version of these reports, FAFG, *Informe de la Fundación de Antropologia Forense de Guatemala: Cuatro Casos Paradigmaticos por la Comisión para el Esclarecimiento Historico de Guatemala* (Guatemala City: Editorial Serviprensa, 2000) also date the Acul massacre on April 21, 1981, and the Chel massacre as April 3, 1982.

37. Acul testimony no. 13, 11 December 1997.
38. Acul testimony no. 1, 10 December 1997.
39. Acul testimony no. 7, 12 December 1997. Don Sebastian shifts to the present tense when remembering this fear—his living memory of terror.
40. Acul testimony no. 13, 11 December 1997.
41. Acul testimony no. 7, 10 December 1997.
42. Acul testimony no. 13, 11 December 1997.
43. Acul testimony no. 7, 10 December 1997.
44. Acul testimony no. 13, 11 December 1997.
45. Acul testimony no. 7, 10 December 1997.
46. Acul testimony no. 7, 10 December 1997.
47. See Laurence Langer, *Holocaust Testimonies—The Ruins of Memory* (New Haven: Yale University Press, 1991). Langer has written extensively about the relationship between the witness and the person giving testimony. His work studying Holocaust survivor testimonies on video revealed a number of interviewer/witnesses who sought to curtail continued testimony when it became discomfiting for the interviewer or failed to meet the interviewer's expectation of "heroic memory." Dominick LaCapra's work on witnessing, trauma, and history indicates that a type of transference takes place between the interviewer/witness and the survivor. Moreover, he concludes that the form this transference takes has much to do with interpretation. See LaCapra, *History and Memory.* In addition to these authors, I am grateful to William Quick, Warren Sibilla, and the works of Carl Jung for helping me to reflect upon the influence of this transference in my writing and in my life.
48. Throughout the hundreds of testimonies, when survivors have sought to demarcate time, they have often done so with reference to twenty days. This reflects contemporary measurement of time with the Maya calendar, which is based on twenty-day cycles. For more on the Maya calendar, see Susan Milbrath, *Star Gods of the Maya: Astronomy in Art, Folklore and Calendars* (Austin: University of Texas Press, 1999); Vincent Herschel Malmstrom, *Cycles of the Sun, Mysteries of the Moon: The Calendar in Mesoamerican Civilization* (Austin: University of Texas Press, 1997); and Marco de Paz, *Calendario Maya: el camino infinito del tiempo* (Guatemala City: Ediciones Gran Jaguar, 1991). See also B.N. Colby and L. Colby,

The Daykeeper: The Life and Discourse of an Ixil Diviner (Cambridge: Harvard University Press, 1969), and Barbara Tedlock, *Time and the Highland Maya* (Albuquerque: University of New Mexico Press, 1982).

49. Acul testimony no. 13, 11 December 1997.

CHAPTER FOUR

1.   Acul testimony no. 31, 15 December 1997.
2.   Acul testimony no. 8, 10 December 1997.
3.   Acul testimony no. 13, 11 December 1997.
4.   Acul testimony no. 8, 10 December 1997.
5.   Acul testimony no. 12, 11 December 1997.
6.   Acul testimony no. 15, 11 December 1997.
7.   Acul testimony no. 19, 11 December 1997.
8.   Acul testimony no. 21, 12 December 1997.
9.   Acul testimony no. 18, 12 December 1997.
10. Acul testimony no. 9, 10 December 1997.
11. Acul testimony no. 11, December 10, 1997.
12. See Department of Defense, United States Marine Corps (MCI), *Operations Against Guerrilla Units,* July 15, 1997, 2–25: "*Fire Flush.* In this method the government forces leave avenues of escape open to the guerrillas. These 'avenues of escape' are turned into 'avenues of death' by covering them with heavily armed ambushes."
13. See MCI, *Operations Against Guerrilla Units,* 1–8: "Mao Zedong says that the guerrilla is like a fish swimming in water. If the water is hostile to the fish, then the fish cannot survive."
14. Acul testimony no. 13, 11 December 1997.
15. Central Intelligence Agency, *Document Secret G5–41* (February 1982): 2. Declassified February 1998.
16. Acul testimony no. 12, 11 December 1997.
17. Acul testimony no. 15, 11 December 1997.
18. Acul testimony no. 24, 15 December 1997.
19. Acul testimony no. 12, 11 December 1997.
20. Acul testimony no. 28, 16 December 1997.
21. Acul testimony no. 25, 15 December 1997.
22. Acul testimony no. 26, 15 December 1997.
23. Acul testimony no. 30, 15 December 1997.
24. This was repeated to me in multiple testimonies.
25. Acul testimony no. 22, 13 December 1997. This story of guerrilla hangings of civilians trying to flee the mountain was repeated by numerous survivors who saw the bodies of five families hanging from trees on the path to Nebaj.
26. Acul testimony no. 28, 16 December 1997.
27. Acul testimony no. 2, 10 December 1997.
28. For an in-depth description and analysis of the Fusiles y Frijoles campaign, see chapters six and seven. See also, Jennifer Schirmer, *The Guatemalan Military Project: A Violence Called Democracy* (Philadelphia: University of Pennsylvania Press, 1998); Tom Barry, *Guatemala: The Politics of Counterinsurgency* (Albuquerque: Inter-Hemispheric Education Center, 1986); and Hector Gramajo, *De la guerra . . . A la guerra* (Guatemala City: Fondo de Cultura Editorial, S.A., 1995).
29. Acul testimony no. 4, 10 December 1997.
30. Guatemala City testimony no. 31, 14 September 1997.
31. Acul testimony no. 1, 10 December 1997.
32. Acul testimony no. 13, 11 December 1997.

33. Acul testimony no. 11, 10 December 1997.

34. Acul testimony no. 2, 10 December 1997.

35. Acul testimony no. 14, Dec. 10, 1997.

36. Acul testimony no. 17, 11 December 1997.

37. Acul testimony no. 33, 16 December 1997.

38. The literal translation of "susto" is fright. For many Maya (and rural ladinos as well), to die from susto is to die from a reconfiguration of the individual body and soul, which cannot bear the weight of fear in the physical and spiritual realms.

39. Acul testimony no. 28, 16 December 1997.

40. Acul testimony no. 21, 11 December 1997.

41. Acul testimony no. 4, 10 December 1997.

42. Acul testimony no. 15, 11 December 1997.

43. Acul testimony no. 7 10 December 1997.

44. Acul testimony no. 4, 10 December 1997.

45. Acul testimony no. 28, 16 December 1997.

46. *Libros de Defunciones de la Municipalidad de Nebaj* 1977–82: 56–59.

47. Acul testimony no. 15, 11 December 1997.

48. "Lamina" is the term used for corrugated aluminum and asbestos roofs.

49. Acul testimony no. 12, 11 December 1997.

50. In 2002, this forced labor with no remuneration remains a highly volatile and contentious issue in rural Guatemala. Indeed, on June 18, some 1,000 former civil patrollers blockaded fifty-seven international tourists visiting the Tikal ruins of Petén. Their demand was for the state to compensate them for their years of free labor as civil patrollers. See "Guatemala—57 Tourists Trapped by Ex-Paramilitaries," *Boston Globe,* 19 June 2002: A8. On July 8, 2002, the Guatemalan government proposed a special tax to provide monetary compensation to past patrollers. See David Gonzalez, "World Briefing: Americas," *New York Times,* July 9, 2002, NYTimes.com. See David Gonzalez, "A Dig in Guatemala Strips Bare a Time of Terror," *New York Times,* 30 August 2002.

51. David Stoll, *Between Two Armies in the Ixil Towns of Guatemala* (New York: Columbia University Press, 1994): 289.

52. Acul testimony no. 12, 11 December 1997.

53. Acul testimony no. 6, 10 December 1998.

54. Acul testimony no. 41, 17 December 1997.

55. Acul testimony no. 12, 11 December 1997.

56. Acul testimony no. 15, 11 December 1997.

57. Acul testimony no. 26, 15 December 1997.

58. Acul testimony no. 6, 10 December 1997.

59. Acul testimony no. 7, 10 December 1997.

60. Acul testimony no. 28, 16 December 1997.

CHAPTER FIVE

1. For an excellent analysis of urban political movements, see Deborah Levenson-Estrada, *Trade Unionists Against Terror: Guatemala City 1954–1985* (Chapel Hill: University of North Carolina Press, 1994); Susanne Jonas, *The Battle for Guatemala. Rebels, Death Squads and US Power* (Boulder: Westview Press, 1991); Jonathan Fried, ed., *Guatemala in Rebellion: An Unfinished History* (New York: Grove Press, 1983); and Eduardo Galeano, *Pais Ocupado* (Mexico: Nuestro Tiempo, 1967). For a comparative analysis of Latin American movements, see Arturo Escobar and Sonia Alvarez, eds., *The Making of Social Movements in Latin America* (Boulder: Westview Press, 1992). For more on urban state terror in Guatemala, see Carlos Figueroa Ibarra, *El Recurso del Miedo—Ensayo sobre el Estado y el Terror en Guatemala* (San Jose, Costa Rica: EDUCA, 1991) and Gabriel Aguilera Peralta, *Di-*

alectica del Terror (San Jose, Costa Rica: EDUCA, 1981). See also, Juan Corradi, ed., *Fear at the Edge—State Terrorism in Latin America* (Boulder: Westview Press, 1992). For an eloquent fictional portrayal of urban life during La Violencia, see Arturo Arias. *After the Bombs* (Willimantic: Curbstone Press, 1990).

2. Tom Barry, *Guatemala: The Politics of Counterinsurgency* (Albuquerque: Inter-Hemispheric Education Center, 1986): 36. For excellent maps of military bases in Guatemala, see also Comisión para el Esclarecimiento Histórico (CEH), *Guatemala Memoria del Silencio*, vols.1–12 (Guatemala City: CEH, 1999), vol. 2, 524–525.

3. See Victoria Sanford. "Child Soldiers, Guerrillas and Civil Patrollers—The Forced Recruitment of Maya Youth," in Siobhan McEvoy, ed., *Reconciliation and Ethnic Conflict* (forthcoming, University of Notre Dame Press).

4. CEH, *Memoria*, vol. 7: 53.

5. CEH, *Memoria*, vol 7: 10. While the CEH provided comprehensive documentation of Guatemalan army human rights violations throughout the country, international and national human rights groups had been reporting these violations for years. See, for example, Americas Watch (hereafter AW), *Closing Space: Human Rights in Guatemala*. (New York: AW, 1988) and *Clandestine Detention in Guatemala* (New York: AW, 1993); Amnesty International (hereafter AI) "Guatemala: A Government Program of Political Murder," *New York Review of Books*, 19 March 1981: 38–40; AI, *Guatemala: The Human Rights Record* (London: AI, 1987). Shelton Davis and Julie Hodson, *Witness to Political Violence in Guatemala. Impact Audit 2* (Boston: Oxfam America, 1982); Ricardo Falla, ed., *Voices of the Survivors: The Massacre at Finca San Francisco* (Cambridge: Cultural Survival and Anthropology Resource Center, report no. 10, 1983). See also Arturo Arias, "Changing Indian Identity: Guatemala's Violent Transition to Modernity," in Carol Smith, ed., *Guatemalan Indians and the State* (Austin: University of Texas Press, 1990), 230–257; Martin Diskin, *Trouble in Our Backyard: Central America and the United States in the 1980s* (New York: Pantheon Books, 1983).

6. "Phenomenology," as a term, is used here not in the philosophical tradition of Husserl, but rather as the application of the term as used in psychology to identify and delineate a series of related phenomenon. See Paul Ricoeur, *Husserl—An Analysis of His Phenomenology* (Evanston: Northwestern University Press, 1967).

7. Helena Pohlandt-McCormick, telephone conversation with author, October 27, 1998.

8. I developed the seven phases of terror based on twenty-four months of ethnographic and archival research between 1994 and 2000, and the collection of more than 400 testimonies in villages and municipalities in Guatemala. I gratefully acknowledge the very useful comments and feedback I received from Lynn Eden and Pamela Ballinger at Stanford's Center for International Security and Cooperation and from John Mowitt at the University of Minnesota.

9. Campesino Unity Committee (*Comité de Unidad Campesino*—CUC). See CEH, *Memoria*, vol. 10, 812–13.

10. CEH, *Memoria*, vol. 10, 813.

11. CEH, *Memoria*, vol. 10, 814.

12. Though the army's Scorched Earth campaign is usually dated between 1981 to 1982 or 1981 to 1983, I argue that this campaign was continued as new campaigns of genocide were initiated and did not end until the bombing and destruction of displaced communities was halted in 1990.

13. CEH, *Memoria*, vol. 7, 56.

14. CEH, *Memoria*, vol. 7, 57.

15. French anthropologists have longstanding generational relationships with the SAS community. For an excellent ethnography of SAS, see Henri Lehmann, ed., *San Andrés Sajcabajá: peuplement, organisation sociale et ancadrement d'une population dans les hautes terres de Guatemala* (Paris: Éditions Recherche sur les Civilisations, 1983). For an excellent history

of SAS, see Jean Piel, *Sajcabajá—Muerte y resurrección de un pueblo de Guatemala 1500–1970* (Mexico City: Centro de Estudios Mexicanos y Centroamericanos, 1989).

16. CEH, *Memoria,* vol. 7, 59.

17. All phases in the phenomenology of terror are based on author's ethnographic research and more than 400 interviews and testimonies with survivors of massacres in villages in Chimaltenango, San Martin Jilotepeque, San Andrés Sajcabajá, Chinique, Santa Cruz del Quiché, Chichicastenango, Cunen, Nebaj, Cotzal, Chajul, Ixcan, Panzos, La Tinta, El Estor, Senahu, Rabinal, Cubulco, Salama, Coban, San Miguel Acatan, San Miguel Chicaj. In addition to author's fieldwork, quantitative and comparative analysis of massacres in Guatemala includes review of primary and secondary literature including: Beatriz Manz, *Refugees of a Hidden War—The Aftermath of Counterinsurgency in Guatemala* (Albany: State University of New York Press, 1988); David Stoll, *Between Two Armies in the Ixil Towns of Guatemala* (New York: Columbia University Press, 1994); Yvon Le Bot, *La guerra en las tierras mayas: Comunidad, Violencia y modernidad en Guatemala 1970–1992* (Mexico City: Fondo de Cultura Económica, 1995); Oficina de Derechos Humanos del Arzobispado de Guatemala (ODHA), *Guatemala—Nunca Más, vols. 1–4, Informé Proyecto Interdiocesano de Recupaeración de la Memoria Histórica (REHMI)* (Guatemala City: ODHA, 1998); George Black, *Garrison Guatemala* (London: Zed Books, 1984); Americas Watch (hereafter AW), *Guatemala: A Nation of Prisoners* (New York: AW, 1984); AW, *Civil Patrols in Guatemala* (New York: AW, 1986); AW, *Closing Space: Human Rights in Guatemala* (New York: AW, 1988); AW, *Persecuting Human Rights Monitors: The CERJ in Guatemala* (New York: AW, 1989); AW, *Messengers of Death: Human Rights in Guatemala* (New York: AW, 1990); AW, *Clandestine Detention in Guatemala* (New York: AW, 1993); Carlos Figueroa Ibarra, *El Recurso del Miedo—Ensayo sobre el Estado y el Terror en Guatemala* (San Jose, Costa Rica: EDUCA, 1991); Robert Carmack, *Harvest of Violence: The Maya Indians and the Guatemalan Crisis* (Norman: University of Oklahoma Press, 1988); Grupo de Apoyo Mutuo (GAM), *Quitar el Agua al Pez* (Guatemala City: GAM, 1996); Amnesty International (hereafter AI), *Guatemala: Massive Extrajudicial Executions in Rural Areas Under the Government of Efrain Rios Montt* (New York: AI, 1982); AI, *Guatemala: The Human Rights Record* (London: AI, 1987); AI, *Guatemala: Human Rights Violations under the Civilian Government* (London: AI, 1989); AI, *Annual Report* (London: AI, 1990); AI, *Guatemala. Lack of Investigations into Past Human Rights Abuses: Clandestine Cemeteries* (London: AI, 1991); Ricardo Falla, *Masacres de la Selva* (Guatemala City: Editorial Universitario, 1992); Victor Montejo, *Testimony: Death of a Guatemalan Village* (Willimantic: Curbstone Press, 1987); Carol Smith, "The Militarization of Civil Society in Guatemala: Economic Reorganization as a Continuation of War—Military Impact in the Western Highlands of Guatemala," *Latin American Perspectives* 17, no. 4 (1990): 8–41; Judith Zur, *Violent Memories—Mayan War Widows in Guatemala* (Boulder: Westview Press, 1998); Kay Warren *The Violence Within: Cultural and Political Opposition in Divided Nations* (Boulder: Westview Press, 1993); Richard Wilson, *Maya Resurgence in Guatemala* (Oklahoma City: University of Oklahoma Press, 1995); Linda Green, "The Paradoxes of War and its Aftermath: Mayan Widows in Rural Guatemala," *Cultural Survival Quarterly* (spring, 1998): 73–75; CEH, *Memoria,* vols. 1–7; and FAFG reports (available at FAFG offices) on massacres in Chel, Acul, Panzós, San José Ojetenam, Laguna Seca, Dinelda, Tusbilpec, San Andrés Sajcabajá, El Coyolar, Monte Redondo, El Chal, El Amaté, El Tablón, Agua Fría, Josefinos, Las Pozás, Pinares, Plan de Sánchez, Chisec, San Diego, Chorraxaj, Las Flores, La Amistad, San Andrés Chapil, Cortijo de las Flores, Río Negro, Chichupac, Tunajá, and San José Pácho Lemóa.

18. "Responsable" is a term used to identify a supervisor at a place of employment. In guerrilla terminology, responsable is a guerrilla-appointed community leader. For more on the Guatemalan guerrilla, see Mario Payeras, *Days of the Jungle: The Testimony of a Guatemalan Guerrillero, 1972–1976* (New York: Monthly Review Press, 1983) and Payeras, *Los fusiles de Octubre—Ensayos y artículos militares sobre la revolución guatemalteca, 1985–1988* (Mex-

ico City: Juan Pablos Editor, 1991). On the guerrilla in El Salvador, see Joaquin Villalobos, "Popular Insurrection—Desire or Reality? *Latin American Perspectives* issue 62, vol.16, no. 3 (summer 1989): 5–37. On the Zapatista uprising, see Sub-Comandante Marcos, *Shadows of Tender Fury* (New York: Monthly Review Press, 1995). For an academic analysis of Latin American guerrilla movements, see Brian Loveman and Thomas Davies, *Guerilla Warfare* (Wilmington: SR Books, 1997).

19. For more on civil patrols, Patrullas de Auotdefensa Civil—PACs, see CEH, *Memoria,* vol. 10; Montejo, *Death of a Village;* Procuraduria de los Derechos Humanos de Guatemala (PDH), *Los Comités de Defensa Civil en Guatemala* (Guatemala City: PDH, 1994); Margaret Popkin, *Civil Patrols and Their Legacy—Overcoming Militarization and Polarization in the Guatemalan Countryside* (Washington, D.C.: Robert F. Kennedy Center for Human Rights [RFKC], 1996); Joel Solomon, *Institutional Violence: Civil Patrols in Guatemala* (Washington DC: RFKC, 1995); and Alice Jay, *Persecution by Proxy—The Civil Patrols in Guatemala* (Washington, D.C.: RFKC, 1993). Also, see more on PACs in chapter six.

20. Specifically violated were Articles 3, 5, 6, 9, 12, 17.2, and 20.1 of the UDHR; Articles 6, 7, and 9 of the ICPR; and, Articles 1 and 2 of the Convention against Torture. For an excellent handbook of human rights instruments, see Ian Brownlie, ed., *Basic Documents on Human Rights* (Oxford: Clarendon Press, 1992).

21. Convention Against Torture, Article 2.1.

22. Guatemala became a signatory to the UDHR in 1948, the same year it was adopted by the UN. The Genocide Convention was adopted by the UN in 1948 and has been in effect since 1951. Guatemala approved signing the Genocide Convention in Decree 704 on November 11, 1949, and became an official signatory June 1, 1950. The ICPR was adopted by the UN in 1966 and has been in effect since 1976; adopted by the UN in 1984, the Convention against Torture has been in effect since that same year. While Guatemala did not sign the ICPR until 1992 and the Convention against Torture until 1990, each of these conventions has been adopted and come into force with a majority of state signatories. When a majority of states agree to an international convention or protocol, it can be argued that this majority commitment represents a new standard of international customary law to which all states can be held accountable.

23. Jennifer Schirmer writes: "No distinction is made between combatant and noncombatant. . . ." See *The Guatemalan Military Project,* 45.

24. See chapter six for in-depth, comparative analysis of massacres.

25. CEH, *Guatemala Memory of Silence—Conclusions and Recommendations* (Guatemala City: CEH, 1999), 10.

26. CEH, *Memory,* 10.

27. CEH, *Memoria,* vol. 2, 226–7.

28. CEH, *Memoria,* vol. 2, 181.

29. CEH, *Memoria,* vol. 7, 164.

30. CEH, *Memoria,* vol. 7, 165.

31. CEH, *Memoria,* vol. 7, 166.

32. CEH, *Memoria,* vol. 7, 164

33. Despite tendencies to romanticize life in the mountains, one cannot help but be deeply moved by Jennifer Harbury, *Bridge of Courage: Life Stories of the Guatemalan Compañeros and* Compañeras (Monroe, ME: Common Courage Press, 1995).

34. This same method of armed assault can be found in the United States Marine Corps Institute (MCI). *Operations Against Guerrilla Units* (Washington, D.C.: July 15, 1997), 2–15. In the MCI manual, a drawing depicts a "Guerilla Camp" surrounded by "cutoff groups" on all but one side where the "assault group" is located. Thus, Maya civilians were subjected to assault operations designed to target guerrillas. The similarity of military tactics between the Guatemalan army and U.S. marines is not surprising given the large number of Guatemalan officers trained in counterinsurgency at the U.S. School of Americas

(SOA). In fact, between 1947 and 1991, SOA records (Department of Defense, School of the Americas Academic Records 1947–1991, School of the Americas Yearly Lists of Guatemalan military officers trained at SOA released under Freedom of Information Act) show 1,598 members of the Guatemalan army were trained at the SOA and that thirteen Guatemalan army officials served as instructors. See Department of Defense, School of the Americas Academic Records, released under the Freedom of Information Act. School of the Americas Yearly lists of Guatemalan military officers trained at SOA 1947–1991. If one were to develop a per capita relationship between army members trained at SOA and the 200,000 dead or disappeared of La Violencia, the calculation would reveal an average of 125 violent deaths or disappearances for each army member trained at SOA.

35. These guerrilla massacres are already well documented. See David Stoll, *Between Two Armies in the Ixil Towns of Guatemala* (New York: Columbia University Press, 1994) and CEH, *Memoria*. My final tabulation of massacres documented during fieldwork will most likely exceed this number because I have yet to conduct a comprehensive review of testimonies from Chimaltenango and Huehuetenango.

36. For more on the Beans and Bullets campaign, see Schirmer, *The Guatemalan Military Project* and CEH, *Memoria*. For the view from within the Guatemalan army, see Hector Gramajo, *De la guerra . . . A la guerra* (Guatemala City: Fondo de Cultura Editorial, S.A., 1995).

37. See Guatemalan Church in Exile, *Guatemala: Security, Development and Democracy* (Location not identified: Guatemalan Church in Exile, 1989); ODHA, *Nunca Más*; CEH, *Memoria*.

38. *Bulletin from the CPR Support Group,* no. 1 (1993): 2.

39. See chapter four for more of Eulalio's experience. Acul testimony no. 21, 12 December, 1997.

40. Kenneth Freed, "Guatemala 'Model Cities' Prove More Like Prisons," *Los Angeles Times,* 13 February 1989, 2.

41. Kenneth Freed, "Prisons," *Los Angeles Times,* 13 February 1989, 2.

42. *Guatemalan Church in Exile* 4, no. 5 (Sept/Oct 1984), 7.

43. *Central America Report* 29 (July/August 1986): 12.

44. *Guatemalan Church in Exile* 4, no. 5 (Sept/Oct 1984): 6.

45. *Central America Report* 29 (July/August 1986):12.

46. Loren Jenkins, "Guatemala's 24 'Model Villages,'" *San Francisco Chronicle,* 23 January 1985: F5. In numerous testimonies in the Ixil Area as well as other Maya communities throughout the country, survivors consistently gave testimony to the need for permission from the army for any movement between or outside of villages and towns. Moreover, these authorizations quickly became a source of income through illegal taxing by military commissioners.

47. Guatemala Human Rights Commission, *Counterinsurgency and Development in the Altiplano: The Role of Model Villages and the Poles of Development in the Pacification of Guatemala's Indigenous Highlands* (October 1987): 11.

48. Stoll, *Between Two Armies,* 289.

49. See Jay, *Persecution by Proxy,* 23.

50. Jay, *Persecution by Proxy,* 23.

51. This was the case in San Andrés Sajcabajá, where the military commissioners used threats of turning in the sons of neighbors to the army in order to gain land titles. In 1995, 1996, and 1997, local women gave testimonies naming local military commissioners who would grab local women on the way to market and rape them.

52. Jay, *Persecution by Proxy,* 34.

53. Jay, *Persecution by Proxy,* 36.

54. CERJ—*Consejo de Etnias Runujel Junam* (The Council of Ethnic Communities—"We are all Equal").

55. Jay, *Persecution by Proxy*, 41.
56. Amilcar Mendez, conversation with author, August 3, 1997.
57. Jay, *Persecution by Proxy*, 27.
58. Jay, *Persecution by Proxy*, 29.
59. See above, footnote seventeen, for fieldwork locations.
60. Jennifer Schirmer, *The Guatemalan Military Project: A Violence Called Democracy.*
61. See also, CEH, *Memoria,* and Jan Perlin, "The Guatemalan Historical Clarification Commission Finds Genocide," *ILSA Journal of International and Comparative Law,* vol.6 (2000): 389–413.
62. In a June 1999 conversation with an investigator for the CEH, I was told of a debate among the writers of the commission's report. This debate centered on Stoll's thesis of guerrilla responsibility for army massacres and civilians being "caught between two armies." If the writers of a report for a truth commission believed that a guerrilla force was responsible for provoking massacres committed by the army, this, no doubt, would have had an impact on the final report. Indeed, the CEH writers felt compelled to respond to Stoll's argument. The CEH specifically concluded that the "caught between two armies" thesis did not provide an explanation of La Violencia. See CEH, *Memoria,* 5: 27.
63. Victoria Sanford, "From *I, Rigoberta* to the Commissioning of Truth," *Social Justice* 27, no.1 (June 2000).
64. See chapters three and four for extensive discussion of Ixil experiences in civil patrol.
65. Michael Taussig, "Culture of Terror—Space of Death. Roger Casement's Putumayo Report and the Explanation of Torture," *Society for Comparative Study of Society and History* (1984): 482.

CHAPTER SIX

1. Specifically violated were Articles 3, 5, 6, 9, 12, 17.2, and 20.1 of the Universal Declaration of Human Rights (UDHR); Articles 6, 7 and 9 of the International Covenant of Civil and Political Rights (ICPR); and, Articles 1 and 2 of the Convention against Torture. See chapter three for more on these violations.
2. This shift from crimes against humanity to genocide is not unique to Guatemala. Indeed, the Nazi death camps were preceded by the brutal wave of selective killings by the *Einsatzgruppen* (mobile killing units) from 1941 to late 1942, which took the lives of approximately 1.5 million Jews as well as communists, partisans, and Polish intellectuals, among others. See Richard Rhodes, *Masters of Death: The SS-Einsatzgruppen and the Invention of the Holocaust* (New York: Knopf, 2002). For an excellent analysis of genocide in Bosnia and Rwanda, see Elizabeth Neuffer, *The Key to My Neighbor's House—Seeking Justice in Bosnia and Rwanda* (New York: Picador, 2001). On Rwanda, see also Mahmood Mamdani, *When Victims Become Killers: Colonialism, Nativism, and the Genocide in Rwanda* (Princeton: Princeton University Press, 2001), and Phillip Gourevitch, *"We Wish to Inform You that Tomorrow We Will Be Killed With Our Families"—Stories from Rwanda* (New York: Farrar, Strauss & Giroux, 1999).
3. George Andreopoulos, ed., *Genocide—Conceptual and Historic Dimensions* (Philadelphia: University of Pennsylvania Press, 1994), 14–15.
4. George Black, *Garrison Guatemala* (London: Zed Books, 1984), 11.
5. U.S. Department of State, "Secret Memorandum. Reference: Guatemala 6366," October 5, 1981, 1–2. Declassified January 1998.
6. CEH, *Guatemala Memoria del Silencio,* vols.1–12 (Guatemala City: CEH, 1999), vol. 5: 42.
7. For known impact of La Violencia before CEH report, see Amnesty International (hereafter AI), *Guatemala: Massive Extrajudicial Executions in Rural Areas Under the Government of Efrain Rios Montt Special Briefing* (New York: AI, 1982); AI, *Guatemala. Lack of Investigations into Past Human Rights Abuses: Clandestine Cemeteries* (London: AI, 1991); AI,

Human Rights Violations Against Indigenous Peoples of the Americas (New York: AI, 1992); AI, *Guatemala. All the Truth, Justice for All* (New York: AI, 1998); Americas Watch (hereafter AW), *Little Hope: Human Rights in Guatemala, January 1984 to January 1985* (New York: AW, 1985); AW, *Guatemala: A Nation of Prisoners* (New York: AW, 1984); Robert Carmack, *Harvest of Violence: The Maya Indians and the Guatemalan Crisis* (Norman: University of Oklahoma Press, 1988); Ricardo Falla, *Masacres de la Selva* (Guatemala City: Editorial Universitario, 1992); Fundación de Antropología Forense de Guatemala (Guatemalan Forensic Anthropology Foundation—FAFG), *Las Masacres de Rabinal* (Guatemala City: FAFG, 1995); FAFG Exhumation Reports 1992 to 1998 on file in FAFG office; Oficina de Derechos Humanos del Arzobispado de Guatemala (ODHA), *Guatemala—Nunca Más*, vols. *1–4, Informé Proyecto Interdiocesano de Recupaeración de la Memoria Histórica (REHMI)* (Guatemala City: ODHA, 1998); Shelton Davis and Julie Hodson, *Witness to Political Violence in Guatemala. Impact Audit 2* (Boston: Oxfam America, 1982); Beatriz Manz, *Refugees of a Hidden War—The Aftermath of Counterinsurgency in Guatemala* (Albany: State University of New York Press, 1988); Carlos Figueroa Ibarra, *El Recurso del Miedo—Ensayo sobre el Estado y el Terror en Guatemala* (San Jose, Costa Rica: EDUCA, 1991).

8. Article II of the convention. For complete convention, see Ian Brownlie, ed., *Basic Documents on Human Rights* (Oxford: Clarendon Press, 1992), 31–34.

9. For more on "intentionality," see Helen Fein, "Genocide, Terror, Life Integrity, and War Crimes: The Case for Discrimination," in Andreopoulos, *Genocide;* Alexander Laban Hinton, *The Dark Side of Modernity: Toward an Anthropology of Genocide* (Berkeley: University of California, 2002); Dinah Shelton, *Remedies in International Human Rights Law* (Oxford: Oxford University Press, 1999); Peter Ronayne, *Never Again?: The United States and the Prevention and Punishment of Genocide since the Holocaust* (Lanham: Rowman and Littlefield Publishers, 2001); John G. Heidenrich, *How to Prevent Genocide: A Guide for Policymakers, Scholars, and the Concerned Citizen* (Westport, CT: Praeger, 2001); Alex Alvarez, *Governments, Citizens and Genocide: A Comparative and Interdisciplinary Approach* (Bloomington: Indiana University Press, 2001); Ben Kiernan, ed., *Genocide and Democracy in Cambodia: The Khmer Rouge, the United Nations and the International Community* (New Haven: Yale University Southeast Asia Studies,1993).

10. CEH, *Memoria*, 2:315.

11. CEH internal document, "Was there a genocide?" no date, 1.

12. Falla, *Masacres.*

13. CEH, "Was there a genocide?" 1.

14. CEH, "Was there a genocide?" 1.

15. Dinah Shelton, e-mail communication with author, March 12, 2002. I gratefully acknowledge Dinah's contribution to my understanding of international human rights and genocide laws.

16. "Political group" was a protected category in Rafael Lemkin's original draft of the convention submitted to the United Nations. Political group was removed in General Assembly debate on the convention. See Andreopoulos, *Genocide.* See also, Raphael Lemkin, *Axis Rule in Occupied Europe* (Washington, D.C.: Carnegie Endowment for International Peace, 1944).

17. CEH, "Was there a genocide?" 2.

18. CEH, "Was there a genocide?" 3.

19. Jan Perlin, "The Guatemalan Historical Clarification Commission Finds Genocide," *ILSA Journal of International and Comparative Law* 6 (2000), 396. See also Bernard Duhaime, "Le Crime de Génocide et le Guatemala—Une Analyse Juridique," *Recherches Amérindiennes au Québes* 29, no.3 (1999): 101–106.

20. Central Intelligence Agency, "Document Secret G5–41," February 5, 1982, 2. Declassified January 1998.

21. CIA, "Document Secret," 2–3.
22. Perlin, "The Guatemalan Commission Finds Genocide," 398.
23. Department of State, "Secret Memorandum. Reference: Guatemala 6366. October 5, 1981," 1–2. Declassified January 1998.
24. CIA, "Document Secret," 2–3.
25. See Ben Kiernan, March 8, 2002.
26. Kiernan, points out that intention is determined by acts carried out deliberately rather than simply the motive behind them. Likewise, Shelton (e-mail) argues that if genocide is the method to obtain land, the goal of obtaining the land does not preclude the intentionality of genocide.
27. Jennifer Schirmer, *The Guatemalan Military Project: A Violence Called Democracy* (Philadelphia: University of Pennsylvania Press, 1998), 45.
28. Dinah Shelton, e-mail communication with author, March 12, 2002. For more on the Velasquez-Rodriguez case, see Shelton, *Remedies in International Human Rights Law*, 221.
29. Kiernan, March 8, 2002.
30. Dinah Shelton, e-mail communication with author, March 12, 2002.
31. Kiernan, March 8, 2002.
32. Alan Riding, "Guatemalans Tell of Murder of 300," *New York Times*, 5 October, 1982, 7.
33. Riding, "Guatemalans Tell of Murder of 300," 7.
34. Perlin, "The Guatemalan Historical Clarification Commission Finds Genocide," 399.
35. In the summer of 1995, I witnessed FRG campaign tactics firsthand in the K'iche' communities of San Andrés Sajcabajá. A group of party officials came to town with some "engineers," who were ostensibly taking census information in order to bring electricity to these villages. As the "engineers" wrote down the information and took measurements for the power lines, they explained that only houses with a blue flag (like the blue background of FRG) would receive electricity and that to obtain a blue flag, adults in the household needed to present their cédulas (national identification cards) and sign a document. The document turned out to be FRG party registration. Given that the majority of local community members signed the document with their thumbprint, only those who were literate were able to see that they were not signing up for electricity, but rather for the FRG party.
36. Analysis on massacres in this section is based on massacre data presented in CEH, *Memoria*, vol. 10.
37. CEH, *Memoria*, vol. 10.
38. For more on Plan Victoria, see Schirmer, *Guatemala Military Project*; Tom Barry, *Guatemala: The Politics of Counterinsurgency* (Albuquerque: Inter-Hemispheric Education Center, 1986); Guatemalan Church in Exile, *Guatemala: Security, Development and Democracy* (n.p.: Guatemalan Church in Exile, 1989); Hector Gramajo, *De la guerra . . . A la guerra* (Guatemala City: Fondo de Cultura Editorial, S.A., 1995).
39. Perlin, "The Guatemalan Commission Finds Genocide," 407.
40. Perlin, "The Guatemalan Commission Finds Genocide," 411. The CEH also found that that 16 percent of Achi-Maya were killed.
41. CEH, *Memoria*, vol. 10: 1012–1213; vol. 11:1384–1388.
42. For excellent analysis on the history and systematic incorporation of PACs into military strategy, see CEH, *Memoria*, vol. 2: 158–234; ODHA, *Nunca Más*, vol. 2: 113–158.
43. Everett, G. Martin, "The Right Way to Fight Anti-Guerrilla Warfare," *Wall Street Journal*, 30 July 1981, 5.
44. Department of Defense, School of the Americas Academic Records 1947–1991, School of the Americas Yearly Lists of Guatemalan military officers trained at SOA released under Freedom of Information Act. The U.S. Marines receive this same training. See Department of Defense, United States Marine Corps (MCI) 15 July 1997, *Operations Against Guerrilla Units*, 1–23: "Your objective is to KILL GUERRILLAS, NOT to hold terrain" (emphasis in original).

45. Like many Maya communities, survivors recount what might initially appear to be conflicting dates. However, once all testimonies are gathered and dates and massacre locations are compared among testimonies and to whatever other archival or documentary information may be available, one soon discovers that it is not that the massacre has conflicting dates, rather the community suffered more than one massacre prior to its final razing. In the case of Tzalbal, two different massacres are registered in 1981 (CEH, *Memoria,* vol.10: 1020, 1031) and five different massacres are registered in 1982 (1061, 1078, 1081, 1101).
46. Doña Eugenia uses the term "populations" which means civilian populations.
47. Nebaj testimony 3N2, 9 March 1997, 1 of 2.
48. Nebaj testimony 22 3N15, 15 March 1997.
49. Primo Levi, *The Drowned and the Saved* (New York: Vintage, 1988), 41.
50. This 30 percent draws on testimonies from massacres survivors in Ixil, K'iche', Achi, Keq'chi', and Kaqchiquel communities.
51. Nebaj testimony 6a C 3N6, 15 March 1997, 2.
52. Nebaj testimony 4A 3N2, 9 March 1997, 2 of 2a.
53. Nebaj testimony 3n16, 15 March 1997, 3 of 3, b.
54. Levi, *The Drowned,* 17.
55. Primo Levi, *Survival in Auschwitz* (New York: Simon and Schuster, 1958), 123.
56. Levi, *The Drowned,* 18.
57. Nebaj testimony 6a C 3N6, 15 March 1997, 1 of 3, 5a.
58. Levi, *The Drowned,* 79.
59. Nebaj testimony C 18 BN12, 14 March 1997, 1 of 1, b.
60. Comité de Unidad Campesina (CUC), "Public Communiqué," May (1982): 4.
61. Richard, J. Meislin, "Guatemalan Chief Says War Is Over," *New York Times,* December 10, 1982, 4.
62. Marilyn Moors with Lars Schoultz and Robert Trudeau, "Guatemala: A Brief Legislative History," Guatemala Scholars Network, n.d.
63. Nebaj testimony 25, 3n17, 15 March 1997.
64. Levi, *The Drowned,* 49.
65. Nebaj testimony 6a C 3N6, 15 March 1997, 1 of 3, 5a.
66. Nebaj testimony 6a C 3N6, 15 March 1997, 1 of 3, 5a.
67. Guatemalan army re-education camps had much in common with the Nazi re-education and factory-work camp ideologies. See "History of Nazi Concentration Camps Studies, Reports, Documents," *Dachau Review* 2 (1990); Barbara Distel and Ruth Jakusch, eds., *Concentration Camp Dachau, 1933–1945* (Brussels: Comité Internacional de Dachau, 1978).
68. Central America Report, "Development as Counterinsurgency," *Central America Report* (July/August 29, 1986): 3.
69. Central American Report, "Development as Counterinsurgency," 3.
70. Barry, *Politics of Counterinsurgency,* 53.
71. Barry, *Politics of Counterinsurgency,* 53.
72. Eureka-based Gospel Outreach was begun in 1971 by real estate agent Jim Durkin, who was born-again with "inspiration from God" to start a rehabilitation project for alcoholics. By 1982, Gospel Outreach was at the center of "International Love Lift," which provided food aid to the army for its counterinsurgency projects. Shortly after Ríos Montt came to power through a military coup, Gospel Outreach's relief director Bob Means met with the U.S. ambassador to the Organization of American States (also at this meeting were Edwin Meese, James Watt, and Jerry Falwell). See Paul Goepfert, "The Lord and Jim Durkin," *California* (February 1983): 2. By 1983, Gospel Outreach had a national newsletter, *Radiance Monthly.* In May 1982, A "Special Report" was distributed on "The Coup in Guatemala" and celebrated "A firsthand account of how a brother in the Gospel Outreach church in Guatemala became the leader of his country," *Radiance Monthly* (May 1982): 1.

73. See Barry, *Politics of Counterinsurgency,* 46–72; Guatemalan Church in Exile, *Informé Especial—FUNDAPI* (June 1983): 1–20; Guatemala Human Rights Commission, *Counterinsurgency and Development in the Altiplano: The Role of Model Villages and the Poles of Development in the Pacification of Guatemala's Indigenous Highlands* (October 1987); Pacific News Service, "Inside the 'New Guatemala'—A New War for the Hearts and Minds of Guatemala's Indians," April 27, 1983; Kenneth Freed, "Guatemala 'Model Cities' Prove More Like Prisons," *Los Angeles Times,* 13 February 1989, 2; Loren Jenkins, "Guatemala's 24 'Model Villages,'" *San Francisco Chronicle,* 9 January 1985, F3; Mary Jo McConahay, "A Vengeance Descends on Guatemala," *San Francisco Examiner,* 16 July 1985, B–16.

74. Nebaj testimony C 23 3N16, 15 March 1997, 2 of 3, 3a.

75. For more on the punishment holes and U.S. denial of their existence, see Julia Lieblich, "Pieces of Bone," AGNI 47 (1998).

76. Nebaj testimony C23, 3N16, 15 March 1997, 2 of 3, 3a.

77. Levi, *Survival in Auschwitz,* 22.

78. Central America Report, "Development as Counterinsurgency," *Central America Report* (July/August 29, 1986): 1.

79. Guatemalan Church in Exile (GCE), "Las Coordinadores Interinstitucionales," *Guatemalan Church in Exile,* 5, no.2 (August 1985): 21.

80. GCE, "Las Coordinadores Interinstitucionales."

81. Alex Michaels, "Poverty and Despair Prevail in Guatemala's 'Model Villages,'" *The Guardian,* 16 September 1987, 11.

82. Barry, *Politics of Counterinsurgency,* 23.

83. Human Rights Watch (HRW), *Guatemala: A Nation of Prisoners* (New York: HRW, 1984), 1.

84. Marlise Simons, "Massacres Spreading Terror in the Villages of the Maya," *New York Times,* 15 September 1982, 4. This article by Simons and articles by other journalists previously cited indicate there was international knowledge of the massacres and the incarceration of survivors by the Guatemalan army as the events unfolded—despite President Reagan's support of the regime. Indeed, a coalition of Native American organizations, Oxfam, and Cultural Survival, among others, ran a full-page advertisement in the *New York Times* denouncing the massacres. See "Help Stop the War Against the Mayan Indians of Guatemala," *New York Times,* 3 January 1984, 9.

85. Nebaj testimony 3N5, 9 March 1997, 1of 1.

86. Communities of Populations in Resistance Support Group, *Bulletin from the CPR Support Group* 1 (1993): 2.

87. Guatemala Health Rights Support Project, *Communities of Population in Resistance (CPR)* (Washington, D.C.: Guatemala Health Rights Support Project, 1992).

88. When Tomuschat was named to lead the CEH, the Ixiles were delighted because he was remembered as the man who had stopped the army bombings. Nebaj testimony no. C20 CBN13, 14 March 1997, 2 of 2.

89. Taussig, "Culture of Terror," 469.

90. Miguel Angel Asturias, *Men of Maize,* trans. Gerald Martin (Pittsburgh: University of Pittsburgh Press, 1993), 11.

91. See "Popol Vuh," trans. Dennis Tedlock, in *Popol Vuh—The Definitive Edition of the Mayan Book of the Dawn of Life and the Glories of Gods and Kings* (New York: Simon and Schuster, 1985); Patricia Mcanany, *Living with the Ancestors—Kinship and Kingship in Ancient Maya Society* (Austin: University of Texas, 1995); and Miguel Angel Asturias, *Men of Maize.*

92. Perlin, "The Guatemalan Commission Finds Genocide," 402.

93. Perlin, "The Guatemalan Commission Finds Genocide," 402.

94. Perlin, "The Guatemalan Commission Finds Genocide," 402–403.

95. Nebaj testimony 3N8, 11 March 1997, 1 of 1.

CHAPTER SEVEN

1.   See Primo Levi, *Survival in Auschwitz* (New York: Simon and Schuster, 1958); Phillip
     Gourevitch, *"We Wish to Inform You that Tomorrow We Will Be Killed With Our Families"—*
     Stories from Rwanda (New York: Farrar, Strauss & Giroux, 1999); Marguerite Feitlowitz, *A*
     Lexicon of Terror—Argentina and the Legacies of Torture (New York: Oxford University
     Press, 1998); Elizabeth Neuffer, *The Key to My Neighbor's House: Seeking Justice in Bosnia*
     and Rwanda (New York: Picador USA, 2001).
2.   See Irina Carlota Silber, "A Spectral Reconciliation: Rebuilding Post-War El Salvador"
     (Ph.D. diss., New York University, 2000), and Shannon Speed, "Global Discourses on the
     Local Terrain: Grounding Human Rights in Chiapas, Mexico" (Ph.D. diss., University of
     California at Davis, 2002).
3.   Michel Foucault, *Fearless Speech* (Los Angeles: Semiotext(e), 2001), 11–32.
4.   I thank Akhil Gupta for his insistence on the inclusion of life histories in my ethnography.
5.   Charles Hale, "Consciousness, Violence and the Politics of Memory in Guatemala," *Cur-*
     rent Anthropology 38, no.5 (November 1997): 822; Arturo Arias, "Comments," *Current*
     Anthropology 38, no.5 (November 1997): 824.
6.   David Stoll, *Between Two Armies in the Ixil Towns of Guatemala* (New York: Columbia Uni-
     versity Press, 1994); Yvon Le Bot, *La guerra en las tierras mayas: Comunidad, Violencia y*
     modernidad en Guatemala 1970–1992 (Mexico City: Fondo de Cultura Económica, 1995);
     Hector Gramajo, *De la guerra . . . A la guerra* (Guatemala City: Fondo de Cultura Editor-
     ial, S.A., 1995); Ricardo Falla, *Masacres de la Selva* (Guatemala City: Editorial Universi-
     tario, 1992); Ranajit Guha, "The Prose of Counterinsurgency," in Ranajit Guha and
     Gayatri Spivak, eds., *Selected Subaltern Studies* (New York: Oxford University Press, 1988).
7.   Kaibiles are the elite fighting forces of the Guatemalan army.
8.   "Masa" is a dough of ground corn and water used to make tortillas. During our interview,
     a woman from the village brought Juana enough masa for one meal's worth of tortillas for
     her family. Without this kind of collaboration from other villagers, Juana and her children
     would not have enough food to eat.
9.   At the time of the interview in 1995, the exchange rate was 6.8 quetzales to the dollar. Ten
     quetzales for a day's work was worth $1.47.
10. The phrase "levantamiento del venado" combines two common phrases: *levantamiento de*
     la veda (opening of the hunting season) and *levantamiento del cadáver* (removal of the
     corpse).
11. See chapter two for more on Esperanza's pre-EGP experiences.
12. "Chaparrita" is a colloquial expression meaning short, petite, or tiny. Esperanza's height is
     4 feet, 8 inches.
13. National Direction (Dirección Nacional) was the high command of the EGP.
14. Hale, "Consciousness, Violence and the Politics of Memory," 822.
15. Arias, "Comments," 824.
16. Stoll, *Between Two Armies*, 95.
17. Public statement at 1998 Latin American Studies Association meeting, Chicago.
18. Stoll, *Between Two Armies,*132. This representation of a homogenized Ixil consciousness of
     neutrality allows Stoll to conclude that the Ixiles transformed the army-controlled civil pa-
     trols into autonomous entities.
19. "Indigenista" refers to scholars who have self-identified with and support so-called fourth-
     world struggles.
20. Le Bot, *Masacres en tierras mayas,* 129.
21. Le Bot, *Masacres en tierras mayas,* 292.
22. Author's interview, July 1994. Official requested anonymity and that I not name location
     of interview or exact date.
23. I thank Kathleen Dill and David Stoll for a lively conversation on this topic.

24. After a little more than a year in the army, Mateo escaped. He walked to the United States.
25. Author's interview, January 1992, San Francisco, California.
26. Guha, "The Prose of Counterinsurgency," 47.
27. U.S. Department of State, "Secret Memorandum. Reference: Guatemala 6366," October 5, 1981. Declassified January 1998.
28. Department of State, "Secret Memorandum," 1.
29. Department of State, "Secret Memorandum," 1–2. Emphasis with italics is mine. Emphasis with quotation marks is from original document.
30. Department of State, "Secret Memorandum," 2.
31. Number of massacre victims based on Amnesty International (hereafter AI) reports and Americas Watch (hereafter AW) Reports. See AI, *Guatemala: Massive Extrajudicial Executions in Rural Areas Under the Government of General Efrain Rios Montt* (New York: AI, 1982); AI, *Testimony on Guatemala: Submitted by Amnesty International USA to the Subcommittee on International Development Institutions and Finance of the Banking Committee of the U.S. House of Representatives* (Washington D.C.: AI, August 5, 1982); AI, *Torture in the Eighties* (London: AI, 1984); AW, *Human Rights in Guatemala: No Neutrals Allowed* (New York: AW, 1982); AW, *The Reagan Administration's Human Rights Policy: A Mid-term Review* (New York: AW, 1982); AW, *Creating a Desolation and Calling it Peace: May 1983 Supplement to the Report on Human Rights in Guatemala* (New York: AW, 1983); AW, *Guatemala: A Nation of Prisoners* (New York: AW, 1984). See also Shelton Davis and Julie Hodson, *Witness to Political Violence in Guatemala. Impact Audit 2* (Boston: Oxfam America, 1982).
32. CIA, "Document Top Secret G5–41," February 5, 1982, 2.
33. CIA, "Document Secret," February 1982, 1.
34. CIA, "Document Secret," 2–3.
35. Number of massacre victims based on Amnesty International reports 1982, 1984; Americas Watch reports 1982, 1983, 1984; Guatemalan Forensic Anthropology Foundation internal exhumation reports 1994–98; Oficina de Derechos Humanos del Arzobispado de Guatemala (ODHA), *Guatemala—Nunca Más, vols. 1–4, Informé Proyecto Interdiocesano de Recupaeración de la Memoria Histórica (REHMI)* (Guatemala City: ODHA, 1998);. See also Davis and Hodson, *Witness to Political Violence in Guatemala* and Fundación de Antropología Forense de Guatemala (Guatemalan Forensic Anthropology Foundation—FAFG), *Las Masacres de Rabinal* (Guatemala City: FAFG, 1995).
36. Guha, "The Prose of Counterinsurgency,"50–51.
37. Guha, "The Prose of Counterinsurgency," 51.
38. In abstentia, Gramajo was found liable for the majority of damages sought based on his command responsibility. For example, Sister Diana Ortiz, one of the plaintiffs in the civil suit, was tortured by army personnel under the command of Gramajo. See Dinah Shelton, *Remedies in International Human Rights Law* (Oxford: Oxford University Press, 1999), 87. See also Gramajo, *De la Guerra.* . . .
39. Author's interview, Guatemala City, September 1997.
40. Guha, "The Prose of Counterinsurgency," 53.
41. Guha, "The Prose of Counterinsurgency," 59.
42. Guha, "The Prose of Counterinsurgency," 70.
43. Guha, "The Prose of Counterinsurgency," 70.
44. Guha, "The Prose of Counterinsurgency," 74. Here Guha is making reference to what he calls the "context-event-perspective ranged along a historical continuum."
45. Guha, "The Prose of Counterinsurgency," 71.
46. Guha, "The Prose of Counterinsurgency," 71.
47. Guha, "The Prose of Counterinsurgency," 71.
48. Guha, "The Prose of Counterinsurgency," 72.
49. Guha, "The Prose of Counterinsurgency," 72.

50. Guha, "The Prose of Counterinsurgency," 77. Emphasis in original.

51. Guha, "The Prose of Counterinsurgency," 82.

52. See Duncan Earle, "Menchú Tales and Maya Social Landscapes: The Silencing of Words and Worlds," in Arturo Arias, ed., *The Rigoberta Menchú Controversy* (Minneapolis: University of Minnesota Press, 2001), and Mario Roberto Morales, *La Ideologia y la lírica de la lucha armada* (Guatemala City: Editorial Universitaria de Guatemala, 1994).

53. Guha, "The Prose of Counterinsurgency," 77.

54. New scholarship on local Maya political processes by Mathilde Gonzalez, Kathleen Dill, Betsy Konefal, and Carlota McCallister will no doubt further challenge those who believe that the Maya are not agents in their own history. See Konefal, "In the Name of the Pueblo: Indigenous Organizing in Guatemala since 1960" (Ph.D. diss., University of Pittsburgh, forthcoming), and Mathilde Gonzalez, "The Man Who Brought the Danger to the Village: Representations of the Armed Conflict in Guatemala from a Local Perspective," *Journal of Southern African Studies* 26, no.2 (June 2000): 317–335. See also Santiago Bastos and Manuela Camus, *Quebrando el Silencio: Organizaciones del Pueblo Maya y sus Demandas* (Guatemala City: FLACSO, 1993).

55. In 1985, Colonel Rene Amadeo Morales Pais told U.S. journalist Mary Jo McConohay that the Ixiles have "always been the most rebellious." See Mary Jo McConohay, "Guatemalan Town Gets a Road," *The Tribune,* 21 July 1985, C–10.

56. Acul testimony no. 7, 10 December 1997.

57. George Orwell, *Nineteen Eighty-Four* (New York: Knopf, 1992), 36.

58. CEH, *Guatemala Memoria del Silencio,* vols.1–12 (Guatemala City: CEH, 1999), vol.1: 34–35.

59. CEH, *Memoria,* 5:24.

60. CEH, *Memoria,* 5:22–3.

61. CEH, *Memoria,* 5:27.

62. CEH, *Memoria,* 5:27.

CHAPTER EIGHT

1.   See Katherine Verdery, *The Political Lives of Dead Bodies: Reburial and Postsocialist Change* (New York: Columbia University Press, 1999); Richard Werbner, ed., *Memory and Post-colony—African Anthropology and the Critique of Power* (London: Zed Books, 1998); Linda Green, *Fear as a Way of Life—Mayan Widows in Rural Guatemala* (New York: Columbia University Press, 1999); Judith Zur, *Violent Memories—Mayan War Widows in Guatemala* (Boulder: Westview Press, 1998).

2.   Veena Das, "The Act of Witnessing—Violence, Poisonous Knowledge, and Subjectivity," in Veena Das, Arthutr Kleinman, Mamphela Ramphele, and Pamela Reynolds, eds., *Violence and Subjectivity* (Berkeley: University of California, 2000), 221. I gratefully acknowledge Veena Das for her support and mentorship.

3.   Judith Herman, *Trauma and Recovery* (New York: Basic Books, 1992), 37.

4.   Herman, *Trauma and Recovery,* 37.

5.   Herman, *Trauma and Recovery,* 41.

6.   Victoria Sanford "The Silencing of Maya Women from Mamá Maquín to Rigoberta Menchú," *Social Justice* 27, no. 1 (June 2000): 128–156.

7.   San Miguel was not the only community attacked by the army that day. On September 15, 1981, the people of Rabinal went to the plaza to celebrate Independence Day. The army had obligated everyone to participate and attend the Independence Day parade. Accompanied by judiciales, military commissioners, and civil patrollers, the soldiers opened fire on the crowd and killed some 200 people. See CEH, *Guatemala Memoria del Silencio,* vols.1–12 (Guatemala City: CEH, 1999), vol. 8:144.

8.   "Oreja" is a colloquialism for army spy.

9. With these statements, he was attempting to protect himself from forced recruitment because by law, recruitment age was eighteen. Here again is another example of rural Maya consciousness of rights.

10. Rabinal testimony no. 6–4, 17 June 1997.

11. All names of survivors have been changed except for Juan Manuel Gerónimo and Jésus Tec, who requested that their real names be used. Juan Manuel has been interviewed and quoted extensively by name (at his own request) in the national and international press, including the *New York Times*. Jésus Tec, a Río Negro massacre survivor, has also been in national and international press. He received the Reebok Human Rights award for his efforts seeking the prosecution of massacre perpetrators.

12. Juan Manuel was twenty-four in 1967.

13. "Básico" is the equivalent of junior high school.

14. He is referring to the FAR (Fuerzas Armadas Rebeldes—Rebel Armed Forces) of the 1960s, which was based in eastern Guatemala and had also organized in Baja Verapaz, including the municipalities of Salamá, Rabinal, and Cubulco.

15. Fuerza Armada de los Pobres. A confusion with the Fuerzas Armadas Rebeldes (FAR), which had organized in Rabinal in the 1960s, and the Ejercito Guerrillero de los Pobres (EGP), which organized in the early 1980s.

16. Rabinal testimony no. 6–3, 6 June 1997.

17. The survival of these three young girls is attributed to local soldiers from Rabinal who participated in the massacre and allowed them to escape.

18. The Camino Antiguo is the prehispanic foot path from Rabinal to Guatemala City. Despite the distance from Rabinal to Guatemala, from the village of Joya de Ramos (which is about two miles beyond Plan de Sánchez) it is possible to see Guatemala City on a clear day. Roads from Rabinal to the capital are through Salama. The Camino Antiguo remains unpaved.

19. Rabinal testimony no. 6–4, 17 June 1997.

20. Plan de Sánchez, collective meeting, July 4,1994.

21. A "licenciado" is someone with a university bachelor's degree.

22. Rabinal testimony no. 3, 16 June 1997, 1 of 3.

23. Giorgio Agamben, *The Coming Community* (Minneapolis: University of Minnesota Press), 13.

24. Agamben, *The Coming Community,* 13.

25. Michel Foucault, *Power and Knowledge* (New York: Pantheon Books, 1980), 79.

26. Francesca Polletta, *Freedom is an Endless Meeting: Experiments in Participatory Democracy from Pre-War Pacifism to the Present* (forthcoming).

27. Martha Nussbaum, *Upheavals of Thought—The Intelligence of Emotions* (Cambridge: Cambridge University Press, 2001), 407.

28. Michael Taussig, "Culture of Terror—Space of Death: Roger Casement's Putumayo Report and the Explanation of Torture," *Comparative Studies of Society and History* 26 (1984).

29. Foucault, *Power and Knowledge,* 131.

CHAPTER NINE

1. Xococ testimony no. 1, 28 June 1994.

2. Xococ testimony no. 2, 4 July 1994.

3. 1994 was the year of the *Roboniños* national panic in Guatemala. Several North American women were attacked and severely beaten in rural communities. They were accused of stealing babies to sell their organs. Like other international women, Kathleen and I were frequently viewed with suspicion, and parents would spirit their children out of our paths, sometimes saying, "*Vienen las lobas*" (Here come the wolves). For more on roboniños, see Abigail Adams, "Word, Work and Worship: Engendering Evangelical Culture Between

Highland Guatemala and the United States" (Ph.D. diss., University of Virginia, 1999), and Diane Nelson, *A Finger in the Wound* (Berkeley: University of California Press, 1999). On worldwide organ-stealing rumors, see Nancy Scheper-Hughes, "Theft of Life: The Globalization of Organ Stealing Rumors," *Anthropology Today* 12, no. 3 (June 1996): 3–11.

4. Xococ testimony no. 3, 14 July 1994.

5. For more on the therapeutic testimonial model, see Yael Fischman and Jaime Ross, "Group Treatment of Exiled Survivors of Torture," *American Journal of Orthopsychiatry* 60, no. 1 (January 1990): 135–141; Patrick Morris, Derrick Silove, Vijaya Manicavasagar, Robin Bowles, Margaret Cunningham, and Ruth Tarn, "Variations in Therapeutic Interventions for Cambodian and Chilean Refugee Survivors of Torture and Trauma: A Pilot Study," *Australian and New Zealand Journal of Psychiatry* 3 (September 1993): 429–435; Patrick McGorry, "Working with Survivors of Torture and Trauma: The Victorian Foundation for Survivors Perspective," *Australian and New Zealand Journal of Psychiatry* 29, no. 3 (September 1995): 463–472; Ronan McIvor and Stuart Turner, "Assessment and Treatment Approaches for Survivors of Torture," *British Journal of Psychiatry* 166 (1995): 705–711; Maritza Thompson and Patrick McGorry, "Psychological Sequelae of Torture and Trauma in Chilean and Salvadoran Migrants: A Pilot Study," *Australian and New Zealand Journal of Psychiatry* 29, no. 1 (March 1995): 84–95; Stevan Weine and Dori Laub, "Narrative Constructions of Historical Realities in Testimony with Bosnian Survivors of 'Ethnic Cleansing,'" *Psychiatry* 58 (August 1995): 246–261; Howard Waitzkin and Holly Magaña, "The Black Box in Somatization: Unexplained Physical Symptoms, Culture, and Narratives of Trauma," *Social Science and Medicine* 45, no. 6 (September 1997): 811–825.

6. See Thomas Gavagan and Antonio Martinez, "Presentation of Recent Torture Survivors to Family Practice," *The Journal of Family Medicine* 44, no.2 (February 1997): 209.

7. Patrick McGorry, "The Clinical Boundaries of Posttraumatic Stress Disorder," *Australian and New Zealand Journal of Psychiatry* 29, no. 3 (September 1995): 385.

8. McGorry, "Working with Survivors of Torture and Trauma," 463.

9. See, for example, Jerzy Krupinski, "Psychiatric Disorders of East European Refugees Now in Australia," *Social Science and Medicine* 7 (1973): 31–49; Elizabeth Lira, "Sobrevivir: Los Limites de la psicoterapia," in E. Lira and E. Weistein, eds., *Psicoterapía y represión política* (Mexico City: Sigo Veintiuno Editores, 1984); A. J. Cienfuegos and C. Monelli, "The Testimony of Political Repression as a Therapeutic Instrument," *American Journal of Orthopsychiatry* 53 (1983): 43–51.

10. See, for example, Fischman and Ross, "Group Treatment of Exiled Survivors of Torture"; Morris, et al., "Variations in Therapeutic Interventions"; McGorry, "Working with Survivors of Torture and Trauma"; Thompson and McGorry, "Psychological Sequelae of Torture and Trauma"; Weine and Laub, "Narrative Constructions"; Harvey Weinstein, Laura Dansky, and Vincent Iacopino, "Torture and War Trauma Survivors in Primary Care Practice," *Western Journal of Medicine* 165, no. 3 (September 1996): 533–538.

11. Weine and Laub, "Narrative Constructions of Historical Realities," 246.

12. Nancy Caro Hollander, *Love in a Time of Hate—Liberation Psychology in Latin America* (New Brunswick: Rutgers, 1997),85.

13. McIvor and Turner, "Assessment and Treatment Approaches for Survivors of Torture."

14. McGorry, "Working with Survivors of Torture and Trauma."

15. Weine and Laub, "Narrative Constructions," 260.

16. Fischman and Ross, "Group Treatment of Exiled Survivors of Torture," 137.

17. Fischman and Ross, "Group Treatment of Exiled Survivors of Torture," 137.

18. Weine and Laub, "Narrative Constructions of Historical Realities," 247.

19. McIvor and Turner, "Assessment and Treatment Approaches for Survivors of Torture," 706.

20. FAFG, *Las Masacres de Rabinal* (Guatemala City: FAFG, 1995). Other contributing authors included Fernando Moscoso and Ronaldo Sánchez. At the time of the publication of

Las Masacres en Rabinal in 1995, it was still considered safer for the security of the authors that the publication carry no names other than the institutional name of the FAFG.

21. In 1997, ECAP replicated the Rabinal healing project in Nebaj and began to accompany the FAFG during exhumations.

22. This is not an uncommon occurrence within human rights NGOs. Without salaries, FAFG staff continued exhumations for nearly six months between 1996 and 1997. Sometimes funding agencies change their funding priorities or funding schedules without notice, and sometimes the NGOs are too overwhelmed with work and/or lack sufficient staff to keep track of application deadlines. The decision to continue to work without salaries was made at great personal and familial sacrifice. All the staff members of the FAFG and ECAP as well as their families depend upon their modest NGO salaries for their livelihoods.

23. Rolando Alecio, interview with author, Guatemala City, August 28, 1997.

24. Francesca Polletta, *Freedom is an Endless Meeting: Experiments in Participatory Democracy from Pre-War Pacifism to the Present* (forthcoming).

25. See ECAP, *Técnicas de Escucha Responsable. Cuadernos de Salud Mental No. 1* (Guatemala City: ECAP, September 1998); ECAP, *Nuestras Molestias—Técnicas Participativas de Apoyo Psicosocial. Cuadernos de Salud Mental No. 2* (Guatemala City: ECAP, October 1998); ECAP, *El Sistema de Vigilancia de la Salud Mental Comunitaria. Cuadernos de Salud Mental No. 3* (Guatemala City: ECAP, November 1998); ECAP, *Psicología Social y Violencia Política* (Guatemala City: ECAP, 1999). An interesting and unexpected outcome of this process has been that parties in conflict often request arbitration by ECAP staff when they are unable to independently reach agreement. In such cases, the parties in conflict further develop their skills by resolving the real-life dispute and laying a framework for peaceful resolution of future village conflicts.

26. Rabinal testimony no. 6–3, 6 June 1997.

27. Plan de Sánchez interview no.3, 18 July 1997.

28. Rabinal interview no. 1, 19 July 1997.

29. Rabinal testimony no. 6–3, 6 June 1997.

30. Rabinal testimony no. 6–4, 17 June 1997.

CHAPTER TEN

1. For a range of perspectives, see Larry Diamond and Marc F. Plattner, eds., *The Global Resurgence of Democracy* (Baltimore: The John Hopkins University Press, 1996). For the classic argument against redress for human rights violations, see Samuel Huntington, *Political Order in Changing Societies* (New Haven: Yale University Press, 1968). For his more recent analysis with little fundamental change, see Samuel Huntington, *The Third Wave: Democratization in the Late Twentieth Century* (Norman: University of Oklahoma Press, 1991).

2. For insightful analysis beyond elections equal democracy, see Terry Lynn Karl and Philippe Schmitter, "What Democracry Is . . . and Is Not," in Marc Plattner and Larry Diamond, eds., *The Global Resurgence of Democracy.* See also Scott Mainwaring, Guillermo O'Donnell, and Samuel Valenzuela, *Issues in Democratic Consolidation: The New South American Democracies in Comparative Perspective* (Notre Dame: University of Notre Dame, 1992). For the major contribution to theorizing democratization, which remains essential to contemporary analyses, see Guillermo O'Donnell and Philippe Schmitter, *Transitions from Authoritarian Rule: Tentative Conclusions about Uncertain Democracies* (Baltimore: Johns Hopkins University Press, 1986). See also, Manuel Antonio Garreton, "Human Rights in Processes of Democratization," *Journal of Latin American Studies* 26 (1994): 221–234; Neil Harvey, *The Chiapas Rebellion—The Struggle for Land and Democracy* (Durham: Duke University Press, 1998); Alison Brysk, *The Politics of Human Rights in Argentina: Protest, Change and Democratization* (Stanford: Stanford University Press, 1994); Rachel Seider,

Derecho Constuetudinario y transción democratica en Guatemala (Guatemala City: FLACSO, 1996).

3. For what remains the classic piece connecting accountability and rule of law, see Diane F. Orentlicher, "Settling Accounts: The Duty To Prosecute Human Rights Violations of a Prior Regime," *Yale Law Journal* (June 1991). See also Naomi Roht-Arriaza, "State Responsibility to Investigate and Prosecute Grave Human Rights Violations in International Law," *California Law Review* (March 1990). See also Irwin Stotzky, *Transition to Democracy in Latin America: The Role of the Judiciary* (Boulder: Westview Press, 1993).

4. See, for example, Patrick Breslin, *Development and Dignity* (Rosslyn, VA: Inter-America Foundation, 1987); Charles Reilly, ed., *New Paths to Democratic Development in Latin America—The Rise of NGO-Municipal Collaboration* (Boulder: Lynne Rienner Publishers, 1995).

5. See Lionel Cliffe and Robin Luckham, "Complex Political Emergencies and the State: Failure and the Fate of the State," *Third World Quarterly* 20, no.1 (1999): 27–50; Mark Duffield, "NGO Relief in War Zones: Towards an Analysis of the New Aid Paradigm," *Third World Quarterly* 18, no. 3 (1997): 527–542; Tom Keating and Francis K. Abiew, "Outside Agents and the Politics of Peacebuilding and Reconciliation," *International Journal of the Canadian Institute of International Affairs* 55, no. 1 (winter 1990/2000): 80–106; Donna Pankhurst, "Issues of Justice and Reconciliation in Complex Political Emergencies: Conceptualizing Reconciliation, Justice and Peace," *Third World Quarterly* 20, no. 1 (1999): 239–256.

6. See Scott R. Appleby, *The Ambivalence of the Sacred* (New York: Rowman and Littlefield Publishers, Inc., 1996); John Borneman, *Settling Accounts: Violence, Justice and Accountability in Postsocialist Europe* (Princeton: University of Princeton Press, 1997); Alex Borraine, Janet Levy and Ronel Scheffer, *Dealing with the Past—Truth and Reconciliation in South Africa* (Cape Town: IDASA, 1997); John Paul Lederach, *Building Peace—Sustainable Reconciliation in Divided Societies* (Washington, D.C.: United States Institute of Peace Press, 1997); James McAdams, ed., *Transitional Justice and the Rule of Law in New Democracies* (Notre Dame: University of Notre Dame Press, 1988); Aryeh Neier, "The Quest for Justice," *The New York Review* 48, vol. 4, no. 8 (March 2001): 31–35; Robert I. Rotberg and Dennis Thompson, eds., *Truth v. Justice—The Morality of Truth Commissions* (Princeton: Princeton University Press, 2000); Paul Van Zyl, "Dilemmas of Transitional Justice: The Case of South Africa's Truth and Reconcilation Commission," *Journal of International Affairs* (spring 1999): 648; Jose Zalaquett, "Balancing Ethical Imperative and Political Constraints: The Dillemma of New Democracies Confronting Past Human Rights Violations," *Hastings Law Journal* (August 1992). See also, Martha Minow, *Between Vengeance and Forgiveness: Facing History after Genocide and Mass Violence* (Boston: Beacon Press, 1998); Mario Benedetti, "The Triumph of Memory," *NACLA Report on the Americas* 29, no. 3 (1995): 10–12; Raul Alfonsin, "'Never Again' in Argentina," *Journal of Democracy* 6, no.1 (1992): 15–19. For an eloquent reading of the inherent conflicts presented by truth commissions, see Ariel Dorfman, *Death and the Maiden* (New York: Penguin Books, 1994). See also Eric Stener Carlson, *I Remember Julia—Voices of the Disappeared* (Philadelphia: Temple University Press, 1996).

7. This section draws on an opinion editorial I co-authored with Fernando Mosocoso. "Along with the Poor, the Powerful Must Face Prosecution, Too," Opinion Editorial, *Los Angeles Times,* 22 October 1999, as well as interviews with survivors between 1994 and 1998.

8. For forensic details on the massacre, see FAFG, *Las Masacres de Rabinal* (Guatemala City: FAFG, 1995).

9. See CEH, *Guatemala Memoria del Silencio,* vols. 1–12 (Guatemala City: CEH, 1999); FAFG, *Informe de la Fundación de Antropologia Forense de Guatemala: Cuatro Casos Paradigmaticos por la Comisión para el Esclarecimiento Historico de Guatemala* (Guatemala City: Editorial Serviprensa, 2000); FAFG, *Las Masacres de Rabinal.*

10. The UN Human Rights Committee (Geneva Subcommittee for the Prevention of Discrimination and Minority Protection) issued its first statement condemning government practices on March 14, 1979. This was followed by subsequent statements in March 1980, March 1981, March 1982, March 1984, and August 1984. The subcommittee also issued Resolutions 1982/7 (September 1982) and 1983/12 (September 1983) condemning human rights violations in Guatemala. The UN General Assembly also condemned Guatemala's human rights violations in Resolutions 37/184 (December 1982) and 1983/12 (September 1983). See Louis Goodman, ed., *The Military and Democracy: The Future of Civilian-Military Relations in Latin America* (Washington, D.C.: Lexington Books, 1990).

11. Interview by author. Army official requested anonymity. San Jose, Costa Rica, July 7, 1994.

12. Jonathan Fried, ed., *Guatemala in Rebellion: An Unfinished History* (New York: Grove Press, 1983), 331–332.

13. Margaret Crahan, ed., *Human Rights and Basic Needs in the Americas* (Washington D.C.: Georgetown University Press, 1982), 101. See also, Thomas Burgenthal, *Protecting Human Rights in the Americas* (Kehl: N.P. Engel, 1982), and Julian Burger, *Report from the Frontier: The State of the World's Indigenous Peoples* (Atlantic Highlands: Zed Books, 1987).

14. Crahan, *Human Rights and Basic Needs in the Americas,* 110.

15. Commission for Historical Clarification (CEH), *Guatemala Memory of Silence—Conclusions and Recommendations* (Guatemala City: CEH, 1999), 20. On Guatemalan National Security Doctrine, the CEH wrote: "Anti-communism and the National Security Doctrine (DSN) formed part of the Anti-Soviet strategy of the United States in Latin America. In Guatemala, these were first expressed as anti-reformist, then anti-democratic policies, culminating in criminal counterinsurgency" (19). See also Cynthia Enloe, *The Morning After: Sexual Politics at the End of the Cold War* (Berkeley: University of California Press, 1993), and Cynthia Enloe, *Bananas, Beaches and Bases: Making Feminist Sense of International Politics* (Berkeley: University of California Press, 1990).

16. Crahan, *Human Rights and Basic Needs in the Americas,* 118.

17. CEH, *Memory of Silence,* 20.

18. Federación Latinoamericano de Asociaciones de Familiares de Detenidos-Desaparecidos (FEDEFAM), *Encuentro Regional Contra La Impunidad* (Santiago: FEDEFAM, 1987), 22. On impunity in Guatemala, see Luisa Cabrera, "Efectos de la Impunidad en el Sentido de Justica," *Psicologia Politica* 23 (2001): 37–58; Luisa Cabrera and Carlos Martin Beristain, "Resistiendo la impunidad en Guatemala—La Dimensión psicosocial en un proceso político-judicial," *Nueva Sociedad* 175 (Septiembre/Octubre 2001): 43–58; Alianza Contra la Impunidad, *Efectos de la Impunidad en Guatemala. Estudio Comparativa de los Casos: Aurora 8 de Octubre—Finca Xamán—Cándido Noriega—Finca Tululché—Jorge Carpio Nicolle* (Guatemala City: Alianza Contra la Impunidad, 2001).

19. Lawrence Weschler, *A Miracle, A Universe: Settling Accounts with Torturers* (New York: Penguin, 1990), 188; Luis Salas, *La Justicia Penal en Guatemala* (Guatemala City: Editorial Universidad Centroamericana with Florida International University, 1989). See also Mark Danner, *The Massacre at El Mozote: A Parable of the Cold War* (New York: Vintage Books, 1994). For a moving fictional account of life in El Salvador during the war, see Manlio Argueta, *One Day of Life* (New York: Vintage International, 1983). See also Philippe Bourgois, "The Continuum of Violence in War and Peace: Post–Cold War Lessons from El Salvador," *Ethnography* 2, no. 1 (2001): 5–37.

20. Author's interviews with various army officials requesting anonymity, Guatemala City, summer 1994.

21. CEH, *Memory of Silence,* 19.

22. CEH, *Memory of Silence,* 24.

23. Author's summer 1994 interviews with army officials (base commanders to generals) who requested anonymity.

24. Amnesty International (hereafter AI), *Human Rights Violations Against Indigenous Peoples of the Americas* (New York: AI, 1992), 11.

25. Amnesties were granted in 1982, 1986, and 1988. For more on these amnesties, see Gregory Jowdy, "Truth Commissions in El Salvador and Guatemala: A Proposal for Truth in Guatemala," *Boston College Third World Law Journal* (spring 1997).

26. FEDEFAM, *Encuentro Regional Contra La Impunidad,* 22.

27. AI, *Human Rights Violations Against Indigenous Peoples of the Americas,* 11.

28. CEH, *Memory of Silence,* 26.

29. CEH, *Memory of Silence,* 26.

30. CEH, *Memory of Silence,* 38.

31. CEH, *Memory of Silence,* 58.

32. CEH, *Memory of Silence,* 58.

33. CEH, *Memory of Silence,* 26.

34. Rotberg and Thompson, *Truth v. Justice—The Morality of Truth Commissions,* 157.

35. Carlos H. Acuña and Catalina Smulovitz, "Guarding the Guardians in Argentina: Some Lessons About the Risks and Benefits of Empowering the Courts," in James McAdams, ed., *Transitional Justice and the Rule of Law in New Democracies,* 95, 107.

36. Clifford Krauss, "Argentine Court Ruling Could Open the Military to Prosecution," *New York Times,* 9 March 2001, A9.

37. Chilean National Commission on Truth and Reconciliation, *Report on the Chilean National Commission,* trans. Berryman (Notre Dame: University of Notre Dame Press, 1993).

38. Although the Chilean Appeals Court reduced charges against Pinochet, in another action the Court also rejected a motion to nullify the order placing him under house arrest. See Clifford Krauss, "Chile: Pinochet Charges Reduced," *New York Times,* March 9, 2001, A6.

39. United Nations Commission on the Truth about Atrocities in El Salvador, *Summary Report of the UN Commission on the Truth about Atrocities in El Salvador* (New York: UN, 1993).

40. Jowdy, "Truth Commissions in El Salvador and Guatemala: A Proposal for Truth in Guatemala."

41. Interview by author with local official who requested anonymity, Rabinal, July 29, 1994.

42. South Africa Truth and Reconciliation Commission, *Truth and Reconciliation Commission of South Africa Report* (Cape Town: The Commission, 1998).

43. CEH, *Memoria.*

44. "South Africa: Township Clash," *New York Times,* 14 February 2001, A6.

45. ABC Evening News, 14 February 2001.

46. Van Zyl, "Dilemmas of Transitional Justice: The Case of South Africa's Truth and Reconcilation Commission," 1.

47. Van Zyl, "Dilemmas," 1.

48. Elizabeth Kiss, "Moral Ambition Within and Beyond Political Constraints: Reflections on Restorative Justice," in Rotberg and Thompson, eds., *Truth v. Justice—The Morality of Truth Commissions,* 80.

49. Comments of Jose Zalaquett in Alex Borraine, Janet Levy and Ronel Scheffer, eds., *Dealing with the Past—Truth and Reconciliation in South Africa* (Cape Town: IDASA, 1997), 105. This volume has one of the most eloquent and moving summary transcriptions of a meeting of some of the world's greatest thinkers and practitioners of human rights law as they contemplate what a post-apartheid South Africa might be and how South Africans might come to terms with their past. Zalaquett, Juan Mendez, Aryeh Neier, and Laurence Weschler were among the participants.

50. Zalaquett in Borraine, Levy, and Scheffer, *Dealing with the Past,* 105.

51. Comments of Juan Mendez in Borraine, Levy, and Scheffer, *Dealing with the Past,* 88.

52. Mendez in Borraine, *Dealing with the Past,* 88.

53. Comments of Aryeh Neier in Borraine, *Dealing with the Past,* 7.

54. Neier in Borraine, *Dealing with the Past,* 7 and 101.

55. Baltasar Garzón comments at the Center for Latin American Studies, Stanford University, February 23, 2001.
56. Neier in Borraine, *Dealing with the Past,* 3.
57. Borneman, *Settling Accounts: Violence, Justice and Accountability in Postsocialist Europe,* 7. See also David Holliday, "Guatemala's Long Road to Peace," *Current History* (February 1997): 68–74.
58. Borneman, *Settling Accounts,* 13.
59. This section draws on Sanford and Moscoso, "Along with the Poor, the Powerful Must Face Prosecution, Too," *Los Angeles Times,* 22 October 1999, as well as interviews with survivors between 1994 and 1998.
60. U.S. Department of State, "Secret Memorandum. Reference: Guatemala 6366," October 1981. Declassified January 1998.
61. I thank Fernando Moscoso, Kathleen Dill, and an anonymous international observer for sharing information about the court proceedings.
62. Bishop Gerardi was killed after the Archbishop's office released the REHMI project's *Nunca Más* report, which Gerardi had supervised.
63. Personal communication, November 17, 2000. International observer spoke on condition of anonymity.
64. CEH, *Memory of Silence.*
65. Primo Levi, *Survival in Auschwitz* (New York: Simon and Schuster, 1958), 87.
66. Levi, *Survival,* 91.
67. Author's interview with witness in 1997 and survivors in 1994.
68. CEH, *Memoria,* 2:226–227.
69. CEH, *Memoria,* 181.
70. CEH, *Memoria,* 234.
71. CEH, *Memoria,* 226–227.
72. Marlise Simons, "Three Serbs Convicted In Wartime Rapes," *New York Times,* 23 February 2001, A7.
73. Daniel Goldhagen, *Hitler's Willing Executioners* (New York: Knopf, 1996). See also Christopher Browning, *Ordinary Men—Reserve Batallion 101 and the Final Solution* (New York: Harper Perennial, 1992).
74. Author's interview with Fernando Moscoso, Portola Valley, California, November 14, 1999.
75. In villages in the Ixil Area, I was frequently told of civil patrol and military commissioner abuses continuing long after the army had changed its strategic policies about treatment of civilians. Specifically, I was told of civilians going to the army base commanders to seek protection from military commissioners who were extorting and abusing their neighbors.
76. Neier in Borraine, *Dealing with the Past,* 7.
77. *Prensa Libre,* October 14, 1999, 1.
78. Rabinal interview no. 2, 23 July 1997.

INDEX

Printed in the United States
87168LV00003B/223-228/A